Geography of Economics in New Millennium

Geography of Economics in New Millennium

Dr. Ashok Purohit

RANDOM

RANDOM PUBLICATIONS

NEW DELHI (INDIA)

Geography of Economics in New Millennium

ISBN 978-93-5111-814-5

Published in 2016 in India by

RANDOM PUBLICATIONS

4376-A/4B, Gali Murari Lal, Ansari Road
New Delhi-110 002
Phone : +9111-43580356, 011-23289044, 011-43142548
e-mail: sales@randompublications.com,
info@randompublications.com, randomexports@gmail.com

Reprinted 2026

Type Setting by : Friends Media, Delhi-110089

Preface

Geography of Economics is the study of the location, distribution and spatial organization of economic activities across the world. It represents a traditional subfield of the discipline of geography. However, in recent decades, many economists have also approached the field in ways more typical of the discipline of economics. Economic geography has taken a variety of approaches to many different subject matters, including but not limited to the location of industries, economies of agglomeration, transportation, international trade, development, real estate, gentrification, ethnic economies, gendered economies, core-periphery theory, the economics of urban form, the relationship between the environment and the economy, and globalization. The subject matter investigated is strongly influenced by the researcher's methodological approach. Neoclassical location theorists, following in the tradition of Alfred Weber, tend to focus on industrial location and use quantitative methods. Since the 1970s, two broad reactions against neoclassical approaches have significantly changed the discipline: Marxist political economy, growing out of the work of David Harvey; and the new economic geography which takes into account social, cultural, and institutional factors in the spatial economy. Economists such as Paul Krugman and Jeffrey Sachs have also analyzed many traits related to economic geography. Krugman has gone so far as to call his application of spatial thinking to international trade theory the "new economic geography", which directly competes with an approach within the discipline of geography that is also called "new economic geography". The name geographical economics has been suggested as an alternative.

– Author

Contents

1

Understanding the Economic Geography

Economic geography is a sub–discipline that uses a geographical approach to study the economy. It is a vibrant and exciting branch of geography. Its name would suggest that economic geography lies somewhere between, or at the overlap of, the disciplines of geography and economics. This is true to some extent. In fact, both geographers and economists use the term 'economic geography'. However, they mean different things by it. Indeed, it is important to stress from the outset that the approach that geographers are using to study the economy is very different from that used by most economists.

In line with the terminology used by the key textbook for this course unit Economic Geography: A Contemporary Introduction written by Neil Coe and his colleagues, this subject guide uses the term economic geography and economic-geographical approach to describe the approach used by geographers.

On the other hand, the type of 'economic geography' that economists are using, can be best described as 'geographical economics' or 'spatial economics'. More generally, this distinction between 'economic geography' and 'geographical economics' reflects fundamental differences between the way the economy is treated by geographers on the one hand, and economists on the other. In other words, an economic–geographical approach to studying the economy is very different from the one used by mainstream economics.

KEY DIFFERENCES BETWEEN ECONOMIC GEOGRAPHY AND ECONOMIC'S APPROACHES

The key difference is that mainstream economists usually pay little attention to the geographical dimensions of economic processes while economic geographers consider geography as being essential for the understanding of the ways economies work. From this, two completely different views of the economy, and the way it operates, emerge. Most mainstream economists see the economy as a machine that works according to certain principles and whose behaviour can be predicted using modelling techniques. Mathematics is therefore the main 'language' economists 'speak'. The body of thought that underpins such a conceptualisation of the economy can be referred to as 'economic orthodoxy'. Let us first explore the key components of economic orthodoxy before introducing the key concepts of an economic-geographical perspective.

MAINSTREAM ECONOMICS

Key components of economic orthodoxy could be simply summarised as follows:

- One of the key assumptions of the economic orthodoxy is that all people are behaving in a rational, self–interested and economising, profit–maximising manner. This type of rational individual is sometimes referred to as 'economic man' or homo economicus.
- Economic orthodoxy assumes that these rational individuals are competing against each other on the market. Mainstream economists believe that the market is the best mechanism to ensure economic efficiency since, they believe, perfect competition on the market guarantees that supply will meet demand at a particular price and the economy will be in equilibrium. The notion of equilibrium is one of the central assumptions of mainstream economic thought and shapes the way in which economists see the world around them.
- Mainstream economists believe that the market economy operates according to certain laws and principles that could be studied as a 'science'. One of the main concerns of this economic 'science' is to predict the behaviour of the economy using mathematical models and equations. The achievement of the aforementioned equilibrium is one of the key concerns of such modelling.
- Mainstream economists believe that these laws and principles work everywhere and therefore economic models are applicable to them in every context. In other words, economic orthodoxy believes in certain universalism.

Some would argue that such a portrayal of economic orthodoxy is somewhat simplistic, a caricature of an increasingly diverse body of economics. However, a tendency among economists to assume some sort of universal applicability of basic economic 'laws' is rather pervasive. Within this world of universal laws there is a little room for local differences and geography in general. Indeed, geography rarely enters economists' equations. The use of geography by economists is somewhat limited.

There are some important exceptions, however. Among them is Paul Krugman, US economist and the Nobel Prize winner for economics in 2008. Over the years, Krugman has made an important contribution in terms of bringing geography into economics and is seen as a leading figure of the so-called 'New Economic Geography'. However, his notion of geography is still somewhat limited and narrow, especially when compared with the conceptualisation of geography used by the economicgeographical perspective.

Indeed, as you will see, there are stark differences between the 'New Economic Geography' used by economists and the 'new economic geography' used by geographers.

AN ECONOMIC–GEOGRAPHICAL PERSPECTIVE

In contrast to a rather limited appreciation of geography by most economists, geographers emphasise the fact that no economy can function at the head of a pin. In other words, 'all economies must take place'. Geography, therefore, is always intrinsically present in all economic processes. One could therefore argue that, in fact, there are 'no economies, only economic geographies'. It follows then, that the kind of universalism that mainstream economics assumes is somewhat problematic. Indeed, if all economic processes have a geographical dimension, then it is difficult to imagine that economic rules can apply equally to all places.

Another major difference between an economic–geographical perspective and the assumptions of economic orthodoxy concerns the notion of a 'rational man'—homo economicus. Mainstream economists assume that people are always behaving as rational, profitmaximising individuals responding to market signals. However, life is more complex than that and people's behaviour is not always the outcome of rational decision-making. Rather, it can be influenced and conditioned by their gender, race, age, class, religion, culture, health or disability. Geographers are keen to take these aspects on board when studying economies. A 'geographical man/woman'—or what I will call here homo geographicus—can behave very differently from the way they are supposed to behave according to economic orthodoxy.

This has important implications for the remaining assumptions of economic orthodoxy. Indeed, if people are not behaving in a predictable way, than it is hard to expect that the entire economy will behave according to some predictable laws and principles. However sophisticated, mathematical models may not be able to capture all the complexity of economic processes happening in the real world. Worse still, mathematical models are not very helpful in elucidating the ways people relate to each other within societies and economies. In other words, 'the language of mathematics limits the ways in which economists can think about questions of power and social relations'. However, the questions of power and social relations are crucial in understanding economies because people do not live and work in isolation. We are connected to each other in complex ways and economic geography helps us to explore these connections and relations.

This exploration becomes more important in the age of globalisation. Further to this, it could be argued that these connections and relations are not limited to market exchanges and transactions. Indeed, there is a wide range of economic processes happening outside the scope of the market. The diversity of forms of economic processes, both within and outside the scope of the market, means that many economic geographers are not talking about 'the economy' but about 'economies'. In recent years, the notion of 'diverse' or 'alternative' economies attracted much interest among geographers. The notion of 'diverse economies' further undermines the universalism of economic orthodoxy and paves the way for alternative explanations of what the economy is and how it works.

Thus, one way or another, geographers in general, and economic geographers in particular, help to build a much richer, and perhaps more accurate, picture of the contemporary globalising economy. Coe and his colleagues go as far as to suggest that 'the set of approaches offered by the field of economic geography is best placed to help us appreciate and understand the modern economic world in all its complexity'. They identify the following key concepts that form part of the economic-geographical approach: space, place and scale.

KEY CONCEPTS OF ECONOMIC GEOGRAPHY: SPACE, PLACE AND SCALE

An economic–geographical approach puts spatial concepts such as space, place and scale at the centre of the analysis. These concepts form part of the common language that is shared among professional geographers. It is therefore essential that you familiarise yourself with these concepts right at the start:

- *Space*: The concept of space refers to physical distance and area. The concept of space allows us to ask simple questions such as where a particular process is happening. Four interrelated elements of the concept of space can be identified:
  - Territoriality and form (*i.e.,* a territorial form of a particular country)
  - Location (*i.e.,* a location of a particular country)
  - Flows across space (*i.e.,* trade flows between countries)
  - The concept of uneven space as a necessary condition of a capitalist system.
- *Place*: The concept of place aims to capture the specificity or uniqueness of particular places that are carved out of space. Through the notion of place, geographers are able to explore the richness and complexity of particular places and economic processes which are always embedded in environmental, social, cultural, institutional and political contexts. The idea of being embedded is very important because environmental, social, cultural, institutional and political contexts influence economic processes. Many Western values, for instance, may be alien to many other cultures, societies or nations. Therefore, the way economies are constructed and performed may

be very different in different places. Despite its importance for geographical research, the notion of place is somewhat vague because it can take various shapes and sizes.

- *Scale*: The concept of scale therefore helps us to organise places through a typology of spatial scales. Spatial scales that are commonly used by economic geographers include:
  - Global scale
  - Macro–regional scale (*i.e.,* South–East Asia, Europe or North America)
  - National scale (*i.e.,* USA, UK, France, Niger, Japan)
  - Regional scale (*i.e.,* California or South East of England)
  - Local scale (*i.e.,* Silicon Valley, Manhattan or the City of London)
  - Lived places (*i.e.,* workplaces and homeplaces).

It is worth noting that the precise typology is sometimes problematic. The terms 'local' and 'regional', for instance, are often used rather loosely. In some cases (*i.e.,* Hong Kong, Singapore or Trinidad), it is difficult to establish whether we are looking at a national, regional or local scale (or a combination of these). When reading economic geography literature, you should always pay attention to what definition of scale a particular author is using.

Further to this, it is important to realise that the above three key concepts are not simply neutral tools for describing the world—they can also be seen as representations of the world. Indeed, the way these concepts are used by academics, the media or politicians influences the way we look at the world and how we understand its problems.

MAJOR THEORETICAL PERSPECTIVES IN ECONOMIC GEOGRAPHY

place and scale, it is important to realise that concepts of space, place and scale are themselves subject to debate and alternative interpretations in geography. For instance, some geographers use the term space to describe absolute geographical space while others are using the term to describe relative space or relational space. You need to keep this in mind when reading some geography texts. More generally, you need to be aware of the fact that economic geography is a vibrant, dynamic and continuously evolving sub-discipline composed of a diverse set of approaches and concepts.

This subject guide will help you to learn about the key approaches and concepts that contemporary economic geography has to offer. These approaches and concepts will be explained in some detail in subsequent stages. However, already at this point, it is useful to highlight the various intellectual traditions within which these approaches and concepts are anchored.

Four main theoretical perspectives in economic geography are:

1. *Neo-classical location theory*: Location theory flourished in the 1950s

and the 1960s and was primarily interested in establishing and explaining patterns in the distribution of economic activities across space. This type of economic geography was firmly anchored in a neoclassical economics theory and used a model-based approach to study the location of economic activities (*i.e.,* firms) in space. This period in the development of economic geography is often called a 'quantitative revolution' which provided foundations for 'regional science', 'geographical economics' and 'spatial economics'. However, many economic geographers became dissatisfied with this approach and started exploring alternatives. More recently, the interest in regional science and geographical economics has been revived through the work of economist Paul Krugman and his 'New Economic Geography' (NEG).

2. *Behavioural approach*: A behavioural approach emerged in the late 1960s as one of the reactions to the 'quantitative revolution'. It moved away from a simple neo–classical assumption of homo economicus and explored a wider range of factors that influence economic decisionmaking of human actors in various situations. The problem with this approach, however, is that it fails to explore fully the relationships between individuals and society.
3. *Structuralist approach/Marxist political economy*: By contrast, a Marxist political economy approach, places social relations at the centre of its analysis, with an emphasis on class. Since the 1970s Marxist views started to influence geography and still have a significant influence on economic geography today. Importantly, Marxist–inspired economic geography moved the attention from spatial patterns and locational issues to questions of social relations and economic structures of capitalist economies.
4. *Post–structuralist approaches/New economic geography/ Cultural turn*: However, since the mid–1990s, a new type of economic geography has started to emerge from post–structuralist ideas. An important contribution of the new economic geography is its insistence that economic process cannot be seen in isolation from social, cultural and political contexts. In fact, new economic geography argues that social, cultural and/or institutional factors are central to the functioning of the economy/economies. Thus the emphasis on the notion of class has been replaced by the interest in categories such as gender, race, age, religion and culture. This change of emphasis is often referred to as the 'cultural turn'. This emphasis on cultural factors also represents one of the key differences between the 'new economic geography' used by geographers and the one used by economists. Furthermore, the cultural turn brought with it a change of focus away

from structural (general) features towards more particular features of societies and economies.

You will familiarise yourself with these major theoretical perspectives step by step in this subject guide. The important thing to remember is that economic geographers do not always agree which approach is best and concepts they are working with are continually tested and contested. None of the theoretical perspectives is perfect; each of them has its strengths and weaknesses.

However, collectively, they provide critical insights into the ways in which societies and economies work. The importance of economic geography for understanding the economic world around us will be explored in the subsequent part. However, before moving on to the next part, let me reiterate the difference between the 'new economic geography' described by geographers and the 'New Economic Geography' (NEG) described by economists. The difference between the two reflects a fundamental difference of understanding concerning what economic geography is about.

Paul Krugman, the key proponent of NEG, economic geography is about 'the location of production in space'; in other words, it is a 'branch of economics that worries about where things happen in relation to one another'. In investigating the patterns of location of production in space, Krugman uses complex economic models in which geography (often simply in the form of transport costs) is inserted as an important factor. In this way, Krugman's NEG has much in common with neo–classical location theory. This subject guide will not explore Krugman's theory in any detail.

However, by learning about neoclassical location theory you will gain a good understanding of the basic principles on which Krugman's theory builds. This, in turn, will help you to study Krugman's work in the future should you choose to do so. In contrast to NEG, the 'new economic geography' described by geographers as part of the 'cultural turn' is not represented by one single theory. Rather it is very much a diverse set of approaches. More importantly, the new economic geography of the cultural turn represents a dramatically different view of economies and their geographies. While there have been attempts to foster a dialogue between geographers and economists the gap between the two types of new economic geographies is rather noticeable.□

WHY IS ECONOMIC GEOGRAPHY IMPORTANT?

ISSUES FOR ECONOMIC GEOGRAPHY

We highlighted the fact that economic geography can be seen as a diverse set of approaches and concepts that economic geographers use to study economic processes. In turn, this diversity of economic geography approaches allows economic geographers to engage with a diverse set of questions about the economy and society. Concrete questions often depend on a theoretical standpoint.

Peter Dicken and Peter Lloyd in their book Location in Space argue that:

- 'Fundamentally, the economic geographer is concerned with the spatial organisation of economic systems: with where the various elements of the system are located, how they are connected together in space, and the spatial impact of economic processes.'

On the basis of this, they argue that economic geographers are interested in three interconnected questions.

- In what ways are economic activities organised spatially on the earth's surface, and how do such spatial forms or patterns change over time?
- Why are economic activities organised spatially in particular ways; that is, what are the underlying processes at work?
- How does the spatial organisation of economic activities itself influence economic and other social processes?

On the other hand, Roger Lee suggests that economic geography is 'a geography of people's struggle to make a living' and should therefore concern itself with 'the sustainable and humane production, use and reproduction of the social, natural and material conditions of human existence'.

On the basis of this, Lee argues that an 'inclusive economic geography' should include the study of:

- The cultural and environmental origins of economic activity, articulated through socially constructed gender and kinship relations; and the struggle to establish a particular set of social relations of production and their geographical extent
- The conceptualisation of nature
- The forms of calculation and measurement of value
- The processes and forms of production and consumption generated by such relations and value systems
- The division of labour
- The conditions of development within a particular set of social relations
- The forms of state and politics which support and legitimise particular social relations and processes of production and consumption
- The construction of cultural and ideological forms which shape the basis of discourse within a particular value system
- The structuring of relationships within and between different sets of social relations
- The conditions of transformation from one set of social relations of production to another.

This is a long list indeed—it reflects the view discussed earlier that there are 'no economies, only economic geographies'. Put differently, given that all economic processes are inherently spatial, economic geographers should be concerned about all the processes related to the people's struggle to make a living. However, an important question arises about whether such an approach is still needed in the era of globalisation in which space is apparently being dissolved by modern information and communication technologies.

THE AGE OF GLOBALISATION: THE END OF GEOGRAPHY?

Powerful arguments have been put forward about the impact of globalisation in general, and the effects of the ICT revolution in particular, on economic activities. Some observers have come to the conclusion that electronic communications have 'space–shrinking' effects and will bring about the 'death of distance' and thus, ultimately, the 'end of geography'.

The 'death of distance' thesis has been expressed by Cairncross as follows:

- 'Distance will no longer determine the cost of communicating electronically. Companies will organize certain types of work in three shifts according to the world's three main time zones: the Americas, East Asia/Australia, and Europe...No longer will location be key to most business decisions. Companies will locate any screen–based activity anywhere on earth, wherever they can find the best bargain of skills and productivity.'

A similar argument has been put forward by O'Brien who argued that ICTs will allow money to be moved around the globe without constraints, thus spelling the 'end of geography':

- 'The end of geography, as a concept applied to international financial relationships, refers to a state of economic development where geographical location no longer matters, or matters less than hitherto. In this state, financial market regulators no longer hold sway over their regulatory territory; that is rules no longer apply to specific geographical frameworks, such as the nation–state or other typical regulatory/jurisdictional territories. For financial firms, this means that the choice of geographical location can be greatly widened... Stock exchanges can no longer expect to monopolize trading in the shares of companies in their country or region... For the consumer of financial services, the end of geography means a wider range of services will be offered, outside the traditional services offered by local banks.' Economic geography is the study of the location, distribution and spatial organization of economic activities across the world. The subject matter investigated is strongly influenced by the researcher's methodological approach. Neoclassical location theorists, following in the tradition of Alfred Weber, tend to focus on industrial location and use quantitative methods. Since the 1970s, two broad reactions against neoclassical approaches have significantly changed the discipline: Marxist political economy, growing out of the work of David Harvey; and the new economic geography which takes into account social, cultural, and institutional factors in the spatial economy.

These statements attempt to convince their readers that, thanks to ICTs, space and place no longer matter or at least they matter much less than before. Indeed, they both seem to suggest that location in space is no longer an issue for firms as they can locate 'anywhere on earth'. Also, the role of place is apparently greatly diminished. Cairncross, for instance, suggests that the only place characteristics that firms may be interested in can be reduced to 'the best bargain of skills and productivity'. O'Brien, in the meantime, does not seem to recognise any role that places may play in the globalised financial markets.

But, interestingly, both Cairncross and O'Brien seem to imply that the national scale is increasingly irrelevant in the global economy. Indeed, O'Brien specifically points out that (national) financial market regulators 'no longer hold sway' and that rules no longer apply to nation-states, because financial flows are spilling over traditional national boundaries. Similarly, Cairncross seems to suggest that the (macroregional) time zone is the only geographical scale that holds any relevance in the new era of global electronic communications.

What is interesting about the statements of Cairncross and O'Brien is that they both see globalisation as something positive. Note, for instance, Cairncross's suggestion that companies will benefit from the new locational freedom by allowing them to find and exploit 'the best bargain of skills and productivity'. O'Brien, meanwhile, suggests that the 'end of geography' will be beneficial for both financial firms and their customers. Views such as these can be labelled as 'hyperglobalist'.

Some of them go as far as to suggest that freeing economic activities from their traditional geographical constraints will bring benefits to all people in all corners of the globe. However, this, manifestly, does not seem to be the case. Today's world is ridden with sharp inequalities both within and between countries and geography plays an important role in understanding economic and social processes and their uneven manifestations in the age of globalisation.

IMPORTANCE OF ECONOMIC GEOGRAPHY IN THE ERA OF GLOBALIZATION

Despite the hyperglobalist views, the role of space, place and scale do not diminish in the globalising world. Quite the opposite perhaps. Indeed, as economic activities are increasingly internationalised, interconnections between various places increase, competition between them intensifies and inequalities are on the rise, so geography becomes more important than ever.

And as we have pointed out earlier, an economic–geographical approach is perhaps 'best placed to help us appreciate and understand the modern economic world in all its complexity'. This conviction is based on the knowledge that economic geography offers powerful tools for analysing and understanding contemporary economies and societies. Economic geography, for instance, can help us to understand that, despite years and decades of economic globalisation, the pattern of investment, production, trade and consumption is highly uneven. Economic geography can also help us to understand that even footloose multinational corporations (MNCs) have to be 'grounded' in specific locations and often 'embedded' in places and their socio–political, institutional and cultural contexts.

Economic geography also helps to elucidate the ways in which MNCs and other economic activities are 'governed' at various geographical scales from local and regional to national, macro–regional and global levels. Economic geography also helps us to understand that despite the widespread use of ICTs, trading places for global financial capital remain stubbornly located in a small number of global cities and these global cities, in turn, influence economic processes around the world. Thanks to these and other insights, economic geography can thus contribute to our understanding of inequalities at various geographical scales from poverty in urban areas to global uneven development.

No other discipline can claim such a wide scope of interest and relevance to today's rapidly changing world. By following this subject guide, you will gain solid foundations in economic geography approaches, concepts and theories and their applicability to the contemporary world and policy-making.

KEY APPROACHES IN ECONOMIC GEOGRAPHY

DEFINING THE ECONOMY

Let us start with a definition of 'the economy'. The term is used in everyday life with such frequency that we rarely pause to think what the economy actually is. Most people take the notion of the economy for granted. In fact, many economics dictionaries and textbooks take it for granted too and do not even bother defining it. The term 'economy' had not featured in the original version of Raymond Williams' *Keywords* either.

So what is 'the economy'? *The Concise Oxford English Dictionary* suggests that the word 'economy' is in fact of Greek origin. The Greek term 'oikonomia' basically means 'household management'—from *oikos* 'house' and *nomos* 'managing' from *nemein* 'manage'. The hint of this original meaning still survives today and 'economy' can mean 'careful management of available resources'. In travel this can mean that you buy the cheapest air or rail ticket and travel 'economy class'.

However, since about the eighteenth century the term economy also began to gain a new meaning and now can refer to economic affairs at a much larger geographical scale, namely that of a nation. Nowadays, the notion of 'the economy' is perhaps still most commonly used to describe the economic processes of a country. *The Concise Oxford English Dictionary* defines the economy as 'the state of a country or area in terms of the production and consumption of goods and services and the supply of money'. However, as it will become apparent below, even this latter definition is somewhat problematic.

MEASURING THE ECONOMY

Perhaps the most common way of measuring 'the state in which a country is in terms of the production and consumption of goods and services' is an indicator called Gross Domestic Product. GDP measures, in money terms, the total market value of production in a particular economy in a given year. It is usually calculated as a sum of expenditures by households, firms and the government plus net exports.

By household expenditure we mean the total amount spent by individuals in a given year including their expenditure on food, fuel, housing, clothing, household appliances, leisure, etc. Expenditure by firms is measured as investment expenditure by which we mean the amount invested by businesses in future productive capacity. Government expenditure is the amount spent by the government to build infrastructure or provide services. Finally, net exports represent the value of goods and services sold to other countries minus the value of goods and services imported from abroad.

Fig. Division of Labour in a Pin–making Factory

PROBLEMATISING AND RE-DEFINING THE ECONOMY

GDP represents a fairly standard way of measuring the economy. It captures three key economic agents—namely households, firms and the government—all of which play important roles in the economy. Yet measuring the economy in this way can be highly problematic. One of the key problems is that GDP measurement is derived from a definition of the economy that is rather narrow—it includes certain things and processes but excludes others. Coe et al. offer a very good example of this problem.

If you have taken a bus or drive a car to your place of work or study then you have engaged in an economic act. Your bus fare or your fuel bills and parking costs would be included in your individual consumption and therefore included in the conventional definition of the economy. But if you decide to cycle or walk instead, no money will change hands and, therefore, oddly, you have not engaged in an economic act! Another good example is unpaid work. Since no wages are paid, unpaid work occurs outside the formal monetary economy and therefore is not included in the consideration of the state of the economy. This way, not only is the economy miscounted, but also the work of certain people is discounted.

A similar problem arises with the 'black economy'. In the 'black economy', money can indeed change hands, but because these monetary transactions are not recorded by the government, they are not included in what counts as 'the economy'. Yet, the livelihoods of millions of people around the world may be dependent on such transactions. Thinking about what constitutes an economic act or process is crucial for our understanding of the economy and is, therefore, a point of contention.

The way in which cultural, social, political and environmental processes are related to the economic processes is another contentious issue. A conventional definition of the economy supports the impression that the economy is somewhat separated from other dimensions of our lives. This in turn helps to create the impression that the economy is something 'out there', which affects our lives, but which we, as individuals, cannot control. This impression is often reinforced by the way the economy is represented in everyday use and policy documents. Indeed, the economy is often represented by metaphors such as a 'machine', an 'organism' or a 'body'; that presumably has a life of its own. However, it could be argued that the economy is inseparable from cultural, social, political and environmental processes.

Ray Hudson, for instance, understands 'the economy' as referring to:

- Those simultaneously discursive and material processes and practices of production, distribution and consumption, through which people seek to create wealth, prosperity and wellbeing and so construct economies; to circuits of production, circulation, realisation, appropriation and distribution of value.

However, he is quick to add that value is 'always culturally constituted and defined' and that '[w]hat counts as "the economy" is, therefore, always cultural, constituted in and distributed over space, linked by flows of values, monies, things and people that conjoin a diverse heterogeneity of people and things'. He further argues that '[e]qually importantly, the social processes that constitute the economy always involve biological, chemical or physical transformation via human labour of elements of the natural world'. This also means that thinking about 'the economy' in terms of evergrowing GDP, for instance, may not be a universally shared, nor necessarily desirable, concept.

Indeed as Hodder and Lee have argued several decades ago, that it is 'all too easy, for instance, to assume that the dream of each less–developed country is to become developed'. Indeed, 'such a view can easily disregard highly developed local cultures'. They add that 'self–respect is at least as important a measure of social and economic progress as are increases in… material wealth'. Similarly, studying 'the economy' without considering the environmental dimension of economic processes is problematic, not least because 'economic activities are taking an increasing toll of balanced interactions within the life–giving ecosystem'.

Another way to approach a definition of 'the economy' is to remind ourselves of the notion introduced in that there are 'no economies, only economic geographies'. In turn, economic geographies can be defined as 'geographies of people's struggle to make a living'. Importantly, this struggle to make a living is framed in both material and social processes.

In other words, 'all economies and economic geographies are both material and social constructs'. What is more, in the construction of economic geographies the relations between the material and the social are 'inseparable and mutually formative'. The recognition of this further undermines the notion of the economy as simply being 'the state of production and consumption of goods and service and the supply of money' or as being measurable by GDP.

HOW DOES THE ECONOMY WORK?

We have attempted to answer the question 'what is the economy?'. The process of defining the economy can be problematic. What should and should not be included in the notion of 'the economy' remains a contentious issue.

In this part as suggested, attempt to address an issue which is even more contentious: 'How does the economy work?' As already pointed out in the introductory part, the answer to this question is in part influenced by the way we define the economy. However, even people who would share the view about what the economy is can disagree profoundly on the question of how it works. Large numbers of economists and social scientists work on this question every day and we have no space here to review all of their theories.

Instead, what as suggested, attempt to do in this stage is to identify three basic theoretical perspectives on the economy:

- First, as suggested, examine the mainstream economic perspective, which sees the functioning of the economy through the lens of market forces and which maintains that individual self–interest mediated by the 'invisible hand' of the market leads to equilibrium and prosperity.
- Second, as suggested, introduce the Marxist perspective which, in contrast, argues that the capitalist market economy is ridden by internal contradictions and produces both inequality and instability.
- Finally, as suggested, have a look at the alternative approaches, especially those associated with evolutionary and institutionalist economics, which try to go beyond the boundaries of market–based

processes and which pay attention to wider social, cultural and institutional contexts in order to explain how economies function.

MAINSTREAM ECONOMIC VIEWS

The mainstream economic perspective is mainly associated with neoclassical economic theory. The neo–classical school of thought has been developing since the late nineteenth–century and currently represents the dominant way of looking at the economy. Neo–classical economics is rooted in the belief that the market is the most efficient mechanism for the allocation of resources and hence the creation of prosperity.

The neo-classical school of economic thought has been built on the foundations laid down by Adam Smith, a Scottish economist and the founder of the classical political economy. Back in the eighteenth century, Smith devised an economic theory, the features of which remain with us today. This includes his concepts of rational self-interest and the 'invisible hand' of the market, concepts that underpin much of contemporary mainstream economic thinking.

In seeking to identify how wealth is created, Adam Smith argued that the main cause of prosperity is the division of labour. Smith expressed his arguments in his famous work titled *An Inquiry into the Nature and Causes of the Wealth of Nations* published in 1776. In it, Smith used an example of a factory making pins to explain the power of the division of labour and the productivity that can be achieved from this. He argued that a single worker working alone at home would be lucky to produce even one pin per day and certainly not 20. However, he observed that in a pin-making factory 10 workers can engage in the production of pins by dividing 18 specialised pin–making tasks between them:

- One man draws out the wire, another straights it, a third cuts it, a fourth points it, a fifth grinds it at the top for receiving the head; to make the head requires two or three distinct operations; to put it on, is a peculiar business, to whiten the pins is another; it is even a trade by itself to put them into the paper; and the important business of making a pin is, in this manner, divided into about eighteen distinct operations, which, in some manufactories, are all performed by distinct hands, though in others the same man will sometimes perform two or three of them... Smith.

By dividing the work between them in this way, Smith argued, 10 workers can together produce about 48,000 pins per day. That is 4,800 pins per worker per day, representing a massive improvement of productivity when compared to the output achievable without the division of labour. The improvement of productivity in the pin-making factory is impressive indeed. But how does the pin-making factory know how many pins to produce and at what price to sell them?

Mainstream economists, this problem will be solved by what Smith called the 'invisible hand' of the market. The market will determine both the quantity of goods produced and the price at which these goods will be sold, by matching supply with demand. This is how it works. From a producer's point of view, the higher the price customers are prepared to pay for a product the more the producer will be prepared to produce. This is represented by the upward–sloping supply curve in Figure.

However, the higher the price, the less the goods will be in demand by the customers—shown as the downward-sloping demand curve in Figure. Under perfect market conditions, supply and demand curves will intersect in the middle, thus fixing both the quantity of goods to be produced and the price under which they will be sold. In other words, the markets will achieve equilibrium.

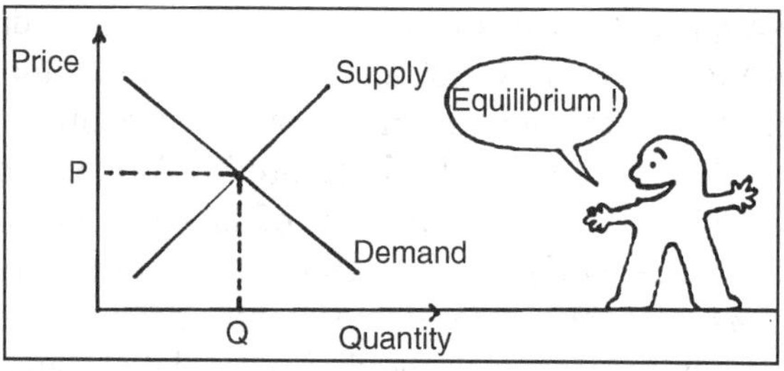

Fig. Market Economy: The Equilibrium Relationship of Demand, Supply and Price.

However, the functioning of the economy in the way described, is based on the expectation that both producers and consumers are acting in a rational, economising or profit-maximising way. In other words, they are behaving as *homo economicus*. Adam Smith argued that such behaviour is motivated by 'self–interest'. He further argued that by pursuing their own self–interests, individuals, led by the 'invisible hand' of the market, are unintentionally contributing to a greater societal good, a win–win situation, from which everybody will benefit.

If pin–makers, shoe–makers, butchers and bakers all pursue their individual self-interest, the market will ensure that everybody will be better off. Since the times of Adam Smith, economic theory has developed a lot, but the key principles he introduced are still with us. The analysis of the workings of the economy through the lens of rational profit–making agents and the belief that markets are capable of delivering both equilibrium and efficiency, is central to neo–classical economic theory. However, such an understanding of the economy has been challenged by Marxist and other alternative approaches which as suggested, examine in turn.

THE MARXIST APPROACH

The Marxist perspective on the economy is derived from the work of Karl Marx and Friedrich Engels, two German philosophers of the late nineteenth–

century. Like Adam Smith, Karl Marx was interested in the question of how wealth is created in the economy and how wealth is distributed among members of society. However, in stark contrast to the win–win situation alluded to by Smith, Marx pointed out that wealth will increasingly concentrate in the hands of the few. How so? To answer this question, Marx devised his labour theory of value.

In order to explain the basics of the labour theory of value as devised by Marx, let us go back to the pin-making factory described earlier. The productivity gains from organising pin production in the pin factory were substantial. But who reaps the benefits? If the factory was jointly owned by the 10 workers who work there, it is possible to imagine a situation in which they could split the benefits of their production between themselves.

However, in the capitalist market economy, the factory is likely to be privately owned. The owner, the capitalist, would own the land on which the factory is built, the factory building itself, the raw materials needed to produce the pins and all the machinery and tools used by the workers. In other words, he or she would own the means of production. Workers, on the other hand, do not own the means of production and the only way they can sustain themselves is to sell their own work to capitalists.

Thus, in the capitalist market economy, labour itself becomes a commodity—labour power can be bought and sold like any other commodity. So, workers sell their labour and receive wages in exchange for their work and that looks fine on the surface. However, the question arises as to what capitalists do to sustain themselves? They have to engage in the circuit of capital and make profit. The way Marx described how the circuit of capital works is presented in Figure.

Fig 2.3: Circuit of Capital in the Capitalist Economy

- M = Money capital,
- C = Commodity capital,
- LP = Labour power,
- MP = Means of production,
- P = Production process,
- C' = Increased commodity capital,
- s = Surplus value,
- M' = Increased money capital.

Imagine a capitalist who has capital in the form of money —money capital (M)—to invest. He or she can turn this money capital into productive capital (P) by purchasing two commodities—the labour power (LP; *i.e.,* labour of 10 workers) and the means of production (MP; *i.e.,* pin-making factory, raw materials, machinery, tools, etc., needed to produce pins).

The labour power and the means of production are then combined in the process of production to produce 48,000 pins a day—representing another form of capital—commodity capital (C). Commodity capital can be turned back into money capital when the factory owner sells pins on the market at a certain price (and this price represents what Marxists call exchange value). For the capitalist to survive, he or she has to make a profit. This means that the money he or she receives in exchange for the commodities produced must be greater than the money originally invested in the enterprise ($M' > M$). The search for profit is the motivating force of the capitalist economy.

The crucial point in the Marxist analysis is a recognition that, ultimately, all value comes from human labour and the only way for a capitalist to make profit is to appropriate surplus value (s). Surplus value is the difference between the wages the factory owner pays workers for their labour and the value these workers produce for him or her in the factory while making pins. To frame it differently, workers add value to the commodities they produce by applying their labour, and this value is greater than the reward they get in exchange for their efforts in the form of wages. This is the basis of exploitation in the capitalist economy.

However, capitalists have to engage in it, if they are to survive the cut–throat competition from other capitalists, who have to do exactly the same. Those capitalists who fail to generate profit (or enough profit) go out of business. The effort to maximise profit is therefore an imperative of the capitalist economy. All capitalists, individually, have to act in a profit–maximising manner, which echoes the self–interested behaviour described by Adam Smith. Such behaviour, in turn, further exacerbates competition and so it could be argued that one of the key features of capitalism is that it is inherently competitive.

However, Marx argued that such individual action will not lead to the equilibrium and win-win situation envisaged by Smith—far from it. Marx argued that capitalism (the system based on capital) is both unequal and unstable. He argued that inequalities within society will increase as capitalists try to increase their profits and squeeze worker's wages, by introducing machines, intensifying labour processes or simply by forcing workers to work longer hours, for example.

Capitalists can also endeavour to replace workers by machines and by doing so, they create a growing pool of the unemployed, which in turn will push wages down further still. The result of this process will be an increasing concentration of wealth in the hands of a few (the capitalist class) and the impoverishment of the working class masses (proletariat). Simply put, the capitalist system will ensure that the rich will become richer and the poor will become poorer.

Ethical issues aside, Marx argued that such a system is unlikely to reach an equilibrium of the kind envisaged by Adam Smith, because sooner or later the fundamental economic contradiction arises: too many commodities (*i.e.,* pins) will be produced, but there will be too few people able to buy them. Marxists call this situation an overaccumulation. Overaccumulation can take various forms, but overaccumulation of capital in the form of unsold commodities is one of the most striking symptoms.

Ian Craib offers a very good illustration of how such a crisis of overaccumulation can happen, using a crucial distinction in Marxist theory between use value and exchange value:

- 'If I am a worker and I produce £50 worth of goods in a day (the use value of my labour to my employer), and I receive £10 a day in wages (the exchange value of my labour power), then I do not receive in wages sufficient to buy back the value of goods I have produced. This applies right across the system, so that if stocks of unsold goods build up, workers have to be laid off, and the economy enters a crisis, a depression, or slump, until the stock of goods are used up and firms go back into production. There is a cycle of growth and slump, something that capitalist economies have been trying to deal with for over a century and a half.'

This is then one of the possible causes of the familiar boom-and-bust cycle. Each boom is followed by a crisis in which devaluation must take place to kickstart the accumulation process all over again. For Marx then, the capitalist economy is neither equal nor stable—it is inherently unequal and crisisprone. The profit–making imperative that drives the capitalist economy and makes it dynamic, is also a source of its fundamental contradiction.

Marxist conceptualisation of the economy therefore represents a stark contrast to the equilibrium-prone and win–win expectations of mainstream economics. Importantly, Marx also argued that in the long run, the capitalist system is unsustainable, because the increasing contradictions will reach a tipping point at which the system will eventually collapse. This, according to Marx will happen in the most advanced capitalist countries, where the contradictions between labour and capital will be the greatest. The collapse of capitalism will pave a way for a new social and economic order (communism). Marx said very little about how such a new system would operate. However, for a system to be freed from exploitation, both private property and class relations based on property rights would have to be abolished.

While Marxism provides a powerful analysis of the way the economy works, it also leaves us with a number of important issues. Indeed, the economy does not always work as predicted by Marx and, so far, the socialist revolution has failed to materialise in the most advanced capitalist countries. One of the key questions therefore is how can we account for the fact that the capitalist system manages to survive despite its contradictions? Economic geographers have made an important contribution to the debate on this question. But for now, let's turn to the alternative approaches.

ALTERNATIVE APPROACHES

It is clear from the two sub-sections that mainstream economic and Marxist perspectives differ dramatically in their analysis of the workings of the economy. However, despite the differences, these two perspectives also share one common feature—they both focus on formal market transactions. Indeed, mainstream economics is concerned with the relationship between the demand and supply of goods or services as expressed by a price fixed through the market mechanism.

The Marxist analysis, meanwhile, focuses on the difference between the price of labour (exchange value of labour power) and the exchange value of the commodities produced by the labour. However, what constitutes 'the economy' and 'the economic' is a contentious issue. Echoing these concerns, a number of alternative economic approaches have emerged. These approaches usually fall within a category of heterodox economics since they are providing a counterbalance to the established mainstream (orthodox) economic views. One of the leading heterodox approaches is associated with evolutionary and institutional economics.

Evolutionary and institutional economics is in itself a diverse set of approaches, but there are some key shared characteristics that clearly distinguish these approaches from both the mainstream economics and Marxist perspectives. The starting point of evolutionary/institutional and other alternative approaches is their insistence that the economy cannot be reduced to market transactions only. Instead, they argue that wider social, cultural and institutional contexts need to be taken into consideration if one is to explain how economies work. Institutional contexts are defined broadly here and may include both formal institutions (*i.e.,* laws, regulations, formal procedures) and informal institutions (*i.e.,* habits, customs, conventions, cultural norms, etc.) at various scales—from the level of the firm to the institutional landscapes underpinning the whole economy.

The inclusion of the wider social, cultural and institutional considerations has profound implications for the understanding of the ways economies work. Importantly, such an inclusion challenges the neo–classical notion of the rational behaviour of 'economic man' guided by the 'invisible hand' of the market. Instead, it emphasises the way in which social institutions play an essential role in guiding the action of economic agents. (This also differs from the Marxist view that the role of economic agents is structured by the prevailing social relations of production). In the evolutionary/ institutionalist view, firms, for instance, are not seen as atomistic units competing against each other on the free market. Rather, firms are perceived as being embedded within wider socio–economic relations and networks. These networks may include various formal and informal links with suppliers, customers and competitors. Importantly, transactions within these networks are not simply guided by market competition. Rather they often involve valuable elements of coordination and cooperation.

This is important because such cooperative networks are often crucial for fostering innovation which is seen as vital for economic development or economic evolution. In turn, this raises the question whether the 'pure market' is the best mechanism for ensuring economic progress. Evolutionary and institutionalist economists would argue that successful economies are neither pure markets nor pure hierarchies.

Instead, successful economies are 'mixed economies' with important roles for the public sector and for different kinds of policy. Mixed economic systems are also seen as capable of producing a diversity of economic forms which contributes to the adaptability and longterm survival of economic systems (rather than just the simple short–term 'survival of the fittest' enforced by unfettered markets).

Another line of argument advanced by alternative approaches relates to the claim that successful economies are increasingly knowledge-intensive or knowledge-based. The knowledge–based economy can be simply defined as an economy in which knowledge becomes the key economic resource. While all economies can be seen as knowledge–based, there is a perception that we witness a major shift in the relative importance of land, physical capital and knowledge capital, in favour of the latter. For some observers, the shift towards the knowledge–based economy represents an epochal transformation.

As Burton–Jones vividly put it:

- 'Since ancient times, wealth and power have been associated with the ownership of physical resources. The traditional factors of production, materials, labour, and money, have been largely physical in nature. Historically the need for knowledge has been limited, and access to it largely controlled by those owning the means of production. Steam power, physical labour, and money capital largely facilitated the Industrial Revolution... In contrast, future wealth and power will be derived mainly from intangible, intellectual resources: knowledge capital. This transformation from a world largely dominated by physical resources, to a world dominated by knowledge, implies a shift in the locus of economic power as profound as that which occurred at the time of the Industrial Revolution. We are in the early stages of a "Knowledge Revolution."'

The notion that the economy is moving towards a post–industrial, knowledge–intensive phase, in turn, opens up a whole set of questions. Both mainstream (neo–classical) economics and Marxist approaches have been devised in the context of an (emerging) industrial era. But will the same principles apply to the new knowledge economy?

Evolutionary and institutionalist economists have devised their own approaches to account for the ways knowledge economies work. One of the most influential concepts is that of the 'learning economy' introduced by Lundvall and Johnson. The starting point of the 'learning economy' concept is the argument that if knowledge is the most fundamental resource in our contemporary economy, then learning is 'the most important process'. Although Lundvall and Johnson admit that knowledge always has been a 'crucial resource' for the economy, and was in the past 'layered in traditions and routines', they argue that knowledge and learning have more recently become much more fundamental resources than before.

They argue that the economy is now characterised by 'new constellations of knowledge and learning in the economy' mainly through the development of ICTs, flexible specialisation and, finally, changes in the process of innovation. These changes are bringing challenges that firms have responded to by changing organisational forms and by building alliances in order to gain access to a more diversified knowledge base. This implies 'broader participation in learning processes' to include all layers within the firm, the development of 'multiskilling and networking skills' and enhancing the 'capacity to learn and to apply learning to the processes of production and sales'. This is why Lundvall and Johnson 'regard... capitalist economies not only as knowledge–based economies but also as "learning economies"'.

They offer the following definition of the 'learning economy':

- 'The learning economy is a dynamic concept; it involves the capacity to learn and to expand the knowledge base. It refers not only to the importance of the science and technology systems—universities, research organisations, in-house R&D departments and so on—but also to the learning implications of the economic structure, the organisational forms and the institutional set–up.'

At the core of the 'learning economy' are apparently firms that 'start to learn how to learn' and which are able to handle various types of knowledge. Lundvall and Johnson distinguish at least four categories of knowledge: know–what, know–why, know-who and know-how. The first category, know-what, represents knowledge about 'facts'. The meaning of this is probably close to that of 'information'. The, second category, know–why, refers to scientific knowledge of principles and laws of motion in nature and in society. This kind of knowledge, Lundvall and Johnson argue, is extremely important for technological development.

The third term, know-who, (together with know-when and know–where) is already a more complex construction that reaches a sphere of specific social relations and time–space dimension. A simple example of know–who can be a situation when, for a successful innovation, it is more important to know key persons than to know basic scientific principles. Know–when and know–where refers to economically useful knowledge about markets with their temporal and spatial dimensions, for instance. Finally, knowhow refers to practical skills in production or other spheres of economic activity.

Lundvall and Johnson also address different aspects of learning. Importantly, they do not understand learning as a simple absorption of science and technical knowledge. Rather, they define it more broadly as learning changes in economic structures, organisational and institutional forms. Learning is presented as a dynamic and interactive process aimed at the accumulation of knowledge at the level of the firm and the economy as a whole. Learning is present in both production and consumption processes and is expressed through 'learning by doing' and 'learning by using'. From the point of view of permanent renewal (learning) and adaptation of economic and organisational structures, Lundvall and Johnson have also introduced an innovative term 'forgetting'.

They argue that the 'learning economy' should not only preserve and store its pool of knowledge, but also should be able to 'forget'. 'Forgetting' at the level of individual workers refers to their ability to abandon obsolete skills and professional expertise. An example of 'forgetting' at the level of the firm or economy includes closing down ailing branches or whole sectors. Thus, the 'learning economy' is supposed to intelligently manage continuous self–organised learning.

The work of Lundvall and Johnson and other evolutionary/institutionalists has proved highly influential in framing the discussion on contemporary economic geographies, despite the fact that there remain questions about the precise nature of the supposed transformation of the economy towards the 'knowledge–based economy' or 'learning economy'. One contentious issue relates to the question of whether the transformation beyond an old industrial economy also signifies a move beyond a capitalist economy.

Geoffrey Hodgson—one of the prominent evolutionary/ institutionalist economists—contributed to the debate by offering his own definitions of the 'knowledge–intensive economy' and 'learning economy'. Hodgson has argued that the 'knowledge-intensive economy' would still be a capitalist one but it would be an economy in which an 'enlightened group of business leaders' is 'aware of the kind of democratic culture and participatory industrial relations that facilitate productivity'. Alongside 'collaborative and co-operative relationships between firms… against the neo–liberal insistence on fierce, price driven, market competition', Hodgson suggests that:

- '[s]uch a progressive movement of business people could find valuable allies among trade unionists and the population as a whole'. However, for Hodgson, the 'learning economy' or 'market cognitism', in contrast, is a scenario clearly 'beyond capitalism' where the 'degree of control by the employer over the employee is minimal'. Hodgson has argued that such an economy, 'would not be socialist, in any common sense of the word', but nevertheless, 'it is not capitalism' presumably because the means of production are effectively controlled by the workers themselves, not by the employers (capitalists). Such a benign view of the emerging new 'knowledge era' thus implies that the contradictions identified by Marx as inherent to the capitalist economy may be waning. This point is hotly debated but if proven true, it can have potentially important implications for the way we conceptualise economic geographies of the 'new era'.

HOW DOES THE ECONOMY WORK OVER SPACE?

The perspectives on the economy presented offer a good starting point to explore the question of what the economy is and how it works. However, the problem is that all views presented could be seen as 'aspatial'. Indeed, they do not tell us much about how the economy or economies work over space. Economic and geographical considerations are, in other words, impossible to separate. The question of how the economy (or economies) work(s) over space, across scales and in particular places, is the key question of economic geography.

This is an important question, economic processes are enfolding in space in a highly uneven way and are engaged in producing and reproducing inequalities at various spatial scales. How can we explain this uneven and unequal development? The three perspectives on the economy presented in the previous part provide three very different (in fact, contrasting) ways of approaching this question. In other words, different perspectives on 'the economy' have profound implications for the theoretical conceptualisation of economic geographies.

NEO–CLASSICAL APPROACH, LOCATION THEORY AND BEYOND

Let us start with the neo–classical approach. The application of the neoclassical model for the understanding of the ways in which the economy works over space looks straightforward enough. Echoing the view that the 'invisible hand' of the market will ensure equilibrium between demand and supply, neo–classical theory of spatial development implies that any uneven development is temporary, because market forces will ensure that some sort of spatial equilibrium or balanced development will be achieved in the long run. This view is based on the assumption that, following the logic of the rational economic man, both producers (firms) and consumers (workers) will move between regions in search of the most profitable location. Simply put, labour will move from poorer to richer regions (in search of higher wages) and capital will move in the opposite direction (in search of cheaper labour and land).

Even more complex neo–classical models that involve other factors of production (*i.e.,* technology) are all built around the assumption that some sort of spatial equilibrium will be achieved in the long run, because such factors of production will inevitably spread or disperse over space. The processes of spatial dispersal can indeed be observed in reality. However, the examples of spatial equilibrium that the neo-classical theory envisages, are hard to find.

One way of accounting for this discrepancy is to acknowledge that, in real life, factors of production cannot move 'freely' over space. Indeed, there are various constraints involved. One of the obvious obstacles is the friction of distance. The calculation of the cost associated with moving people, machinery, materials or goods across space and the implication of this for location in space forms the basis of the neo–classical location theory. Key concepts that build upon the location theory include the central place theory, urban hierarchy, market potential and accessibility. These concepts help us to understand how the friction of distance influences the location of economic activities in space.

Further insights into why economic activities simply do not disperse in space are, among others, offered by the concepts of agglomeration economies, increasing returns and cumulative causation. These latter concepts identify additional market advantages arising from the spatial concentration of economic activities. In essence, these concepts show that rather than having a self–correcting dispersal effect, market forces can in fact reinforce existing inequalities in space. The kind of spatial equilibrium envisaged by the neo–classical theory is therefore hard to achieve. It could be argued that these latter concepts 'use the approach and language of neo–classical economics to reach contrary conclusions'.

MARXIST–INSPIRED APPROACHES AND UNEVEN DEVELOPMENT

Marxist–inspired approaches in economic geography also challenge the neoclassical idea of spatial equilibrium, although coming from a completely different perspective. Marxist theory sees capitalism as a system based on the exploitation of labour. The profit imperative makes such a system incredibly dynamic, yet, at the same time, inherently unequal and crisis-prone. Internal contradictions mean that crises of overaccumulation are inevitable in such a system. Devaluation must take place to kick–start the accumulation process all over again. Building on these systemic features of capitalism, Marxist economic geographers do not see inequalities in space as disappearing with the operation of market forces.

Instead they consider uneven development as a permanent, unavoidable and, in fact, necessary feature of the capitalist market economy. Indeed, in Marxist–inspired approaches, uneven development is usually seen as both the necessary precondition and the unavoidable consequence of capitalist economic growth. Several concepts have been put forward that try to describe the way capitalist economies work over space. One of them uses a 'see-saw' metaphor to describe the ebb and flow of capital from one region to another in search of profit. Destruction and devaluation of places left behind may create pre-conditions for future renewed growth.

In a similar vein, the concept of spatial fix recognises that geographical space is an important element in the functioning of the capitalist economy and its ability to contain, absorb or delay crises. This includes the expansion of the spatial horizons of the capitalist system, for example, in the form of new (more profitable) spaces of production or new regional markets. Such a spatial expansion (or spatial fix) is perhaps one of the ways in which the capitalist system is able to postpone the collapse predicted by Marx.

In this view, geographical space plays a crucial role in the workings of the capitalist system. Another concept that tries to capture the operation of the capitalist economy over space is that of spatial divisions of labour. It describes the way in which capitalism creates spatial structures that assign distinct economic functions to particular regions.

The economic fortunes of these regions are thus linked to their position in the spatial division of labour within the wider economic structure. Related to this is a concept of core–periphery which conceptualises uneven development as a set of uneven economic relations between a (dominant) core region and (dominated) periphery region(s). Somewhat echoing the exploitative nature of capitalist class relations, the core-periphery concept suggests that rich regions (or countries) exist thanks to the exploitation of peripheral regions (or countries). One way or other, in Marxist–inspired approaches, uneven development is always linked to the structural features of the economy. This is in stark contrast to some alternative approaches that are going to be examined in turn.

EVOLUTIONARY/INSTITUTIONALIST APPROACHES AND NEW ECONOMIC GEOGRAPHY

Economic geography approaches that draw from heterodox economics and the evolutionary/institutionalist perspective represent a diverse and evolving group. However, some common features are discernible. The evolutionary/ institutionalist perspective emphasises the importance of social, cultural and institutional factors for the understanding of the ways economies work. This is in contrast to both neo-classical views (that largely disregard such factors) and the Marxist approach (that assumes that such factors are determined by, rather than being determinants of, the economy).

However, the evolutionary/ institutionalist perspective sees the economy as always embedded in, and constituted by, social, cultural and institutional spheres. Economic geography approaches developed from this perspective thus see uneven development as inextricably linked to (or shaped by) institutional contexts. One of the key points that such economic geography approaches are making is that social, cultural and institutional contexts are placespecific. In other words, economic fortunes of regions (or whole countries) depend on the institutional arrangements that these regions (or countries) are able to create.

At the regional level, for instance, the concept of 'institutional thickness' has been proposed to capture the strength of local/regional institutions, their ability to cooperate and to promote a coherent development strategy. In line with the view that successful economies are increasingly knowledge-based or learning economies, successful regions have also been conceptualised as learning regions. The key feature of such regions is their ability to innovate, to learn and to accumulate knowledge in various forms, thanks to their institutional set-up.

It is argued, for instance, that the capacity to innovate and to learn depends on various collaborative networks, which are sustained thanks to the institutions of trust, shared culture and social capital, all of which are dependent on particular regional settings. In this view then, regions are in fact seen as key engines of the knowledge economy and uneven development in such an economy is a result of differences in regional 'institutional thickness', innovation capacity, learning and knowledge accumulation.

Interestingly, there are two opposing views with regard to the prospect of achieving balanced development in the knowledge–based or learning economy. The first view is based on the assumption that economically lagging regions (or nations) can catch–up because favourable conditions for growth can be created locally by making appropriate institutional arrangements. This view is further supported by the assumption that thanks to information and communication technology (ICT), the key resource in the knowledge economy—knowledge—can move freely around the world. It should therefore be possible for previously underdeveloped regions to emulate the success of leading regions such as Silicon Valley. The second, and opposing, view suggests that uneven development will continue to be a feature in the knowledge–based economy.

This view is based on the assumption that the key sources of competitiveness and economic success is non–standardised tacit knowledge (as opposed to standardised, written, explicit knowledge). Tacit knowledge, the argument goes, is embedded in local/regional institutions, regional innovation cultures and clusters and these are apparently place-specific to the extent that they cannot be replicated by regions elsewhere. One way or another, the interest in regional institutional settings has been associated with the emergence of so–called new economic geography. While the term 'new economic geography' is used by some economists to describe recent advances in economics in relation to space, in geography the term is used to describe an economic geography approach which moves away from viewing economic processes as separate from social, cultural and political contexts and emphasises that these contexts are crucial for understanding economic dynamics. New economic geography therefore also enthusiastically embraces the notions of culture, social capital, ethnicity and gender in its study of the economy, reflecting a wider 'cultural turn' in social sciences.

CONCEPTS AND THEORIES IN ECONOMIC GEOGRAPHY NEO–CLASSICAL APPROACH, LOCATION THEORY AND BEYOND

This part will examine concepts and theories in economic geography that use the mainstream perspective of the economy as their starting point. This will include a discussion on neo–classical spatial equilibrium which presupposes that factors of production will disperse across regions to create a balanced and efficient pattern of development. This will be followed by a discussion on the neo-classical location theories, one of which is the central place theory.

The central place theory shows that even under perfect market conditions economic activities will cluster in certain locations creating a dynamic equilibrium in space and a distinct urban hierarchy. Such an urban hierarchy, in turn, creates different levels of market potential and connectivity–accessibility, concepts that will be examined subsequently.

Finally, the part will turn attention to the concepts of agglomeration economies and increasing returns and the theory of cumulative causation, all of which help to explain why the spatial equilibrium envisaged by the neo–classical theory is hard to achieve. These latter concepts demonstrate that rather than having a self–correcting dispersal effect, market forces can in fact reinforce existing inequalities in space.

NEO–CLASSICAL SPATIAL EQUILIBRIUM

The simplest version of the neo-classical spatial model involves the movement across space of the two key factors of production—capital and labour.

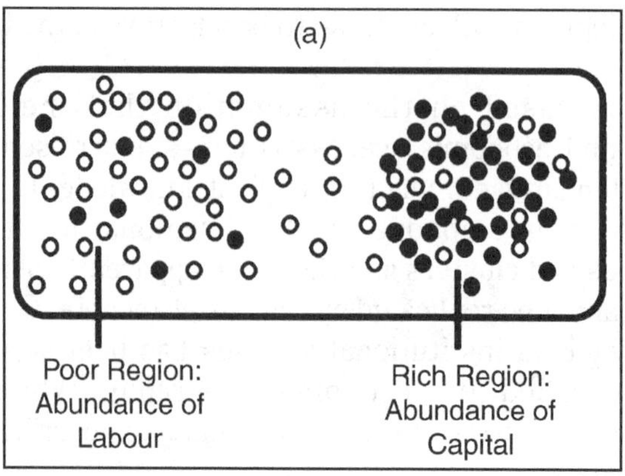

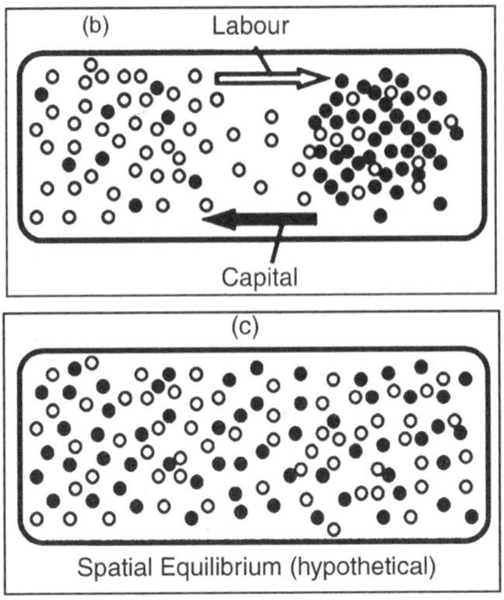

Fig. Neo–classical Spatial Equilibrium

Imagine a country—an island—that has two regions, one 'rich' and one 'poor'. In the rich region, there is a great supply of capital, but a relative shortage of labour. As a result of this labour shortage, the wages in the rich region will be very high. In the poor region, wages are much lower, due to the abundance of labour and a relative lack of capital. The neo–classical model, labour will move from the poor region to the rich region in search of higher wages, while the capital will move in the opposite direction in search of cheaper labour. This is fully in line with the expected behaviour of a rational 'economic man'. Importantly, individual actions of this kind will ensure that the system as a whole will reach spatial equilibrium.

The economic geographer, Diane Perrons, summarises the neo–classical hypothesis as follows:

- 'Labour and capital are predicted to move from areas of surplus to areas of deficit, stimulated by higher returns—wages or profits respectively. Thus, labour should move from poor to rich regions and capital should move in the opposite direction until wages and profits are equalised across regions resulting in an efficient and balanced pattern of development.'

Even more complex neo–classical models that involve other factors of production are all built around the assumption that some sort of spatial equilibrium will be achieved in the long run, because such factors of production will inevitably spread or disperse over space. The processes of spatial dispersal can indeed be observed in reality. However, the examples of spatial equilibrium that the neo–classical theory envisages are hard to find. Firms, for instance, do not disperse over space but cluster in particular locations. The explanation for this has been offered by the neo–classical location theory to which we now turn.

NEO–CLASSICAL LOCATION THEORY

One way of accounting for the fact that spatial equilibrium does not occur, is to acknowledge that in real life, factors of production cannot move 'freely' over space. Indeed, there are various constraints involved. One of the obvious obstacles is the friction of distance. In other words, moving people, machinery, materials or goods over geographical distance usually involves a cost. For workers, there is usually a price tag associated with travelling to work, for instance. For firms, there is a cost involved in moving raw materials from the source to the factory and there is a cost associated with delivering finished products from the factory to consumers. Thus, for both people and businesses, location in space is a crucial part of their strategy of self–interest and profit–maximisation. The calculation of the cost associated with moving across space and the implication of this for location in space, forms the basis of the neo–classical location theory. Key concepts that build upon the location theory include central place theory, urban hierarchy, market potential and connectivity-accessibility, all of which will be explored in turn.

CENTRAL PLACE THEORY AND URBAN HIERARCHY

Central place theory helps us to understand how the friction of distance influences the pattern of the location of economic activities in space, while focusing on the issue of the delivery of goods and services from producers/providers to customers/clients. In order to explain central place theory, let's return to our imaginary island. The starting point of central place theory is the observation that even if the population of the island were distributed evenly over space, firms would still tend to cluster in particular locations.

Walter Christaller, a German scholar and the key proponent of central place theory called these locations central places. Why would firms want to locate in central places? The friction of distance, and the cost associated with overcoming it, is the central element in the explanation offered by location theorists. Central place theory highlights the fact that firms do not simply have 'markets'—they have 'market areas'.

Geography is a factor in the operation of the market, because there are transport costs associated with delivering finished products to customers. The longer the delivery distance, the higher the final price of a product. In order for a firm to survive, it clearly needs a certain minimum market area. The pin–making factory, for instance, needs a certain minimum market area to be viable. This minimum market area must contain a sufficient number of potential customers which would create a sufficient demand for its products. This minimum market area is called threshold.

Of course, it is in the interest of every factory to extend its market area well beyond the threshold. However, due to the transport costs, a market area cannot be infinitely large. Indeed, with each mile or kilometre of distance from the factory, the final price of a product will increase. Following the neo–classical reasoning of supply and demand, with each price increase, the number of customers willing to pay for the product will decrease.

As the price of our box of pins increases with distance, less and less customers will be willing to pay for it, until we reach a point where a box of pins becomes too expensive for anyone to buy it. In central place theory this is called a market area range. Beyond the range, there is no market for our pins due to the transport costs involved. It goes without saying that for a company to be profitable, the market area range must be bigger than the threshold. In general, the bigger the overall market area, the better.

However, central place theory rightly points out that different products have market areas of different sizes. In fact, one can imagine a hierarchy of goods and services, each having different market areas and therefore prompting a different location in space for their providers. A simple ranking may include higher–order, medium–order and lower–order goods and services. Higher–order goods would include high–value items that are bought infrequently. Lower–order goods would include the least expensive items that customers demand on a frequent basis. This logic, butchers, bakers, pin–makers, shoe–makers, car–makers would locate in central places of relevant order, because those locations offer the best opportunity to serve the market.

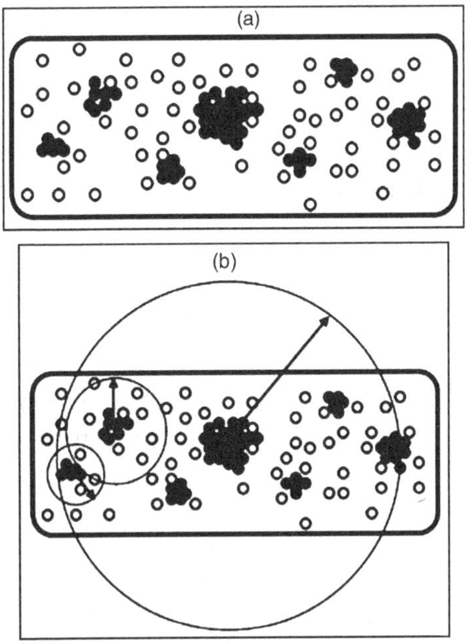

Fig. Central Place Theory: Hierarchy of Central Places

What central place theory does then, is apply the principles of neoclassical thought to location in space, while incorporating the role of distance. In doing so, it shows that spatial equilibrium characterised by the total dispersal of economic activities is unlikely to happen. However, the theory remains firmly within the neo–classical framework. It suggests that a dynamic equilibrium will emerge out of the balance between the inputs of money and the outputs of goods and services.

A dynamic equilibrium will be achieved as firms move around and locate in central places until the island is covered by overlapping market areas of various hierarchical order, ensuring that demand by local consumers is met by producer's supply in the most efficient manner. One important implication of the central place theory model is that the hierarchy of central places can be translated into an urban hierarchy. Higher–order central places become higher–order urban centres, while lower-order central places correspond to lower–order settlements.

A simple urban hierarchy that can emerge out of Christaller's conceptualisation of central places may involve five levels, namely:

- Metropolis
- City
- Town
- Village
- Hamlet

While central place theory does represent a major improvement on the original simple spatial equilibrium model, it has its own shortcomings. One of the key limits is that population is never spread evenly over space. Rather, population is likely to concentrate in urban centres of various sizes, perhaps reflecting the urban hierarchy. This also means that market opportunities are not spread evenly over space. This in turn, may have important implications for the location of firms. One concept that is used to capture this is called market potential and this will be examined in turn alongside the concepts of connectivity and accessibility.

MARKET POTENTIAL AND CONNECTIVITY–ACCESSIBILITY

Connectivity–accessibility, in its simplest terms, can be defined as the ease with which people, materials and information can be moved from one location to another. In contemporary economies, these movements are usually supported by dedicated transport infrastructure and telecommunication networks. Therefore, regional connectivity accessibility could also be seen as a measure of the ability of these infrastructures and networks to reduce the friction of distance within and between regions. While the two terms are often used interchangeably, there are in fact subtle differences between the concept of connectivity and the concept of accessibility.

Connectivity usually relates to the features of a given transport or communications network and can be measured in two basic ways. The first one is to measure the level of connectivity of an entire network. Numerous indices have been devised to measure such connectivity. One of the most frequently used is the beta index, which is calculated as the ratio of links to nodes. The higher the number of links to nodes, the higher the degree of connectivity of a given network. Figure a shows an example of a calculation of beta index for our imaginary island which has 15 urban centres connected by a simple road network grid.

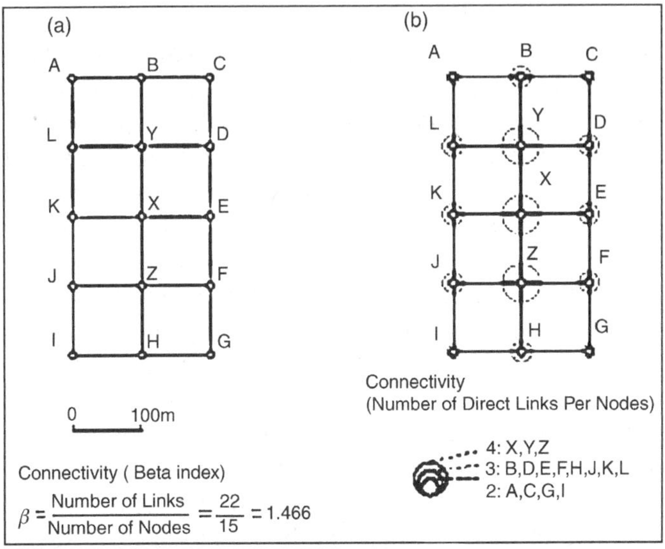

Fig. Connectivity

The second option is to measure the level of connectivity of individual places within a network. In other words, node connectivity measures the degree to which individual nodes are connected with other nodes within the network. Again, this can be done in a number of ways. The simplest measure of node connectivity is the number of direct links that a particular node has with other nodes. The more direct links a particular node has, the higher its degree of connectivity.

The measures of connectivity may be useful in some cases and some firms may choose to locate in certain places thanks to their higher level of connectivity. However, if firms want to achieve the best possible access to the largest share of markets, then the concepts of accessibility and market potential may be more relevant for their location decisions.

The concept of accessibility is based on the explicit recognition of the importance of both the geographical distances between nodes and the characteristics of the nodes. The characteristics of the nodes are sometimes called the 'attributes of destinations'. Within the concept of accessibility, the aspect of geographical distance is considered as an impedance for the movement of people, materials and information. While transport and telecommunication infrastructures may reduce the friction of distance, it still takes a certain amount of time, money and/or effort to move people, goods and services around. Travel time and travel cost is often a direct function of the distance covered. One way or another, the level of impedance is clearly important to economic agents, as we have already learned in the case of central place theory.

The crucial difference is that the concept of accessibility explicitly recognises the fact that population represent the second dimension of the concept of accessibility. From an economic point of view, the level of attractiveness of destinations is frequently associated with the size of their markets, which can be expressed as an economic mass or volume of economic activity either in terms of population size, income, spending power, gross domestic product, opportunities to be reached, or similar characteristics.

This is based on an assumption that the bigger the market a firm has access to, the better the prospects for the firm's profitability and growth. This way, the level of accessibility is directly associated with the expected economic performance and competitiveness of firms. In other words, it is expected that a firm will be more successful if it locates in places with high levels of accessibility. In turn, regions with high levels of accessibility are expected to be more economically viable.

This assumption is encapsulated in the market potential or economic potential model, which represents the most frequent way of measuring accessibility. In this model, the economic potential of a region is a positive function of the size of markets that can be accessed from the region, and a negative function of impedance that needs to be overcome when reaching those markets. In the simplest measure of regional accessibility, the potential of any region can be calculated by summing the population of all other regions in the system and dividing these by some measure of their intervening distance. The potential of region i, thus can be calculated as:

$$Pi = (j = 1 \rightarrow j = n) \Sigma Mj / Dij$$

where Pi is the potential of region i, Mj is a measure of economic mass in region j and Dij is a measure of impedance from region i to region j, and n is the total number of regions in the system. The regions located closest to the biggest markets would be seen as having the highest economic potential. The way in which the size of markets influences the market potential of different places is captured in Figure.

If all the urban centres on our island were of equal size then the picture of accessibility measured through the market potential model would be simple: the urban centres located in the geographical centre of the island would display the highest level of accessibility. Meanwhile the urban centres located at the geographical periphery of the island would be considered as the least accessible.

However, if, for whatever reason, the populations of these urban centres start to vary, the picture of accessibility can change considerably, due to the changing market potential. If, for instance, urban centre G were to become a city with a population of 500,000, the picture of accessibility for this regional economy would be dramatically transformed. Indeed, city G with its population of half a million people would several times exceed the population of the rest of the island.

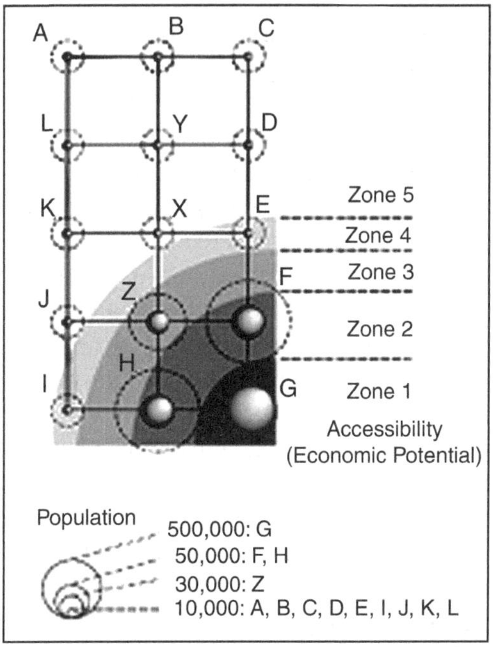

Fig. Market Potential and Accessibility

Therefore, due to the weight of its own self-potential, city G would become the most accessible place on the island. Thanks to their proximity to city G, urban centres F and H, would overnight become the second–best 'accessible' places on the island, perhaps attracting some population growth, thus further strengthening their own market potential, while having a similar knock-on effect on town Z. Looking at the question of industrial location from the point of view of market potential and regional accessibility, our pin-making factory will be best located in city G, where the biggest market can be reached with the least effort or cost. The economic mass has a major influence on the level of accessibility of different regions. The concept of market potential using two variables is ultimately more satisfactory than the Christaller's concept of central places which operates with one variable only. The concept of market potential, in other words, helps us to better understand the economic pull that is created when markets are being concentrated in particular places. Further insights into why economic activities simply do not disperse in space are offered by the concepts of agglomeration economies, increasing returns and cumulative causation, which will be examined in turn.

AGGLOMERATION ECONOMIES

The market potential model is based on the assumption that the bigger the market a firm has access to, the better the prospects for the firm's profitability and growth. But this is not the end of the story. By pursuing the strategy of locating close to large markets, firms inevitably end up locating close to each other. This, in itself, can be a source of an additional advantage. Indeed, firms can derive further advantages from simply co–locating in particular places. In other words 'clustering itself offers further economies'.

Economies derived from colocated firms are called agglomeration economies or economies of agglomeration. In order to explain how agglomeration economies work, as suggested, introduce the concepts of economies of scale and increasing returns to scale. Let us start with the concept of economies of scale. There are two types of scale economies—internal economies of scale and external economies of scale. In order to explain how internal economies of scale work, let us return to our pin–making factory. Adam Smith described a situation in which major productivity gains were achieved by introducing a division of labour.

There are about 18 specialised tasks to be performed in the pin–making process. One worker alone would find it difficult to produce one pin a day. However, productivity can increase dramatically if 10 workers are employed to do the job. It could be argued that further productivity gains are possible if 18 workers were employed, each performing just one particular task. Internal economies have emerged in our pin–making factory thanks to the division of labour. Importantly, these economies have been growing as we have been up-scaling our production, by employing more and more workers.

The bigger the operation, the higher productivity per worker has been achieved. In other words, we have achieved increasing returns to scale. Unfortunately, returns to scale are not increasing indefinitely. One can imagine that our pin–making factory can employ more workers still. For instance, a cleaner, a machine repair specialist, an accountant, advertising/ marketing people and selling agent(s) may all come in useful. Also, employing a worker responsible for delivering boxes of pins to our customers in our market area would be of benefit.

So, one can imagine that the factory can probably profitably employ up to 23 or 25 workers. But beyond this number, the return to scale would start to decline dramatically. In other words, we would not gain much by employing additional workers as the existing workforce is already covering all the tasks in an efficient manner. In fact, employing an extra pair of hands would probably be more of a hindrance than a benefit—the profit per worker would decline. In other words, we would experience decreasing or diminishing returns to scale. Consider now what options are available to firms if they 'cluster' in certain locations.

It is possible that if such a geographical concentration of firms was large enough, certain specialised tasks can be performed by specialist firms. For instance, there may be scope for a professional accountant who can provide comprehensive accountancy services to all firms in the agglomeration—and at a much smaller cost to the firms involved. Our pin–making factory would benefit from this, because the need to employ our own full–time accountant would disappear.

Similar economies can be achieved if other tasks or sub–processes were performed by specialist firms, rather than employing in–house workers. One can imagine that a cleaning company, a machine repair company, an advertising agency or a transport company can be set up if sufficient demand exists within the agglomeration. In effect, division of labour would emerge in such an agglomeration.

The benefits of such a division of labour between firms would be similar to those derived from a division of labour within firms. Economies of scale can be realised, but this time these economies would be external to any one firm. Our pin–making factory would benefit from this development and its profitability would increase. In other words, our pin–making factory would reap the benefits of agglomeration economies.

Such benefits of agglomeration were originally described more than a century ago by Alfred Marshall in Principles of Economics. Marshall also argued that, in addition to agglomerated firms providing each other with key inputs and markets, there are two further major benefits of agglomeration. First, the availability of a local pool of skilled labour may be an advantage, and second, firms within an agglomeration may benefit from knowledge spillovers.

This latter point about knowledge spillovers is interesting, because it diverts from a strict neo–classical framework. More recently, it has been re-discovered by the new economic geography approaches. Meanwhile, you will find that literature usually describes two types of agglomeration economies—localisation economies and urbanisation economies. Localisation economies are agglomeration economies that emerge between specialised suppliers, collaborators, sub-contractors or competitors within a single industry located together in a particular place.

Urbanisation economies, on the other hand, refer to agglomeration economies shared by all firms in all industries in one location. In real life, localization economies and urbanisation economies are sometimes hard to distinguish, as the boundaries between these two notions are rather porous.

One way or another, firms co-locating in particular locations can often benefit from agglomeration economies which can include:

- The collective use of transport infrastructure and communication facilities
- The local availability of skilled labour force

- A technical college or university offering relevant training
- Access to research facilities
- Proximity to ancillary industries among others

Further to this, it is important to recognise that agglomerations are usually underpinned by two types of linkages between firms. The first type is referred to as traded interdependencies, the second one as untraded interdependencies. Traded interdependencies are created by firms having formal trading relationships between them within a given agglomeration. For instance, our pin–making factory has a formal contractual relationship with a professional accountant, with a cleaning company, or with a local courier service.

These arrangements benefit from agglomeration economies. On the other hand, untraded interdependencies refer to the less tangible benefits of being located in the same place. Untraded interdependencies may include various informal links and interactions between firms and between firms and other economic actors. Untraded interdependencies thus relate to various social and cultural bases of agglomerations that go beyond the narrow neo–classical definitions of the 'economic'. The concept of untraded interdependencies is linked to the notion of clusters which will be examined in more detail in the final part of this stage, alongside the alternative and new economic geography approaches.

CUMULATIVE CAUSATION

Important advantages occur for firms locating close to each other in specific locations. We can now ask the question: what are the implications of this for uneven development? The theory of cumulative causation introduced by a Swedish scholar Gunnar Myrdal argues that a circular chain reaction will emerge leading to a greater polarisation between rich and poor regions. In the rich regions with strong agglomeration economies, a virtuous circle of growth and development may emerge in which 'success breeds success'.

In part, this is possible thanks to the multiplier effect, a mechanism in which each dollar spent in the local economy generates further income down the line. Indeed, it is not difficult to imagine that existing agglomeration economies may attract further firms into the region. If this happens then a circular chain reaction will begin. Indeed, jobs created by new or expanding firms will increase employment and the population of the region. This in turn will increase local demand for goods and services, thus leading to an enlarged local supply base and expanded service sector. This in turn will enlarge the local financial base and spending power of the local government, which will allow for local infrastructure to be upgraded.

This in turn will increase agglomeration economies. The increased agglomeration economies will again attract more firms into the region, fuelling a virtuous circle of growth and development. This is then a principle of circular and cumulative causation in which one event triggers a sequence of causal links in a circular and self–reinforcing way. What we observe could also be described as a process of the increasing returns to scale, although this time at the level of the entire agglomeration.

If in operation, such a process would ensure that the bigger the agglomeration gets, the bigger the agglomeration economies that can be achieved. In addition to the advantages, such a growing agglomeration may go hand in hand with an increasingly diverse economic base characterised by a complex division of labour. Indeed, as a given agglomeration grows, there is a possibility that more and more specialised tasks will be carried out by specialist firms, contributing to the increasing division of labour between firms, thus increasing economies of agglomeration further still. While the increasing dynamism of successful regions may be welcome, the problem is that their expansion may be happening at the expense of other regions.

Indeed, it may well be the case that firms that are being attracted by the vibrant economic climate of large agglomerations relocate there from poorer, 'less developed' or less favoured regions. The loss of a firm in a less favoured region generates a negative chain reaction that mirrors the process of cumulative causation in an adverse sense. Indeed, it is not difficult to imagine that the closure of a firm leads to the loss of employment and possibly to a loss of population too, via out–migration. Either way, the spending power of the local population decreases, reducing the local demand for goods and services and in turn undermining the local tax base, leading to the reduced ability of the local government to maintain local infrastructure.

This, in turn, affects the agglomeration economies and reduces the attractiveness of the peripheral region further still. More firms may choose to relocate to richer regions, and the younger and skilled workforce may follow suit. In essence, this constitutes what Myrdal called a backwash effect—a flow of capital and labour from lagging regions to developed regions. Contrary to the neo–classical assumption of spatial equilibrium, the backwash effect will cause the economic gap between rich and poor regions to widen further.

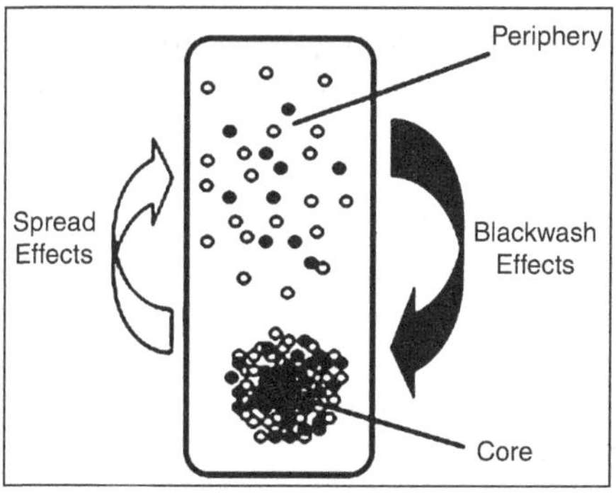

Fig. Cumulative Causation

The rich regions will end up with increasing levels of investment, young workers, growing purchasing power and improving local services and infrastructure, while less developed regions will be characterised by a lack of investment, an ageing labour force, a decline in local services and a dilapidated infrastructure. This polarised spatial pattern is often referred to as core–periphery. The important question is whether such a core–periphery pattern will remain in place once established. This is a difficult question.

Some economists and economic geographers believe that just as is the case with individual firms, agglomerations too have their limits, beyond which diminishing returns will kick-in. Indeed, the dis-economies that may occur in large cities may include the prohibitive cost of land, the cost of labour, pollution and congestion. Such dis–economies may indeed encourage the decentralisation of operations or whole firms to less developed regions. In other words, spread effects may emerge, as predicted by the neo–classical spatial equilibrium model. However, according to cumulative causation theorists, backwash effects will always be greater than spread effects, thus contributing to the polarisation, rather than the dispersal, of economic fortunes between regions.

This is because:

- 'Market forces, if left to their own devices, are spatially disequilibriating. Economies of scale and agglomeration lead to the cumulative concentration of capital, labour, and output in certain regions at the expense of others: uneven regional development is self–reinforcing'

In essence, the theory of cumulative causation provides further evidence that, rather than having a self–correcting effect, market forces can in fact reinforce existing inequalities in space. The kind of spatial equilibrium envisaged by neo–classical theory is therefore difficult to achieve. Importantly, this conclusion has been reached while using the neo–classical conceptual framework. It could therefore be argued that the cumulative causation theory and similar concepts 'use the approach and language of neo–classical economics to reach contrary conclusions'.

MARXIST–INSPIRED APPROACHES AND UNEVEN DEVELOPMENT

We have examined concepts and theories of spatial development whose starting point is the neo–classical framework of selfinterest and the profit-maximising behaviour of economic agents. We have seen that after a thorough application of neo–classical principles, the original neo–classical ideal of spatial equilibrium is in fact hard to achieve. Some of these concepts and theories show that market forces can reinforce, rather than reduce, existing inequalities in space. The issue of unequal and uneven development will be taken further in this part, although from a completely different perspective. The part will examine concepts and theories associated with the Marxist perspective. This will include a discussion on wealth, value and circuits of capital, with an emphasis on the concepts and theories which help to elucidate the circuits of capital over space. Subsequently, the related concept of spatial fix will be examined, highlighting the role of space and uneven development as fundamental to the functioning of the capitalist economy.

Further to this the concept of spatial divisions of labour will be introduced alongside a discussion on the technical and social division of labour. The concept of the spatial divisions of labour helps us to appreciate how the economic fortunes of regions are associated with their position in the spatial division of labour within the wider economic structure. The part will conclude by examining the core-periphery concept which conceptualises uneven development as a set of uneven economic relations between a core region and periphery regions.

WEALTH, VALUE AND CIRCUITS OF CAPITAL

Wealth can be defined as 'a cumulative share of the rewards created in the economic process of adding value'. The creation of value is therefore central to the discussion on economic development in general and uneven development in particular. But what is value and how is value created? Marxist theory, all value ultimately comes from human labour.

In other words, 'value is always created by people' such as our workers in the pin-making factory. Workers engage in a labour process, that is, they apply their labour on raw materials to produce new goods and these goods embody values. Marxist theory distinguishes several types of value embodied in commodities. The key distinction can be made between exchange value and use value. Exchange value is a value expressed in money for which a particular commodity has been sold on the market.

A pair of shoes, a coat, a bottle of milk or an apple can all be commodities for which you need to pay a certain price to buy them. Use value, on the other hand, is the value of a commodity to the person who uses it—the pleasure, for instance, of drinking a glass of milk. Use value is therefore harder to express in terms of money. For instance, a coat can be bought via the Internet for the same price anywhere around the world but the use value of having such a coat and keeping oneself warm is definitely higher for those living in cold climates. For Marxists, the key problem of the capitalist system is that labour power itself is a commodity which is bought and sold on the market for an exchange value.

A capitalist only employs workers if their use value to him or her is greater than the exchange value of their labour. The difference between the two is surplus value. Capitalists accumulate wealth by appropriating surplus value through the exploitation of workers. Capitalists have to do this if they are to survive competition from their rivals. The creation of the little 's' is absolutely essential for the operation of the capitalist system and this is done via a circuit of capital we have described earlier.

However, capitalists need to make a decision about what to do with the little 's' they 'create'. One option is to simply consume it, for example, by indulging in the luxuries of life. This creates a situation which Marxists call a simple reproduction.

Fig. Circuit of Capital: Simple Reproduction

The other option is to re-invest the surplus value in the production process. For instance, the owner of the pin-making factory may decide to use the profit to hire a few more workers. In other words, the owner will engage in expanded reproduction. With each run of the circuit of capital, the little 's' gets bigger and bigger. The rate at which surplus value is expanding is usually referred to as accumulation.

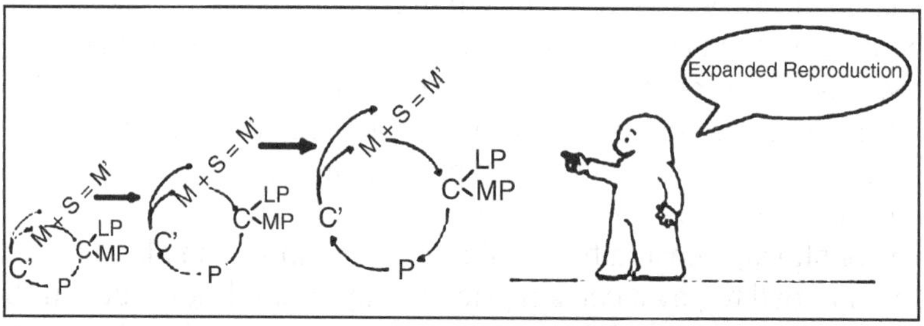

Fig. Circuit of Capital: Expanded Reproduction

What we have just described is a circulation of value in the primary circuit of capital. The re–investment of surplus value in production involves continuously putting capital to work within the primary circuit of capital. This can work well, but there are limits. Indeed, as we have already learned, the capitalist system is crisis-prone. It is likely that, sooner or later, a crisis of overaccumulation will surface. This can happen in a number of ways, but usually such a crisis is caused by over–production and/or under–consumption. In other words, too many pins or cars will be produced and too few people will be able to afford them. One way or another, the crisis of overaccumulation will mean falling rates of profit for the capitalist. The circuit of capital is broken, the surplus value cannot be created. Existing surplus value has nowhere to go to be profitably employed.

The way in which the capitalist system copes with this has been described by economic geographer David Harvey in his influential book The Limits to Capital a new edition of which was published more recently. Let us examine David Harvey's hypothesis in a bit more detail. One obvious 'solution' to the crisis of overaccumulation is devaluation. However, Harvey has pointed out that another way of coping with this is capital switching. Capital switching involves re-directing capital surpluses to various other circuits of capital. This can happen at various levels and scales.

It may be possible that profitable opportunities still exist within the primary circuit of capital. If a pin-making business goes bust, capital can be redirected to a mobile phone business; if a car-making business is in difficulty, money can be invested in the production of computers. Capitalists do not care which business their money is in, unless it produces the precious little 's'. However, if the crisis engulfs the entire economy, then switching capital within the primary circuit is not going to help. The system then enters a 'switching crisis'.

However, David Harvey has identified two other circuits in which capital can be invested: secondary and tertiary circuits of capital. The secondary circuit involves investing surplus value in fixed capital. Fixed capital includes all the elements of the built environment such as factories, dams, offices, shops, warehouses, roads, railways, docks, power stations, water supply and sewage disposal systems, schools, hospitals, parks, cinemas, restaurants, etc.

Capitalists investing in the secondary circuit are doing so in the expectation of realising their profits either in the form of rental income, or from the enhanced future sale price of the building. The tertiary circuit involves investment in science and technology, education, health care, etc. Although usually undertaken by the state, investment in these latter areas may eventually improve the profitability of capital via increased productivity and improving labour capability. The secondary and tertiary circuits are very different in character, but they share an important common feature.

In both cases, there is a potentially considerable time lag between the time when investment is made and the time when profits are eventually realised. In other words, both these circuits have a capacity to absorb surplus value for a long time before releasing it back into circulation many years later. In other words, both these circuits have a temporal dimension and both may be part of what can be called a 'temporal fix'. The other important point to note is that circuits of capital also have their spatial dimension.

Indeed, capital switching may happen both within and between regions. Some regions may be engaged in specific circuits of capital and the crises of those circuits may be translated into regional crises. Capital switching thus may involve not only moving surpluses into secondary and tertiary circuits of capital within a given region, but also into various circuits outside the regional economy in question. One way or another, geography plays an important role in the operation of the capitalist system. Spatial structures created around us can be seen as being part of the circuits of capital. As such, they can also be part of the answer to the question of why capitalism has managed to avoid terminal collapse despite its inherent contradictions. This leads us to the concept of a spatial fix.

UNEVEN DEVELOPMENT AND 'SPATIAL FIX'

Spatial fix, or more precisely, spatio–temporal fix is another concept developed by David Harvey. The concept refers to the way in which both time and space play a central role in the operation of the capitalist system. The word 'fix' has a double meaning here. On the one hand, it describes a situation in which a certain portion of capital is 'literally fixed in and on the land in some physical form for a relatively long period of time'. On the other hand, the term 'fix' is used as 'a metaphor for a particular kind of solution to capitalist crises through temporal deferral and geographical expansion'.

There are several ways in which capitalism can cope with crises:

- Devaluation
- Macro–economic management
- Temporal displacement of capital
- Spatial displacement of capital.

Devaluation may involve the devaluation of money, devaluation of labour as well as the devaluation of productive capacities. Macro–economic management involves attempts to bring together idle capital and idle labour back into productive use through government intervention. This can be done by curbing excessive labour exploitation or through increased government spending, for instance. An example of such an approach to the economic crisis is Keynesianism. More generally, various modes of regulation may be instituted to prevent the system from collapsing.

A temporal displacement of capital involves placing surplus capital in long-term ventures. This may include the investment in secondary and tertiary circuits of capital. Social expenditures and long–term investments in infrastructure of various kinds are examples of this, as is the advancement of loans. The effect of such temporal displacements of capital is that they avert crises at the present and delay them into the future. A temporal fix is therefore responsible for expanding the time horizons of the circuits of capital.

The spatial displacement of capital on the other hand, expands the spatial horizons of the capitalist system. The spatial fix includes the opening of new spaces of production; spatial expansion into new markets; finding new sources of raw materials; or the re-creation of old places.

The logic behind the spatial fix has been summarised by Harvey as follows:

- If the surpluses of capital and of labour power exist within a given territory and cannot be absorbed internally then they must be sent elsewhere to find a fresh terrain for their profitable realization if they are not to be devalued..

In other words, capital constantly searches for the spaces in which surplus value can be created. This search for new spaces of capital accumulation may involve re-investment in previously devalued old spaces or pushing the boundaries of capitalist enterprise beyond the established circuits of capital. Understanding the operation of the economy in this light opens up new ways of looking at processes such as globalisation. One way or another, it is important to note that Harvey's conceptualisation of economic geographies include the notion that uneven development 'is not only an inevitable feature of capitalism, but also a necessary one'.

This is because:

- [s]pace is not just the container in which capitalism takes place. Rather, economic geography is fundamental and inherent to the successful operation of the system.

To put it differently, 'uneven development is both a cause and an outcome of capitalist growth'. Further insights into the issue of uneven development in the capitalist economy have been offered by the concept of spatial divisions of labour to which we now turn.

SPATIAL DIVISIONS OF LABOUR

The concept of spatial divisions of labour has been developed by a British geographer Doreen Massey in her highly influential book Spatial Divisions of Labour: Social Structures and the Geography of Production. In it, Massey has discussed the geography of production and uneven development through the prism of the social relations of production.

Under capitalism, social relations of production revolve:

- Around the social relations between capital and labour, employers and employees, investors and wage earners. These are essentially relations of economic power, within which control lies with capital, employers, and investors.

Another way of putting this would be to say that social relations under capitalism are structured along the relations based on class. Massey's point is that social relations are also organised spatially and this is captured in her concept of spatial divisions of labour. In order to explain the concept of spatial divisions of labour, as suggested, first examine two key related concepts—technical division of labour and social division of labour. Technical division of labour, in its simplest form, involves the division of labour within a firm.

As we have seen in the example of the pinmaking factory, the process of making pins involves 18 distinct stages. The technical division of labour implies a division of the production process into distinctive tasks and the assignment of workers to these tasks. In the pin–making factory described by Adam Smith,

10 workers covered 18 tasks. But it is possible to imagine that a more refined technical division of labour can be achieved if an additional eight workers were hired so that each worker specialises in one task.

Fig. Technical Division of Labour

Social division of labour, on the other hand, is a more general concept which goes beyond the boundaries of a firm to describe the roles performed by various people or groups of people within a society at large. Social divisions of labour thus may refer to the division of labour between various sectors or to workers in different jobs or professions. One way or another, the concept helps us to understand that we rely on each other for society to function. In the capitalist society, however, both technical and social divisions of labour reflect the underlying capitalist social relations of production.

The idea of spatial divisions of labour is based on the recognition that the economy is characterised by complex technical and social divisions of labour which are reflected in complex spatial structures. Massey argues that the economy cannot work at the 'head of a pin'—therefore the spatial dimension is always present. Inevitably, the economy is stretched over space and so are social relations of production. In other words, social relations are organised spatially. The spatial organisation of the economy is rather complex, reflecting complex spatial divisions of labour.

A simple example of the spatial division of labour involves the division of labour within a firm, in which different tasks are undertaken in different locations. For instance, head office functions, administrative functions, research and development and production functions can all be located in different regions. Also it is possible to imagine a situation where the different stages of production are located in different regions.

Another example of the spatial division of labour involves the division of labour between firms and sectors— *i.e.,* the steel industry, the electronics industry, financial services) concentrating in certain locations. One way or other, at the level of the national economy, all regions are functionally inter-connected through economic linkages and social relations of production. Individual regions thus must be seen as parts of a wider economic structure.

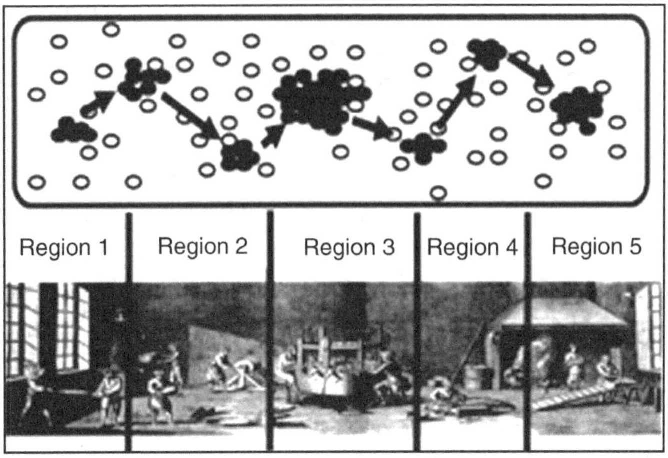

Fig. Spatial Division of Labour

The economic power and fortunes of particular regions depend on their position within the wider social relations of production. The position within the spatial divisions of labour, in turn, is modified or maintained by successive rounds of investment. Uneven development, therefore, cannot be understood in relation to the characteristics of individual regions only. Rather it involves a recognition that the roles the regions are playing are mutually constituted.

In addition, it involves a recognition that uneven development can vary not only in degree but also in character. Simply put, high–level strategic, control and R&D functions would remain concentrated in major metropolitan regions in core countries; management of operations would be delegated to regional capitals; while routine operations and production itself would be based in the periphery. Doreen Massey offers an example of London and the south–east of England which, she argues, 'was the prime locus of control, of strategic planning, of finance, of the resources for research and innovation'. Because of the social relations involved, the southeast of England is, Massey argues, 'in a position of structural dominance in comparison with, and in relation to, other regions of the country'.

Many of the other regions of the country, meanwhile, remained dominated by branch plant manufacturing, simple line assembly or other, subordinate tasks. Thus, Massey insists, this is not about the geography of jobs, but rather the geography 'of power relations, of dominance and subordination, of enablement and influence, and of symbols and signification'. Massey is well aware that the power relations of 'dominance and subordination' are not confined to the national space.

Rather, the spatial divisions of labour within a national economy are embedded within a wider international context of economic and social relations.

Simply put, national economies are themselves part of much wider international divisions of labour and power relations that such a division of labour entails. The significance of the international divisions of labour has been growing hand-in-hand with the processes of globalisation. The way in which regional economies are economically inter–dependent on each other is also reflected in the concept of the core–periphery model to which we now turn.

CORE–PERIPHERY

The key idea of the core–periphery model is that uneven development results from a set of uneven economic relations between a core region and periphery regions. Simply put, economically advanced regions become rich by exploiting economically less developed regions. The idea of domination and subordination between regions has a strong resonance with the principle of exploitation of labour under capitalism. According to the Marxist–inspired core–periphery models, the economic fortunes of regions are dependent on their economic power within the uneven economic relations which allow for an unequal exchange to take place between regions.

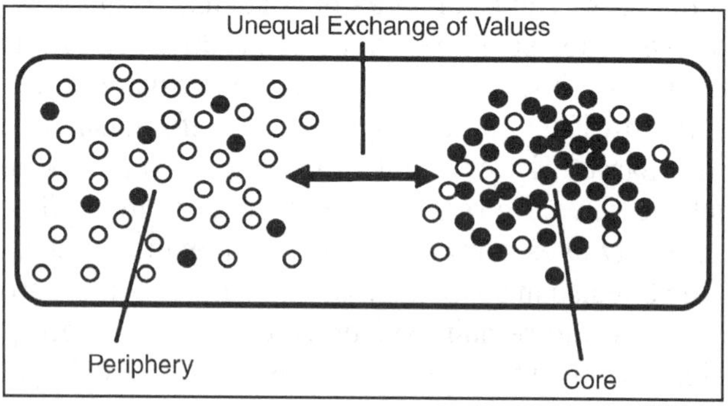

Fig. Core–periphery

Unequal exchange, in turn, contributes towards uneven development between regions. The insistence by the core-periphery model that the fortunes of regions are mutually linked thus echoes both the concepts of spatial divisions of labour reviewed above and that of cumulative causation introduced in the first part of this stage. The core–periphery model offers a simple way of looking at economic dependency between economies and has been applied at various spatial scales from national to international and global.

For instance, South–East of England may be seen as a core region of the UK national economy. In relation to this, the extent to which Britain is economically divided into prosperous South and declining North by the North–South divide has been debated. Meanwhile, at the European level, the south–east of England can be seen as but a part of a much larger core area which stretches from London through Germany to Northern Italy. With the fall of state–socialism in Central and Eastern Europe, the extent to which the East–

West development divide characterises the New Europe has become an issue. Finally, at the global level, the reference is frequently made to the advanced 'core economies' of the Global North and the extent to which the global North–South divide is a useful way of describing divisions within the global economy. While the core–periphery model has its limits, it nevertheless alerts us to some important issues about the mutual interdependencies within and between economies and the creation of 'core' and 'peripheral' spaces at various spatial scales.

ALTERNATIVE APPROACHES AND NEW ECONOMIC GEOGRAPHY

The third and final part of this stage will examine concepts and theories associated with various alternative approaches to economies and their geographies. In doing so, the part will provide basic insights into concepts associated with new economic geography. Most of these concepts have been developed from intellectual vibrations of the evolutionary–institutionalist perspective. New economic geography approaches thus often provide a stark contrast to both the neo–classical and Marxist approaches in the way they see the operation of economies over space.

Indeed, by taking on board various social, cultural, institutional and other factors, new economic geography approaches are shedding a new light on the issue of uneven development. This is a vibrant area of geography and one that has seen many exciting developments in recent years. Having said that, it is important to recognise that some of the new concepts are still hotly debated. You need to be aware of this and keep a critical eye on whatever you read. Also, you need to be aware that many scholars use a combination of various approaches in their study of economic geographies.

Therefore, a sharp delineation of boundaries between various perspectives is sometimes not easy. However, some key differences between the neo-classical and Marxist approaches on the one hand, and new economic geography and other alternative approaches on the other hand, are apparent and will be highlighted in this part. The part will begin by discussing geographical implications of broad sectoral shifts between agriculture, manufacturing and services, stages of product and industry life cycles and technological shifts.

This will set a stage for the examination of selected new economic geography concepts. The part will specifically focus on the role of technical change, innovation and the emergence of knowledge–based and learning economies in the form of regional innovation systems, clusters and learning regions. In relation to this, the part will also discuss the role of networks, trust and social capital in regional economic development. Finally, the part will examine aspects of cultural economies, ethnicity and gender.

STAGES THEORY: AGRICULTURE, MANUFACTURING AND SERVICES

Stages theory is the first of a group of theories that look upon economic development as 'historical and evolutionary processes'.

The starting point of the stages theory is a recognition that the economy is composed of four major sectors:

1. Primary (agriculture and extractive activities)
2. Secondary (manufacturing)
3. Tertiary (services)
4. Quaternary (research and knowledge-intensive activities).

Statistical offices around the world are routinely using the split of economic activities into these major sectors to capture the economic structure of national and regional economies. The key idea of the stages theory is that as societies and economies develop, they move through 'stages' of economic growth from agriculture to manufacture to services to knowledge–based forms of development, each representing a more advanced stage of development. Sectoral shifts from primary to secondary to tertiary and quaternary activities can indeed be observed in the real world.

The importance of each of the sectors changes over time, and this can be measured both in terms of the share of employment and the relative importance of these sectors in the economic output of a given economy. Advanced economies are said to be characterised by a very small agricultural sector, continuously declining manufacturing sector, large and expanding service sector and, more recently, growing quaternary sector.

The growth of the tertiary and quaternary sectors, in turn, fuels the views that advanced economies are in fact entering a stage of the knowledge–based economy. Seen in this light, uneven development can be considered as a consequence of the unevenness in development stages between various regions. However, things are probably more complicated than that. Regions are functionally inter–dependent and their roles may be determined by their position within the wider spatial divisions of labour.

CYCLE THEORIES: PRODUCTS AND PROFITS

Cycle theories are also concerned with the process of economic evolution. However, they focus on the stages of development of individual products or industries. In its simplest version, the product life cycle theory suggests that products progress through various stages of development— from a product's introduction to growth to maturity to saturation and decline. Each stage of the product life cycle is associated with different locational patterns: the conception of a new product results from an innovation, the original location of which can be a historical accident. However, it is likely that innovative firms introducing new products are located close to key supplier and research and development facilities. As the product matures and the markets for it expand, however, there is a scope for a mass production to be moved to less developed regions where cheaper labour can be found. A more sophisticated version of the product life cycle theory is a profit cycle theory which focuses on the product's profit stages and associated locational patterns.

WAVE THEORIES, TECHNICAL CHANGE AND INNOVATION

Wave theories are based on the idea that economic growth occurs in a series of 50–year long-waves. Such long–waves are also known as Kondratiev waves after the Russian economists who first identified them.

Each Kondratiev wave may be divided into four phases:

1. Prosperity,
2. Recession,
3. Depression and
4. Recovery.

Importantly, each wave is associated with 'particularly significant technological changes around which other innovations—in production, distribution and organization—cluster and ultimately spread through the economy'.

In other words, each wave is underpinned by a progressively more advanced 'techno–economic paradigm'. So far, five Kondratiev waves have been identified, each underpinned by a specific set of technologies and type of industry and associated with particular locations in which these industries flourished. The first Kondratiev wave is sometimes referred to as the 'early mechanisation' wave. Lasting from about the 1780s through to the 1830s and being mostly associated with regions in Britain, France and Belgium, the first wave was associated with textile industries, iron working/casting and water power.

The subsequent second Kondratiev wave, of 'steam power and railway' was based on steam engine technologies, steamships, machine tools, iron and steel industries and railway equipment. Regions associated with the second wave regions are: Britain, Germany, France, Belgium and USA.

The third wave of 'electrical and heavy engineering' was associated with electric power and the emergence of electrical engineering, electrical machinery, heavy engineering and armaments, heavy chemicals and synthetic dyestuffs. The spatial core of the third Kondratiev wave included regions in Germany, USA, Britain, France, Belgium, Netherlands and Switzerland. The fourth wave coincided with the post-War boom years and is known as the 'Fordist mass production' Kondratiev wave.

The main industrial branches that were associated with this wave included: automobiles; trucks; tractors; tanks; aircraft; consumer durables; process plant; synthetic materials and petrochemicals. The 'Fordist mass production' wave was led by the USA, Germany, Switzerland, Sweden and other European countries, Japan, Canada and Australia. Finally, it has been argued that we are now in the midst of the fifth Kondratiev wave.

This is based mostly on computers; digital information technology; the internet; software; telecommunication; optical fibres; robotics and biotechnology; it is often referred to as the 'information and communication' wave or the post–Fordist wave. Again, there are specific geographical locations associated with this current technological wave. However, apart from the 'core' economies, countries like Taiwan and Korea are also claimed to be part of this wave.

REGIONAL INNOVATION SYSTEMS AND CLUSTERS

While the concepts such as techno–economic paradigm, post—Fordism and the long–waves of development continue to be debated, they are nevertheless useful in that they highlight the importance of the link between technology and economic development. More specifically, they make the point that economic growth is dependent on either the technological innovation or the adoption of new technologies. In terms of the technological innovation, the literature distinguishes between two basic models: the linear innovation model and the interactive innovation model.

The linear innovation model involves the linear stage of innovation from:

- Idea/invention,
- Design and development of prototypes;
- Production; and finally
- Sale.

The interactive innovation model, on the other hand, recognises that innovation is an interactive social process and cannot be reduced to a one–way linear process. Instead, the interactive innovation model emphasises mutual/ two–way interactions between various stages of innovation and between producers and users. The concept of the interactive innovation model has been influenced by evolutionary and institutional approaches. Originally, it has been applied at the national level in the form of the national innovation systems model.

However, economic geographers quickly pointed out that the kinds of interactions implied in the national innovation systems model are probably best achieved at the regional level. Indeed, within the regional context, interactions between individual firms; firms and public R&D laboratories; firms and universities; and firms and their customers may benefit from close geographical proximity and evolve into regional innovation systems. There are a large number of other, similar concepts that you may encounter in the literature, all of which try to describe the phenomenon of innovative regions.

Such concepts include:

- Flexible specialisation districts
- High–technology districts

- Innovative milieus
- Intelligent regions.
- New industrial districts
- New industrial spaces
- Sunbelt regions
- Technolopoles

More recently, the concepts of clusters and learning regions have gained considerable currency among academics and policy–makers alike. It is therefore worth examining both these concepts in a bit more detail. As suggested, first start by discussing the concept of clusters before examining learning regions in the following sub–section. Clusters have been defined as the 'geographic concentration of interconnected companies, specialised suppliers and service providers, firms in related industries, and associated institutions in particular fields that compete but also cooperate'.

The notion of the 'geographic concentration' evokes the concept of agglomeration discussed earlier in this stage. Indeed, the two terms are often used interchangeably. However, one could argue that there are a small number of important differences between the two concepts. Two such differences will be highlighted here.

First, it is important to notice that the definition provided by Porter already signals one important feature of clusters, which clearly distinguishes them from agglomerations: while the neo–classical approach emphasises competition between firms as the key economic driver, the concept of clusters recognises that interactions between various economic agents may involve the elements of both competition and cooperation.

Moreover, some would argue that the element of active cooperation may not only apply to economic agents such as firms, trade associations and universities, but also to actors such as trade unions and local and regional government. A term associational economy has been coined to capture this cooperative nature among principal economic players. This is an important point, because it implies that the contradictions between capital and labour can somehow be overcome. Indeed, it has been argued that, in successful regions, cooperative institutional arrangements exist to coordinate the actions of regional players. This also represents another important contrast to the neoclassical framework, which sees the 'invisible hand' of the market as the key mechanism for guiding the actions of economic agents.

The ability of institutional arrangements to guide collective action in successful regions has been referred to as institutional thickness. Institutional thickness arises from coordination between a plethora of regional institutions, which include firms, financial institutions, local chambers of commerce, training agencies, trade associations, local authorities, development agencies, innovation centres, clerical bodies, marketing boards, government agencies and trade unions. Another important difference between agglomerations and clusters lies in a type of interaction between various regional players.

Both neo–classical and Marxist approaches focus on formal market transactions. Formal market transactions are transactions that have a price tag attached to them. Such transactions are also called traded interdependencies; that is, formal trading relationships between economic agents. An example of a formal market transaction or a traded interdependency includes a formal contract between a supplier and a client. Firms may also use formal contracts to regulate relationships in joint co-operative projects, for instance.

It is these traded transactions that form an agglomeration in the neo–classical, strictly economic, sense. However, the economy cannot be reduced to market transactions only. Indeed, in addition to traded interdependencies, regional economies are made up of a vast array of exchanges that are not based on formal market relationships. Such nonmarket exchanges are also called untraded interdependencies.

These are less tangible, but not less important, interactions between economic agents. Examples of such interactions include informal information exchanges and various forms of cooperation happening through informal networks and inter-personal contacts. Often, such exchanges are based on trust and reciprocity, and are lubricated by a shared culture. What emerges from this process are so-called 'relational assets', which are not based on economic, but primarily on social and cultural factors. This then, constitutes the second major difference between a cluster and a economic agglomeration.

In other words, cluster is perhaps much closer to Alfred Marshall's century old concept of 'industrial districts'. Indeed, contemporary innovative regions have been described as 'neo-Marshallian nodes in global networks'. It has been argued that in successful regions, untraded interdependencies foster technology spillovers, innovation, learning, and ultimately competitiveness of the firms involved and of the entire regional economy.

However, the reality is perhaps more complex and confusing and the ability of the cluster concept to explain regional economic success has been questioned. Important criticisms have been levied upon the concept of clusters.

KNOWLEDGE ECONOMIES AND LEARNING REGIONS

Learning region is another influential concept that aims to account for dynamic innovative regions. However, unlike the regional innovation system and cluster, the concept of the learning region focuses less on technological innovation. Instead, it emphasises the importance of 'learning'. From this point of view, the learning region can be seen as a regional dimension of the knowledge–based, learning economy. In the definition provided by Richard Florida, learning regions '...function as collectors and repositories of knowledge and ideas, and provide the underlying environment and infrastructure which facilitates the flow of knowledge, ideas and learning'. The process of 'learning' is defined very broadly here and goes beyond the usual meaning of individual learning. Instead, in line with the view that learning is a social process, the notion of 'learning' encompasses a range of situations. Various versions of the learning region concept exist and we have no space to review them all here. However, it could be argued that 'learning region' theorists build on several commonly held positions.

These positions could be tentatively summarised as follows:

- There is a commonly shared conviction that the role of knowledge in the economy and society is indeed growing and that the current economy is best described as the 'learning economy', 'knowledge economy' or 'knowledge-based economy'. Within such an economy, knowledge is considered as 'the most important resource and learning the most important process'. Consequently, '[k]nowledge has become a central organising concept for those concerned with regional economic development' and 'learning has become the best way to understand regional economic change'. In effect, the region has become conceptualised as a 'nexus of learning processes'.
- It is maintained that learning is a collective process. Therefore, it is not confined to individuals, or even individual firms, rather it is conceptualised as occurring between firms; between firms and consumers; and between firms and a plethora of local or regional institutions.
- The result of this learning process, resulting knowledge, is however a rather 'leaky phenomenon'. Indeed, as soon as it is codified, the global knowledge economy renders knowledge ubiquitous and makes it open to competitors' appropriation and replication. Therefore, it is non-codified or tacit knowledge that is a crucial source of competitive advantage.
- Tacit knowledge requires regular face-to-face contacts of involved actors. It is assumed that in the absence of 'magic carpets' these face-to-face relations are only sustainable within a certain spatial proximity.
- Besides, what is needed for successful 'collective learning' is a set of informal institutions such as habits, conventions, rules of conduct, lubricated by cooperative culture and trust. These factors, it is believed, are place–specific and supported by regionally based formal institutions that facilitate the exchange of knowledge and ideas between regional actors, guarantee continuous innovation and ensure coordination of regional action for the benefit of all participants. Thanks to 'localised learning' and 'institutional endowments', 'learning regions' can thrive in the 'global knowledge economy', while becoming the basic organisational units of such an economy.

To conclude, it could be said that in comparison to economics-based approaches, the conceptualisation of 'learning regions' brings very different answers to the questions of economic agglomeration and competitiveness. As Peter Maskell and his colleagues assert, 'it has to do with knowledge creation and with the development of localised capabilities that promote the learning process'. Learning, knowledge creation and localized capabilities are believed to lie behind the success of advanced regions, such as Silicon Valley. What is more, some commentators believe that less–favoured regions can emulate the success of advanced regions by mimicking their institutional structures and creating favourable conditions for 'learning'.

In other words, it is believed that the new 'knowledge' era offers opportunities to eradicate/overcome uneven development. However, it needs to be noted that the concept of the learning region and its ability to act as a catalyst for a more balanced development has been questioned.

NETWORKS, TRUST AND SOCIAL CAPITAL

New economic geography approaches such as regional innovation systems, clusters and learning regions, differ substantially from both the neo–classical and conventional Marxist perspectives on economies and their geographies. Indeed, the notions of networks, trust and social capital, help to shed a new light on the way regional economies work.

The focus on networks is important, because they are seen as intermediate and institutionalised forms of social organisation that are neither markets nor hierarchies. Instead, networks are seen as cooperative and reciprocal, especially when they are lubricated with mutual trust and shared culture. What emerges from such trustful relations and networks is 'social. New economic geography approaches such as regional innovation systems, clusters and learning regions, differ substantially from both the neo–classical and conventional Marxist perspectives on economies and their geographies.

Indeed, the notions of networks, trust and social capital, help to shed a new light on the way regional economies work. The focus on networks is important, because they are seen as intermediate and institutionalised forms of social organisation that are neither markets nor hierarchies. Instead, networks are seen as cooperative and reciprocal, especially when they are lubricated with mutual trust and shared culture. What emerges from such trustful relations and networks is 'social

CULTURAL ECONOMIES, ETHNICITY AND GENDER

The final sub–section of this stage is devoted to economic geographies of culture, ethnicity and gender. This is an area of geography which has recently seen dramatic developments, in part reflecting the rise of the feminist approaches and the 'cultural turn' in geography and in social sciences more widely. In many ways, these approaches challenge the very notion of 'the economic'. Indeed, the boundaries and the relations between 'the economy' and 'culture' are being questioned and problematised. The mutual constitution of 'the economic' and 'the cultural' is being emphasised. The terms such as 'cultural economies' and 'economic cultures' have been used to highlight this point. Furthermore, the ways in which ethnicity and gender are intertwined with economies and their geographies have received a lot of attention. In order to get a good understanding of this vibrant and often contested area of 'economic' geography.

ECONOMIC GEOGRAPHY AND REGIONAL PRODUCTION STRUCTURE

Why is there trade? This is a fundamental question for international economists. And it is equally so for those who consider trade across regions. Theory has provided two principal answers: comparative advantage and increasing returns. Comparative advantage holds that trade across geographical units arises to take advantage of inherent differences. Increasing returns says that trade arises to take advantage of scale and variety gains from specialization.

While theorists have devoted great energy to developing myriad models of comparative advantage and increasing returns, empirical research has had next to nothing to say about the relative importance of these two forces in driving world trade At one time, researchers might have pointed to the large volume of intra–industry trade or of North–North trade as confirming the importance of increasing returns.

Yet closer examination has proven that these phenomena do not distinguish the increasing returns theory from that of comparative advantage. Renewed hope for distinguishing the theories arises if we restrict ourselves to the class of increasing returns models that Krugman has labeled "economic geography." The defining characteristic of these theories is the interaction of increasing returns and costs of trade. As Krugman showed, this does allow one to identify a critical test distinguishing a world of comparative advantage from one with increasing returns.

In a world of comparative advantage, unusually strong demand for a good, cet. par., will make that good an import. In a world with increasing returns, typically each good will have only one site of production. When there are trade costs, a country with unusually strong demand for a good makes that an excellent site to locate production, hence makes that country the exporter of that good. These •ghome market effects•h of demand on trade patterns thus provide a key feature to distinguish a world of comparative advantage from one of increasing returns.

In Davis and Weinstein, we made this search for home market effects the centerpiece of our effort to distinguish the two theories. We noted that the home market effect has an equivalent characterization as a "magnification effect" from idiosyncratic components of demand to output. We then applied this to explain the structure of OECD production. Our null hypothesis was that the conventional Heckscher–Ohlin model explains production structure at the 4–digit ISIC level.

The alternative hypothesis was that Heckscher–Ohlin explains only the broad industrial structure of production in these countries at the 3–digit ISIC level, and that this must be augmented with a model of economic geography to account for the finer 4–digit production structure. Within this overarching structure, we identify three possibilities: a frictionless world (comparative advantage or IRS); comparative advantage with positive trade costs; and economic geography. Our results did not support the proposition that economic geography plays an important role in determining the structure of OECD production. The data strongly rejected a frictionless model, since in such a model demand would have no influence on the location of production. Yet 3 the results also rejected the economic geography framework in *favour* of a model of comparative advantage with trade costs. Some specifications did indicate significant economic geography effects in a number of important industries. However, all specifications which allowed for inclusion of factor endowments as predictors of fine production structure show that the economic geography effects were not robust.

The same question that we ask of countries can be asked of sub–units of countries: Why do regions trade? This is an important and fascinating problem in its own right. Moreover it promises to yield insights of broader applicability. From a theoretical standpoint, we should expect that the same basic forces are at work in the regional and international cases. However, from an empirical standpoint, there is no necessary reason that the answers of their relative importance be the same. It is perfectly conceivable that economic geography could have little influence on the structure of production across countries, yet be very important in explaining the structure of production across regions within a country. This could arise, for example, due to lower interregional trade costs, which theory suggests should strengthen economic geography effects. Thus an investigation that examines the trade of regions may provide the best hope for identifying such effects, and so also provide a *favour*able experiment to distinguish the microeconomic stories underlying the comparative advantage and economic geography approaches.

THEORETICAL FRAMEWORK

A REGIONAL APPROACH

The seminal theoretical contribution underlying our work is Krugman's model of the "home market effect." In Davis and Weinstein, we showed how to nest his model of economic geography with a model of comparative advantage, the aim being to identify and estimate the importance of such home market effects on OECD production structure. Since the basic theoretical framework in the present document follows that developed in our earlier work, as suggested, here provide a more compact presentation. However, there are some important issues that must be addressed in moving from an international to a regional setting before we turn to the specifics of our framework.

A conventional contrast between international and regional economics is the greater degree of factor mobility across regions within a country than across countries. This could in principle be very important. Large countries or regions have highly diversified products available without trade costs, so tend to have low price indices. Under certain conditions, large countries may be desirable locations for producers to locate, so they may tend to pay high wages.

As well, if some of the differentiated goods themselves serve as inputs to production of differentiated goods, then labor may be more productive in large economies, again tending to raise wages there. All of these suggest that large countries or regions may also attract large numbers of immigrants, tending to empty national or international hinterlands. The greater mobility of factors across regions within a country tends to raise the salience of this issue.

Of course, the extensive literature on economic geography has considered at length the tensions between these pressures for concentration and the counteracting pressures for dispersion of economic activity. We choose to sidestep these issues, even as we recognize their importance. As suggested, assume that within the economic geography part of our model, there are in fact some countervailing forces at work that prevent all economic activity from locating on a single point without inquiring the nature of those forces.

As suggested, assume that the economy is in equilibrium. If this is so, then imposing a further condition that factors are not allowed to move ex post will not disturb the nature of the equilibrium. In other words, we are going to treat the regional model as a special case of the international model in which the specific combination of centrifugal and centripetal forces are such that in equilibrium no one would migrate even if they could.

The legitimacy of treating a model of regions as if it were a model of countries depends on the questions one addresses. Clearly, the comparative statics of the two models will not be the same. However, our interest is precisely in the static equilibrium, which we believe justifies this approach.

PREVIOUS EMPIRICAL STUDIES

The role that scale economies, internal or external, play in production has been an important topic in a wide range of contributions from the regional economics literature. These studies have typically searched for the existence of economies of scale or spillovers by estimating production functions or growth specifications with aggregate industry or city–size variables on the right–hand side. The present study differs from the regional contributions in two important respects. The first is that we articulate our empirical specification from a general equilibrium perspective. The second is that within our general equilibrium framework we are able to identify precise null and alternative hypotheses. The focus on general equilibrium is valuable because it allows us to draw on the wealth of analytic results from the international trade literature. In the present study, it allows us to focus on a particularly surprising result known as the ghome market effect. “home market effects”.

The full specification of null and alternate hypotheses is valuable, since it allows us to be precise about which hypotheses may be distinguished by the evidence. This is particularly important when searching for evidence of scale economies, as these may easily be confounded with omitted factors in regressions of industry output on aggregate regional variables, such as city size or employment. This difficulty common to many of the regional studies is voiced, for example, in Ellison and Glaeser’s conclusion that their own “analysis of the mean concentration of industries [the principle dependent variable in their study]... is compatible with a pure natural advantage model, a pure spillover model, or models with various combinations of the two factors.”

The combination of a general equilibrium perspective with the explicit specification of a null and alternative hypothesis is particularly important in comparing our study with related work in the regional literature. An example is the suggestive work of Justman which also considers a variant of the Linder hypothesis. Justman approached the problem by calculating industry correlations between supply and demand across regions, and then regressing these correlations on industry characteristics. Justman argued that in industries in which the Linder hypothesis is valid there should be strong correlations between supply and demand. Our study, focused on home market effects, imposes a more stringent test on the data—not only must supply and demand be correlated, but demand must move supply more than one-for-one.

One might reasonably ask whether our more stringent test is justified or whether one might want to settle for correlations as in the Justman study. To understand this, we must return to the distinguishing prediction of the Linder hypothesis. Virtually any model with trade costs will have the feature that local demand and supply are correlated. The critical feature of the Linder hypothesis is that demand deviations cause more-than-proportional supply responses. Thus it can be problematic if one focuses simply on correlations instead of magnitudes.

Suppose that a demand deviation of ten causes output to rise by one but that the observed data is very tightly distributed around a line of slope one–tenth. The Linder hypothesis is clearly not valid, but the correlation might be quite high. Similarly, if a demand deviation of one caused output to move by ten, but the data are very noisy, one would have a low correlation but clear evidence of the Linder hypothesis. In other words, in order to test for the home market effects characteristic of the Linder hypothesis, one cannot search simply for correlations between supply and demand. Rather one must focus on the magnitude of the relationship.

ECONOMIC GEOGRAPHY, COMPARATIVE ADVANTAGE, AND THE HOME MARKET EFFECT

The key theoretical insight underlying our empirical work. Building on an insight from Linder, Krugman posed a simple question: Can idiosyncratically high demand for a good in a country or region, ceteris paribus, make that good an export?

It is worth considering his intuitive argument before developing the formal models:

- In a world characterized both by increasing returns and by transportation costs, there will obviously be an incentive to concentrate production of a good near its largest market, even if there is some demand for the good elsewhere. The reason is simply that by concentrating production in one place one can realize the scale economies, while by locating near the larger market, one minimizes transportation costs. This point—which is more often emphasized in location theory than in trade theory—is the basis for the common argument that countries will tend to export those kinds of product for which they have relatively large domestic demand. Notice that this argument is wholly dependent on increasing returns; in a world of diminishing returns, strong domestic demand for a good will tend to make it an import rather than an export.

This role for idiosyncratically high demand to lead a good to be exported—"home market effect"—is our central focus. Its value from an empirical standpoint is that, conditional on costs of trade, it provides a clear contrast between the diminishing returns, comparative advantage theory, and that of increasing returns and economic geography.

Krugman develops a special case of the Dixit–Stiglitz model of monopolistic competition. The crucial departure from Krugman is the introduction of iceberg costs of trade between economies. The particular example that he works with assumes that there are two types of consumers in the world, each of which demands only one of the two classes of differentiated varieties available in the world. He further assumes that the two equa–sized economies have the consumers in mirror proportions. Symmetry insures nominal factor price equalization. Wellknown properties of the Dixit–Stiglitz iso–elastic case insure that output per variety is the same for all varieties of both types in each country. The only thing to be determined is how many of each variety are produced in each country. Assume that the majority–type consumers in each country exist in relative proportion $\lambda \geq 1$. Because of trade costs, consumers will demand smaller quantities of imported than of locally–produced varieties. Let the ratio of the typical consumption of an imported to a local variety be given by $\sigma < 1$. Finally, let the number of varieties produced in a country tailored to the tastes of the majority be given by μ. Krugman shows that for the range of incomplete spxecialization,

$$\mu = \frac{\lambda - \sigma}{1 - \lambda\sigma}$$

If there were no idiosyncratic component to demand, *i.e.*, $\lambda = 1$, then each country would produce the same number of varieties of each of the two classes of goods, *i.e.*, $\mu = 1$. This is important, since it suggests that the "baseline" composition of production will be similar across countries, absent idiosyncratic demand. However, when there are idiosyncratic elements of demand, $\lambda > 1$, then it is easily verified that a country produces a larger number of the varieties preferred by its majority–type consumers, so $\mu > 1$.

The home market effect, though, requires a yet stronger result. Krugman asked if idiosyncratically high demand could lead a good to be exported. If high demand is to lead the good to be exported, then production must rise by even more than demand. That is, the home market effect requires that idiosyncratically high demand have a magnified impact on production of the relevant good. These are equivalent statements. From above, and again for the range of incomplete specialization, we see that:

$$\frac{\partial \mu}{\partial \lambda} = \frac{1 - \sigma^2}{(1 - \sigma\lambda)^2} > 1$$

That is, Krugman has shown that precisely this kind of •gmagnification effect•h from idiosyncratic demand to production holds in this model. When we turn to the empirical work, this will provide the foundation for deviations from the •gbaseline•h composition of production.

Weder extends this result to the case in which countries differ in size. His principal result is contained in his Proposition 3: "In the open–economy equilibrium, each country is a net exporter of that group of differentiated goods where it has a comparative home–market advantage." And a country has a comparative home-market advantage when it has a higher proportion of demanders of one type relative to the other. The insight is simple but powerful.

Producers of varieties of the different classes of goods must compete for resources within a market. Absolute market size alone leads all producers to want to locate in the larger market. But the aggregate resource constraint in the large market forces an ordering of priorities. It is intuitively pleasing that it is the relative strength of demand that is in fact the deciding factor in determining the pattern of exports. It is straightforward to derive simple extensions considering separately more countries and more goods, indicating some robustness for the basic home market relation.

We have seen that in the world of economic geography, unusually strong demand for a good leads that good to be an export, reflecting the home market effect. This contrasts with the results in a comparative advantage world. Krugman argued that "... in a world of diminishing returns, strong domestic demand for a good will tend to make it an import rather than an export." Let us think about the underlying logic in a simple import–demand exportsupply framework.

Consider a small idiosyncratic component of demand in a country. In a competitive world with rising marginal opportunity costs, this will be met with additional local supply only if the price rises. Will a home market effect arise? Note that with a fixed trade–cost wedge, the local price can rise in equilibrium only if the foreign price rises as well. But if the foreign export supply curve has the conventional slope, then this must also imply larger foreign net exports of this good.

Hence the local idiosyncratic demand is met in part by a rise in local supply and in part by greater imports— hence local supply rises less than one-for-one with idiosyncratic demand. If the good in question were non–traded both before and after the demand perturbation, then local supply would rise exactly one-for-one. But unless the foreign export supply curve has a perverse slope, local supply will never rise more than one-for-one with idiosyncratic local demand. That is, in the comparative advantage world, home market effects will not arise.

EMPIRICAL SPECIFICATION

We turn now to translating this theory to an implementable empirical specification. The model of Krugman cannot be taken directly to data. The one–factor model that he develops is entirely appropriate for theory. But it can be rejected without recourse to data if the suggestion is that endowment differences are not important for the structure of production.

Thus, if we are to give Krugman's theory a chance, as suggested, need to build into it a structure in which endowments are allowed to matter at one level of aggregation, and economic geography to matter at a finer level of disaggregation. Such an approach is suggested by the work of Helpman and this is broadly the course that we take. However, we caution that the literature has not developed the economic geography model in sufficient generality to deal simultaneously with differences in the size of regions, goods, and industries, as well as to allow for differences in input composition and demand structure. We cannot fully remedy this shortcoming, but we do believe that the framework we develop presents a highly structured and sensible interpretation of Krugman that focuses on a central feature of the theory.

In the discussion that follows, it will prove useful to distinguish three levels of production. The broadest level is what we term industries, with each industry composed of many goods. In the empirical section, as suggested, have six industries covering the nineteen goods that form the basis of our analysis. For the case of monopolistic competition, each good will feature many varieties. While the varieties play an important theoretical role as the locus of increasing returns, they are never directly observed.

Let us begin with the comparative advantage theory. Our representative of this class for the purpose of our empirical work is the square Heckscher–Ohlin model. Assume that all regions r of Japan share identical constant returns to scale technologies. Assume as well that these technologies are Leontief. Let there be F factors of production. Let there be N industries with G_n goods in industry n. Assume that the total number of goods is the same as the number of primary factors, so

$$\sum_{n=1}^{N} Gn = F$$

Assume that the F×F technology matrix mapping output into factors is invertible, where the inverse is given by Ω. Assume that all regions are diversified in production.

Letting the vector of goods output for region r and good g in industry n be X_g^{nr} the vector of factor endowments be, V^r and Ω_g^n be the corresponding row of Ω, there is an exact relation:

$$X_g^{nr} = \Omega_g^n V^r$$

In this framework, endowments fully suffice to determine the structure of goods production.

The alternative that we develop is in the spirit of Helpman's nesting of the Heckscher–Ohlin and simple monopolistic competition models. There endowments served to determine the broad industrial structure of a country while monopolistic competition led to intraindustry specialization. We follow the same division, assuming that Heckscher–Ohlin determines the output by regions of industries, while économic geography determines the output of goods within industries. Let A be a technology matrix, with A_n a column reflecting input usage n within industry n. Within industry n, there are G_n goods.

We assume that demand arises from n Dixit-Stiglitz iso–elastic preferences, and that the elasticity of substitution between varieties of a good is common for all varieties of all goods within an industry. This implies that the equilibrium scale of production of each variety of each good within an industry is common. If we further assume that both fixed and marginal costs are in scalar proportion to A_n, then we can take that column as the total input coefficients for a variety of any good in n industry n. We assume that the coefficients of A are fixed.

Here, as in Helpman endowments serve to determine the exact structure of production by industry. This can be expressed as:

$$X^{nr} = \sum_{g=1}^{G_n} X_g^{nr} = \bar{\Omega}^n V^r,$$

where $\bar{\Omega}$ is an N×N matrix. However endowments provide no information about a region's production structure within an industry—*et al.,* the goods composition of production within the industry. For example, they tell us which regions have a large textile industry, but not whether this will be occupied producing carpets, rugs, etc.

We now need to specify how the location of goods production within industries is determined for the economic geography specification. Absent idiosyncratic components of demand, regions will divide production across goods within an industry in the same proportion as all other regions. Hence regions with a large industry n will produce absolutely large amounts of all goods within n, but cet. par. will have the same composition across goods as regions with a smaller industry n. This base level of production of a particular good for a region, which depends on that region•fs overall commitment to the encompassing industry and to the importance of that good in the aggregate within that industry, is what as suggested, refer to as SHARE.

However, in the spirit of Krugman, we posit that this base level of production of a good must be adjusted to reflect the influences of idiosyncratically high demand. Our specification is influenced by Weder to focus on differences in the relative importance of a good for the specific region relative to all the regions taken together. The magnitude of this influence is, of course, also influenced by that region•fs total commitment of resources to the industry of interest.

This will give rise to a variable that we term IDIODEM. This will play a key role when we turn to hypothesis testing, since the economic geography framework predicts that the responsiveness of goods production to movements in IDIODEM will be more than one-to-one.

We can state this hypothesis first in a general form. Let

$$\lambda_g^{nr} \equiv \frac{X_g^{nr}}{X^{nr}}, \delta_g^{nr} \equiv \frac{D_g^{nr}}{D^{nr}},$$

and ROJ stand for the rest of Japan. Then goods production is modeled as:

$$X_g^{nr} = f\left(\gamma_g^{nROJ} X^{nr} \left(\delta_g^{nr} - \delta_g^{nROJ}\right) X^{nr}\right)$$

where D denotes absorption in either the region, r, or Japan as a whole, J, and the first derivatives are expected to be non–negative. The first term in f captures the tendency for each region to produce the same relative shares of each good as other regions.

Specifically, we postulate that a region's output of any good X_g^{nr} is going to be centered around the product of:

- The share of that good in that industry•fs output for the rest of Japan; and
- A scale term reflecting that industry•fs total size within the region,X^{nr} The second term in f measures the demand deviation.

If all regions demanded the same share of each good, this term would equal zero. If a good comprises a greater (smaller) share of demand within an industry, however, this term will be positive (negative) indicating that the region is an idiosyncratically high (low) demander of that good. Again this is scaled by region refers output in industry n.

As suggested, estimate a linear of version of presented below:

$$X_g^{nr} = \alpha_g^n + \beta_1 \gamma_g^{nROJ} X^{nr} + \beta_2 \left(\delta_g^{nr} - \delta_g^{nROJ}\right) X^{nr} + \epsilon_g^{nr}$$

or equivalently

$$X_g^{nr} = \alpha_g^n + \beta_1 SHARE_g^{nr} + \beta_2 IDIODEM_g^{nr} + \epsilon_g^{nr}$$

While we believe this exercise is informative, we do not want to stop with estimation of equation. The reason is that such a specification may suffer from an omitted variables bias, as it assumes that endowments play no role in the location of goods production once we know the level of industry output. Thus we estimate a nested model:

$$X_g^{nr} = \alpha_g^n + \beta_1 SHARE_g^{nr} + \beta_2 IDIODEM_g^{nr} + \Omega_g^{nr} V^r + \epsilon_g^{nr},$$

We want to verify that the conclusions derived from our earlier tests are robust to allowing endowments to matter for output at a finer level of production. The structure that we have placed on the analysis enables us to directly test the hypothesis of whether economic geography can improve our understanding of production patterns at the goods level relative to the hypothesis that all production is determined by endowments.

A few more words are in order about the specification. If the production of goods within a region is proportional to production of these goods in the rest of Japan, then SHARE will equal the expected level of production of a good given output at the industry level. In the specification without endowments, one should expect the coefficient on SHARE to be unity.

Our main interest is in testing a null that Heckscher–Ohlin predicts the level of goods output against an alternative that an augmented economic geography model does so. However, it will prove informative to postpone this test and first consider directly several hypotheses concerning equation. The key is the interpretation of the coefficient β_2, for which we distinguish three hypotheses. In a frictionless world, the geographical structure of demand should have no influence of production patterns, so $\beta_2 = 0$.[5]

In a comparative advantage world with trade costs, the geographical location of demand does matter. But so long as import demand and export supply curves have the conventional slopes, the response of local supply to idiosyncratic components of demand should be at most one-to-one.

Finally, in the presence of economic geography, we expect the response of local production to idiosyncratic components of demand to be more than one-to-one.

Summarizing:

Interpretation of β_2

- $\beta_2 = 0$: Frictionless World (Comparative Advantage or IRS) 2
- $\beta_2 \in (0, 1]$: Comparative Advantage with Trade Costs 2
- $\beta_2 > 1$: Economic Geography 2

EMPIRICS

ECONOMETRIC ISSUES

Equations can be estimated at various levels of aggregation, separately or as a system of seemingly unrelated regressions. The latter yields maximum power to discern the average impact of economic geography in our sample. Alternatively, we can allow the coefficients on the parameters to vary at the goods or industry level.

Direct estimation of is not possible because of a simultaneity problem. Because X_g^{nr} is X^{nr} an element of Xnr one cannot treat them as independent observations. Davis and Weinstein show however, that if we assume that factor endowments drive aggregate production, then as suggested, have a theoretically consistent set of instruments: factor endowments. In what follows, we therefore always instrument X^{nr} on factor endowments.

Second, there are two types of heteroskedasticity in these data. Errors are likely to be correlated with the size of both regions and industries. These two types of heteroskedasticity can be corrected for by postulating that for each good the error process is of the form given below:

$$\nu ar\left(\epsilon_g^{nr}\right) = \phi_g^n \, GDP_r^{\theta_g^n}$$

where ϕ_g^n and θ_g^n are parameters. We corrected for heteroskedasticity by first estimating the system and generating the squared residuals. Following Leamer. We then regressed the log of this series on the log of regional GDP and then used the fitted values to form our weighting series for the heteroskedasticity correction.

DATA ISSUES

We provide an overview of the data used in the document. Our data set contains output, endowment, and absorption data for the 47 prefectures/cities of Japan. However, we were concerned that people in the cities of Tokyo and Osaka might be working in the city but living and consuming in an adjacent prefecture, so we were forced to aggregate some of the data. We formed two aggregates: Kanto, out of the city of Tokyo and the prefectures of Yamanashi, Kanagawa, Chiba, and Saitama; and Kinki, out of the prefectures/cities of Hyogo, Kyoto, Nara, and Osaka. This reduced our sample to 40 observations, but enabled us to significantly increase the probability that anyone within a region consumed largely within that region.

Our next problem was how to define industries and goods. Ideally, we would like to rely on industry classifications based on technological criteria rather than substitutability in demand. Unfortunately, industry classification schemes are typically based upon the latter more than the former. There is some evidence that standard industry definitions do contain information about production technologies. However, since we had access to the Japanese technology matrix, we decided that we could provide more theoretically sensible classifications than those typically found in statistical annuals.

In earlier work, we had constructed a technology matrix for Japan. This matrix enabled us to have direct information on college, non–college, and capital usage for 30 sectors. Of these 30 sectors, we dropped eight non–tradable goods sectors and two agricultural sectors. We felt it necessary to drop the agricultural sectors because large–scale Japanese industrial policy interventions, such as price supports, marketing boards, tax breaks, subsidies, zoning laws, etc. significantly distort demand and supply in these sectors. Indeed, this accounts for the fact that in our data 13 per cent of private land in the city of Tokyo is farmland. Finally we also dropped mining since it is obviously an endowment–based sector.

The nineteen sectors that we eventually used are reported in Table.

Table. Aggregation Scheme

Sector	College/Non–College	Capital/Non–College	Capital/College
Textiles	1	1	4
Apparel	1	1	2
Lumber & Wood	1	1	5
Furniture	1	1	3
Ceramics, Stone, Clay, Glass	2	3	5
Iron and Steel	2	5	6
Paper and Pulp	3	4	5
Rubber	3	3	4
Fabricated Metal Products	3	2	3
Transportation Equipment	4	4	5
Other Manufacturing	4	3	4
Leather & Leather Products	5	1	1
Non-Ferrous Metals	5	4	5
General Machinery	5	3	3

Electrical Machinery	5	3	3
Precision Instruments	5	2	2
Printing and Publishing	6	2	2
Chemicals	6	5	4
Petroleum and Coal Products	6	6	6

Davis and Weinstein argued that in international data one can reject the economic geography specification in *favour* of the Heckscher–Ohlin specification for these industry categories. However, as we have suggested earlier, there is reason to be more optimistic that we can identify home market effects in Japanese data. Bernstein and Weinstein argue that the reason for the good fits in international data is the interaction between transaction costs and Heckscher–Ohlin effects. These authors demonstrate that on Japanese data, where transactions costs are small, there is substantial production indeterminacy at this level of aggregation. This has two important implications for our work. First, since endowments do not predict output as well on regional data as on international data, there is more latitude for other factors, such as economic geography, to determine regional production.

Second, the fact that transportation costs are substantially smaller between regions means that the observed economic geography effects will be stronger. Both of these reasons suggest that we should be more optimistic about finding a role for economic geography in determining regional production.

In some of the exercises that as suggested, carry out, aggregation of goods into industries may in principle matter a great deal. The theory literally holds that all varieties of all goods within an industry use common input coefficients. Obviously this is too much to hope for with real data. So we are required to aggregate the goods into industries in a way that respects the underlying theoretical requirement that goods within an industry use similar input coefficients. Unfortunately, in a world with more than two inputs, there is no theoretically compelling manner for performing this aggregation.

Hence we took a pragmatic approach of considering aggregation based on factor–intensity ratios, taking two factors at a time. Unfortunately, although ranking sectors by college to non–college ratios and capital to non-college ratios yields similar orderings, one obtains radically different orderings if one looks at capital to college ratios. Ultimately, we decided to form industry aggregates on the basis of college to non–college factor ratios, because this scheme yielded the most plausible aggregates. The other aggregations schemes, especially the capital to college scheme, had enormous outliers and produced very odd mixes of industries.

We calculated the ratio of college to non–college workers in each sector and then divided the 19 goods into six industry aggregates based on the similarity of these ratios. The last columns of Table present these aggregates. Larger numbers indicate an industry composed of goods with higher factor-intensity ratios. The commodity groupings for the college/non–college aggregation scheme seem quite sensible, although there are a few anomalies, *i.e.,* leather in industry

Variable	Obs	Mean	Std. Dev.	Min	Max
SHARE/X^{nr}	760	0.3158	0.2113	0.0108	0.7746
IDIODEM/X^{nr}	760	0.0000	0.0824	–0.4037	0.4037
Non–College	40	1585633	2500886	372125	14500000
College	40	426592	1063285	62628	6443185
Capital	40	7559625	13400000	1469625	79100000
Land	40	2034	2570	555	16487

Table presents sample statistics for our data set using the college/non–college aggregation scheme. These reveal that the typical good constitutes about one-third of the typical industry and that there is substantial variation in idiosyncratic demand, which is important because we need variation in the latter to drive the home market effects.

ESTIMATING THE HECKSCHER–OHLIN PRODUCTION MODEL

Since our theoretical framework requires us to find a level of aggregation for which factor endowments drive aggregate production, it is reasonable to ask whether our aggregation scheme enables us to explain much of the variance at the three–digit level.

Table. Aggregated Production on Factor Endowments (40 Regions, Heteroskedasticity Corrected Estimates)

	t–statistics					$F_{.01,5,35}$ =3.6	
	Constant	College	Non–College	Capital	Land	F–Statistic	Adjusted R^2
Aggregate 1	–0.343	–3.389	1.29	1.715	–3.823	14.77	0.5854
Aggregate 2	–1.208	–2.413	–0.085	2.432	–3.522	24.02	0.7024
Aggregate 3	–3.317	–2.286	3.255	0.266	–3.503	78.45	0.8882
Aggregate 4	–2.702	–1.758	1.213	1.209	–3.422	11.86	0.5268
Aggregate 5	–2.086	0.396	3.182	–0.946	–2.621	70.19	0.8765
Aggregate 6	0.467	4.994	1.323	–1.098	–0.534	1192.63	0.9919

Table presents results of estimating equation for our sample of 40 regions. What is striking in our results is the fact that fits of the regressions are quite high. Indeed, our results indicate that, on average, factor endowments can explain almost 80 per cent of the variation of our aggregates.

It is worth remembering, however, that there are two sources of variation in these data. One source is pure size–based variation: larger regions produce more output. If all of our explanatory power came from this source of variation, it would be somewhat disturbing, since one would like to believe that endowments should tell us something about the relative sizes of industries within regions. In other words, we would like endowments to also tell us about crosssectional variation within regions of similar size. One way to eliminate this size–based variation and examine the cross-sectional variation is to force the exponent on GDP to equal two in our heteroskedasticity correction. This is equivalent to estimating a version of equation in which both sides have been deflated by GDP.

When we estimated this version of the equation we obtained an average R^2 of 0.4. This suggests that even after controlling for size based variation, endowments explain almost half of the variance of aggregate output. Furthermore, our data revealed that endowments had a more difficult time explaining more disaggregated output levels. Using the same specification, we only obtained an average R^2 of only 0.3 when we ran the same specification on the most disaggregated data. This is consistent with the theoretical notion that the Heckscher–Ohlin framework performs better using aggregates of industries with similar factor intensities than using disaggregated data.

Overall, our results suggest that endowments and output are highly correlated on regional data, and we have therefore established that the idea that endowments matter in determining the location of production is a credible null hypothesis.

3.4 TESTING FOR HOME MARKET EFFECTS

Before presenting our regression evidence, we begin by plotting our data. Our formulation of the theory, given in equation suggests that we have a multivariate relationship

between the variables. If, however, we impose that s equals 1, divide through by industry level output, and carry the SHARE variable over to the left-hand side, we obtain

$$\gamma_g^{nr} - \gamma_g^{nJ} = \frac{\alpha_g^n}{X^{nr}} + \beta_2\left(\delta_g^{nr} - \delta_g^{nJ}\right) + \epsilon_g^{\sim nr}$$

The left–hand side of this equation measures how the share of industry output within a prefecture deviates from that share for the rest of Japan, while the term in parentheses indicates the deviation in absorption. We refer to these two variables as the "Production Deviation" and the "Absorption Deviation."

If economic geography has some role to play in these data one should expect to see absorption deviations produce more than one-for-one movements in output. This would result in a line with a slope of more than one. On the other hand if comparative advantage determined production, then one would expect to see a line with a slope of less than one. The slope of the fitted line is 1.7. This suggests economic geography effects. Based on the slope of the fitted line in this figure, a rise in a prefecture of idiosyncratic demand leads net exports to rise by 70 per cent of the increment to local demand.

These results are surprising in light of our earlier work on international data. We conducted a similar experiment for the OECD using 2–and 3–digit ISIC classifications. In the international data, the fitted line was significantly below the diagonal at this level of aggregation, with a slope of only 0.66. In other words, international data revealed no economic geography effect at this level of aggregation, and only a very weak relationship at greater levels of disaggregation.

Although this graph is quite suggestive that economic geography might matter for regional specialization, regression analysis will allow us to examine these relations more precisely. We begin by estimating equation. The results from this exercise are presented in

Table. Seemingly Unrelated Regression Results Dependent Variable is Production

IDIODEM	1.416	0.888
	0.025	.070
SHARE	1.033	–1.7441
	0.007	0.211
FACTORS	No	Yes
Observations	760	760

When we do not include factor endowments in the specification, our econometric results confirm the general impression of the data. Although the coefficient is slightly smaller, its value of 1.42 is clearly in the range of economic geography.

The results presented thus far have examined economic geography against a very weak null hypothesis: *et al.,* that factor endowments do not matter at all at the goods level. Davis and Weinstein, however, show that factor endowments play an important role in determining production at this level of aggregation on international data. This suggests that by leaving out factor endowments from our estimating equations we may be creating an omitted–variables bias.

Consider the following possibility. We know that an important component of absorption is demand for intermediate goods. Demand for intermediates is determined by the production of final goods, but, if one believes in equation, production of the latter is driven by endowments.

This implies that demand for intermediates may be driven by endowments. In other words, if one believes that endowments determine production, then it would not be surprising to find that there is a correlation between production and absorption because both are driven by endowments.

The obvious solution is to estimate equation since it includes factor endowments on the right–hand side.

Interestingly, this causes the coefficient on IDIODEM to decline to 0.9. This implies that once we account for factor endowments, it no longer is the case that movements in demand produce more than proportionate movements in production. In other words, this specification rejects economic geography.

This result is troubling, especially in light of our earlier work. On international data, we also rejected the economic geography specification, but when we did so in the specification with factor endowments, we obtained a coefficient on IDIODEM of 0.3. This implies that in international data, on average less than one-third of any deviation in demand was met by higher domestic production, the rest being met by imports.

This result makes sense in light of the existence of international transaction costs which theoretically can cause demand and production to covary. What is more puzzling is that if one believes that comparative advantage drives production then one should also believe that in regional data, where transportation costs are presumably lower, one should obtain an even smaller coefficient on IDIODEM. Instead we have a coefficient that is too large to plausibly be generated by comparative advantage and transport costs, but too small to signal economic geography.

One explanation for these results is that not all sectors are composed of monopolisticallycompetitive industries. Suppose that only a few of our aggregates actually contain sectors exhibiting increasing returns. Then our system of equations would be pooling together industries in which the coefficient on IDIODEM is greater than unity with sectors in which the coefficient is less than unity. This pooling could be the explanation for a coefficient that is too high to plausibly describe a comparative advantage world, but too low to lead us to believe that economic geography matters. Fortunately, it is straightforward to modify our theory to address this problem. Assume that some of our aggregates are composed entirely of constant returns to scale sectors and others of increasing returns to scale sectors. Then the correct test would be to run equation separately for each aggregate. This should result in aggregates without monopolisticallycompetitive sectors exhibiting low coefficients on IDIODEM, but sectors with increasing returns producing coefficients over unity. The results from this exercise are presented in Table

Table. Estimation by Aggregate Dependent Variable is Output

Aggregate	IDIODEM	SHARE	Obs
1	0.1052	–2.864	160
	0.1628	0.9320	
2	1.0320	–1.6958	80
	0.3328	2.2646	
3	0.4272	–10.681	120
	0.1480	1.6466	
4	1.4757	2.6239	80
	0.2521	0.7825	
5	1.3575	–3.1882	200
	0.1430	0.8202	
6	0.8808	–0.2538	80
	0.2230	0.2766	

In the three least skilled–intensive aggregates, we detect no significant economic geography effect.

However, in the more skill–intensive aggregates 4 and 5 we find a coefficient that is larger than unity and significant at the 10 and 5 per cent levels respectively. The fact that these sectors contain such plausible economic geography candidates as general machinery, electrical machinery, transportation equipment, and precision instruments makes it even more believable that economic geography effects may be present in these data.

However, it is also important to focus on economic, not only statistical, significance. While we have been able to detect the presence of economic geography effects, it remains to be seen whether it matters much for production. To assess the latter we consider β–coefficients. These statistics tell us how sensitive production is to movements in idiosyncratic demand. Formally, a β–coefficient tells us how many standard deviations the dependent variable is predicted to move if the independent variable moves one standard deviation. As discussed by Leamer, these statistics are useful in answering questions regarding which independent variables are important in determining movements in the dependent variable.

In earlier work on international data, we found that often even when we could detect economic geography in the sample, this impact was economically small. While we find larger effects in the regional data, they nonetheless remain modest. A one–standard–deviation movement in idiosyncratic demand moves production by 0.22 standard deviations in aggregate 4, and by 0.09 standard deviations in aggregate 5. In other words, knowing the variation in idiosyncratic demand does not provide much information about the variation in production. Indeed, these numbers are not that different than what we found on international data, suggesting that even in the sectors where economic geography matters, the effects are relatively modest.

These results, however, are obviously very sensitive to the aggregation scheme. For example, the inclusion of an unlikely economic geography candidate, leather, in aggregate 5 may dilute the overall impact of economic geography in these data. In fact, while we found that changing the basis of our aggregation scheme had little impact on estimates obtained in the full system, changing the mix of goods within our industry definitions could cause different groups of industries to be labeled as sectors with significant economic geography effects.

One solution to this theoretical and empirical mire is to foreswear aggregation altogether, and allow all coefficients to vary at the goods level. This might be appropriate if, contrary to our initial theoretical specification, the elasticity of substitution between varieties of a good is different for the various goods within an industry. The results from this exercise are presented in Table.

Table. Disaggregated Estimation Dependent Variable is Output

Industry	IDIODEM	SHARE	Factors	Adjusted R^2	Observations
Textile	3.9532 0.4570	0.5932 3.2302	Yes	0.8468	40
Apparel	–1.5866 0.2843	–24.3909 4.3741	Yes	0.5725	40
Lumber	1.0622 0.4440	4.1937 1.8351	Yes	0.8106	40
Furniture	–0.5538 0.2765	–5.1598 1.4389	Yes	0.988	40
Pulp, paper	1.9913 0.3150	–8.9731 1.7861	Yes	0.8917	40
Printing	0.7269 0.2296	–0.3423 0.2876	Yes	0.9979	40
Chemicals	6.6781 1.2454	0.9248 1.1038	Yes	0.9928	40
Petrol, Coal products	–0.4655 2.3048	–6.3220 4.2047	Yes	0.9934	40
Rubber	–0.1081 0.1763	–24.5223 5.78042	Yes	0.8454	40
Leather, leather products	0.1643 0.4053	–7.1330 1.7866	Yes	0.9412	40
Stone, clay, glass	–0.6454 0.4148	–5.0674 2.4824	Yes	0.7681	40
Iron, steel	3.9294 0.5613	–3.9582 6.2968	Yes	0.7663	40
Non–ferrous metals	1.5932 0.1741	2.5509 3.1334	Yes	0.962	40
Fabricated metal	–0.8197 1.0820	–14.0257 7.0734	Yes	0.5972	40
General machinery	–0.4219 0.9524	–4.4744 2.6163	Yes	0.7802	40
Electrical machinery	6.2713 1.3552	5.6614 3.7628	Yes	0.9002	40
Transport equipment	6.7060 0.5024	1.2685 0.9336	Yes	0.8826	40
Precision instruments	4.32139 0.8115	–3.9460 1.8107	Yes	0.7477	40
Other manufacturing	0.0655 0.3824	1.1179 1.4888	Yes	0.5307	40

The coefficient on IDIODEM is significantly larger than unity for eight of the nineteen sectors: textiles, paper and pulp, iron and steel, chemicals, transportation equipment, precision instruments, non–ferrous metals, and electrical machinery. With perhaps the exception of paper and pulp, all of these seem like plausible candidates for monopolistic competition, with textiles, transportation equipment, iron and steel, and electrical machinery providing canonical examples of the power of the economic geography framework.

Furthermore, our results are robust to whichever aggregation scheme we choose. The variables SHARE and IDIODEM will vary depending on whether we group industries on the basis of college to non–college, capital to non–college ratios, or capital to college ratios. However, we found that all of these sectors except paper and pulp were identified as exhibiting economic geography effects regardless of the aggregation scheme.

We can run an additional robustness check to confirm that we are identifying economic geography effects here. We posit that the R&D-intensity of an industry may be used as a proxy for the increasing returns and monopolistic competition that underlie the economic geography theory. Plots our estimated coefficients against sectoral R&D expenses divided by sales.

The correlation is 0.62, indicating that high R&D is associated with identification of economic geography sectors. In fact, the four most R&D–intensive sectors are also the four sectors for which we obtain the highest coefficients on IDIODEM. Once again we confront the issue of economic significance. We repeat our experiment with beta-coefficients, only this time we use the disaggregated results presented in Table.

Table reports the β-coefficients for the 8 sectors for which we obtained statistically significant economic geography coefficients. For these sectors, economic geography seems quite important.

Table. Beta Coefficients for Goods with Significant Coefficients on IDIODEM

Sector	Beta Coefficient
Textiles	0.82
Iron and Steel	0.40
Paper and Pulp	0.51
Transportation Equipment	0.74
Non-Ferrous Metals	0.42
Electrical Machinery	0.37
Precision Instruments	0.42
Chemicals	0.53

A one standard deviation movement in idiosyncratic demand on average moves production by half a standard deviation. In other words, observed fluctuations in idiosyncratic demand seem to provide a lot of information about production patterns. Furthermore, in the important sector of transportation equipment, these effects are very strong. Although economic geography may not be that important for international specialization, there appears to be strong evidence that it matters for certain sectors on a regional level.

CONCLUSION

This stage introduced economic geography as a dynamic, diverse and contested sub–discipline of geography that uses a geographical approach to study the economy. The stage emphasised that an economicgeographical approach to studying economies is very different from the one used by mainstream economics. In highlighting these differences, the stage introduced the key concepts of an economic–geographical approach, namely the concepts of space, place and scale. Having these and other concepts at its disposal, economic geography is uniquely placed to help us appreciate and understand the modern economic world in all its complexity.

2

Population Geography

INTRODUCTION

Human beings evolved under conditions of high mortality due to famines, accidents, illnesses, infections and war and therefore the relatively high fertility rates were essential for species survival. In spite of the relatively high fertility rates it took all the time from evolution of mankind to the middle of the 19th century for the global population to reach one billion. The twentieth century witnessed an unprecedented rapid improvement in health care technologies and access to health care all over the world; as a result there was a steep fall in the mortality and steep increase in longevity. The population realised these changes and took steps to reduce their fertility but the decline in fertility was not so steep. As a result the global population has undergone a fourfold increase in a hundred years and has reached 6 billion.

DEMOGRAPHIC TRANSITION

Demographers refer to these changes from stable population with high fertility and mortality to a new stability in population due to low fertility and mortality patterns as demographic transition. Demographic transition occurs in four phases; of these the first three phases are characterized by population growth. In the first phase there is a fall in death rate and improvement in longevity; this leads to population growth. In the second phase there is a fall in birth rate but fall is less steep than fall in death rates and consequently there is population growth. In the third phase death rates plateau and replacement level of fertility is attained but the population growth continues because of the large size of population in reproductive age group.

The fourth phase is characterized by fall in birth rate to below replacement level and reduction in the proportion of the population in reproductive age group; as a result of these changes population growth ceases and population stabilizes. Experience in some of the developed countries suggest that in some societies even after attainment of stable population there may be a further decline in fertility so that there is a further reduction in the population-so called negative population growth phase of the demographic transition. Different countries in the world have entered the demographic transition at different periods of time; there are also substantial differences in the rate of demographic transition and time taken to achieve population stabilization.

<table>
<tr><th colspan="4">Global Population Scenario</th></tr>
<tr><th colspan="2">Population in Billion</th><th colspan="2">Total Fertility Rate</th></tr>
<tr><td>1901</td><td>1.4</td><td>1969</td><td>6.0</td></tr>
<tr><td>1960</td><td>3.0</td><td>1999</td><td>3.0</td></tr>
<tr><td>1987</td><td>5.0</td><td></td><td></td></tr>
<tr><td>1999</td><td>6.0</td><td></td><td></td></tr>
<tr><td colspan="2">Population growth</td><td colspan="2">Population growth Rate</td></tr>
<tr><td colspan="2">1989–86 million</td><td colspan="2">1969–2.4%</td></tr>
<tr><td colspan="2">1989–78 million</td><td colspan="2">1999–1.8%</td></tr>
<tr><td colspan="4">Showing of population growth is due to:</td></tr>
<tr><td colspan="4">1. Global decline in fertility
2. Increase in mortality in some regions e.g. HIV related increase in mortality in subsahar as Africa</td></tr>
</table>

GLOBAL POPULATION SCENARIO

In 1901 the world population was 1.6 billion. By 1960, it became 3 billion, and by 1987, 5 billion and in 1999, 6 billion. Currently, one billion people are added every 12-13 years. During the last decade there has been substantial decline in birth rate.

The reasons for decline vary from society to society; urbanization, rising educational attainment, increasing employment among women, lower infant mortality are some major factors responsible for growing desire for smaller families; increasing awareness and improved access to contraception have made it possible for the majority of the couple to achieve the desired family size.

In some countries slowing of the population growth has been due to an increase in mortality (*e.g.* HIV related mortality in sub-saharan Africa). As a result of all these the decline in the global population growth during the nineties is steeper than the earlier predictions.

Currently, the annual increment is about 80 million. It is expected to decrease to about 64 million by 2020-25 and to 33 million by 2045-50; 95% of the growth of population occurs in developing countries. Most demographers believe that the current accelerated decline in population growth will continue for the next few decades and the medium projections of Population Division of United Nations, that the global population will grow to 8.9 billion by 2050 is likely to be achieved.

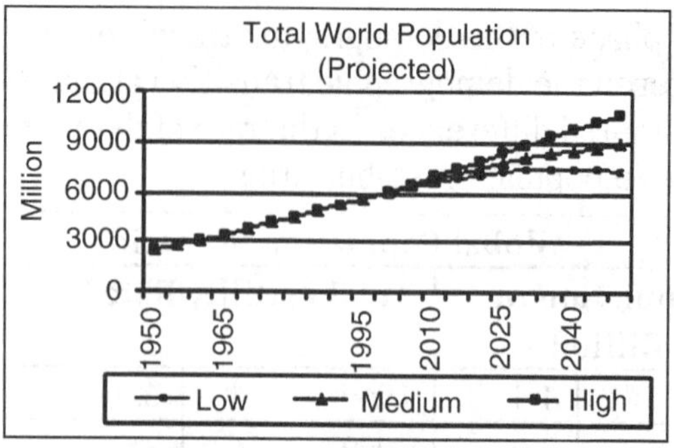

CHANGING AGE STRUCTURE OF THE POPULATION

During demographic transition along with the growth in number there are changes in the population age structure. While the importance of the population growth as a determinant of quality of life is universally understood, the profoundly serious consequences of changing age structure especially if it occurs too rapidly is not understood by many. Population pyramids graphically represent complex changes in age structure of the population so that it can be readily understood and interpreted.

The population pyramids for the global population, developed and developing countries is shown in Figure. Currently nearly half of the global population is below 25 years of age and one sixth are in the age group 15-24. Their choices, efforts and lifestyles will determine not only the population growth but also future improvement in the quality of life in harmony with global ecology.

In developed countries the reproductive age group population is relatively small; their fertility is low and the longevity at birth is high. Population profiles of these countries resemble a cylinder and not a pyramid.These countries have the advantages of having achieved a stable population but have to face the problems of having a relatively small productive workforce to support the large aged population with substantial non-communicable disease burden. Some of the developing countries have undergone a very rapid decline in the birth rates within a short period.

This enabled them to quickly achieve population stabilization but they do face the problems of rapid changes in the age structure and workforce which may be inadequate to meet their manpower requirements. In contrast the population in most of the developing countries (including India) consist of a very large proportion of children and persons in reproductive age. Because of the large reproductive age group (Population momentum) the population will continue to grow even when replacement level of fertility is reached (couples having only two children).

It is imperative that these countries should generate enough employment opportunities for this work force and utilise the human resources and accelerate their economic growth. Planners and policy makers in developing countries like India have to take into account the ongoing demographic changes (number and age structure of the population) so that available human resources are optimally utilised as agents of change and development to achieve improvement in quality of life.

DEMOGRAPHIC TRANSITION IN INDIA

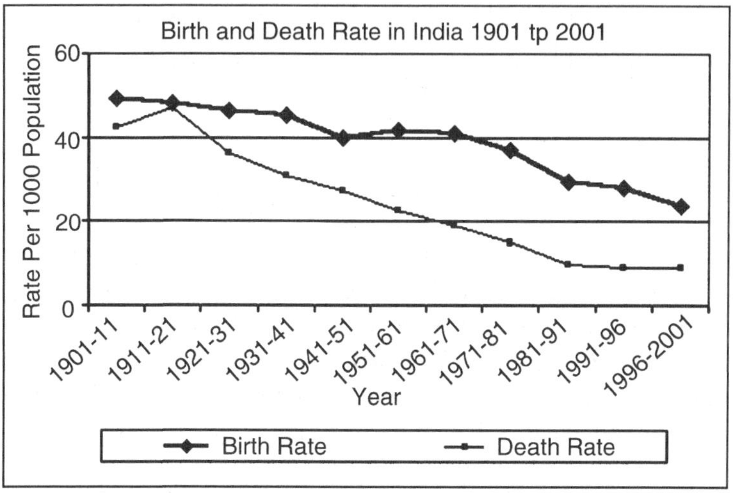

Over the last four decades there has been rapid fall in Crude Death Rate (CDR) from 25.1 in 1951 to 9.8 in 1991 and less steep decline in the Crude Birth Rate (CBR) from 40.8 in 1951 to 29.5 in 1991.

The annual exponential population growth rate has been over 2% in the period 1961-90. During the nineties the decline in CBR has been steeper than that in the (CDR) and consequently, the annual population growth rate has fallen below 2%.

The rate of decline in population growth is likely to be further accelerated during the next decade. The changes in the population growth rates have been relatively slow, steady and sustained. As a result the country was able to achieve a relatively gradual change in the population numbers and age structure.

The short and long term adverse consequences of too rapid decline in birth rates and change in age structure on the social and economic development were avoided and the country was able to adapt to these changes without massive disruptions of developmental efforts.

In spite of the uniform national norms set under the 100% Centrally Funded and Centrally Sponsored Scheme (CSS) of Family Welfare, there are substantial differences in the performance between States as assessed by IMR and CBR. Though the decline in CBR and IMR has occurred in all States, the rate of decline is slower in some States.

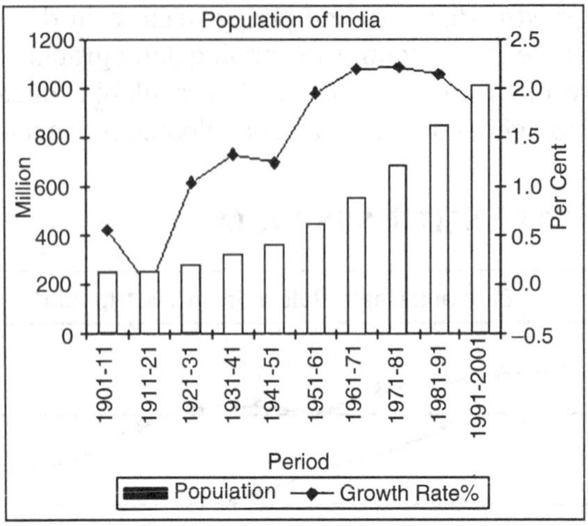

At one end of the spectrum is Kerala with mortality and fertility rates nearly similar to those in some of the developed countries. At the other end, there are four large northern States with high Infant Mortality Rate and Fertility Rates. Though the decline in CBR, IMR and CDR has occurred in all States, the rate of decline was slower in some States like U.P. and Bihar. There are substantial differences in CBR and IMR not only between States but also between the districts in the same state.

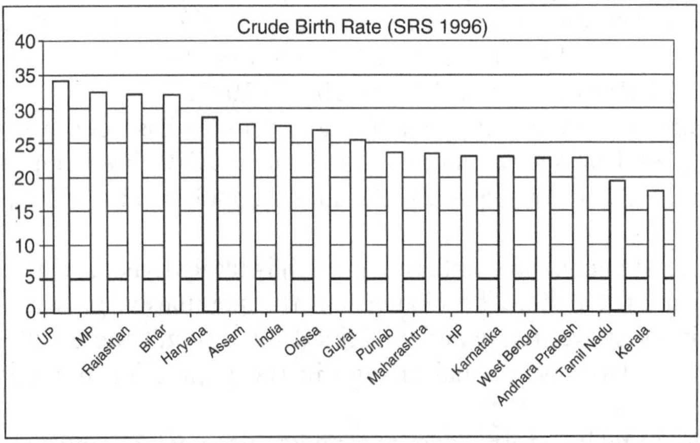

In view of these findings, the NDC Committee on Population recommended that efforts should be made to provide reproductive and child health services at district level and undertake decentralized area-specific micro planning and implementation of appropriate interventions. In response to this recommendation Dept of Family Welfare has abolished the practice of fixing targets for individual contraceptives by the Central Government from April 1996 and had initiated decentralized district based, planning (based on community need assessment), implementation, monitoring and midcourse corrections of FW programme.

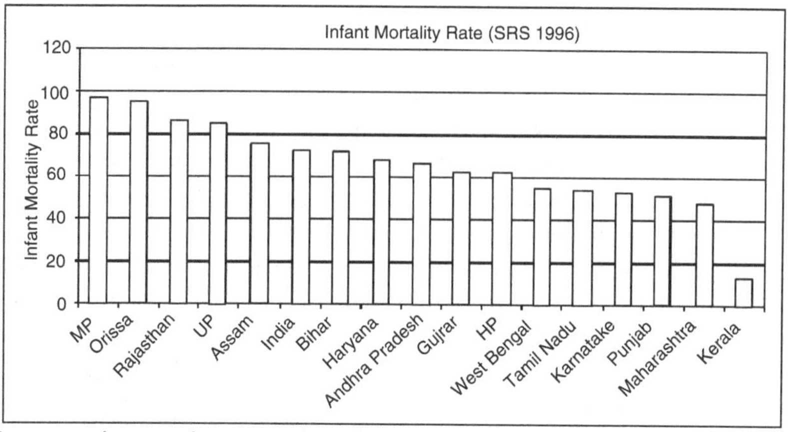

The experience of states with district based planning, implementation and the impact are being closely monitored.

CONSEQUENCES OF POPULATION GROWTH

ENVIRONMENTAL AND ECOLOGICAL CONSEQUENCES

The already densely populated developing countries contribute to over 95% of the population growth and rapid population growth could lead to environmental deterioration. Developed countries are less densely populated and contribute very little to population growth; however, they cause massive ecological damage by the wasteful, unnecessary and unbalanced consumption the consequences of which could adversely affect both the developed and the developing countries.

The review on "Promotion of sustainable development: challenges for environmental policies" in the Economic Survey 1998-99 had covered in detail the major environmental problems, and policy options for improvement; the present review will only briefly touch upon some of the important ecological consequences of demographic transition.

In many developing countries continued population growth has resulted in pressure on land, fragmentation of land holding, collapsing fisheries, shrinking forests, rising temperatures, loss of plant and animal species. Global warming due to increasing use of fossil fuels (mainly by the developed countries) could have serious effects on the populous coastal regions in developing countries, their food production and essential water supplies.

The Intergovernmental Panel on Climate Change has projected that, if current greenhouse gas emission trends continue, the mean global surface temperature will rise from 1 to 3.5 degrees Celsius in the next century. The panel's best estimate scenario projects a sea-level rise of 15 to 95 centimeters by 2100. The ecological impact of rising oceans would include increased flooding, coastal erosion, salination of aquifers and coastal crop land and displacement of millions of people living near the coast. Patterns of precipitation are also likely to change, which combined with increased average temperatures, could substantially alter the relative agricultural productivity of different regions.

Greenhouse gas emissions are closely linked to both population growth and development. Slower population growth in developing countries and ecologically sustainable lifestyles in developed countries would make reduction in green house gas emission easier to achieve and provide more time and options for adaptation to climate change. Rapid population growth, developmental activities either to meet the growing population or the growing needs of the population as well as changing lifestyles and consumption patterns pose major challenge to preservation and promotion of ecological balance in India.

Some of the major ecological adverse effects reported in India include:

- Severe pressure on the forests due to both the rate of resource use and the nature of use. The per capita forest biomass in the country is only about 6 tons as against the global average of 82 tons.
- Adverse effect on species diversity:
- Conversion of habitat to some other land use such as agriculture, urban development, forestry operation. Some 70-80% of fresh water marshes and lakes in the gangetic flood plains has been lost in the last 50 years.
- Tropical deforestation and destruction of mangroves for commercial needs and fuel wood. The country's mangrove areas have reduced from 700,000 ha to 453,000 ha in the last 50 years.
- Intense grazing by domestic livestock
- Poaching and illegal harvesting of wildlife.
- Increase in agricultural area, high use of chemical fertilizers pesticides and weedicides; water stagnation, soil erosion, soil salinity and low productivity.
- High level of biomass burning causing large-scale indoor pollution.
- Encroachment on habitat for rail and road construction thereby fragmenting the habitat. Increase in commercial activities such as mining and unsustainable resource extraction.
- Degradation of coastal and other aquatic ecosystems from domestic sewage, pesticides, fertilizers and industrial effluents.
- Over fishing in water bodies and introduction of weeds and exotic species.
- Diversion of water for domestic, industrial and agricultural uses leading to increased river pollution and decrease in self-cleaning properties of rivers.
- Increasing water requirement leading to tapping deeper aquifers which have high content of arsenic or fluoride resulting health problems.
- Disturbance from increased recreational activity and tourism causing pollution of natural ecosystems with wastes left behind by people.

The United Nations Conference on Environment and Development acknowledged population growth, rising income levels, changing technologies, increasing consumption pattern will all have adverse impact on environment. Ensuring that there is no further deterioration depends on choices made by the population about family size, life styles, environmental protection and equity. Availability of appropriate technology and commitment towards ensuring sustainable development is increasing throughout the world. Because of these, it might be possible to initiate steps to see that the natural carrying capacity of the environment is not damaged beyond recovery and ecological balance is to a large extent maintained. It is imperative that the environmental sustainability of all developmental projects is taken care of by appropriate inputs at the planning, implementation, monitoring and evaluation stages.

URBANIZATION

The proportion of people in developing countries who live in cities has almost doubled since 1960 (from less than 22 per cent to more than 40 per cent), while in more developed regions the urban share has grown from 61 per cent to 76 per cent. Urbanization is projected to continue well into the next century. By 2030, it is expected that nearly 5 billion (61 per cent) of the world's 8.1 billion people will live in cities. India shares this global trend towards urbanisation.

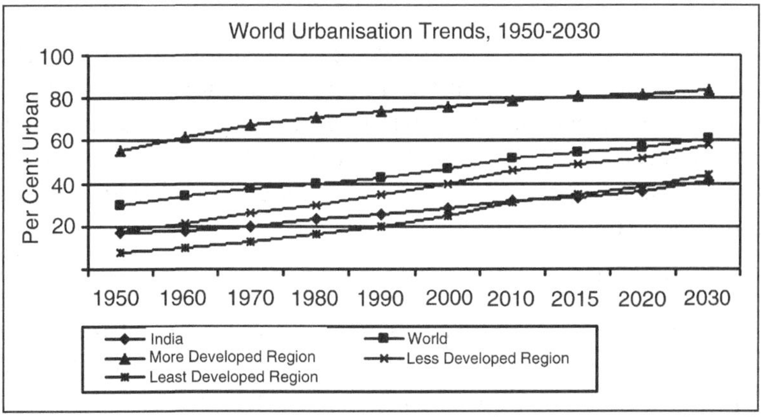

Globally, the number of cities with 10 million or more inhabitants is increasing rapidly, and most of these new "megacities" are in developing regions. In 1960, only New York and Tokyo had more than 10 million people. By 1999, the number of megacities had grown to 17(13 in developing countries). It is projected that there will be 26 megacities by 2015, (18 in Asia; of these five in India); more than 10 per cent of the world's population will live in these cities (1.7% in 1950). India's urban population has doubled from 109 million to 218 million during the last two decades and is estimated to reach 300 million by 2000 AD.

As a consequence cities are facing the problem of expanding urban slums. Like many other demographic changes, urbanization has both positive and negative effects. Cities and towns have become the engines of social change and rapid economic development. Urbanisation is associated with improved access to education, employment, health care; these result in increase in age at marriage, reduction in family size and improvement in health indices. As people have moved towards and into cities, information has flowed outward. Better communication and transportation now link urban and rural areas both economically and socially creating an urban-rural continuum of communities with improvement in some aspects of lifestyle of both.

The ever increasing reach of mass media communicate new ideas, points of reference, and available options are becoming more widely recognized, appreciated and sought. This phenomenon has affected health care, including reproductive health, in many ways. For instance, radio and television programmes that discuss gender equity, family size preference and family planning options are now reaching formerly isolated rural populations. This can create demand for services for mothers and children, higher contraceptive use, and fewer unwanted pregnancies, smaller healthier families and lead to more rapid population stabilisation.

But the rapid growth of urban population also poses some serious challenges. Urban population growth has outpaced the development of basic minimum services; housing, water supply, sewerage and solid waste disposal are far from adequate; increasing waste generation at home, offices and industries, coupled with poor waste disposal facilities result in rapid environmental deterioration. Increasing automobiles add to air pollution. All these have adverse effect on ecology and health. Poverty persists in urban and peri-urban areas; awareness about the glaring inequities in close urban setting may lead to social unrest.

RURAL POPULATION AND THEIR DEVELOPMENT

Over seventy per cent of India's population still lives in rural areas. There are substantial differences between the states in the proportion of rural and urban population (varying from almost 90 per cent in Assam and Bihar to 61 per cent in Maharashtra). Agriculture is the largest and one of the most important sector of the rural economy and contributes both to economic growth and employment. Its contribution to the Gross Domestic Product has declined over the last five decades but agriculture still remains the source of livelihood for over 70 per cent of the country's population. A large proportion of the rural work force is small and consists of marginal farmers and landless agricultural labourers. There is substantial under employment among these people; both wages and productivity are low. These in turn result in poverty; it is estimated that 320 million people are still living below the poverty line in rural India.

Though poverty has declined over the last three decades, the number of rural poor has in fact increased due to the population growth.

Poor tend to have larger families which puts enormous burden on their meagre resources, and prevent them from breaking out of the shackles of poverty. In States like Tamil Nadu where replacement level of fertility has been attained, population growth rates are much lower than in many other States; but the population density is high and so there is a pressure on land. In States like Rajasthan, Uttar Pradesh, Bihar and Madhya Pradesh population is growing rapidly, resulting in increasing pressure on land and resulting land fragmentation. Low productivity of small land holders leads to poverty, low energy intake and under nutrition, and this, in turn, prevents the development thus creating a vicious circle. In most of the states non-farm employment in rural areas has not grown very much and cannot absorb the growing labour force. Those who are getting educated specially beyond the primary level, may not wish to do manual agricultural work. They would like better opportunities and more remunerative employment.

In this context, it is imperative that programmes for skill development, vocational training and technical education are taken up on a large scale in order to generate productive employment in rural areas. The entire gamut of existing poverty alleviation and employment generation programmes may have to be restructured to meet the newly emerging types of demand for employment. Rural poor have inadequate access to basic minimum services, because of poor connectivity, lack of awareness, inadequate and poorly functional infrastructure.

There are ongoing efforts to improve these, but with the growing aspirations of the younger, educated population these efforts may prove to be inadequate to meet the increasing needs both in terms of type and quality of services. Greater education, awareness and better standard of living among the growing younger age group population would create the required consciousness among them that smaller families are desirable; if all the felt needs for health and family welfare services are fully met, it will be possible to enable them to attain their reproductive goals, achieve substantial decline in the family size and improve quality of life.

WATER SUPPLY

In many parts of developed and developing world, water demand substantially exceeds sustainable water supply. It is estimated that currently 430 millions (8% of the global population) are living in countries affected by water stress; by 2020 about one fourth of the global population may be facing chronic and recurring shortage of fresh water. In India, water withdrawal is estimated to be twice the rate of aquifer recharge; as a result water tables are falling by one to three meters every year; tapping deeper aquifers have resulted in larger population groups being exposed to newer health hazards such as high fluoride or arsenic content in drinking water. At the other end of the spectrum, excessive use of water has led to water logging and increasing salinity in some parts of the country. Eventually, both lack of water and water logging could have adverse impact on India's food production. There is very little arable agricultural land which remains unexploited and in many areas, agricultural technology improvement may not be able to ensure further increase in yield per hectare. It is, therefore, imperative that research in biotechnology for improving development of foodgrains strains that would tolerate salinity and those which would require less water gets high priority. Simultaneously, a movement towards making water harvesting, storage and its need based use part of every citizens life should be taken up.

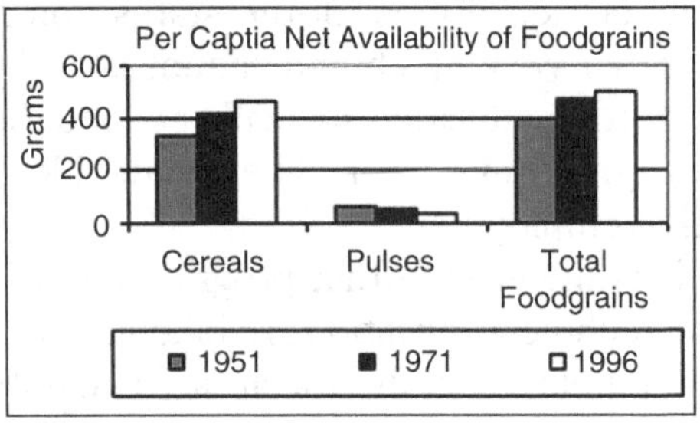

FOOD SECURITY

Technological innovations in agriculture and increase in area under cultivation have ensured that so far, food production has kept pace with the population growth. Evolution of global and national food security systems have improved access to food. It is estimated that the global population will grow to 9 billion by 2050 and the food production will double; improvement in purchasing power and changing dietary habits (shift to animal products) may further add to the requirement of food grains. Thus, in the next five decades, the food and nutrition security could become critical in many parts of the world especially in the developing countries and pockets of poverty in the developed countries.

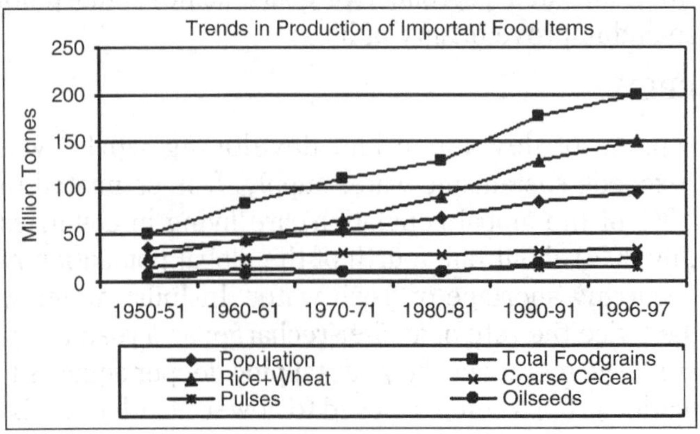

In India one of the major achievements in the last fifty years has been the green revolution and selfsufficiency in food production. Food grain production has increased from 50.82 in 1950-51 to 200.88 million tons in 1998-99. It is a matter of concern that while the cereal production has been growing steadily at a rate higher than the population growth rates, the coarse grain and pulse production has not shown a similar increase. Consequently there has been a reduction in the per capita availability of pulses (from 60.7 grams in 1951 to 34 grams per day in 1996) and coarse grains.

Table. Production of Food grains-Average Annual Growth

						(Million Tonnes)
Year	**Rice**	**Wheat**	**Coarse Cereals**	**Pulses**	**Total Food Grains**	**Compound Annual Growth**
			(Percent)			
1950-51	20.58	6.46	15.38	8.41	50.82	–
1960-61	34.58	11.00	23.74	12.70	82.02	3.22
1970-71	42.23	23.83	30.55	11.82	108.42	1.72
1980-81	52.63	36.31	29.02	10.63	129.59	2.08
1990-91	74.29	55.14	32.7	14.26	176.39	3.54
1997-98	82.3	65.9	31.1	13.1	192.4	1.66
1998-99*	84.50	70.63	30.58	15.2	200.88	

*Estimated

Over the last five decades there has been a decline in the per capita availability of pulses. During the last few years the country has imported pulses to meet the requirement. There has been a sharp and sustained increase in cost of pulses, so there is substantial decline in per capita pulses consumption among poorer segment of population. This in turn could have an adverse impact on their protein intake. The pulse component of the "Pulses and Oil Seeds Mission" need to receive a major thrust in terms of R&D and other inputs, so that essential pulse requirement of growing population is fully met. Rising cost of pulses had a beneficial effect also. Till eighties in central India wages of landless labourers were given in the form Kesari Dal which was cheaper than cereals or coarse grains.

Consumption of staple diet of Kesari Dal led to crippling disease of neuro lathyrism. Over the last three decades the rising cost of pulses has made Kesari Dal more expensive than wheat or rice and hence it is no longer given to labourers as wages for work done; as a result the disease has virtually disappeared from Central India.

Over years the coarse grain production has remained stagnant and per capita availability of coarse grain has under gone substantial reduction; there has been a shift away from coarse grains to rice and wheat consumption even among poorer segment of population. One of the benefits of this change is virtual elimination of pellagra which was widely prevalent among low income group population in Deccan Plateau whose staple food was sorghum. Coarse grains are less expensive than rice and wheat; they can thus provide higher calories for the same cost as compared to rice and wheat.

Coarse grains which are locally produced and procured if made available through TPDS at subsidised rate, may not only substantially bring down the subsidy cost without any reduction in calories provided but also improve "targetting"-as only the most needy are likely to access these coarse grains. Another area of concern is the lack of sufficient focus and thrust in horticulture; because of this, availability of vegetables especially green leafy vegetables and yellow/red vegetables throughout the year at affordable cost both in urban and rural areas has remained an unfulfilled dream. Health and nutrition education emphasizing the importance of consuming these inexpensive rich sources of micronutrients will not result in any change in food habits unless there is harnessing and effective management of horticultural resources in the country to meet the growing needs of the people at affordable cost. States like Tamil Nadu and Himachal Pradesh have initiated some efforts in this direction; similar efforts need be taken up in other states also.

NUTRITION

At the time of independence the country faced two major nutritional problems; one was the threat of famine and acute starvation due to low agricultural production and lack of appropriate food distribution system. The other was chronic energy deficiency due to poverty, low-literacy, poor access to safe-drinking water, sanitation and health care; these factors led to wide spread prevalence of infections and ill health in children and adults.

Kwashiorkor, marasmus, goitre, beri beri, blindness due to Vitamin-A deficiency and anaemia were major public health problems. The country adopted multi-sectoral, multi-pronged strategy to combat the major nutritional problems and to improve nutritional status of the population.

Chronic energy deficiency (CED)–current situation:

- While mortality has come down by 50% and fertility by 40% reduction in under nutrition is only 20%.
- There has been 50% decline in severe under-nutrition
- Reduction in mild under-nutrition is marginal
- India with less than 20% global children accounts for over 40% under nourished children
- Under nutrition in pregnant women and 6-24 months children has not declined
- Major causes of CED remains to be inadequate food intake, infections and poor caring practices..

During the last 50 years considerable progress has been achieved. Famines no longer stalk the country. There has been substantial reduction in moderate and severe undernutrition in children and some improvement in nutritional status of all segments of population. Kwashiorkor, marasmus, pellagra, lathyrism, beri beri and blindness due to severe Vitamin-A deficiency have become rare.

However, it is a matter of concern that milder forms of Chronic Energy Deficiency (CED) and micronutrient deficiencies continue to be widely prevalent in adults and children. In view of the fact that population growth in India will continue for the next few decades, it is essential that appropriate strategies are devised to improve food and nutrition security of families, identify individuals/families with severe forms of CED and provide them assistance to over come these problem

OPERATIONAL STRATEGY TO IMPROVE THE DIETARY INTAKE OF THE FAMILY AND IMPROVE NUTRITIONAL STATUS OF THE RAPIDLY GROWING ADULT POPULATION WOULD INCLUDE

- Ensuring adequate agricultural production of cereals, pulses, vegetables and other foodstuffs needed to fully meet the requirement of growing population.
- Improving in purchasing power through employment generation and employment assurance schemes;
- Providing subsidised food grains through TPDS to the families below poverty line.
- Exploring feasibility of providing subsidized coarse grains to families Below Poverty Line (BPL)

OPERATIONAL STRATEGIES TO IMPROVE HEALTH AND NUTRITIONAL STATUS OF THE GROWING NUMBERS OF WOMEN AND CHILDREN INCLUDE

- Pregnant and lactating women-screening to identify women with weight below 40 Kgs and ensuring that they/their preschool children receive food supplements through Integrated Child Development Services Scheme (ICDS); adequate antenatal intrapartum and neonatal care.
- *0-6 months infants-Nutrition education for*:
  - Early initiation of lactation
  - Protection and promotion of universal breast feeding
  - Exclusive breast feeding for the first six months; unless there is specific reason supplementation should not be introduced before 6 months
  - Immunisation, growth monitoring and health care.

- *Well planned nutrition education to ensure that the infants and children do*:
  - Continue to get breasted;
  - Get appropriate cereal pulse-vegetable based supplement fed to them at least 3-4 times a day–appropriate help in ensuring this through family/community/work place support;
  - Immunisation and health care.
- *Children in the 0-5 age group*:
  - Screen by weighment to identify children with moderate and severe undernutrition
  - Provide double quantity supplements through icds;
  - Screening for nutrition and health problems and appropriate intervention.
- *Primary school children*:
  - Weigh and identify those with moderate and severe chronic energy deficiency;
  - Improve dietary intake to these children through the mid-day meal.
- Monitor for improvement in the identified undernourished infants, children and mothers; if no improvement after 2 months refer to physician for identification and treatment of factors that might be responsible for lack of improvement;
- Nutrition education on varying dietary needs of different members of the family and how they can be met by minor modifications from the family meals. Intensive health education for improving the life style of the population coupled with active screening and management of the health problems associated with obesity.

POPULATION PROJECTIONS FOR INDIA AND THEIR IMPLICATIONS

Populations projections 1996-2016

The population will increase from 934 million in 1996 to 1264 million in 2016.

Between the periods 1996-2001 and 2011-2016 there will be a decline of:

- *CBR from*: 24.10 to 21.41
- *CDR from*: 8.99 to 7.48
- *NGR from*: 1.51% to 1.39%
- IMR
  1. *Male from*: 63 to 38
  2. *Female from*: 64 to 39

Right from 1958 the Planning Commission has been constituting an Expert Group on Population Projections prior to the preparation of each of the Five

Year Plans so that the information on the population status at the time of initiation of the Plan and population projections for future are available during the preparation of the Plan.

Population projections have been utilised not only for planning to ensure provision of essentials necessities such as food, shelter and clothing but also prerequisites for human development such as education, employment and health care.

Over the years there has been considerable refinement in the methodology used for population projections and substantial improvement in the accuracy of predictions. The projections made by the Standing Committee on Population Projection in 1988 for the year 1991 was 843.6 million; this figure was within 0.3% of the 846.3 million reported in the Census 1991.

In 1996, Technical Group on Population Projections, had work out the population projections for the country and the states for the period 1996 to 2016 on the basis of census 1991 and other available demographic data. Population pyramids for the period 1971 to 2016 are shown in Figure.

Economic Implications of Demographic Transition
The next two decades will witness: • Increase in the 15-59 age group from 519-800 million • Low dependency ration *Challenge is to ensure:* • Adequate investment in HRD • Appropriate employment with adequate emoluments for the labour force *Opportunity is to:* • Utilise available abundant human resources to accelerate economic development

ECONOMIC IMPLICATIONS

Population growth and its relation to economic growth has been a matter of debate for over a century. The early Malthusian view was that population growth is likely to impede economic growth because it will put pressure on the available resources, result in reduction in per capita income and resources; this, in turn, will result in deterioration in quality of life. Contrary to the Malthusian predictions, several of the East Asian countries have been able to achieve economic prosperity and improvement in quality of life inspite of population growth.

This has been attributed to the increase in productivity due to development and utilisation of innovative technologies by the young educated population who formed the majority of the growing population. These countries have been able to exploit the dynamics of demographic transition to achieve economic growth by using the human resources as the engine driving the economic development;

improved employment with adequate emoluments has promoted saving and investment which in turn stimulated economic growth. However, not all countries, which have undergone demographic transition, have been able to transform their economies. Sri Lanka in South Asia underwent demographic transition at the same time as South East Asian countries but has not achieved the economic transition. It is now realised that population growth or demographic transition can have favourable impact on economic growth only when there are optimal interventions aimed at human resource development (HRD) and appropriate utilisation of available human resources. For India the current phase of demographic transition with low dependency ratio and high working age group population, represents both a challenge and an opportunity. The challenge is to develop these human resources through appropriate education and skill development and utilise them fully by giving them appropriate jobs with adequate emoluments; if this challenge is met through well planned schemes for HRD and employment generation which are implemented effectively, there will be improved national productivity and personal savings rates; appropriate investment of these savings will help the country to achieve the economic transition from low economic growth-low per capita income to high economic growth-high per capita income. It is imperative to make the best use of this opportunity so as to enable the country and its citizens to vault to the high income-high economic growth status and stabilize at that level.

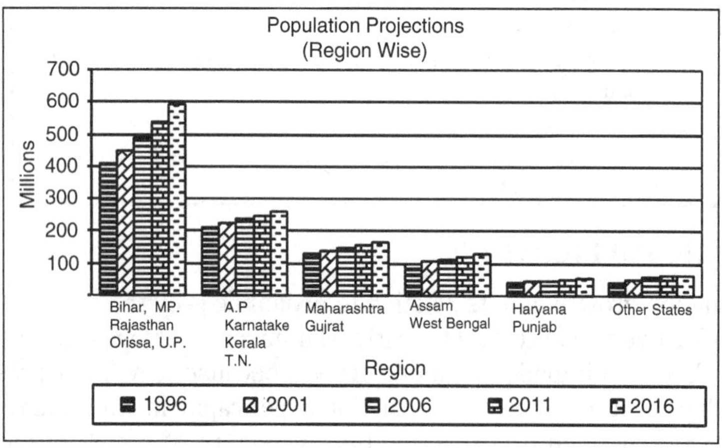

INTERSTATE DIFFERENCES

The projected values for the total population in different regions is shown in Figure. There are marked differences between States in size of the population and population growth rates, the time by which replacement level of fertility is to be achieved and age structure of the population. If the present trend continues, most of the Southern and the Western States are likely to achieve TFR of 2.1 by 2010.

Urgent energetic steps to assess and fully meet the unmet needs for maternal and child health (MCH) care and contraception through improvement in availability and access to family welfare services are needed in the States of UP, MP, Rajasthan and Bihar in order to achieve a faster decline in their mortality and fertility rates. The five states of Bihar, Uttar Pradesh, Madhya Pradesh, Rajasthan and Orissa, which constitute 44% of the total population of India in 1996, will constitute 48% of the total population of India in 2016.

These states will contribute 55% of the total increase in population of the country during the period 1996-2016. In all the states performance in the social and economic sector has been poor. The poor performance is the outcome of poverty, illiteracy and poor development which co-exist and reinforce each other. The quality and coverage under health services is poor and the unmet need for FW services is about 30%. Urgent energetic steps are required to be initiated to assess and fully meet the unmet needs for maternal and child health (MCH) care and contraception through improvement in availability and access to family welfare services in the states of UP, MP, Rajasthan and Bihar in order to achieve a faster decline in their mortality and fertility rates. The performance of these states would determine the year and size of the population at which the country achieves population stabilisation.

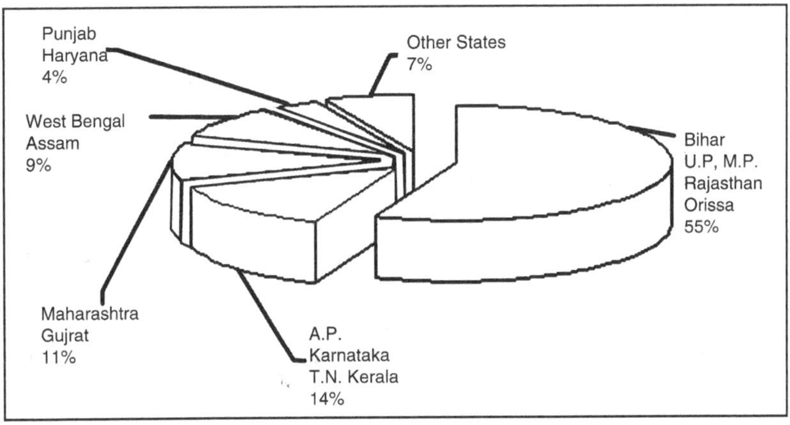

Fig. Share of Regions in Population Growth (1996-2016)

There are also marked differences between States in socio-economic development. Increasing investments and rapid economic development are likely to occur in the States where literacy rates are high; there is ready availability of skilled work force and adequate infrastructure. In these States, population growth rates are low.

If equitable distribution of the income and benefits generated by development is ensured, substantial increase in per capita income and improvement in quality of life could occur in these States in a relatively short time. In majority of States with high population growth rates, the performance in the social and economic sector has been poor. The poor performance could be the outcome of a variety of factors including paucity of natural, financial or human resources. Poverty, illiteracy and poor development co-exist and aggravate each other. In order to promote equity and reduce disparity between States, special assistance has been provided to the poorly performing States.

The benefits accrued from such assistance has to a large extent depended upon:

- The States' ability to utilise the available funds; improve quality & coverage of services and facilities, increase efficiency and improve performance
- Community awareness and ability to utilise the available services.

In spite of the additional assistance provided, improvement in infrastructure, agriculture and industry have been sub-optimal and the per capita income continues to be low in most of the poorly performing States. These States also have high birth rates and relatively low literacy rates. It is imperative that special efforts are made during the next two decades to break this vicious self perpetuating cycle of poor performance, poor per capita income, poverty, low literacy and high birth rate so that the further widening of disparities between States in terms of per capita income and quality of life is prevented. The higher population growth rates and low per capita income in poorly performing States are likely to have a major impact on several social sector programmes. The health status of the population in these States is poor; the health sector programme will require inputs not only for improving infrastructure and manpower, but also increasing efficiency and improving performance. The Family Welfare Programme has to address the massive task of meeting all the unmet needs for MCH and contraception so that there is a rapid decline in mortality and fertility rates. Due to high birth rate, the number of children requiring schooling will be large. The emphasis in the education sector on primary education is essential to ensure that the resource constraints do not result in an increase in either proportion or number of illiterates. Emphasis on prevocational and vocational training in schools will enable these children to acquire skills through which they will find gainful employment later.

MIGRATION

The available data from census shows that until 1991 both internal and international migration has been negligible. The Technical Group while computing the population projection upto 2016, has assumed that the component of migration between major States and from India will be negligible. This assumption may not be valid if there is further widening of the disparity between States in terms of economic growth and employment opportunity. Given the combination of high population growth, low literacy and lack of employment opportunities in the poorly performing States, there may be increasing rural to urban migration as well as interstate migration especially of unskilled workers. Such migration may in the short run assist the migrants in overcoming economic problems associated with unemployment. However, the migrant workers and their families may face problems in securing shelter, education and health care. It is essential to build up a mechanism for monitoring these changes. Steps will have to be taken to provide for the minimum essential needs of the vulnerable migrant population.

LABOUR, EMPLOYMENT AND MANPOWER

Population, which is engaged in any economic activity (employed persons) and population seeking work (unemployed) constitute Labour Force. India has the second largest labour force in the world. Projection of labour force is pre-requisite ensuring optimal utilisation of available human resources. Manpower development is then taken up to provide adequate labour force, of appropriate skills and quality to different sectors so that there is rapid socioeconomic development and there is no mismatch between skills required and skills available.

Planning also attempts to provide enabling environment for employment generation (both self employment and wage employment) in public, private and voluntary sectors in urban and rural areas.

Table. Population and Labour force Projections: 1997-2012.

	1997	2002	2007	2012
Population (Millions)	951.18	1028.93	1112.86	1196.41
Labour Force (Millions)	397.22	449.62	507.94	562.91

Labour force in India will be increasing by more than 10 million per annum during 1997-2012. It will be imperative to plan for and achieve adequate agricultural and industrial growth to absorb this work force. Most of the persons entering the labour force will be educated and have some skills. Increasing literacy and decreasing birth rates may result in more women seeking economically productive work outside home.

It will be important to generate appropriate and renumerative employment at places where labour force are available so as to reduce interstate and urban migration in search of employment. Attempts should be made to eliminate bonded labour, employment of children and women in hazardous industries and minimising occupational health hazards.

Planners face the challenge to have sustained high economic growth rate in sectors that are labour-intensive to ensure adequate employment generation for productively utilising this massive work force. If the massive work force of literate, skilled, aware men and women in age-group 20-60 years get fully employed and adequately paid they could trigger off a period of rapid economic development.

As they have very few dependant children and elders there will be increased savings and investments at household level; this in turn will improve the availability of resources for accelerating economic growth. The current stage of demographic transition thus provides the country with the opportunity window for using human resources as the engine to power economic development and improving the quality of life of all the citizens.

SEX RATIO

The reported decline in the sex ratio during the current century has been a cause for concern. The factors responsible for this continued decline are as yet not clearly identified.

However, it is well recognised that the adverse sex ratio is a reflection of the gender disparity. Higher childhood mortality in girl children is yet another facet of the existing gender disparities and consequent adverse effect on survival.

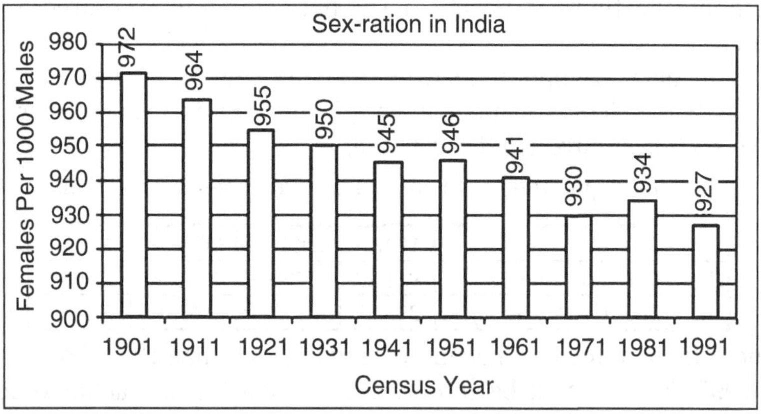

In the reproductive age group the mortality rates among women are higher than those among men. The continued high maternal mortality is one of the major factors responsible for this. Effective implementation of the Reproductive and Child Health Programme is expected to result in a substantial reduction in maternal mortality.

At the moment, the longevity at birth among women is only marginally higher than that among men. However over the next decade life expectancy among women will progressively increase. Once the reproductive age group is crossed, the mortality rates among women are lower as women outlive and outnumber men in the age group 65 and above.

The needs especially of the widowed women have to be met so that quality of life does not deteriorate. The census 2001 will collect and report vital data on sex disaggregated basis; this will be of help in identifying and taking up appropriate interventions in correcting gender disparity; continued collection, collation, analysis and reporting of sex disaggregated data from all social sectors will also provide a mechanism to monitor whether girls and women have equal access to services.

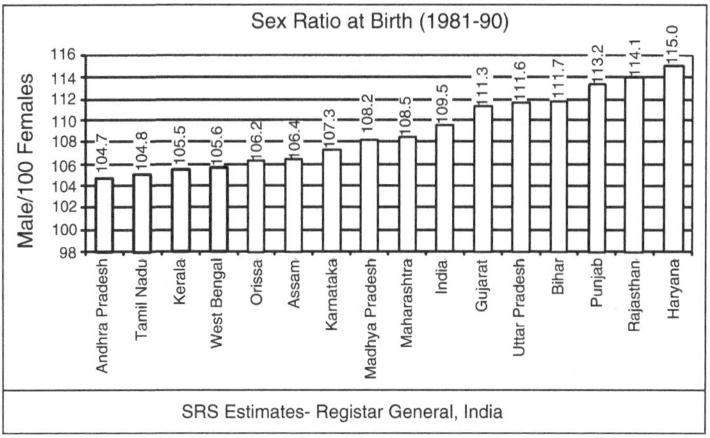

There are substantial differences in sex ratio at birth and in different age groups between states. The SRS based estimates of average sex ratio at birth for the period 1981-90 for the major States and India are given in Figure. The observed sex ratio of 110 is higher than the internationally accepted sex ratio at birth of 106. There are substantial differences among states in the reported sex ratio at birth. There had been speculations whether female infanticide, sex determination and selective female foeticide are at least in part responsible for this. The Government of India has enacted a legislation banning the prenatal sex determination and selective abortion. Intensive community education efforts are under way to combat these practices, especially in pockets from where female infanticide and foeticide have been reported.

INCREASING LONGEVITY

The projected populations of India in the three major age groups (less than 15, 15-59, 60 years or above) are shown in Figure.

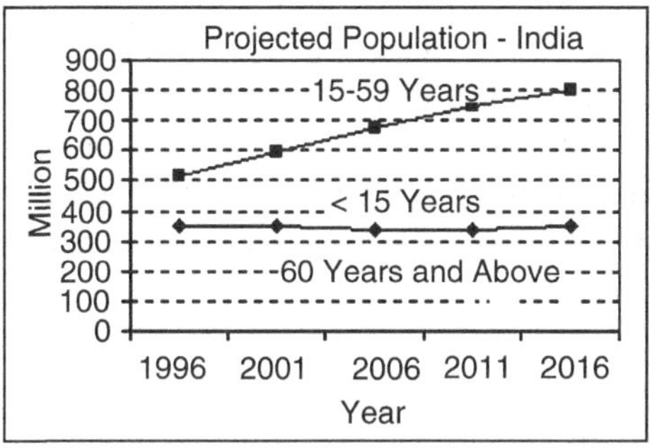

Over the coming decades the country will be facing a progressive increase both in the proportion and number of persons beyond 60 years of age. Over the next 20 years the population of more than 60 years will grow form 62.3 million to 112.9 million; the subsequent decades will witness massive increase in this age group. Increasing longevity will inevitably bring in its wake increase in the prevalence of non-communicable diseases. The growing number of senior citizens in the country poses a major challenge and the cost of providing socio-economic security and health care to this population has to be met. Currently several region and culture specific innovative interventions to provide needed care to this population are underway; among these are efforts to reverse the trend of break up of joint families. If these efforts succeed, it will be possible to provide necessary care for rapidly increasing population of senior citizens in the subsequent two decades within the resources of the family and the country.

Increasing longevity:

- The population of elderly (>60 years) will increase from 62.3 millions in 1996 to 112.9 million in 2016
- Improved health care had added "Years to life"
- Increased social sector investment is needed to add "Quality of life to years"

Majority of the people in their sixties will be physically and psychologically fit and would like to participate both in economic and social activities. They should be encouraged and supported to lead a productive life and contribute to the national development. Senior citizens in their seventies and beyond and those with health problems would require assistance. So far, the families have borne major share in caring for the elderly. This will remain the ideal method; however, there are growing number of elderly without family support; for them, alternate modes for caring may have to be evolved and implemented. Improved health care has "added years to life". The social sectors have to make the necessary provisions for improving the quality of life of these senior citizens so that they truly " add life to years."

HEALTH IMPLICATION OF THE DEMOGRAPHIC TRANSITION

It was earlier assumed that population growth during demographic transition will lead to overcrowding, poverty, undernutrition, environmental deterioration, poor quality of life and increase in disease burden. Experience in the last few decades have shown that this may not always be correct. India is currently in the phase of demographic transition when the increase in population is mainly among younger, better educated and healthy population with low morbidity and mortality rate.

The challenge for the health sector is to promote healthy life styles, improve access to and utilisation of health care so that the country can achieve substantial reduction in mortality and morbidity. Occupational health and environmental health programme need be augmented to ensure that working population remain healthy and productive. If these challenges are fully met, it is possible to accelerate reduction in morbidity and mortality rate in this age group and improve health indices of the country. With growing number of senior citizens there may be substantial increase in health care needs especially for management of non-communicable diseases. Increasing availability and awareness about technological advances for management of these problems, rising expectations of the population and the ever escalating cost of health care are some of the problems that the health care system has to cope with. Health care delivery systems will have to gear up to taking up necessary preventive, promotive, curative and rehabilitative care for growing population of senior citizens.

Age groups < 15 Years
There will be no increase in numbers. *Focus will be to improve*: • Quality and coverage of health and nutrition services and achieve improvement in health and nutrional status • Improve access to education and skill development

Age groups < 15 Years

There will be no increase in numbers.

Focus will be to improve:

- Quality and coverage of health and nutrition services and achieve improvement in health and nutrional status
- Improve access to education and skill development

POPULATION PROJECTIONS AND THEIR IMPLICATIONS FOR THE FW PROGRAMME

There will be a marginal decline in the population less than 15 years of age (352.7 million to 350.4 million).

The health care infrastructure will therefore be not grappling with ever increasing number of children for providing care and they will be able to concentrate on:

- Improving quality of care;
- Focus on antenatal, intranatal and neonatal care aimed at reducing neonatal morbidity and mortality;

Age groups 15-59 years
• There will be an increase from 519-800 million two decades *They will*: • Need wider spectrum of services • Expect better quality of services • Expect fulfillment of their felt need for MCH/FP care Opportunity is that if their felt needs are met through effective implementation of RCH programme, it is possible to accelerate demographic transition and achieve rapid population stabilization. Deptt. of family welfare is now implementing the RCH programme to meet these needs

- Improve coverage and quality of health care to vulnerable and underserved adolescents;
- Promote intersectoral coordination especially with icds programme so that there is improvement in health and nutritional status;
- Improve coverage for immunization against vaccine preventable diseases.

The economic challenge is to provide needed funds so that these children have access to nutrition, education and skill development. The challenge faced by the health sector is to achieve reduction in morbidity and mortality rate in infancy and childhood, to improve nutritional status and eliminate ill-effects of gender bias.

Components of comprehensive RCH programme:

- Effective maternal and child health care
- Increased access to contraceptive care
- Safe management of unwanted pregnancies
- Nutritional services to vulnerable groups
- Prevention and treatment of RTI/STD
- Reproductive health services for adolescents
- Prevention and treatment of gynecological problems
- Screening and treatment of cancers, especially that of uterine cervix and breast

These services are bring provided in all the secondary and tertiary care hospitals. There will be a massive increase of population in the 15-59 age group. The persons in this age group will be more literate and have greater access to information; they will therefore have greater awareness and expectation regarding both the access to a wide spectrum of health care related services and the quality of these services.

Under the Reproductive and child health care programme efforts are underway to provide:

- Needed services for this rapid growing population
- To broaden the spectrum of services available and
- To improve quality and coverage of health care to women, children and adolescents, so that their felt needs for health care are fully met.
- To improve the participation of men in the planned parenthood movement.

The components of the comprehensive RCH services are given in the text box. While providing the package of services, efforts will have to be made to improve the quality of services, make services more responsive to users' needs, ensure that health workers and health care providers have the necessary skills and supplies they need and there is a strong and effective referral system to manage all the risk cases. Family welfare Programme is attempting to improve the logistics of supply of drugs and vaccine to make sure good quality drugs are available at appropriate time.

Simultaneously the IEC efforts are being directed to:

- Ensure responsible reproductive/sexual behaviour;
- Improve awareness about reproductive health needs;
- Promote community participation and optimal utilisation of available services

ESSENTIAL REPRODUCTIVE AND CHILD HEALTH SERVICES

Though it is desirable that the entire package of services indicated under comprehensive RCH care is made available to all those who need it, it will not be possible to immediately implement such a comprehensive package at primary health care level on a nationwide basis. After consultation with experts a package of essential reproductive health services for nationwide implementation at primary health care settings has been identified.

Essential components recommended for nationwide implementation include:

- Prevention and management of unwanted pregnancy,
- Services to provide antenatal, intra-natal and post-natal, and neo-natal care
- Services to promote child health and survival,
- Prevention and treatment of RTI/STD.

Most of these services are already being delivered under the Family Welfare Programme. However, there are wide variations in the quality and coverage of services not only between states but also between districts in the same state. The focus under RCH Programme is therefore on the improvement in the quality and coverage of the services over and above the existing level in all districts/states in an incremental manner so that there is over all improvement maternal and child health indices.

FAMILY WELFARE PROGRAMME IN INDIA

India, the second most populous country in the world, has no more than 2.5% of global land but is the home of 1/6th of the world's population. The prevailing high maternal, infant, childhood morbidity and mortality, low life expectancy and high fertility and associated high morbidity had been a source of concern for public health professionals right from the pre-independence period. The Bhore Committee Report (1946) which laid the foundation for health service planning in India, gave high priority to provision of maternal and child health services and improving their nutritional and health status. It is noteworthy that this report which emphasized the importance of providing integrated preventive, promotive and curative primary health care services preceded the Alma Ata declaration by over three decades.

Under the Constitution of India elimination of poverty, ignorance and ill health are three important goals. In 1951, the infant republic took stock of the existing situation in the country and initiated the first Five Year Development Plan. Living in a resource poor country with high population density, the Planners recognised in the census figures of 1951, the potential threat posed by population explosion and the need to take steps to avert it. It was recognised that population stabilisation is an essential prerequisite for sustainability of development process so that the benefits of economic development result in enhancement of the well being of the people and improvement in quality of life. India became the first country in the world to formulate a National Family Planning Programme in 1952, with the objective of "reducing birth rate to the extent necessary to stabilise the population at a level consistent with requirement of national economy". Thus, the key elements of health care to women and children and provision of contraceptive services have been the focus of India's health services right from the time of India's independence.

Successive Five Year Plans have been providing the policy framework and funding for planned development of nationwide health care infrastructure and manpower. The Centrally Sponsored and 100% centrally funded Family Welfare Programme provides additional infrastructure, manpower and drugs, vaccines contraceptives and other consumables needed for improving health status of women and children and to meet all the felt needs for fertility regulation.

- Basic premises of the Family Welfare Programme are: Acceptance of FW services is voluntary,
  - FW programme will provide:
    1. Integrated Maternal and Child Health (MCH) & FP services
    2. Effective IEC to improve awareness
    3. Ensure easy and convenient access to FW services free of cost

PROGRESS UNDER THE FW PROGRAMME

Major achievements:

- A vast nation wide infrastructure and manpower fro providing FW services has been created
- There is increased access to and utilsation of FW services
- *These has been*:
  - Reduction in Crude Birth Rate (CBR) from 40.8 (1951 Census) to 27.4 in 1996 (SRS 96)
  - Reduction in Infant Mortality Rate (IMR) from 146 in 1951 t0 72 in 1996 (SRS)
  - Increase in couple protection Rate (CPR) from 10.4% (1970-71) to 45.4% (31.3.1997)

CONTRACEPTION

Over the last four decades there has been substantial improvement in the availability and utilization of the and access to FW services and a progressive increase in the acceptance of contraception and couple protection rates. In the initial fifteen years, the rise in the couple protection rate has been steep. The reduction in the CBR was however not commensurate with the increase in couple protection rates. In the last ten years, the rise in CPR is less steep, but the fall in CBR has been steeper than in the earlier years.

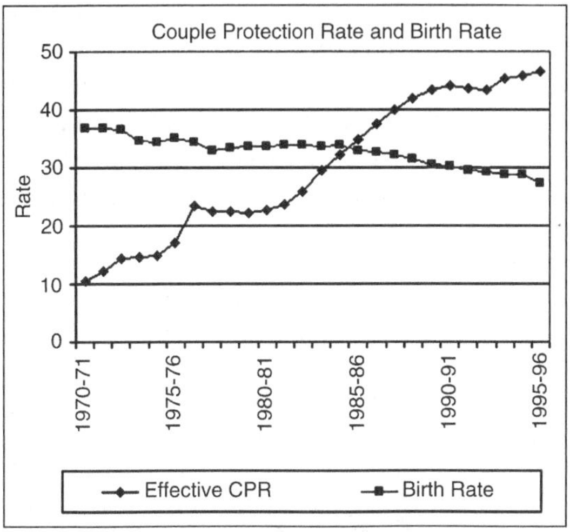

The age and parity of the acceptors of contraception, and the continuation rates of temporary methods of contraception are some of the important factors that determine birth rates. The trends in CPR and CBR over the last 25 years suggest that over the years there has been an improvement in the acceptance of appropriate contraception at appropriate time.

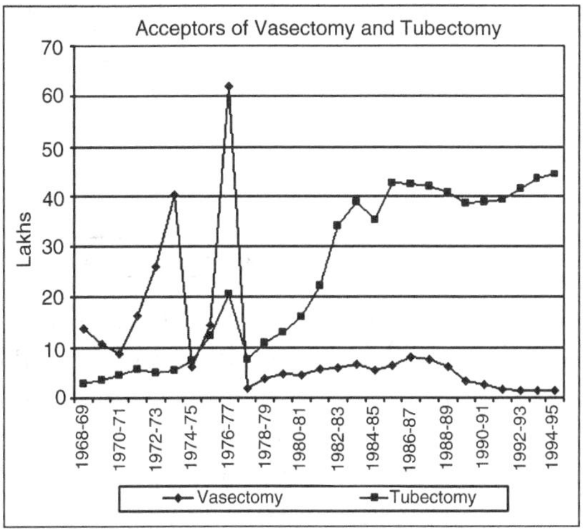

Currently the FW Programme is focusing its attention on need assessment, balanced presentation of advantages and disadvantages about all the available methods of contraception counseling, provision of appropriate contraceptive at the right time and good follow up services. Effective implementation of the

FW programme and ensuring that all the unmet needs for contraception are met will result in substantial improvement in CPR and enable rapid reduction in CBR.

Over the last two decades there has been a steep fall in number of vasectomies. At the moment, over 97% of all sterilisations are tubectomies. If, over the next decade, attempts are made to repopularise vasectomy so that this safe, simple procedure forms at least 50% of all sterilizations, there will be a further improvement in access to sterilization in the primary health care settings, substantial reduction both in the morbidity/mortality associated with terminal methods of contraception and reduction in the cost of permanent methods of contraception. In addition this would be one of the efforts to improve participation of men in planned parenthood.

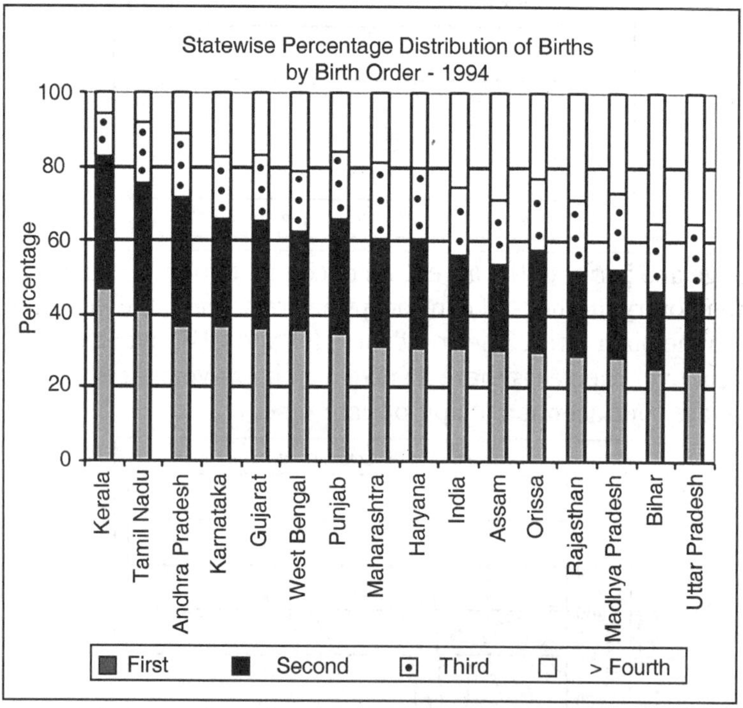

In the past demographers have assumed that access to a wide spectrum of spacing and permanent methods of contraception and achievement of contraceptive prevalence of atleast 60% are essential for achievement of replacement level of fertility. In Kerala and Tamil Nadu sterilisation is the most commonly utilised method of contraception; these States have been able to achieve replacement level of fertility (Total Fertility Rate (TFR) of 2.1) long before there was improved access to a wide spectrum temporary methods of contraception and Couple protection rate of 60% has been achieved. The National FW programme statistics as well as National Family Health Survey have shown in all the states in India sterilization is the most widely accepted method of contraception. Given the fact that most couples in India complete their family by the time they are in their mid-20s and marriage is a stable institution, sterilisation is the most logical, safe and cost effective contraception to protect these young couples against unwanted pregnancies for the next two decades. There are substantial differences between states regarding the need for temporary and permanent methods of contraception.

Percentage distribution of birth order in major states is shown in Figure. It is obvious in most of the poorly performing states over half of the women have two or more children and are likely to require permanent methods of contraception sooner or later. On the other hand in some of the better performing states increasing number of women may desire to postpone the first or second pregnancy and there may be a progressive increase in the need for spacing methods. Contraceptive need assessment, counseling, improved quality of initial and follow up care would go a long way in meeting the felt needs of contraception in the population and accelerate the decline in fertility.

MATERNAL AND CHILD HEALTH

Reduction in the infant and child mortality indices between 1951-1997 is shown in Figure. Even though the decline in IMR and CDR are substantial, it is noteworthy that maternal, perinatal, neonatal mortality rates continue to remain high. This is because the antenatal, intrapartum and neonatal care programmes have, till now, not aimed at screening of all pregnant women for risk factors, identification and appropriate referral of the 'at risk' individuals. Improvement in the contents and quality of antenatal and paediatric care at primary health care level is receiving focussed attention under the RCH programme.

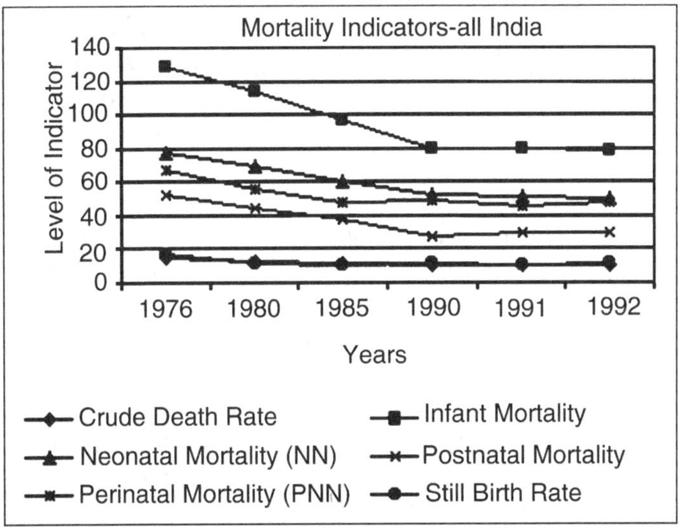

INTER-STATE/INTRA-STATE DIFFERENCES IN FERTILITY AND MORTALITY

The availability and utilisation of family welfare services is the critical determinant of performance in Family Welfare Programme, achievements in terms of reduction in IMR and CBR go hand in hand in most States. However, there are exceptions; both Punjab and Tamil Nadu have good primary health care infrastructure; IMR in both the States are identical and the age at marriage in these States is similar; TFR in Tamil Nadu is 2.1 and in Punjab it is 2.9. In Bihar, IMR is 72 and TFR is 4.6 but Assam with IMR of 75 has a TFR of 3.8. Efforts will have to be made to identify the factors responsible for poor achievements in terms of IMR and TFR and area specific remedial measures have to be planned and implemented in the States.

District wise data on CBR and IMR computed on the basis of Census 1991 show that there are marked differences in these indices not only between States but also between districts in the same State. Census 1991 has confirmed that even in Kerala there are districts where IMR and CBR are higher than national levels.

There are districts in UP with IMR and CBR (Kanpur-Urban) lower than national levels.

The Family Welfare Programme, therefore, has been re-oriented to:

- Remove or minimise the inter and intra-state differences,
- Undertake realistic phc based decentralised area-specific microplanning tailored to meet the local needs and
- Involve panchayati raj institutions in microplanning and monitoring at local level to effective implementation of the programme and ensuring effective community participation.

Under the Reproductive Child Health programme efforts are under way to improve the quality and coverage of FW services in all states. In each state, the success achieved by the better performing districts will have be replicated in poorly performing districts; in addition efforts will have to be made to achieve incremental improvement in performance in all districts so that the performance in the state improves.

States like Kerala and Tamil Nadu have achieved low CBR and IMR at relatively low cost. On the other hand, States like Haryana and Punjab have not achieved any substantial reduction in CBR in spite of higher expenditure per eligible couple.

In States like Bihar and Uttar Pradesh the expenditure is low and performance is poor. In between these extreme categories are States like Orissa and Andhra Pradesh with average or below average expenditure and average or below average performance in MCH or family planning. In some States like Orissa and West Bengal the performance in family planning is better than the performance in MCH or vice versa.

Deptt. of Family Welfare is attempting to implement the recommendation of the NDC Committee on Population, that factors responsible for observed differences in utilisation of funds as well as impact of the programme are to be studied and existing lacunae identified and rectified at the district level. The last five decades have shown that different states used different approaches to achieve improvement in MCH care and improve performance in FW programme. Some of these efforts have been path breaking and have disproved many theories on the essential prerequisites for rapid achievement of decline fertility and mortality.

Some examples of these experiences are indicated below:

- Goa with relatively high income, literacy and good health care infrastructure was the first administrative unit to achieve the replacement level of fertility. This fitted the classical theory; Goa and Pondicherry have been having less than replacement level fertility for over a decade.
- Kerala, the first State to achieve replacement level of fertility did so in spite of relatively low per capita income proving that in the Indian context economic development is not an essential prerequisite for the achieving small family. High status of women, female literacy, age at marriage and low infant mortality were thought to be the factors behind the rapid fall in fertility in Kerala
- Tamil Nadu which was the second state to achieve replacement level of fertility did so in spite of low PCI, higher IMR and lower female literacy rate than Kerala. This is attributed to the strong social and political commitment, backed by good administrative support and ready availability of Family Welfare Services. There have been speculations whether the low PCI in the aware population desiring improvement in quality of care had also acted as factor that accelerated the decline in fertility.
- Andhra Pradesh is likely to achieve replacement level of fertility in the next two years. The State has shown a steep decline in fertility in spite of relatively lower age at marriage, low literacy and poorer outreach of primary health care infrastructure. It has been suggested that the major factors responsible for the success include caring attitude of the government and strong sustained movement to empower women.
- In the North-eastern States of Tripura, Manipur, Mizoram there is substantial difficulty in accessing primary health care facilities, but these States have achieved not only low fertility rates but also low infant mortality, suggesting thereby that a literate aware population can successfully overcome difficulties in access to and availability of primary health care infrastructure.

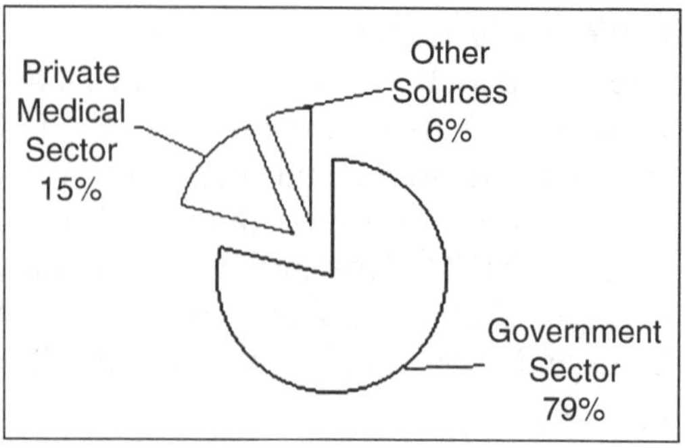

Fig. Sources of Family Planning Services

UNMET NEEDS FOR FAMILY WELFARE SERVICES

The National Family Health Survey (NFHS) 1992-93 had provided an independent nation wide evaluation of the progress and problems in delivery of Family Welfare services in the country. The survey confirmed that in spite of obvious constraints and inadequacies, the governmental network can, and does, provides most of the MCH and contraceptive care; Data from the NFHS showed that:

- There is universal awareness about contraception
- 40.6% of currently married women use contraceptives
- Wanted fertility is lower than the actual fertility
- There is a large unmet need for contraception:-
  - 11.0% for birth spacing methods and
  - 8.5% for terminal method.
- Unmet needs for health and contraceptive care exist in all regions and in all segments of the population irrespective of religion, caste, education and income status.

Lessons learnt during implementation of Family Welfare Programme:

- Governmental network provides most of the MCH and contraceptive care
- Adequate functional health infrastructure is an essential prerequisites for the success of the programme
- Providing efficient and effective integrated MCH and contraceptive care helps in building up rapport with the families
- IEC activities are powerful tools for promoting the small family norm;
- The population is conservative but responsible, responsive and mature; their response is slow but rational and sustained.

There is a popular belief that the population growth is due to poor performance in the health sector. This is not correct. The population growth that the country (and the world) had witnessed in the last five decades is mainly because of rapid reduction in the death rates due to health care and is inevitable during the frist three phases of demographic transition. India's progress in demographic transition has been a slow but sustained; unlike some other developing countries India's population growth never exceeded 2.2% even at its peak; the decline in population growth once started has been sustained. This orderly progression has been achieved through improving access to family welfare services and ensuring peoples participation.

Concern has been expressed by some groups that the RCH programme which essentially aims at improving quality and coverage of the already ongoing maternal and child health and contraceptive care may not be successful in accelerating the decline in fertility and help the country to achieve rapid population stabilization and that there is a need for new path breaking innovations. Ongoing evaluations, however, do not suggest that there is a need for change in policy, strategy and programme content; all these studies have emphasized that there is a huge unmet need for services and there is an urgent need to improve access to good quality services to meet this need, the focus of the RCH initiative is on this task.

APPROACH TO FW PROGRAMME DURING THE NINTH PLAN

Reduction in Population growth is one of the major objectives in the Ninth Plan.

- *The current high population growth rate is due to*: The large size of the population in the reproductive age-group (estimated contribution 60%); higher fertility due to unmet need for contraception (estimated contribution 20%); and high wanted fertility due to prevailing high IMR (estimated contribution about 20%).
- *Rapid reduction in the population growth rate can be achieved by*: Meeting all the felt-needs for contraception; and reducing the infant and maternal morbidity and mortality so that there is a reduction in the desired level of fertility.
- *The Ninth Plan strategies for achieving these objectives are*: To assess the needs for reproductive and child health at PHC level and undertake area-specific micro planning; and To provide need-based, demand-driven high quality, integrated reproductive and child health care.
- *Efforts of the Family Welfare Programme are being directed towards*:
  - Bridging the gaps in essential infrastructure and manpower through a flexible approach and improving operational efficiency through investment in social, behavioural and operational research
  - Providing additional assistance to poorly performing districts identified on the basis of the 1991 census to fill existing gaps in infrastructure and manpower.
  - Ensuring uninterrupted supply of essential drugs, vaccines and contraceptives, adequate in quantity and appropriate in quality
  - Promoting male participation in the Planned Parenthood movement and increasing the level of acceptance of vasectomy.

Under the RCH Programme the focus is on enhancing the quality and coverage of family welfare services through:

- Increasing participation of general medical practitioners working in voluntary, private, joint sectors and the active cooperation of practitioners of ISM&H;
- Involvement of the Panchayati Raj Institutions for ensuring inter-sectoral coordination and community participation in planning, monitoring and management;
- Involvement of the industries, organised and unorganised sectors, agriculture workers and labour representatives.

GOALS TO BE ACHIEVED

The performance under the Family Welfare Programme will depend upon:

- Programme initiatives during the Ninth Plan
- Financial resources available;
- Capability and effectiveness of the infrastructure and manpower to carry out the programme;
- Literacy and economic status of the families particularly of the women;
- Policy support by opinion leaders and the society.

The Deptt. of Family Welfare has launched the RCH intiative during the Ninth Plan. Under the Special Action Plan an additional sum of ₹4700 crores had been provided to the Family Welfare Deptt. and the toal outlay provided the Department of Family Welfare was raised to ₹15120.20 crores for the Ninth Plan period to enable the Dept to implement the RCH programme. In view of the marked differences in the availability and utilisation of family welfare services and IMR CBR and CPR between States and districts within the states, a differential area specific approach to the implementation of Family Welfare Programme is being used. State specific Expected Level of Achievement in terms of process and impact indicators have been worked out for effective monitoring of the programme. Projection of expected levels of achievement for process and impact indicators at the end of the Ninth Plan have taken into consideration the pace of improvement in these indicators during the Eighth Plan and the additional policy and programme measures envisaged to accelerate the pace of achievement during the Ninth Plan and the additional funding being provided under the Programme.

The State-specific projections have been worked out at two different levels of achievement, one on the basis of the assumption that the trend observed with regard to these parameters in the last 15 years will continue during the Ninth Plan period and the second on the assumption that the additional policy and programme initiatives provided during the Ninth Plan period will result in the acceleration of the pace and result in more substantial improvement during the Ninth Plan period. The expected levels of achievement under both these assumptions have been computed State wise The expected levels of achievement at the national level by the terminal year of Ninth Plan (2002) are given below:

Indicator	If current trend continues	If acceleration envisaged in the Ninth Five Year Plan is achieved
C B R	24/1000	23/1000
I M R	56/1000	50/1000
T F R	2.9	2.6
C P R	51%	60%
NNM R	35/1000	
M M R	3/1000	

The expected level of achievement for CBR at national level under these two sets of assumptions is 24 and 23/1000. If the target of 23/1000 is achieved there will be one million less births in 2002 AD alone. Similarly if the Programme achieves, the accelerated decline in IMR (from 56/1000-50/1000) over 140 thousand infant deaths will be averted in 2002 AD. These achievements may be the beginning of a major acceleration in pace of demographic transition and improving health status of the population. If the acceleration begun during the Ninth Plan is sustained the country may achieve replacement level of fertility by 2010, with the population of 1120 million; if this were done the country's population may stabilize by 2045.

SUMMARY

Demographic transition is a global phenomenon; population growth is inevitable in the initial phases of the transition. For India the current phase of the demographic transition is both a challenge and an opportunity. The challenge is to ensure human development and optimum utilisation of human resources. The opportunity is to utilise available human resources to achieve rapid economic development and improvement in quality of life. Over the last five decades the country has built up a massive healthcare infrastructure for delivery of FW services to the population in the Govt, private and voluntary sectors. The RCH programme envisages wider range of services and improvement in quality of services provided.

There is universal awareness about the need for these services. In the next two decades the population growth will be mainly among the young adults who will be more literate, aware and likely to make optimal use of available facilities. India is currently in the phase of demographic transition during which where it will be possible for the country to accelerate the pace of decline in fertility. If the population now has ready access to good quality services at affordable cost, it will be possible for them to meet all their needs, achieve the desired family size and enable the country to achieve population stabilsation rapidly. Demographic transition does not occur in isolation. Simultaneously, there are ongoing economic transition, education transition, health transition and reproductive health transition. All these affect human development. If there is synergy between these transitions; the transitions can be completed rapidly; there will be substantial improvement in human development and economic development. The focus of planners, programme implementers and the people during the next two decades will have to be in achieving the synergy so that India can achieve rapid population stabilization, improvement in economic social and human development.

POPULATION AGEING DEMOGRAPHY

The number of persons aged 60 years or older in the world is estimated to be 605 million in 2000. This number is projected to grow to nearly 2 billion by 2050, at which time it will be as large as the population of children. This historic crossover of an increasing share of older persons and a declining share of children will mark the first time that the number of children and older persons are the same.

Table. Estimated and Projected Percentage of the Population in Selected Age Groups, by Region

Region	1970	2000	2025	2050
Children: Under age 15				
World total	37	30	23	20
More developed regions	26	18	16	15
Less developed regions	42	33	25	20
Least developed countries	44	42	35	24
Africa	45	42	35	24
Asia	40	30	22	19
Europe	25	17	15	14
Latin America and the Caribbean	42	32	24	20
Northern America	29	21	18	17
Oceania	32	25	21	19
Youth: Ages 15-24				
World total	18	18	15	13
More developed regions	17	14	11	11
Less developed regions	18	19	16	14
Least developed countries	18	20	20	17
Africa	18	20	20	17
Asia	18	18	15	13
Europe	16	14	10	10
Latin America and the Caribbean	19	20	16	13
Northern America	17	13	12	12
Oceania	18	15	14	13

Region	1970	2000	2025	2050
Older persons: Ages 60 or over				
World total	8	10	15	22
More developed regions	15	20	28	33
Less developed regions	6	8	13	21
Least developed countries	5	5	6	12
Africa	5	5	6	12
Asia	6	9	15	24
Europe	15	20	28	35
Latin America and the Caribbean	6	8	14	22
Northern America	14	16	26	28
Oceania	11	13	20	24
Oldest old: Ages 80 or over				
World total	1	1	2	4
More developed regions	2	3	5	9
Less developed regions	0.4	1	1	3
Least developed countries	0.3	0.3	1	1
Africa	0.3	0.4	1	1
Asia	0.4	1	2	4
Europe	2	3	5	9
Latin America and the Caribbean	1	1	2	4
Northern America	2	3	4	8
Oceania	1	2	3	6

Persons aged 60 or older currently comprise 10 per cent of the world population. The percentage is much higher in the more developed regions (20 per cent) than in the less developed regions (8 per cent), which are at an earlier stage of the demographic transition. It is especially low in the least developed countries (5 per cent). Among individual countries, the most aged are Greece and Italy, where 24 per cent of the population is aged 60 or older in 2000. Many European countries, as well as Japan, have percentages nearly as high. By 2050, the older ages will make up a projected 22 per cent of the world population—33 per cent in the more developed regions, 21 per cent in the less developed regions and 12 per cent in the least developed countries.

In terms of major regions, the majority of the world's older persons (53 per cent) reside in Asia, while Europe has the next largest share, 24 per cent. Asia's share of the older population will increase to 63 per cent by 2050, while the share of Europe will show the greatest relative decrease of any region, shrinking from 24 per cent to 11 per cent.

The oldest old, persons aged 80 years or older, currently number 70 million, the majority of whom live in more developed regions. Thirty-three million are estimated to be living in less developed regions. They make up about 1 per cent of the world's population and 3 per cent of the population of the more developed regions. This oldest age group is the fastest growing segment of the older population.

Table. Estimated and Projected Regional Distribution of the Population Aged Under 15 Years and the Population Aged 60 Years or Over-1970, 2000 and 2050 (Percentage)

Region	Under age 15			Aged 60 or over		
	1970	2000	2050	1970	2000	2050
World total	100	100	100	100	100	100
More developed regions	19	12	10	47	38	19
Less developed regions	81	88	90	53	62	81
Least developed countries	10	15	20	5	5	9
Africa	12	19	24	6	6	11
Asia	63	61	57	45	53	63
Eastern Asia	27	20	15	23	27	26
China	24	18	14	18	21	22
South-eastern Asia	9	9	9	5	6	9
South Central Asia	24	29	28	15	17	25
India	16	19	17	11	13	16
Western Asia	3	4	5	2	2	3
Europe	12	7	5	33	24	11
Latin America and the Caribbean	9	9	9	6	7	9
Northern America	5	4	4	10	8	6
Oceania	0.4	0.4	0.5	1	1	1

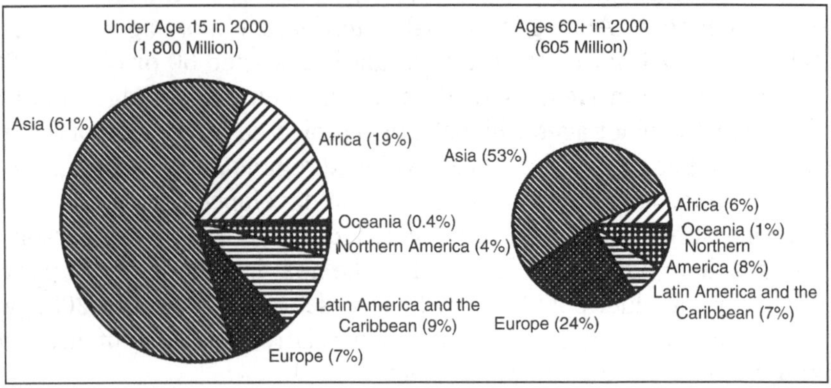

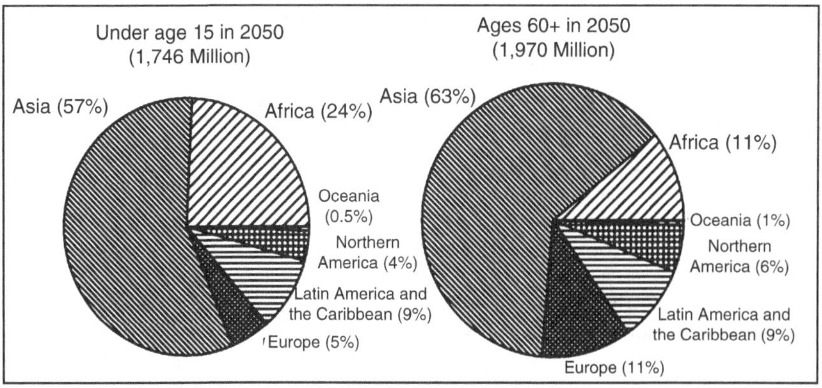

Fig. Geographic Distribution of the Population Aged Under 15 and 60 or over, 2000 and 2050

By 2050, the number of the oldest old is projected to be five times as large as at present. By that date, the oldest old will be 4 per cent of the total world population, and in the more developed regions, one person out of 11 is projected to be aged 80 or older. In the less developed regions, 3 per cent of the population will be 80 years or older. It is necessary to look beyond 2050 to see the full consequences for population ageing of ongoing trends towards lower fertility and mortality rates.

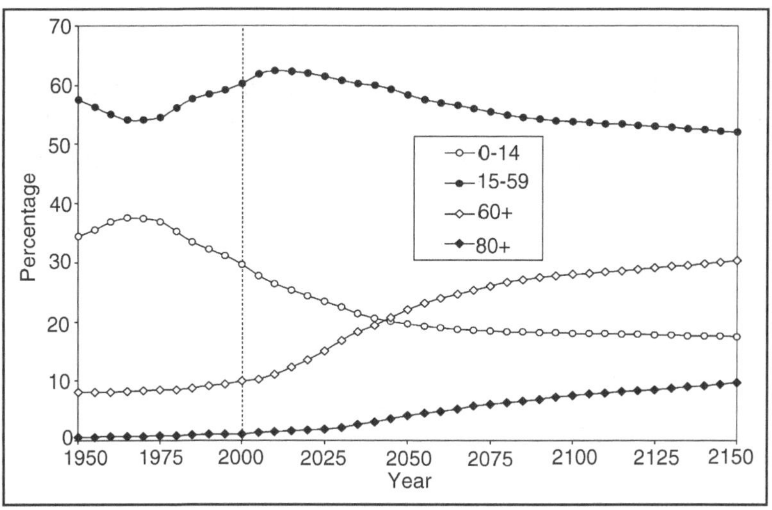

Fig. Percentage of World Population by Age Group, Medium Scenario, 1950-2150

A range of alternative scenarios presented in the United Nations long-range population projections show that future populations will reach a significantly older age structure than the populations of the present, or even of the populations of 2050. Figure shows projected trends in the proportion of the world's population aged 60 or older through the year 2150, from the medium fertility scenario, which assumes that fertility in all major areas will stabilize at replacement level around 2050, and that mortality rates will continue to improve. By 2150, persons aged 60 or older are projected to number 3.0 billion, nearly one person out of every three alive at that time. Over 1.2 billion people, or one in every 10 persons, will be aged 80 or older. Only 18 per cent of the population will be children aged under 15 years, as compared to 30 per cent at present.

SPEED OF AGEING

The growth of the older population often receives attention in connection with the developed countries. However, the tempo of ageing is more rapid in the less developed regions than in the more developed regions. Because rapid changes in age structure may be more difficult for societies to adjust to than change that is spread over a longer time horizon, the speed of population ageing has important implications for government policies, such as pension schemes, health care and economic growth.

Figure shows, for selected countries, the dates when the population reached, or is expected to reach, the point when 7, 14 and 21 per cent of the population was aged 65 or older. (Currently, 6.9 per cent of the world's population is aged 65 or older.) Typically, the transition from 7 to 14 per cent took longer for countries that reached the 7 per cent level at an earlier date. For example, France and Sweden, which reached the 7 per cent point before 1900, took 114 years and 82 years, respectively, to reach 14 per cent.

That same transition required only 24 years in Japan, from 1970 to 1994. Several developing countries shown in figure will also make a rapid transition from 7 to 14 per cent aged 65 or older. Brazil, Indonesia, the Republic of Korea and Tunisia are projected to make this transition in a time-span of under 25 years, and the two most populous countries, China and India, may require only 25 and 28 years, respectively.

Number of People:

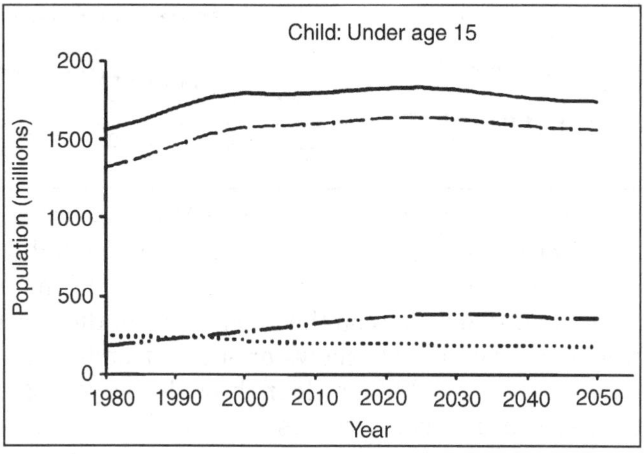

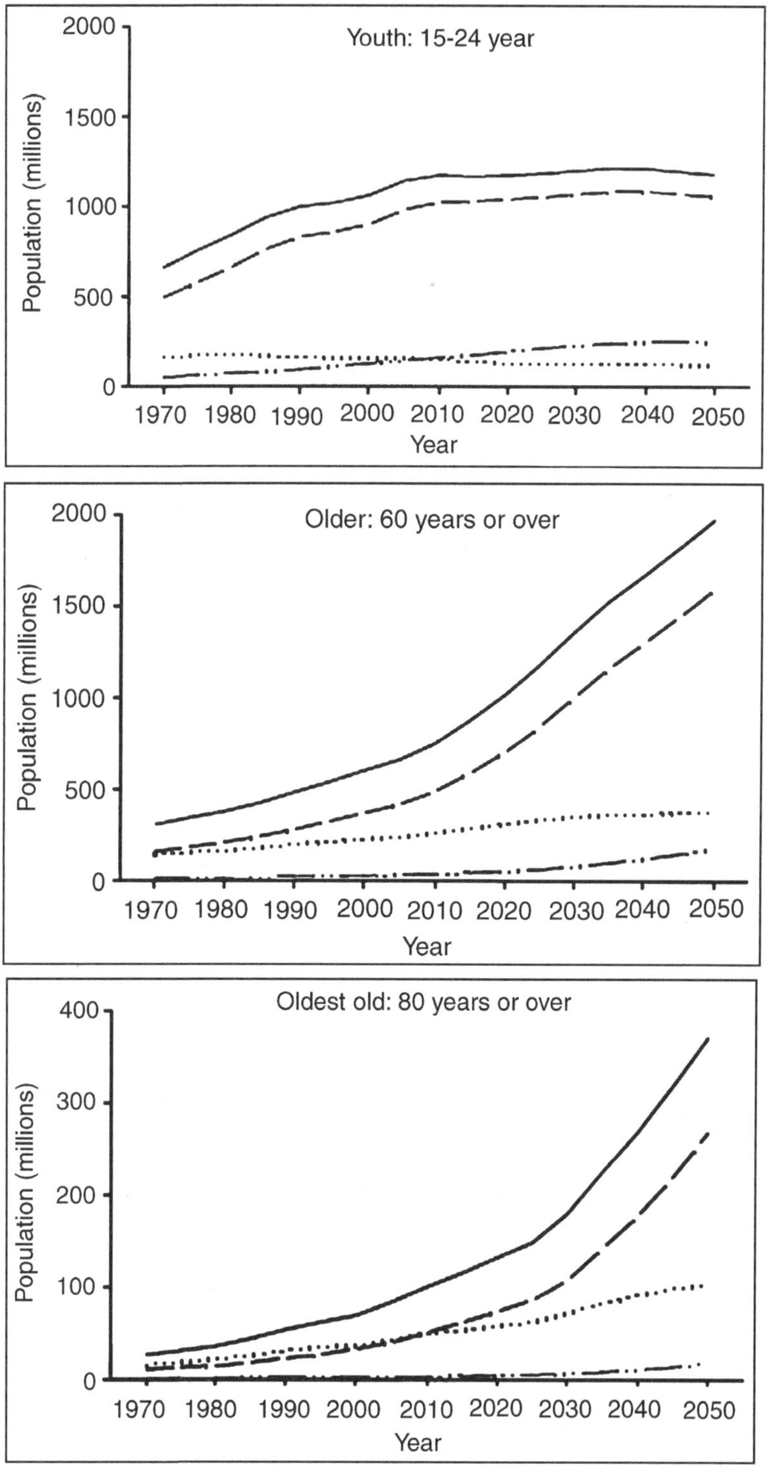
Youth: 15-24 year
Population (millions)
2000
1500
1000
500
0
1970 1980 1990 2000 2010 2020 2030 2040 2050
Year
Older: 60 years or over
Population (millions)
2000
1500
1000
500
0
1970 1980 1990 2000 2010 2020 2030 2040 2050
Year
Oldest old: 80 years or over
Population (millions)
400
300
200
100
0
1970 1980 1990 2000 2010 2020 2030 2040 2050
Year

Average annual growth rate of the Population:

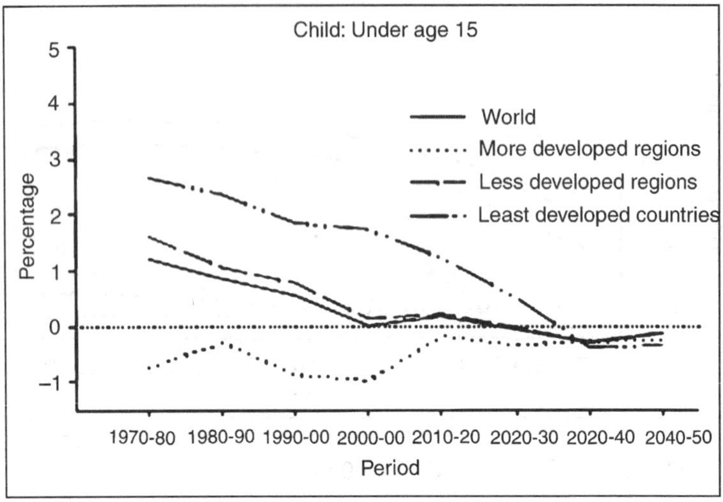

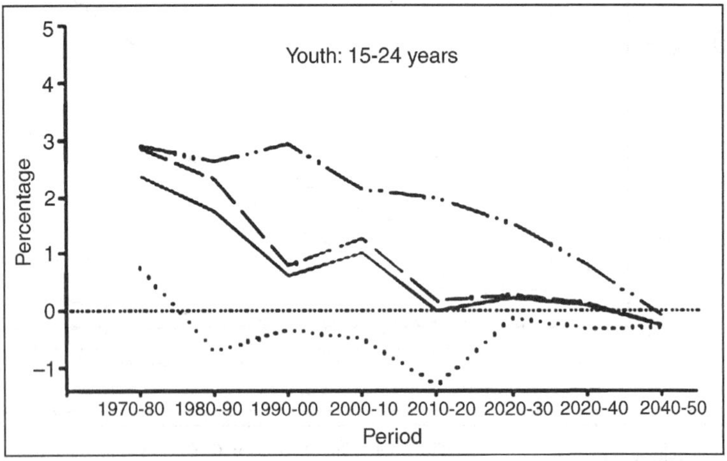

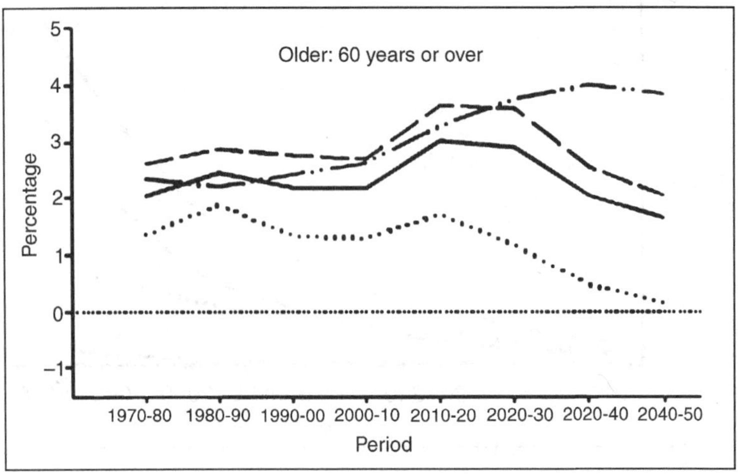

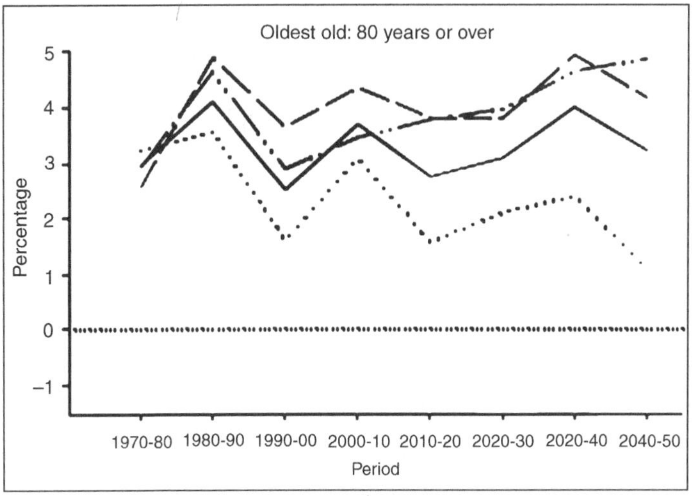

Fig. Growth in Population Size and Age-specific Annual Growth Rates, for the Child, Youth and Older Populations, 1970-2050

In many cases, it will take substantially less time for the transition from 14 to 21 per cent aged 65 years or older than it took to move from 7 to 14 per cent. Although no country has yet reached the point where 21 per cent of the population is aged 65 or older, some countries, including Italy and Japan, are expected to reach that point before 2015; in Japan, the transition from 14 to 21 per cent will have taken only 16 years, and in Italy, 23 years.

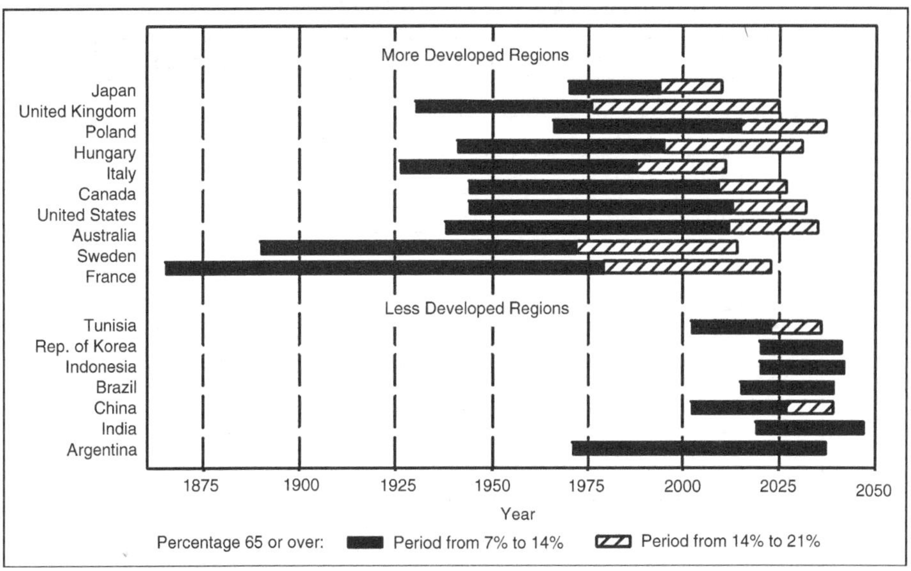

Fig. Time when the Percentage of the Population Aged 65 or Over Reached or will Reach 7, 14 and 21 Per cent: Selected Countries

Note: For countries where the percentage aged over 65 years will reach 21 per cent after 2050, only the period between attainment of the 7 and 14 per cent points is shown.

At a later date, Canada and the United States of America are also expected to make a rapid transition from 14 to 21 per cent aged 65 or older as the large "baby boom" cohorts enter the higher ages.

Thus, in the near future, some societies will be faced not only with older populations than have ever existed at the national level, but also with populations that are ageing at an extremely rapid pace.

AGEING AND GENDER

Population ageing is, in basic demographic respects, not "gender-neutral". The evolution to an older age structure changes the balance in numbers of men and women in the whole population. Men's higher mortality over the life course means that women typically outnumber men at older ages, and the difference is quite large among the oldest old. At ages 60 or older, there were an estimated 81 men for every 100 women globally in 2000, and at ages 80 or older there were only 53 men for every 100 women. The sex ratios of older age groups are lower in the more developed regions than in the less developed regions, since there are larger differences in life expectancy between the sexes in the more developed regions.

In addition, the sex ratio in the oldest age groups in the more developed regions retains the effect of the heavy loss of males in some countries during the Second World War.

Table. Sex Ratios by Age in the More and Less Developed Regions, 2000 (Men per 100 Women)

Age	World	More developed regions	Less developed regions
For broad age groups			
Total	101	95	103
<15	106	105	106
15-59	103	101	104
60+	81	71	88
80+	53	44	64

Age	World	More developed regions	Less developed regions
For 5-Year groups, ages 60 or over			
60-64	94	87	97
65-69	89	82	93
70-74	81	72	86
75-79	69	59	78
80-84	60	51	69
85-89	48	41	59
90-94	36	32	46
95-99	27	23	37
100+	25	19	38

Given the age patterns of the sex ratio, the rapid growth of the elderly population and the increase in the proportion in older age groups imply a decrease in the sex ratio for the total population and a greater increase in the number of older women than of older men. Projected increases between 2000 and 2050 in the number of persons aged 60 or older are 636 million for men and 729 million for women in the world as a whole. Projected increases during the same period in the number of persons aged 80 or older are 116 million for men and 185 million for women.

Concomitant with dramatic improvements in average lifespan has been the widening differential over time between male and female longevity. By 1995-2000, the female advantage in life expectancy at birth has grown to almost eight years in more developed regions and three years in less developed regions. The advantage, however, diminishes during the life course and by age 60, the male-female differential has narrowed to four years in more developed regions and to only two years in less developed regions.

At current mortality rates (for 1995-2000), almost 40 per cent of girls and about one quarter of boys born can expect to survive to the "oldest old" ages, 80 years or older. While the increased likelihood of surviving to older ages is obviously due to mortality declines at younger ages, recent decades have also seen significant mortality improvements among the older population, including the oldest old, and these trends so far have been more beneficial to women than to men. At older ages, women are less likely to be married and more likely to be widowed than are men, not only because they survive on average to higher ages, but also because most women marry men several years older than themselves.

While more than three quarters (79 per cent) of older men are married, on a global basis, less than one half (43 per cent) of older women are married. The longer-term effect of gender differences in marriage age on later widowhood is only one of many ways in which demographic, as well as economic and social circumstances in early life have diverging ramifications for men and women in old age.

DEMOGRAPHIC CAUSES OF POPULATION AGEING

The process of population ageing is determined primarily by trends in fertility rates and secondarily by mortality rates. Any population with a long history of high fertility has a "young" age structure, similar in its general features to the present age structure for the group of least developed countries. The average age of the population starts to rise when fertility rates decline. For the period 1995-2000, 61 countries in the world, representing 44 per cent of the world's population, are at or below replacement fertility. By 2015, the world's population is projected to reach 7.2 billion, of which about two thirds will be living in countries at or below replacement fertility.

The impact of mortality decline is more variable, depending on whether the decline in mortality operates mainly at younger or at older ages. In fact, the first stages of mortality decline have usually particularly benefited infants and children, and have often served to make the population younger. However, changes in mortality may assume a greater importance for population ageing later in the demographic transition.

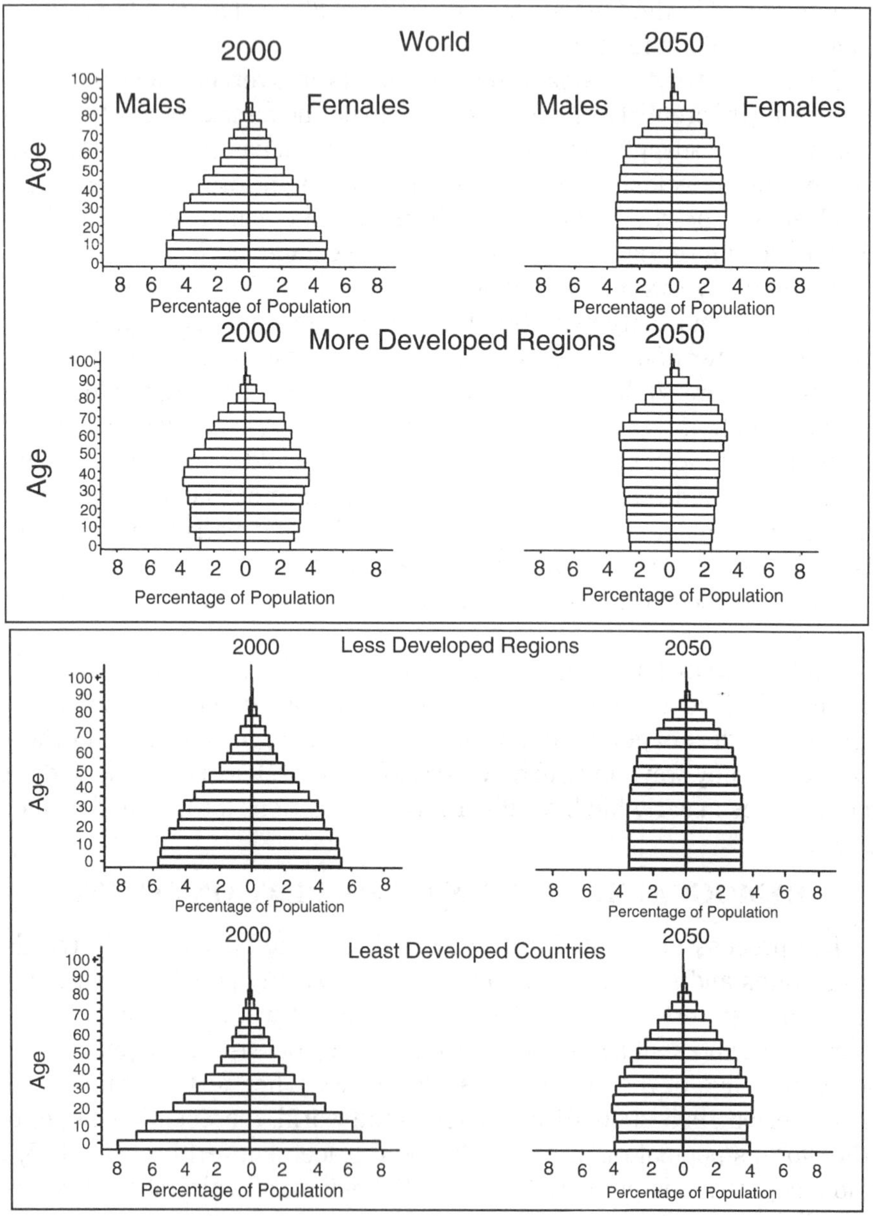

Fig. Population Pyramids: Age and Sex Distribution, 2000 and 2050

In countries where mortality rates at young ages are already low, further declines have tended to affect mainly the adult and older ages, and have contributed to population ageing. For example, Caselli and Vallin have demonstrated the growing impact of mortality change in population projections of France and Italy.

They concluded that even if Italian fertility remained at a very low level of 1.4 children per woman through the year 2040, more than half the increase in the proportion of the population aged 60 or older would be due to mortality change, and less than half to the earlier fertility trends.

TRENDS IN DEPENDENCY RATIOS

Demographic dependency ratios are used as approximate indicators of the relative sizes of the nonworking-age and working-age populations.

The youth-dependency ratio (the number of children per 100 persons of labour force age, ages 15-64 years) and the elderly-dependency ratio (the number aged 65 years or older per 100 persons of labour force age) indicate the dependency burden on workers and how the type of dependency shifts from children to older persons during the demographic transition.

The potential economic implications of falling or rising burdens of demographic dependency have been an area of active research. Since 1970, the youth-dependency ratio has been declining in all regions, while the over-65 dependency ratio is rising.

Trends for the total ratio in different countries and regions depend upon the relative size and speed of these countervailing trends in the older and younger components. In general, the total dependency burden declined between 1970 and 2000. In the more developed regions, the total dependency ratio decreased over that period from 56 to 48 dependent-aged persons per 100 aged 15 to 64. The ratio will increase between the present and 2025 and is projected to rise further, to 70, by 2050.

In the less developed regions, the overall dependency ratio in 1970 was 84, much higher than in the more developed regions, but it decreased rapidly to 60 by 2000, is projected to decline further to 50 by 2025 and then to increase slightly between 2025 and 2050.

The impact of demographic ageing is clearly visible in the old-age dependency ratio, which is increasing in both more and less developed regions during the period from 1970 to 2050. Between 2000 and 2050, the old-age dependency ratio will double in more developed regions and almost triple in less developed regions.

The amount and pace of change in demographic dependency ratios varies greatly between countries. Large swings in dependency ratios are typically initiated or accentuated by rapid fertility declines, but those effects take many years to play out.

Table. Trends in Age-dependency Ratios, by Region-1970 to 2050 (Percentage)

Region	1970	2000	2025	2050
Dependency ratio: Total				
World total	75	58	51	56
More developed regions	56	48	58	70
Less developed regions	84	60	50	54
Least developed countries	90	82	63	47
Africa	92	84	63	47
Asia	80	56	48	57
Europe	56	48	56	72
Latin America and the Caribbean	87	59	50	58
Northern America	62	51	59	64
Oceania	65	54	56	60
Under Age 15				
World total	66	47	36	31
More developed regions	41	27	25	26
Less developed regions	77	52	37	31
Least developed countries	84	77	56	35
Africa	86	78	56	35
Asia	73	47	33	30
Europe	39	26	23	25
Latin America and the Caribbean	79	50	35	32
Northern America	46	32	29	28
Oceania	53	39	33	30
Ages 65 or over				
World total	10	11	16	26
More developed regions	15	21	33	44
Less developed regions	7	8	13	23
Least developed countries	6	6	6	12
Africa	6	6	6	12
Asia	7	9	15	27
Europe	16	22	33	47
Latin America and the Caribbean	8	9	14	27
Northern America	16	19	30	36
Oceania	12	15	23	30

Note: The rations show the ratio of the numbers of persons aged under 15 years and over 65 years to the number aged 15 to 64 years, expressed as a percentage.

Four examples are shown in figure to illustrate a range of situations and trends:

- Argentina has experienced a gradual fertility decline, with relatively minor fluctuations over a long period. It is projected to experience only minor changes in the total dependency ratio, which will remain near 60 over the entire period from 1970 to 2050.

In Italy, the total fertility rate plummeted after the mid-1970s to reach the unprecedentedly low level of 1.2 by the early 1990s. The total dependency ratio initially declined, but increases in the over-65 dependency ratio will dominate the trend into the future, and will produce an especially rapid rise in demographic dependency after 2020. The Republic of Korea experienced a rapid fertility decline after 1970, and the total dependency ratio fell to an unusually low level of 39 by 2000. The overall ratio will not begin to rise appreciably until after 2015, but it will then increase rapidly. Kenya shows an extremely high child-dependency ratio, with a total dependency ratio of 115 in 1980. Kenya had one of the highest levels of fertility in the world, estimated at 8.1 children per woman during the period from 1960 to 1980, before beginning a rapid fertility decline, which is projected to continue. By 2000, Kenya's under-15 and over-65 ratios were similar to those seen in the Republic of Korea 30 years earlier.

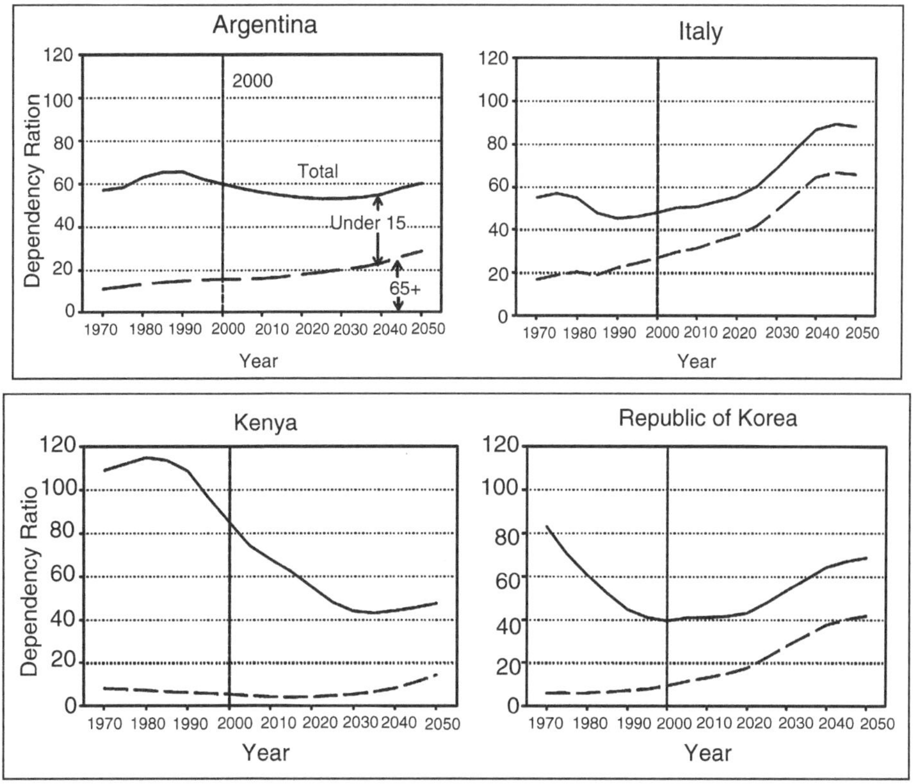

Fig. Estimated and Projected Trends in Age-dependency Ratios in Selected Countries (Persons Aged Under 15 or Over 65 Years Per 100 Persons Aged 15-64 Years)

URBANIZATION

Consistent with the global trend of urbanization, the older population is becoming more concentrated in urban areas. By 2000, the majority of the world's older persons (51 per cent) will live in urban areas; by 2025, this is expected to climb to 62 per cent of older persons. These figures, however, mask the large divergence between more and less developed regions. In the more developed regions, 74 per cent of older persons are urban dwellers, while in the less developed regions, which remain predominantly rural, slightly more than one third (37 per cent) of the elderly reside in urban areas. Despite the increasing urbanization of the older population, rural areas remain disproportionately older than urban areas in many countries as a result of migration of young persons to urban areas and the return migration of older persons to rural areas.

3

Tourism and Resources

GEOGRAPHY EDIFICES AND TOURISM

Places, and images of places, are fundamental to the practice of tourism. The demand for tourism commonly emanates from individual or collective perceptions of tourist experiences that are usually firmly rooted in associations with particular places, whilst the promotion and marketing of tourism depends heavily upon the formation and dissemination of positive and attractive images of destinations as places. Tourism therefore maps the globe in a distinctive, though highly subjective, manner, and one of the ways in which we may view the geography of tourism is as a visible manifestation of perceptions and images of what constitute tourism places.

However, as those perceptions and images are recast and re-formed—in response to changing public expectations, tastes, fashions, levels of awareness, mobility and affluence—new tourism geographies emerge, overlying or even superseding previous patterns as different forms of tourism promote new areas of interest. This chapter explores some of the ways through which such tourism geographies are formed and in concluding the volume as a whole, points up some of the new directions in which tourism appears to be moving.

INVENTING TOURISM PLACES

The construction and subsequent consumption of tourist places is essentially a socio-cultural process. The initial identification of places to which tourism may be drawn reflects an appraisal of resources that is located in cultural evaluations, and the physical development of tourism places typically depends as much upon social and institutional structures and organisations as it does upon the more tangible impacts of (say) innovations in transport technology.

Hence, the original growth of sea bathing resorts in eighteenth-century England mirrored key shifts in health practices and beliefs, whilst the later development of mountain tourism in Alpine Europe owed its impetus to the alternative views of landscape that grew out of the new taste for the picturesque and the romantic that was popularised in the first decades of the nineteenth century. Later still, the growth of mass forms of Mediterranean tourism only became really established with the fashion for sunbathing from about 1920. Railways (and later aeroplanes) may have provided a physical mechanism for moving tourists in large number to new destinations, but it required the transformations in the social organisation of tourism (for example, the guided tour and later the packaged holiday) and the importation of holidaymaking into popular culture to realise that potential to the full.

THE TOURIST GAZE

The spatial pattern of tourism depends very strongly, therefore, upon how we view places—an idea that has been most usefully conceptualised by the sociologist Urry in his notion of the 'tourist gaze'. The concept of the gaze is valuable because it helps us understand the processes both of construction of tourist places and of their consumption, whilst the metaphor of visualisation that is implicit in the term 'gaze' is central to comprehending modern tourism practices and their associated meanings. Tourism is a strongly *visual* practice. We spend time in advance of a tourism trip attempting to visualise the experience by examining guide books and brochures, or in anticipatory day-dreams; we often spend significant parts of the trip itself engaged in the act of sightseeing in which we gaze upon places, people and their artefacts; and we relive experiences as memories and recollections, aided by photographs or home video footage that we have consciously taken to act as visible reminders of the trip. However, the entire process of visualisation, experience and recall is socially constructed and strongly mediated by 'cultural filters'.

We gaze and record places in a highly selective fashion, disregarding some places altogether and, from the remainder, removing the unappealing or the uninteresting. In the process, we are inventing (or reinventing) places to suit our purposes. The gaze is also a detached and superficial process, as the term itself suggests. This superficiality increases the role of cultural signs within the invention and consumption of tourist places—not signs in the literal sense of directional indicators, but figurative signs: places or actions that represent, through simplification, much more complex ideas and practices.

So for the tourist, a prospect of a rose-decked thatched cottage may come to represent or embody a much wider image of 'olde England' and the lifestyles and practices that mythologies associate with the rural past. For some writers, tourism has become an exercise in the collection of such signs—the postcards and the holiday photographs from the great tourism sites of the world conferring a status upon the individual, the true mark of the modern (or post-modern) tourist.

The construction of the tourist gaze is also inextricably bound up in the notion of contrast or difference. Tourism, or at least those leisurely sectors of tourism, is widely conceived as an opposite to work, and the practice of travel takes the tourist away from the familiarity of places of employment or residence and into places that have been consciously selected as providing varying levels of contrast to the familiar. This helps to explain the clear tendency for tourism geographies to change through time, through the quest to discover (or invent) new tourism places to replace established locations that have become unacceptably familiar. This may result in the tourist gaze being focused upon new destinations or perhaps upon elements in existing destinations that had not previously been a part of the tourist circuit and which therefore possess the valued cachet of originality. So, Brighton and Torbay are replaced by Biarritz and St Tropez, whilst the seasoned tourist to Paris, no longer simply content with views of the Eiffel Tower, may now sign up for guided visits to the city's nineteenth-century sewers.

The manner in which we gaze upon tourist sites (and sights) is partly a product of our own social, educational and cultural backgrounds and partly a result of the systematic production and presentation of tourism places within the media in general and the travel industry in particular—a form of 'professional gaze'. Film, television, magazines, travel books and advertisements constantly produce and reproduce objects for the tourist gaze.

This is an enormously powerful influence that infiltrates the subconscious of everyday life, creating new patterns of awareness, fuelling desires to see the places portrayed and instilling within the travelling public new ways of seeing tourism destinations. Research suggests that most visitors' perceptions of tourism places are often vague and ill-formed, unless those perceptions have been sharpened through previous experiences. Hence there is clear potential for marketing and promotional strategies to shape both the character and the direction of the tourist gaze.

PROMOTING TOURIST PLACES

Surprisingly, perhaps, relatively little work has been conducted upon the role of advertising in the cultural representation of tourist places, despite the lengthy—if not always honourable—history of the practice. Some of the first promoters of tourism places were the railway companies, which, in their efforts to secure a commercial market, produced some enduring images of places. Visitors to contemporary Torquay, for example, are still welcomed to the 'English Riviera'—a conception (originally in the more spatially specific guise of the 'Cornish Riviera') of the Great Western Railway in the early 1900s. Under the distinctly patriotic slogan 'See your own country first', it exhorted potential travellers to explore the delights of distant and exotic Cornwall in preference to Italy, with which it drew direct parallels in terms of the mildness of climate, the natural attractiveness of its (female) peasantry and even the shape of the two lands on the map, albeit with some cartographic licence in the case of Cornwall. In so doing, the railway promoters fed off such limited perceptions of Cornwall as may have existed, but primarily they invented an image that was then reinforced through associated guidebooks and literature that presented Cornwall as some form of distant, yet still accessible, Arcadia.

This tradition of creative promotion of tourist places has continued to the present, and content analysis of contemporary tourist brochures reveals texts that are often unashamedly escapist in their tone and which, when combined with photographic representations, emphasise difference; excitement; timelessness or the unspoilt; tradition or romance—according to the perceived market at which the publicity is aimed.

Such creative constructions of tourist places are most prevalent, of course, in the representation of foreign destinations, where fewer people will have had the direct experience needed to balance the claims of the brochures and the guidebooks. Messages are often subtly encoded. A recent study of a cross-section of British travel brochures promoting foreign places found, for example, that 25 per cent of illustrations showed only empty landscapes and, especially, beachscapes (reinforcing ideas of escape); that pictures showing tourists were nine times more common than pictures of local people (reinforcing notions of exclusivity and segregation); and that written text placed overwhelming emphasis upon qualities of naturalness (as an antithesis to the presumed artificiality of the tourists' routine lives) and the opportunities for self-(re)discovery.

Only occasionally were senses of the exotic conveyed by use of images of local people, whilst reassurance that the experience of difference would not be so great as to be disorientating and unpleasant was provided by pictures showing familiar (though culturally displaced) items—typically as background elements. Examples of the latter might include 'English-style' pubs in the Spanish package tour resorts or, most ubiquitously of all, glimpses of the familiar red emblem of the Coca-Cola Company.

Promotional material that presents selective representations of realities is, of course, to be expected. What is more interesting, perhaps, is the emerging trend in some sectors of tourism towards promotion of places that do not actually exist or which are entirely imagined reconstructions of a locality. This has been nicely exemplified in England and Wales by the popular practice within regional and local tourism boards of appropriating legendary, literary or popular television characters or events to provide a form of spatial identity to which tourists will then be drawn. Some are well established.

The term 'Shakespeare Country' to designate the area around Stratford-upon-Avon dates back to railway advertising of the 1930s and, along with similar descriptions of the Lake District as 'Wordsworth Country' or Haworth as 'Brontë Country', possesses some grounding in the real lives of individuals. 'Robin Hood Country' is more problematic given the uncertainties surrounding the actual existence of Robin Hood. However, descriptions of parts of Tyneside as 'Catherine Cookson Country' or the Yorkshire Dales as 'Emmerdale Farm Country' or Exmoor as 'Lorna Doone Country' take the process one stage further removed. They confuse reality with fictional literary and television characters or locales, and tourists are thereby confronted by a representation of what is already a representation. It is then only a short step to the totally artificial worlds of Disney in which cartoon characters—albeit in the form of employees in costume—step into the sunlight of Anaheim or Orlando to be photographed with the tourist.

COMMODIFICATION AND PSEUDO-REALITIES

Such practices represent commodification of tourism in one of its most overt forms. This is the tourism industry constructing a product and marketing it as an inclusive and convenient experience of another place. It draws selectively upon the real nature of places and presents only those elements that will appeal to the market segments at which the holidays are directed. But given the alacrity with which tourists consume such commodified and invented places, a question is raised over the significance, or otherwise, of 'real' experiences of place.

The problem for providers of tourism is that having constructed specific images of peoples and places in order to draw the visitor, it is obligatory for destinations to match the images that are projected. The tourist must confirm his or her expectations, otherwise the return visits, or the visits of others made on the basis of personal recommendation (one of the most important methods for disseminating knowledge of tourism places), will not occur. In this way, tourist images tend to become self-perpetuating and self-reinforcing with the attendant risk that, through time, tourist experiences become increasingly artificial.

The argument that tourist experience is founded on artificial rather than real situations is an idea that has been debated since the early 1960s, when a number of scholars (most notably Boorstin) attempted to argue that the traveller does not experience reality but thrives instead upon 'pseudo-events'—commodified, managed and contrived forms of provision that present a flavour of foreign places in a selective and controlled manner. This is evidenced in several distinct directions.

- *The physical isolation of the tourist from the host environment*: This tendency receives its most obvious expression in the enclavic forms of resort development in the Third World, where visitors are provided with the familiar creature comforts that may literally have been imported from their place of origin, set within a physical environment that has been deliberately contrived to reflect popular images of what an exotic location should be like. But many forms of tourism place visitors in what has been termed an 'environmental bubble': a protective cocoon of Western-style hotels, international cuisine, satellite television, guidebooks and helpful, multilingual couriers—'surrogate parents' that cushion and, as necessary, protect the tourist from harsher realities and unnecessary contacts. As a result, the tourist gaze is often akin to gazing into a mirror. We construct tourism places to reflect ourselves, rather than the places we are visiting.

- *Cultural imposition*: The powerful expectations of tourists often impose particular forms of development and provision upon host communities. Many of us, quite illogically, expect a home-from-home experience, even in foreign lands, and the necessity for local providers to match those expectations inevitably changes the nature of the places that we visit. In the most extreme forms of this phenomenon, places actually begin to lose their sense of identity—they become *placeless* and quite indistinct from other tourist places, and quite unrepresentative of the realities of indigenous places. The mass tourist resorts of the Spanish coast, for example, commonly present a bland, placeless uniformity that says little about the 'real' Spain that exists often only a few miles inland.
- *Staged events*: One of the many ironies in international travel is that a primary motive is exposure to foreign culture and custom, yet this is often met through a quite artificial purveyance of supposed custom, whether via the sale of inauthentic souvenirs or via staged events or places. Sanitised, simplified and staged representations of places, histories, cultures and societies match the superficiality of the tourist gaze and meet tourist demands for entertaining and digestible experiences, yet they provide only partial representations of realities.

NEW TOURISM DIRECTIONS

In some ways, commodification and the pseudo-realities represent an inevitable product of modern tourism if mass markets are to be effectively served, but the visible shift from a natural to an artificial basis to tourism and the lack of authenticity that surrounds many contemporary tourism practices have raised concerns. For some writers (especially MacCannell), tourists embody a quest for authenticity—the act of travelling and the shifting focus of the tourist gaze reflecting a search for an authenticity that many tourists from urban, industrialised countries seem no longer able to detect in their own routine lifestyles. For others, issues of authenticity are much less important than the quest for difference.

The quest for difference has become one of several strands within an emerging pattern of 'new' tourism—alternative tourist geographies that have been variously designated as 'post-industrial', 'post-modern' or 'post-Fordist'. The new tourism industry is characterised by flexibility, by segmentation and by the development of new forms of customised experience that bring a myriad of new choices to tourists and thus offer stark contrasts to the mass, standardised and packaged forms of 'old' tourism. (Fordism, which is derived from the production-line philosophy of the motor manufacturer Henry Ford, is a description given to the hypermodern patterns of mass, standardised forms of production and consumption that prevailed between approximately 1920 and 1970. Post Fordism, therefore, emphasises contrasting patterns centred on flexible production and enhanced consumer choice.)

Table. Tourism and Post-fordist Forms of Consumption

Post-Fordist consumption	Tourist examples
Increased significance of consumers and consumer choices	Rejection of some mass forms of tourism (holiday camps; cheap packages) and increased diversity of preferences
Greater volatility of consumer preferences	Fewer repeat visits and proliferation of alternative attractions
Increased market segmentation	Multiplication of holiday types
More new products with shorter product life	Rapid turnover and change in popularity of sites in response to fashions
Increased preference for non-mass forms of production and consumption	Growth of alternative tourism

The advent of new forms of tourism does not, of course, mean that old tourism in its mass, packaged forms is disappearing. There remain many millions of people committed to such travel who derive sufficient rewards and pleasures from the experience to sustain mass tourism for the foreseeable future.

What is changing is the development of new market segments comprising groups seeking the out of the ordinary, groups that we may expect to see forming alternative tourism geographies that reflect this quest for difference. These trends are revealed within the increasing popularity of, *inter alia:*

- Cultural tourism, which has become a major factor shaping tourism patterns in Europe, refocusing attentions upon major cities both as established tourist destinations—for example, Paris, Amsterdam, Florence and Vienna—and as new centres of culture—for example, Glasgow;
- Heritage tourism, which is especially important in countries such the UK where a wealth of heritage-related sites survive, often in places that represent new locations for tourism;
- Theme parks, which are arguably the outstanding example of the artificial construction of post-modern tourist spaces and are fast becoming major centres of tourist consumption in countries such as the USA, Britain and Japan;

- Adventure tourism, which frequently takes tourists to exotic and unexplored places where notions of difference are often especially prominent; for example, trekking in the Himalayas;
- Eco-tourism, which attempts to combine principles of sustainability in developing new forms of responsible travel to natural areas, particularly to Third World destinations such as Costa Rica, Ecuador and Nepal.

The new tourists—'post-tourists' in the minds of some writers—embody a new spirit of playfulness in tourism as a dominant mode of experience. They are not deceived by the pseudo-realities of contemporary tourism but are happy to accept such constructions at face value as an expected and valued part of new forms of experience.

The broad effect of these demands has been twofold: the reinvention of existing tourist places and, much more widely, the establishment of new ones. We will explore the first theme by briefly revisiting a traditional seaside resort and then examine the latter theme more fully by reference to two contrasting examples: the growth of heritage tourism in Britain and the growth of theme parks, particularly in the USA and Japan.

REINVENTION OF EXISTING TOURIST PLACES

The reinvention of places is a perennial theme within tourism development and many different types of destination have periodically been required to adjust the nature of what they offer to the visitor in order to keep abreast of evolving tastes and fashions. This is most visibly evidenced in the changing role of traditional seaside resorts. We visited Brighton in its formative years and saw how the resort was 'invented' through a particular combination of scientific advocacy, opportunism, patronage, fashion, technology and new social organisation.

Revisiting Brighton today, we find a resort that is busy reinventing itself, partly in an attempt to retain a tourism sector in the face of growing competition from foreign places, and partly to build new images of the town in order to attract alternative populations and enterprises—particularly in commercial services and higher education.

Tourism policies are especially interesting since they reveal a conscious attempt to define a new image for Brighton that actually mirrors its distant past, replacing the vulgar, even seedy, version of Brighton that had developed in the 1950s and 1960s with a more stylish and up-market model that consciously refers to the period of Regency Brighton. Some of the reinvention of Brighton has centred on conference tourism, which has become a major user of the elegant seafront hotels with more than 1,200 conferences hosted in the town in 1994. But more significant has been the growth of heritage tourism, a process in which the townscapes that tourism created in the nineteenth century have now become the object of a new tourist gaze. Urban conservation areas have mushroomed; the Old Town has been pedestrianised and, in the process, the streetscapes have been reconstructed by the implantation of street furniture (signs, seats, litter bins, etc.) designed to look old; whilst the Brighton Festival, once a low-key, local event, has been developed to form a major attraction aimed at high-spending cultural tourists.

The boisterous seaside entertainments that characterised the Brighton of the recent past are now closely contained by local planning controls, and whilst the disused West Pier corrodes away and falls into the sea—a potent symbol of the passing of one tourism era—millions of pounds are being reinvested in restoration of King George IV's Royal Pavilion as a focal point for the new heritage tourist.

THE ESTABLISHMENT OF NEW TOURIST PLACES

HERITAGE TOURISM

Heritage tourism (in which the term 'heritage' is taken to refer to places, objects or ideas that are deemed to be of value or importance and which have been passed from one generation to the next) has, in recent years, developed as one of the main sectors in the establishment of new spatial patterns of tourism, particularly in countries such as Britain. Brighton represents an example of an existing tourism place using its past to sustain its future, but heritage tourism has also been more widely responsible for the introduction of tourism into localities that previously held no pretensions to be tourist places. In Britain (which has a stronger heritage tourism tradition than most), the castles, great houses, museums, galleries and historic towns that have provided the basis of one set of tourist geographies for some time have been supplemented by new tourist spaces that centre upon industrial cities, ports and the working countryside—places which have adapted (and adopted) their pasts as a means to attract visitors. The dramatic expansion of heritage tourism invites both description and explanation. The practice of gazing on the past is not new. The Grand Tourists of the seventeenth and eighteenth centuries focused much of their attention on sites and artefacts that we would today classify as 'heritage', whilst in the nineteenth century, popular rail excursions ferried industrial workers as day trippers to places such as Windermere to enjoy the landscape heritage of the Lake District.

What has changed is the scale, diversity and extent of heritage-based attractions in tourism, which summarises a typology of heritage attractions. Since the mid-1970s, Britain has acquired over 1,000 new registered museums, an additional 210,000 listed buildings (i.e. buildings designated as being of architectural importance), 5,000 new conservation areas and a further 5,400 scheduled ancient monuments.

A typology of heritage tourism attractions:

- *Natural history and science attractions*: Including nature reserves and trails; zoos, aquariums, wildlife parks and rare breeds; technology centres; scientific museums; geomorphological or geological sites (caves, gorges, cliffs or waterfalls)
- *Agricultural and industrial attractions*: Including working farms and farming museums; quarries and mines; factories; breweries and distilleries; museums of industry
- *Transport attractions:* Including transport museums; working steam railways; canals and docks; preserved ships; aircraft and aviation displays
- *Socio-cultural attractions*: Including historic sites; museums of rural or industrial life; museums of costume
- *Built attractions*: Including stately homes; religious buildings (cathedrals, churches, shrines)
- *Military attractions*: including castles, battlefields, naval dockyards and military museums
- *Landscape attractions*: Including historic town- and villagescapes; national parks; heritage coastlines and seascapes
- *Artistic attractions*: Including galleries; theatres or concert halls and their performances; art festivals
- *Attractions associated with historic figures*: Including homes or working places of writers, artists, composers, politicians, military leaders or leaders of popular culture

Over 2,000 historic buildings and monuments are regularly open to the public, and on a recent Heritage Open Day (when sites not normally open received visitors), some 670,000 people took advantage of the opportunity, part of an overall total of an estimated 58.3 million heritage visits made in the same year—1996. Recent trends suggest that although prone to year-on-year fluctuations, the market trend for this form of tourism is still upward.

Explanation for the popularisation of the past in contemporary tourism needs to take account of several factors. First, it is argued that interest in the past is something inbuilt in human nature, and that for many people the remains of the past provide a sense of security and continuity that will be amplified whenever the present becomes uncertain. The concept of nostalgia is important here. Nostalgia was initially recognised as a physical condition (first seen in sailors on long voyages of discovery); we now call it 'homesickness'. The uncertainties surrounding modern lives, so it is argued, produce an equivalent of the sailor's homesickness, but here manifest in sentimental attachments to a past that is variously perceived as safer, more secure and more predictable.

This links to a second idea. One of the abiding themes of contemporary life—and strongly evident in tourism—is globalisation. Yet paradoxically, as our lives become more influenced by globalised processes, so resistance to globalisation becomes more firmly embedded in the reassertion of local places, histories and cultures. Out of this reassertion of the local has arisen a popular preservation movement that has actively reclaimed and restored a wide range of places and associated artefacts as cultural mementoes and, through their active promotion, developed their use as objects of the tourist gaze.

This process has been aided by a third factor. The rapid deindustrialisation of Britain in the 1970s and 1980s—as happened in a number of industrialised economies—created a valuable legacy of redundant sites and buildings that provided natural homes for the new heritage industry. As working industry disappeared, people became increasingly interested by its memory and by the forms of life and practices associated with it.

This trend, in particular, has been responsible for much of the diversification within heritage tourism, focusing popular attention on a wide range of industrial museums, restored mills and factories, working steam railways, canals and dockland, coal mines and slate quarries—places that represent new sites of consumption on the tourist map. The commodified, selective and sanitised ways in which such places tend to present their views of the past have drawn predictable criticism over a lack of authenticity and a tendency to glamorise, yet the majority still convey a valuable sense of the past that many visitors would otherwise struggle to achieve through other media and are consciously valued for this quality.

There have also been important social shifts that have helped to promote heritage tourism. The collective weakening of traditional working classes in many Western economies, which has been partly responsible for the decline of older seaside towns, has been countered by the emergence of new professional and quasi-professional service classes whose lifestyles and aspirations are much more attuned to the enjoyment of cultural and heritage-based attractions. However, one of the great strengths of heritage tourism is its breadth.

The past means different things to different people, and whilst there is still a strong market for 'high' cultural forms of the kind expressed in traditional museums, art galleries, concert halls and theatres, the post-industrial era has been associated with wider promotion of 'low' or 'popular' cultural forms that are far more accessible to people who lack the cultural capital to enjoy—or even make sense of—the high forms of heritage. So the new museums of industry, of transport, or of rural life, for example, succeed because they offer memories to which ordinary people can relate.

DEVELOPMENT OF HERITAGE TOURISM

Bradford Metropolitan District, with its population of 480,000 people, is located on the western fringes of the West Yorkshire conurbation. Bradford is a product of the Industrial Revolution of the nineteenth century, and its economic base until very recently was founded on textiles and engineering, factors which had contributed to a popular image of the place as a grim and grimy northern city, plagued by poor housing and amenities and suffering extreme levels of unemployment. By the 1980s, inevitable decline in traditional industries posed major challenges to attempts to restructure and revive the area. Surprisingly, the new strategies that emerged to address these problems included proposals for the promotion of tourism, using several established or potential attractions as a basis.

These included:

- An existing stock of hotel bed spaces associated with the city's commercial activity;
- A superb Victorian industrial heritage, including the model community of Saltaire;
- Proximity to the Yorkshire Dales National Park and other scenic areas such as Ilkley Moor;
- The village of Haworth (which lies in the Metropolitan District) and which is the centre of 'Brontë Country';
- The Keighley and Worth Valley steam railway;
- Locational settings for the popular TV soap *Emmerdale.*

To these existing attractions, the city was able to add further to its tourism stock, including the National Museum of Photography, Film and Television (which was established in 1983 as a joint partnership between the Science Museum and the city council); the restored Alhambra Theatre (one of Britain's best-preserved

Table. Major Tourism Attractions in the Bradford Metropolitan District, 1994.

Attraction	No. of visitors
Haworth village	1,000,000*
Esholt (Emmerdale)	750,000*
National Museum of Film, Photography and Television	737,098
Ilkley Moor	550,000*
1853 Gallery (Salt's Mill)	500,000*
Bradford Cathedral	202,200
Bradford Industrial Museum	170,000
Keighley and Worth Valley Steam Railway	141,028
Brontë Parsonage	101,900
Cliffe Castle	99,739
Cartwright Hall	90,477
Bolling Hall	37,908
East Riddlesden Hall	34,923
Yorkshire Car Collection	24,000

These attractions have been built into promotional strategies that focus upon short-break forms of tourism with strong thematic foci—'In the Steps of the Brontës', 'Industrial Heritage' and (reflecting the distinctiveness of the Asian community in Bradford) 'Tastes of Asia' all being successful initiatives with clear heritage links. By 1994, estimated annual visitor levels had reached almost 5 million, although a significant proportion of these would be day visitors rather than tourists making overnight stays. Indeed, one of the constraints on the development of tourism in Bradford that has emerged is a shortage of hotel beds, a matter that the city council is now addressing as the values of conference-based tourism have become more apparent.

Overall, tourism is currently estimated to be worth £64 million to the local economy. As a different mark of success, popular destinations are already revealing the stresses and strains of congestion, pollution and disruption to local life that tourism can create. The small village of Esholt (which masquerades as *Emmerdale,* in the TV soap) draws an estimated 500,000 visitors to a settlement without a single public lavatory!

The case of Bradford demonstrates several points. It shows the power of heritage attractions to promote new tourism destinations but, more importantly, it shows the importance of images of places. To succeed, Bradford had to reinvent itself, to cast off the old images of the industrial city and through conscious policies of investment and promotion, construct a new set of images that would appeal to the fickle and unpredictable tastes of the tourist.

The fact that it was able to do so successfully and provide a model for similar places seeking to follow the same path tells us just how flexible the modern geographies of tourism are becoming.Source: Davidson and Maitland (1997).The composite effect of these changes has been to define new tourism geographies in countries such as Britain where heritage promotion forms a central plank in tourism development strategies.

So alongside the established sites of heritage tourism—London, Canterbury, Oxford, Chester, York, Edinburgh—are a host of sites that were once the antithesis of tourism—a source of tourists rather than a destination—but places to which the visitors now flock. Unfashionable places such as Liverpool, Manchester, Wigan, Gateshead, Bradford, Stoke-on-Trent and Dudley now have a local tourist industry, based around heritage, which provides a valuable new medium for economic revival and a reassertion of a distinctive local sense of place.

THEME PARKS

The development of theme parks as tourist attractions illustrates several aspects of the contemporary redefinition of tourism practices and places.

- They are the quintessential post-modern spaces with their overt and conscious mixing of styles and deliberate confusion of the real with the artificial.

- They represent the globalisation and homogenisation of tourism cultures as the parks have spread and multiplied from their origins in North American amusement parks to reach Britain, continental Europe and the Pacific Rim of Asia (Japan, Korea, Australia, etc.).
- They appeal strongly to the 'post-tourists', the playful consumers of superficial signs and surfaces that some writers see as embodying the new age of tourism.
- Theme park developments also illustrate very effectively the idea of invented places.

This operates at two levels. First, in many parks the visual and contextual fabric is often an invention since it portrays imaginary characters and places that circulate around cartoon characters, fairy stories, myths or legends. 'Magic Kingdoms' and 'Fantasy Lands' are popular constructions in theme parks across the world, whilst themes that have a stronger grounding in reality, such as Disney's 'Frontier Land' and 'Main Street USA', present idealised and selective recollections.

Second, theme parks are quite capable of inventing new tourism geographies by the manner in which they are located. Whilst some ventures have gravitated towards established tourism areas, such as the theme park developments in Florida, others have been obliged (through their considerable land requirements) to take on greenfield sites in places where tourism is not currently present. The original Disney development at Anaheim, Los Angeles (opened in 1955), was located in a nondescript zone on the city fringe where the tourist stock amounted to just seven rather modest motels. Similarly, the subsequent development of Euro-Disney on a 2,000-ha site at Marne-la-Vallée, 32 km east of Paris, although close to a major tourism city, also introduced large-scale tourism to an area that had only been lightly affected previously.

The specific character of theme parks varies from place to place, and this has led to some problems in their definition. For purposes of this discussion a theme park is viewed as a self-contained family entertainment complex designed around landscapes, settings, rides, performances and exhibitions that reflect a common theme or set of themes.

The leading exponent of the modern theme park, the Disney Corporation, reveals in its parks a remarkable synergy of resort development, state-of-the-art rides and amusements, as well as integral cross-references to the Corporation's own film and television products. But where Disney leads, others have followed, as the theme park concept has been replicated and reproduced in a growing number of settings across the globe.

Initially, the theme park grew out of fairground-style amusement parks of the 1920s, and a number of successful ventures had been established in North America and Europe prior to the opening of Disney's park at Anaheim. (Disney borrowed several ideas from the Efteling Park in the Netherlands, for example.)

But the success of Disney's initial venture encouraged others to enter the field, including major entertainment corporations and, particularly, film companies. The successful development of American parks encouraged expansion in European theme parks from the late 1970s and East Asian and Australian parks during the 1980s.

The area of fastest growth in theme parks is now centred on the Pacific Rim, the trend with an outline of a case study of theme park development in Japan. Alongside the rapid expansion of theme parks, other tourist attractions have also incorporated themed areas as part of their planned developments. Shopping malls such as West Edmonton (Alberta, Canada) and The Mall of the Americas at Minneapolis (USA) are spectacular examples of new tourist spaces in which theming is a prominent aspect of the appeal.

RECENT GROWTH OF THEME PARKS: THE CASE OF JAPAN

The development of theme parks in Japan illustrates not only the rapidity with which these tourist spaces have become popular, but also the importance of thematic diversity, location and accessibility, effective management and political support in securing the establishment of successful parks.

The first recognised theme park—a reconstruction of a Meiji village—opened in 1965 at Inuyama City, some 200 km west of Tokyo. This was followed in 1975 by a second park at Kyoto that is based on a theme of films. Until 1983, these two parks were Japan's only examples, but between 1983 and 1991 a further twenty-five parks were opened.

The catalyst to this remarkable expansion was the opening in 1983 of Tokyo Disneyland at Urayasu City. Set in the heart of Japan's most populated area, with 30 million people resident within a 50-km radius, the location and the high levels of accessibility to Japan's major cities have been key variables in the dramatic success of this venture. The advantages of location have been further reinforced by the skills of the Japanese as business managers and their instinctive attention to the efficiency of customer services, the cleanliness of the park and the smoothness of its operations. Tokyo Disney also demonstrates the importance of ongoing investment and the production of new rides and attractions as a means of retaining their market share—a lesson that smaller ventures have been slower to learn.

The success of Tokyo Disney spawned a number of direct imitations but also encouraged the promotion of parks centred on other themes. Japanese parks mirror the cultures in which they are produced, so alongside the themes of fantasy and adventure (which seem to possess a universal appeal) are parks that reflect Japanese interest in their history, nature, technology and—rather unusually—the cultures of other countries. The latter theme (which includes parks centred on reconstructions of Nordic villages, German towns of the Middle

Ages, New Zealand farms and Dutch cities) produces decontextualised spaces that often leave foreign visitors who know the originals quite bemused, but which Japanese tourists apparently take in their stride.

Part of the growth and diversification of Japanese theme parks is explained by the natural enthusiasm of the urban Japanese for tourism and travel, but it is also the product of political support from the Japanese government and its prefectures (local authorities), together with substantial investment from enterprises outside tourism. Tokyo Disney, for example, is owned by real estate and railway companies, with local government as a minor shareholder. Several of the less well positioned parks (such as Noboribetsu Nordic Village on Hokkaido and Reoma World Water Park on the island of Shikoko) would not have come into being without strong local political support and investment. In Japan, the theme park is a mark of local success and for some communities is literally a means of getting onto the map.

However, it is becoming clear that there are limits to the growth of theme parks in Japan. Whilst the 1990s have seen several more large projects added to the list, concerns over problems of identity within the market, the spiralling costs of investment and reinvestment, as well as uncertainties over the longer-term impacts of theme park development, have led to cancellations and postponements of other planned ventures.

The spatial expansion of theme parks as tourist attractions is, of course, a reflection of the success of the concept and its almost universal appeal—something that is strongly reflected in their capacity to draw huge numbers of visitors. These are family attractions that, perhaps surprisingly, also appeal to older tourists.

This is especially true when the theme park focuses upon historical, natural or cultural attractions, rather than 'white-knuckle' rides alone. In Britain, Alton Towers and Blackpool's Pleasure Beach consistently dominate the rankings of attractions at which visitors pay for entry, with Alton Towers drawing around 2.5 million visitors in a typical recent year. This pales almost into insignificance, however, compared to the market leaders in North America and the Far East. Tokyo Disney attracted almost 16 million visitors in 1993 while Disney's original venture at Anaheim drew 11.4 million people in the same year. In fact, the combined total attendance at the four Disney parks in the USA (Disneyland, Magic Kingdom, EPCOT and Disney World/MGM—the last three all in Florida) reached a staggering 41 million people. Aggregate attendance at theme parks in the USA and Canada in 1990 touched 160 million, an increase of 24 per cent over the decade since 1980.

The spatial distribution of the major parks is interesting. As the Japanese case shows, there are clear advantages to being close to major urban markets and/or established tourism regions. In the USA, the largest parks generally favour the warmer states such as Florida and California, since these represent the preferred destinations for American tourists in general. The more attractive climates in these locations clearly favour outdoor parks. (This was a requirement that Disney discovered to its cost in the near-disastrous opening of Euro-Disney in the damp and often cold outskirts of Paris.)

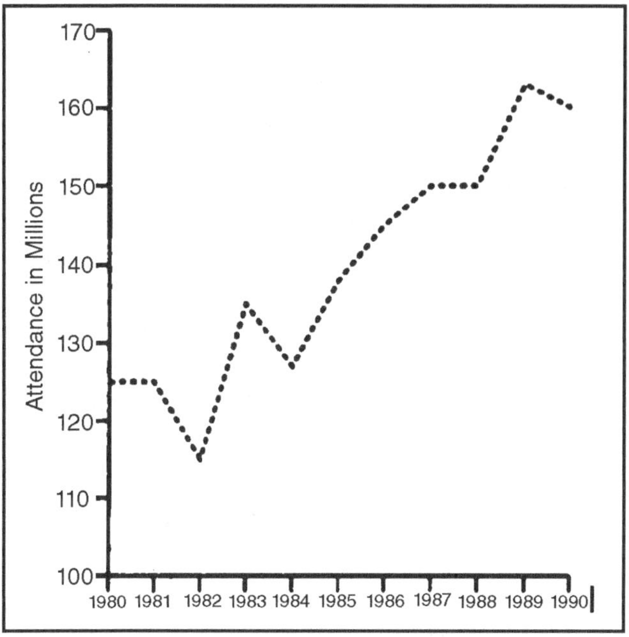

Fig. Growth of Theme Park Attendance.

But interestingly, parks can also be developed successfully in less propitious locations. Some of the most rapid rates of expansion in visits to American theme parks have been recorded in less popular areas such as Illinois, Ohio, Missouri, Tennessee and Kentucky.

Similarly, in Britain, the most popular theme park, Alton Towers, is buried deep in the lanes of rural north-east Staffordshire, one of the least visited counties in England—especially if visitors to the park are deducted from aggregate totals! The capacity of tourism to invent new places is indeed remarkable.

The case studies and examples that have been employed in this final chapter demonstrate particularly well how the dynamic quality of contemporary tourism has become one of its defining features. The traditional patterns of annual holidays by the sea in high summer, which in some locations endured for the best part of a century, are fast receding into individual and collective memories, replaced by new tourism geographies that emphasise different ways of seeing the world we inhabit.

The seasides, lakes and mountains that supported the development of tourism for a large part of the twentieth century still attract, but so, increasingly, do shopping malls, centres of culture and heritage, sporting venues, theme parks, centres of industry, rainforests, savannahs, wildernesses and icefields.

The (post-)modern tourist, no longer confined to traditional times and spaces, has become virtually ubiquitous. So, too, have tourism's effects, impacts and influences.

For human geographers, a central theme within the discipline is interpreting and understanding our changing world—a world in which geographic patterns are constantly being reworked by powerful forces of change: population shifts; new patterns of economic production and consumption; evolving social and political structures; new forms of urbanism; and globalisation and the compressions of time and space that are the product of the ongoing revolutions in information technology and telecommunications.

This book has attempted to show how tourism has also come to be a major force for change—an integral and indispensable part of the places in which we live, their economies and their societies. When scarcely a corner of the globe remains untouched by the influence of tourism, this is a phenomenon that we can no longer ignore.

TOURIST AND RECREATIONAL DEMAND FOR WILDERNESS, NATIONAL PARKS AND NATURAL AREAS

Many values are attached to wilderness in western society. Tourism and recreation has increasingly become significant as one of the main values attached to wilderness and its conservation with substantial increases in demands for access to wilderness in recent years. Demand for tourist or recreational experience of wild country or wilderness may be related to two major factors. First, changing attitudes towards the environment. Second, access to natural areas.

As discussed above, there has been the development of a more favourable response to wild country in western society over the past 200 years. These positive responses have been reinforced in recent years by the overall development of a climate of environmental concern which has served to influence recreation and tourism patterns in natural areas. Going hand-in-hand with the increase in demand for personal contact with nature has been the production of natural areas for tourist consumption. While the setting of a boundary for a national park may be appropriate for assisting conservation management it can also serve as a marker for tourist space on which it is appropriate for the viewer to gaze.

In the same way that notions of rurality are complex spaces of production and consumption, so it is that the ideas of wilderness and naturalness are bound up in the commodification of landscapes for tourist and recreational enjoyment. For some, such a perspective is at odds with the mythology that national parks are ecological rather than cultural landscapes, but the cultural idea of wilderness is implicit in the very notion of wilderness itself. For example, Nash (1982:1) noted that wilderness is 'heavily freighted with meaning of a personal, symbolic and changing kind'. Although the personal meaning of wilderness may not be of great value when it comes to the designation of wilderness areas from a biocentric perspective which concentrates on actual rather than perceived naturalness, it is of value in terms of the recreation and tourism values of wilderness.

The last decade has witnessed growing academic attention in the field of wilderness perception imagery. Stankey and Schreyer (1987), for example, demonstrate that wilderness perceptions may be shaped by a wide range of influences. These include social attitudes, cultural influences, recreational experiences, expectation and personal cognition. It is apparent, therefore, that 'while wilderness environments have an objective physical reality, what makes that reality "wilderness" rests very much with personal cognition, emotion, values and experience'.

Kliskey and Kearsley (1993) argue that, while demand for access to wilderness increases, so too does the need to define the extent to which certain qualities of wilderness are sought. Kearsley (1990) illustrates this point with his proposal for a classification of natural areas based on degrees of naturalness, ease of access and the provision of facilities. Implementation of such a classification would facilitate the use of 'degrees of wilderness'. This would allow custodians of tourist facilities to provide for a wide range of wilderness preferences and utilise a wide range of natural settings.

The wider spatial distribution of recreationists based upon an appreciation of wilderness perceptions could contribute to the attainment of two fundamental goals: the maximising of visitor satisfaction and the mitigation of environmental impact at tourist sites. Kliskey and Kearsley (1993) also identified the need for a tourism development approach that does not impact upon the values sought by those who try to avoid the infrastructure of mass tourism, and to protect the social and environmental values that nature-based tourists, or ecotourists, seek. However, this demands that wilderness imagery assumes a role in the marketing and management of recreational and tourism resources in natural settings.

Higham (1997) examined the dimensions of wilderness imagery by international tourists in the South Island of New Zealand (NZ). This was done via a list of variables that may be considered appropriate or inappropriate to wilderness recreation and tourism. A five-point Likert scale allowed respondents to express the extent to which each variable was considered acceptable or unacceptable. Higham noted that in 'classic' (i.e. high quality in terms of absence of human impact) wilderness terms it should be expected that these variables would be considered to violate or compromise qualities of wilderness recreation. However, only seven of the 21 variables listed received a generally negative response (a mean value less than 3.0). Thirteen variables returned mean values exceeding 3.0 indicating a generally favourable disposition within the sample frame.

In Higham's (1997) study, 'Distance from civilisation' (mean = 4.0) is clearly an important aspect of wilderness recreation to most inbound tourists. The desire for remoteness is reinforced in the similar high regard for the scale of the location ('big enough to take at least two days to walk across' mean = 3.8). However, there is also a desire for the provision of safeguard mechanisms to reduce risk, with the provision of search and rescue operations receiving the highest mean score (4.3) of all listed variables. The desire for swing bridges and walk-wires over watercourses, signposting and well-marked and maintained tracks confirm the widely held desire for wilderness recreation in a natural but relatively safe and humanised environment.

Furthermore, the placement of restrictions upon access and group size, again inconsistent with the notion of wilderness as free from human influences, was widely considered acceptable by inbound visitors. The variables 'restricted access' and 'restricted group size' share a mean of 3.8, placing them favourably. As Higham (1997:83) observed, 'It is quite possible that positive disposition toward these variables derives from trampers visiting high profile tracks on which social carrying capacities are being approached and, at times, exceeded.'

Only seven listed variables returned a mean response which indicated a generally negative disposition. Six of these seven variables described activities that were likely to present associated social or physical impacts. These included commercial recreation and motorised transport, and grazing of stock and hunting/trapping and plantation logging, respectively. The seventh such variable, 'gas provided in huts for cooking', is exceptional in that it described the provision of a facility that may ease the passage of visitors in back-country locations. This was the only such variable that was generally rejected by inbound tourists, all other visitor provisions and facilities (huts, shelters, the provision of water and toilet facilities) being considered generally acceptable or compatible with wilderness recreation and tourism.

Higham's (1997) research raises important questions about the role of accessibility to wilderness areas. Indeed, issues of access are now presenting major management problems in wilderness and national parks. For many years access to wilderness was restricted by both the nature of the terrain and the capacity of individuals to travel there. Up until the Second World War the main means of access to most national parks was by train, with many of the national parks in the New World actually being developed in association with the railroads.

However, in the post-war period there was a substantial increase in the proportion of personal car ownership, thereby increasing accessibility to parks. National park management agencies also promoted themselves to the public through 'parks for the people campaigns'. Herein though lies the critical situation in which many parks and wilderness managers now find themselves. National parks were originally established to provide both recreational enjoyment and conservation. The founders of the park movement, though, such as John Muir, could never have imagined the almost continuous growth in demand for park access from tourists and recreationists seeking to escape the urban environment.

The situation now sees traffic jams occurring in some parks, congestion on walking tracks, displacement of local users by tourists, increased pollution and other adverse environmental impacts, and reduced visitor satisfaction. Within this context, therefore, park and wilderness managers are now seeking both a better understanding of their visitors and how they may be satisfied, and strategies to find a better match between visitor needs and the capacities of the resource to be used, yet to retain the values that attract people in the first place.

Historically, tourist profiles have been generated to assist in the planning and management of visitor demand at a particular destination, attraction or site. Analysing tourist demand has traditionally been based on one of two main approaches: a socio-economic approach and a psychological or psychographic approach. The socioeconomic approach attempts to establish a correlation between a visitor's actions at a particular destination and their social position. Mathieson and Wall (1982) argue that visitor attitudes, perceptions and motivations at a destination are influenced by socio-economic characteristics such as age, education, income, residence and family situation. Representative of this form of research is Blamey's (1995) study of international ecotourists to Australia, a country which has paid particular attention to promoting its natural features to tourists in recent years.

According to Blamey (1995), Japanese and other Asian tourists are the most common inbound visitors to national parks on an absolute basis (21 and 19 per cent respectively of all such visitors), although they have the lowest propensities to do so on a per visit basis. Visitors from Switzerland have the highest propensity to visit natural areas (74 per cent) followed by Germany, Canada, Scandinavia and other European countries (all above 65 per cent). In addition, the economic expenditure of nature-based tourists may be substantial. Blamey (1995) reported that in 1993 the average expenditure per trip for international visitors undertaking bushwalks during their stay was Aus.$2,824 in 1993, or 58 per cent above the average expenditure of all inbound visitors (Aus.$1,788).

Psychographic or psychological approaches classify people into groups according to their lifestyles, including values, motivations and expectations (Blamey and Braithwaite 1997). Lifestyles are distinctions in people's behaviour which are identified and categorised to distinguish different types of respondents. In a comparative study of Canadian tourists, ecotourists were found to be more motivated by features such as wilderness and parks than the rest of the Canadian population in choosing a destination (Kretchmann and Eagles 1990; Eagles 1992).

Higham (1997) investigated a variety of wilderness motivations in an attempt to identify qualities of back-country recreation that motivate tourists to visit tracks in the New Zealand conservation estate. Eighteen wilderness motivation variables were drawn from a review of the wilderness literature.

Motivation variables are listed on this table in order of mean response. Perhaps not surprisingly, natural beauty and outstanding scenery are primary motivations as identified by international visitors. Indeed, Higham (1997:80) argued that this is a result that explains and entrenches the overwhelming popularity of the high-status Great Walks (of New Zealand). The reputations of the Milford, Routeburn and Kepler tracks are, in large part, explained by outstanding opportunities to experience alpine scenery. While these tracks remain those of unequalled scenic repute it is likely that inbound tourist interest in them will remain high.

The 18 variables listed appeared in random order in Higham's (1997) original questionnaire. It is thus interesting to note the order in which variables when listed by mean response. When paired sequentially, the first 10 listed variables demonstrate consistency in terms of both motivation and mean response.

These, in decreasing strength of motivation, were:

- To experience natural beauty and outstanding scenery.
- To experience remote and relatively untouched nature.
- To experience New Zealand's distinctive flora, fauna and natural systems.
- 4 To escape civilisation and engage in something completely new and different.
- 5 To engage in the physical challenge that natural areas present.

The desire to experience solitude, one of the classic principles of wilderness recreation, represents the eleventh variable. This variable receives a mean score of 3.0. The last seven listed variables returned mean scores that described a negative rather than positive disposition. The last two relate to the physical and mental challenges that classic wilderness recreation offers, yet these receive distinctly low levels of endorsement by tourists. Such a situation therefore raises fundamental questions about the benefits which people are seeking when they visit wilderness areas and the extent to which agencies should seek to supply such benefits.

Another major issue in terms of tourism and recreation in national parks and wilderness areas is the extent to which tourism economically benefits such peripheral areas. Researchers disagree on the economic impact of nature tourists on local communities. On the one hand, there is the argument that since these visitors spends most of their time out on the land or in the wilderness their economic impacts on local communities are minimal. On the other, environmentalists have promoted tourism as a non-consumptive use of nature and a win-win development strategy for underdeveloped rural areas. As an influential World Wildlife Fund publication on ecotourism states:

One alternative proposed as a means to link economic incentives with natural resources preservation is the promotion of nature tourism. With increased tourism to parks and reserves, which are often located in rural areas, the populations surrounding the protected areas can find employment through small-scale tourism enterprises. Greater levels of nature tourism can also have a substantial economic multiplier effect for the rest of the country. Therefore, tourism to protected areas demonstrates the value of natural resources to tourists, rural populations, park managers, government officials and tour operators.

Indeed, Boo (1990) found that nature-oriented tourists had higher daily expenditures than those tourists who were not nature oriented. Grekin and Milne (1996) also argued that ecotourism is an industry where the physical isolation of a destination may work to its economic advantage by providing a taste of the unknown and the untouched.

Similarly, Stoffle *et al.* (1979) in a study on indigenous tourism in the south-western United States also found that tourists who felt positive about residents at a particular destination were likely to purchase items to remember their experience. Hull (1998), in examining the average daily expenditure patterns of ecotourists on the North Shore of Quebec, found that package ecotourists had a substantially higher average daily expenditure than did independent tourists.

Accommodation was the area of largest expenditure with package tourists spending on average Can.$42.04 and independent tourists spending Can.$11.76. For package tourists, accommodation costs represented 59.6 per cent of their average daily expenditure while for independent tourists accommodation costs represent only 23.8 per cent. Package tourists' second largest expenditure category was transportation at 22.2 per cent while for independent tourists meals were the second largest category at approximately 17.8 per cent.

Expenditure patterns show that over 75 per cent of the package tourists' costs are restricted to accommodation and transportation while independent tourists, even though they spend less overall, are spending more money in different sectors of the local economy and contributing more to the sustainability of the industry. Hull's findings are supported by those of Place (1998:117) who also noted that ecotourism can provide an economic base, but it does not happen automatically, or without social and environmental impacts. If it is to be sustainable, local populations must be allowed to capture a significant amount of the economic multipliers generated by tourism. Successful reduction of multiplier leakage requires local participation in development planning and outside assistance with the provision of necessary infrastructure, training and credit.

Ecotourism, tourism and recreation in natural environments can undoubtedly bring economic benefits to both communities on the periphery and to the wholesalers and suppliers of such experiences, and it is for this reason that increasing attention is being given to the supply of the experience of wild nature.

OUTDOOR RECREATION EXPERIENCE

In many ways the idea that one can 'supply' a wilderness or outdoor recreation experience seems at odds with the implied freedom of wilderness.

However, the tourism industry is in the business of producing such experiences, while national parks and wilderness areas, by virtue of their formal designation, are places which have been defined as places where such experiences may be found. One of the most important transformations in the production of leisure on the periphery has been the way in which the initial construction of national parks as places of spectacular scenery and national monuments for the few were transformed into places of mass recreation in the 1950s and 1960s and to places of tourist commodification in the 1980s and 1990s, particularly through the notion of ecotourism.

A number of different meanings applied to the concept of 'ecotourism' which range from 'shallow' to 'deeper' statements of the tourism environment relationship:

- Ecotourism as any form of tourism development which is regarded as environmentally friendly and has the capacity to act as a branding mechanism for some forms of tourist products;
- Ecotourism as 'green' or 'nature-based' tourism which is essentially a form of special interest tourism and refers to a specific market segment and the products generated for that segment;
- Ecotourism as a form of nature-based tourism that involves education and interpretation of the natural environment and is managed to be ecologically and culturally sustainable.

The Australian Office of National Tourism (1997), for example, defined ecotourism as 'nature-based tourism that involves interpretation of the natural and cultural environment and ecologically sustainable management of natural areas'.

Ecotourism is seen as ecologically and socially responsible, and as fostering environmental appreciation and awareness. It is based on the enjoyment of nature with minimal environmental impact. The educational element of ecotourism, which enhances understanding of natural environments and ecological processes, distinguishes it from adventure travel and sightseeing. Many countries around the world are now focusing on the supply of an ecotourism product. Unfortunately, much of the ecotourism promotion best fits into the shallow end of the ecotourism spectrum, in that much of it revolves around the branding of a product or destination rather than seeking to ensure sustainability. Indeed, one of the greatest problems of ecotourism is the extent to which such experiences can be supplied without a limit on the number of people who visit natural areas, as visitation may lead not only to environmental damage, but also to perceptions of crowding thereby reducing the quality of the experience. As Kearsley *et al.* (1997:71) noted, 'From the viewpoint of tourism ... it is the impact of tourists upon tourists that has increasingly led to concern. Issues of crowding, displacement and host community dissatisfaction have risen to prominence.'

Crowding is a logical consequence of rising participation in outdoor recreation and nature-based tourism activities. It should therefore be of no great surprise that crowding is the most frequently studied aspect of wilderness recreation. Indeed, many issues in wilderness management and outdoor recreation,

such as satisfaction, desired experiences, carrying capacity and displacement are all related to the primary issue of crowding. Furthermore, social carrying capacity is increasingly being recognised as the most critical of all types of carrying capacity, since ecological impacts can often be controlled by management actions other than limiting use levels; for example, facilities may be extended and made more effective, and physical capacities are usually high (Shelby and Heberlein 1984). Importantly, crowding should not be confused with density. Density refers to the number of individuals in a given area while crowding refers to the evaluation of a certain density. In a review of 35 studies of crowding, Shelby *et al.* (1989) identified four sources of variation in perceptions of crowding:

- *Temporal variation*: Either in terms of time or season within which outdoor recreation activities are taking place. For example, weekends and public holidays are likely to experience higher than average use densities thereby resulting in inflated perceptions of crowding.
- *Resource availability*: Variation of resource availability (e.g. the opening and closing of tracks in alpine areas) may act to alter the presence of people at recreational sites.
- *Accessibility*: Distance (expressed in terms of time, cost, spatial or perceived distance) will affect crowding and densities, particularly if there is little or no recreation resource substitution.
- *Management strategies*: Management can intervene directly (e.g. use restrictions), or indirectly (e.g. de-marketing) to reduce visitor numbers at recreation sites.

Shelby *et al.* (1989) also investigated the hypothesis that crowding perceptions would vary according to the type of recreational use, although they were not able to resolve this hypothesis. However, recent research by Higham (1996) indicates that recreational use history is a substantial factor in influencing perceptions of crowding. Concerns over crowding are closely related to issues of social carrying capacity in wilderness and outdoor recreation areas. Social carrying capacity in recreation areas 'has typically been defined as a use level beyond which some measure of experiential quality becomes impaired'. However, there is no 'absolute value' of social carrying capacity, there is no single response to specific levels of use in a particular area. Instead, indicators of social or behavioural capacity will be dependent on the management objectives for a given recreation site. Shelby and Heberlein (1986:21) therefore refined this definition to read: 'Social carrying capacity is the level of use beyond which social impacts exceed acceptable levels specified by evaluative standards.' Several factors have been identified as influencing crowding norms, with a number of variables contributing to the interpretation of increasing recreational use density as perceived crowding (Manning 1985):

- Visitor characteristics: motivations, preferences and expectations, previous use experiences, visitors' attitudes towards wilderness;
- Characteristics of those encountered: type and size of groups encountered, behaviour of those encountered, perceptions of alikeness;
- Situational variables: type of area and location within an area.

Manning (1985) concluded that crowding norms are extremely diverse, yet the significance of visitor characteristics as a factor and the psychographic variables which comprise this factor indicate the possibility of a high degree of agreement being reached on crowding norms within particular subsets of the recreational population. This latter possibility highlights the importance of managers having a good understanding of the psychographic and demographic profiles of their visitor base in order to optimise levels of visitor satisfaction and attainment of management objectives. Density alone provides no measure of visitor satisfaction. Satisfaction will be determined by expectations, prior experiences and commitment to the recreational activity. Perceptions of crowding are therefore influenced by use densities, but this relationship is mediated by a range of other factors and variables. Indeed, a range of reactions or coping strategies are possible in recreationalist response to decreased recreational satisfaction, which may result not only from crowding, but also from such factors as littering, noise and worn out camp sites (e.g. Anderson and Brown 1984).

Such reactions include:

- Modifying behavioural patterns (e.g. by camping rather than using developed facilities);

- Changing time of visit or use (e.g. visiting in shoulder or off-peak periods in order to avoid conflicts with other users);
- Changing perceptions, expectations and recreation priorities (also referred to as product shift (Shelby *et al.* 1988), e.g. developing a new set of expectations about a recreational setting in order to maintain satisfaction);
- Recreational displacement, where those who are most sensitive to recreational conflicts seek alternative sites to achieve desired outcomes.

Of the above strategies, recreational displacement is probably the most serious from the manager's perspective as displacement appears to be a reality of wilderness use regardless of the level of recreational experience (Becker 1981; Anderson and Brown 1984). Therefore, increases in numbers of visitors to wilderness and other natural areas, particularly at a time when such areas have to cope with their promotion as places for ecotourism experiences as well as the pressures of traditional recreation users, may lead to a decline in wilderness qualities as users are displaced from site to site. For example, in the case of major walking tracks in the South Island of New Zealand, Kearsley (1997:95) observes:

In a context where there is a clear hierarchy of sites, as in Southern New Zealand, displacement down the hierarchy is an all-too-likely possibility ... the very large increase in overseas users of the Routeburn has displaced some domestic recreationists (and perhaps some tourists) to second tier tracks such as the Hollyford or Dart-Rees, or, indeed, out of tramping altogether. Similarly, their arrival might displace others yet further down the hierarchy to even less well known places, and there is a danger that trampers might be forced into wild and remote environments that are beyond their safe capacity.

One consequence of this, if it is happening, is increased visitor pressure on more remote locations and displacement of moderate wilderness purists to a limited reservoir of pristine sites ... with obvious physical impacts. A second consequence is the effect upon host community satisfaction, as domestic recreationists are displaced by overseas visitors. Both of these consequences have serious implications for the sustainability of tourism.

The case of crowding and other variables which influence visitor satisfaction and behaviour, including displacement, highlights the significance of understanding the factors of supply and demand of the recreation and tourist experience. Just as importantly they indicate the need for sound planning and management practice in trying to achieve a balance between the production and consumption of tourism and recreation, particularly in environmentally sensitive areas.

This chapter has highlighted a number of areas in which geographers have contributed to research and scholarship in the tourism and recreation periphery.

From the Topophilia of Tuan (1974), the sacred space of Graber (1978) and the breath-taking historical analysis of Glacken (1967), geographers have been at the forefront not only of understanding the human relationship to the natural environment and wild lands in particular, but also to the behaviours of tourists and recreationists in the wilderness. In addition, geographers have assisted in developing techniques to identify wilderness areas, undertake environmental histories and to cast light on their values.

As a resource analyst, the geographer therefore 'seeks to understand the fundamental characteristics of natural resources and the processes through which they are allocated and utilised'. The geographer's task is also relayed by Coppock (1970:25), who has made remarks of direct relevance to a better understanding of the relationship between tourism, recreation and wilderness conservation: 'A concern with problem solving and with the processes of human interaction with resources, particularly in respect of decision making, will powerfully assist a more effective geographical contribution to conservation.'

ADVENTURE TRAVEL AND SUSTAINABLE TOURISM IN THE PLEASURE PERIPHERY WILDERNESS AND NATIONAL PARKS

Historically, wilderness has been one of the main sources of 'the other' in western society. Wilderness was what lay beyond the boundaries of a 'civilised', ordered landscape. Since the beginning of the nineteenth century however, wilderness and wild areas began to assume a more favourable impression under the influence of the romantic and transcendentalist movements which favoured wild nature as an antidote to an increasingly industrialised and technocratic society.

More recently, the conservation and commodification of wilderness has become entwined with the growth of recreation and tourism which has seen national parks established not only for outdoor and adventure recreation enthusiasts but also as one of the main sites in which eco-tourism occurs. Geographers have long played a significant role in understanding and contributing to the conservation of natural resources and natural areas and their relationship with recreation and tourist activities. Indeed, recreation and tourism has long been used as an economic justification for the conservation and legal protection of such areas. Geographers have contributed to an understanding of a number of different dimensions of the relationship between wilderness and national park concepts and recreation and tourism:

- The changing meaning of wilderness in western society;
- The environmental history of national parks and wilderness areas;
- The value of wilderness;
- The identification and inventory of wilderness;
- The demand for wilderness and natural areas, including visitor profiles, activities and behaviours;

- The development of wilderness and national park policy and the supply of wilderness and natural areas for recreation and tourist activities.

THE CHANGING MEANING OF WILDERNESS IN WESTERN SOCIETY

Definition presents a major problem in the identification of wilderness areas. Definition is important 'because it is the basis for common understanding and communication' and it 'provides a basis for putting a concept into action through creating and preserving a referent'. However, wilderness is an elusive concept with many layers of meaning. Tuan (1974:112) has gone so far as to claim that 'wilderness cannot be defined objectively: it is as much a state of mind as a description of nature'. Wilderness has now become 'a symbol of the orderly progress of nature. As a state of mind, true wilderness exists only in the great sprawling cities'.

The problem of defining wilderness was summarised by Nash (1967:1):

'Wilderness' has a deceptive concreteness at first glance. The difficulty is that while the word is a noun it acts like an adjective. There is no specific material object that is wilderness. The term designates a quality (as the '-ness' suggests) that produces a certain mood or feeling in a given individual and, as a consequence, may be assigned by that person to a specific place. Because of this subjectivity a universally acceptable definition of wilderness is elusive.... Wilderness, in short, is so heavily freighted with meaning of a personal, symbolic, and changing kind as to resist easy definition.

The meaning of wilderness has changed over time but several themes may be distinguished. The word 'wilderness' is derived from the old English word *wilddeoren* meaning 'of wild beasts', which in turn is derived from the Teutonic languages of Northern Europe. In German, for example, *Wildnis* is a cognate verb, and *Wildor* signifies wild game.

The Romance languages have no single word selfless which expresses the idea of wilderness but rely instead on its attributes. In French the equivalent terms are *lieu desert* (deserted place) and *solitude inculte*, while in Spanish wilderness is *la naturaleza, immensidad* or *falts da cultura* (lack of cultivation). 'Italian uses the vivid *scene di disordine o confusione*'. The Latin root of desert, *de* and *serere* (to break apart, becoming solitary) connotes not only the loneliness and fear associated with separation but also an arid, barren tract lacking cultivation. Both the Northern European and the Mediterranean traditions define and portray wilderness as a landscape of fear, which is outside the safer bounds of human settlement. This image was taken up by Nash (1967:2) who noted that the image of wilderness 'is that of a man [*sic*] in an alien environment where the civilization that normally orders and controls life is absent'.

The landscape of fear that dominated early attitudes towards wilderness was noted in the eighth-century classic *Beowulf*, 'where *wildeor* appeared in reference to savage and fantastic beasts inhabiting a dismal region of forests, crags, and cliffs'. The translation of the Scriptures into English from Greek and Hebrew led to the use of wilderness as a description of 'the uninhabited, arid land of the Near East'. It was at this point that wilderness came to be associated with spiritual values. Wilderness was seen as both a testing ground for man and an area in which man could draw closer to God.

The biblical attitude towards nature was an essential ingredient of the Judaeo-Christian or western attitude towards wilderness. According to the dominant tradition within Judaeo-Christianity concerning humankind's relationship with nature, it was 'God's intention that mankind multiply itself, spread out over the earth, make its domain over the creation secure'. This relationship is best indicated in Genesis 1:28 where God said to man, 'Be fruitful and multiply, and fill the earth and subdue it; and have dominion over the fish of the sea and over the birds of the air and over every living thing that moves upon the earth.'

To the authors of the Bible, wilderness had a central position in their accounts as both a descriptive and as a symbolic concept. To the ancient Hebrews, wilderness was 'the environment of evil, a kind of hell' in which the wasteland was identified with God's curse. Paradise, or Eden, was the antithesis of wilderness. The story of Adam and Eve's dismissal from the Garden of Eden, from a watered, lush paradise to a 'cursed' land of 'thorns and thistles', reinforced in western thought the notion that wilderness and paradise were both physical and spiritual opposites. Isaiah (51:3), for instance, contains the promise that God will comfort Zion and 'make her wilderness like Eden, her desert like the garden of the Lord', while Joel (2:3) stated that 'the land is like the garden of Eden before them, but after them a desolate wilderness'.

The experience of the Israelites during the Exodus added another dimension to the Judaeo-Christian attitude towards wilderness. For 40 years the Jews, led by Moses, wandered in the 'howling waste of the wilderness' (Deuteronomy 32:10) that was the Sinai peninsula (Funk 1959). The wilderness, in this instance, was not only a place where they were punished by God for their sins but also a place where they could prove themselves worthy of the Lord and make ready for the promised land.

Indeed, it was precisely because it was unoccupied that it 'could be a refuge as well as a disciplinary force'.

The experience of the Exodus helped to establish a tradition of going to the wilderness 'for freedom and purification of faith'. Elijah spent 40 days in the wilderness in order to draw guidance and inspiration from God. John the Baptist was the voice crying in the wilderness to prepare for the coming of the Messiah, while Christ himself 'was led by the spirit into the wilderness to be tempted by the devil'. It was through the environment of evil and hardship, characteristic of the dominant Judaeo-Christian perception of the wilderness, that spiritual catharsis could occur, a sentiment that exists through to this day. The example of the prophets venturing into the wilderness was followed by early Christian ascetics. Hermits and monks established themselves in wilderness surroundings in order to avoid the temptations of earthly wealth and pleasure and to find a solitude conducive to spiritual ideals. As Tuan (1974:148) recorded:

The monastic community in the wilderness was a model of paradise set in an unredeemed world. Wilderness was often perceived as the haunt of demons but in the neighbourhood of the monastery it could acquire some of the harmony of redeemed nature and the animals in it, like their human suzerains in the monastery, lived in peace.

The desert ascetics drew on an appreciation of nature that sprang from the Bible itself. As Glacken (1967:151) observed, 'The intense otherworldliness and rejection of the beauties of nature because they turn men away from the contemplation of God are elaborated upon far more in theological writings than in the Bible itself'. The desert monks lived in the solitude of the wilderness to remove themselves from man, not from nature. Psalm 104 provides one of the clearest statements of the existence of a sympathetic attitude in Christianity towards nature, noting that everything in nature has its place in a divine order: 'the high mountains are for the wild goats; the rocks are a refuge for the badgers'. 'O Lord, how manifold are thy works! In wisdom hast thou made them all' (Psalm 104:24). As Glacken (1967:157) noted:

It is not to be wondered at that Psalm 104 has been quoted so often by thinkers sympathetic to the design argument and the physico-theological proof for the existence of God. The life, beauty, activity, order, and reasonableness in nature are described without mysteries, joyously - even triumphantly. God is separate from nature but he may be understood in part from it.

The theme of the wisdom of the Lord being shown in the order of nature was similarly indicated elsewhere in the Bible. The psalmist in Psalm 8:1 exclaimed: 'O Lord, our Lord, how majestic is thy name in all the earth!' The notion that 'The heavens are telling the glory of God; and the firmament proclaims his handiwork' proved to be influential throughout Christendom in the Dark and Middle Ages, although by no means enabling a universally sympathetic attitude towards nature. Nature came to be regarded as a book which could reveal the works of the Lord in a manner similar to the Scriptures. In the early exegetical writings God was regarded as being made manifest in his works.'There is a book of nature which when read along with the book of God, allows men to know and understand Him and his creation; not only man but nature suffered from the curse after the Fall; one may admire and love the beauty of the earth if this love and admiration is associated with the love of God'. This view of nature played an important role in establishing a favourable attitude towards wild country. St Augustine (in Glacken 1967:204) wrote, 'Some people in order to discover God, read books. But there is a great book: the very appearance of created things.' Pulpit eloquence was 'adopted by medieval mystico-philosophical speculation, and finally passed into common usage'.

Reading the book of nature for the word of God was eventually to lead to the reading of nature itself, but the notion of nature as a book was also to prepare the way for the development of a natural theology in the writings of St Francis of Assisi, St Bonaventura and Ramon Sibiude. To St Francis, living creatures were not only symbols, but were also 'placed on earth for God's own purposes (not for man's), and they, like man, praise God'. St Francis' theology represented a revolutionary change in Christian attitudes towards nature because of the distinct break they make from the anthropocentric nature of earlier theology.

Upon the foundation built by the natural theologians and their intellectual heirs, such as John Ray and Gilbert White, came to be built the framework for the discovery of nature by the Romantic movement. Nevertheless, despite a continuing appreciation of nature as part of God's divine presence by some theologians, the dominant attitude in the Judaeo-Christian tradition until the seventeenth century was that true appreciation of God could only be gained by looking inwards, not out at nature. Nature was provided for man to utilise. Wilderness and wild lands were to be tamed and cultivated to display the divine order as interpreted by man.

The dominant Judaeo-Christian view of wilderness may be contrasted with that of eastern religions. In eastern thought, wilderness 'did not have an unholy or evil connotation but was venerated as the symbol and even the very essence of the deity'. The aesthetic appreciation of wild land began to change far earlier in the Orient than in the West. By the fourth century AD, for instance, large numbers of people in China had begun to find an aesthetic appeal in mountains, whereas they were still seen as objects of fear in Europe (Nicholson 1962; Tuan 1974).

Eastern faiths such as Shinto and Taoism 'fostered love of wilderness rather than hatred' (Nash 1982:21). Shinto deified nature in favour of pastoral scenes. The polarity that existed between city and wilderness in the Judaeo-Christian experience did not exist outside European cultural tradition (Callicott 1982). Western civilisation has tended to dominate, rather than adapt, to its surrounding landscape whereas traditional eastern and non-European cultures have tended to attempt to blend into their surroundings. As Tuan (1974:148) noted, 'In the traditions of Taoist China and pre-Dorian Greece, nature imparted virtue or power. In the Christian tradition sanctifying power is invested in man, God's vice regent, rather than nature.' However, it should be emphasised that Oriental civilisations, such as those of China, India and Japan, have had highly destructive impacts on the environment and will continue to do so.

The attitude of different cultures to nature and, hence, wilderness is important. As Eidsvik (1980, 1985) has recognised, wilderness has only recently taken on global meaning with the increasing dominance of western culture throughout the world. The perception of wilderness as an alien landscape of fear is derived from the Northern European set of attitudes towards nature, where the Judaeo-Christian perception of nature became combined with the Teutonic fear of the vast northern forests. It is perhaps of no coincidence therefore that the creation of designated wilderness areas began in lands occupied by peoples who have inherited European cultural attitudes. However, despite retaining something of its original attributes the meaning of wilderness has changed substantially over time and now incorporates wider scientific and conservation values.

The classic example of changing popular attitudes towards wilderness is witnessed in the history of the evolution of the wilderness concept in the United States. The founding fathers of the American colonies saw the wild lands before them in classical biblical terms, and although attitudes towards wilderness did change gradually through the seventeenth and eighteenth centuries it was not until the late eighteenth century that positive appreciation of American nature began to emerge. The political independence of the American nation found cultural expression in the extolment of the virtues of American natural scenery. However, a similar cultural expression was not to be found in colonial Canada where untamed nature still assumed the guise of a landscape of fear. Nevertheless, America's cultural independence from the Old World produced a desire to laud the moral purity of the wild forests and mountains of the New World, untainted as they were by the domination of things European, a cultural movement which, perhaps somewhat ironically, sprang from the Romantic movement then sweeping Europe.

The American Romantic movement laid the groundwork upon which a popular appreciation of the value of wild land would come to be based. Artistic, literary and political perceptions of the importance of contact with wild nature provided the stimulus for the creation of positive cultural attitudes towards the American wilderness. Once positive attitudes towards primitive, unordered nature had developed then the emergence of individuals and societies dedicated to the preservation of wilderness values was only a short step away. However, an appreciation of the aesthetic values of wild land was countered by the utilitarian ethic that dominated American society.

The majority of Americans saw the land as an object to be conquered and made productive. The first reservations for the preservation of scenery therefore tended to be established in areas that were judged to be wastelands that had no economic value in terms of agriculture, grazing, lumbering or mining. The aesthetic value of wilderness was upheld by national parks and reserves which were intended to protect national scenic monuments that expressed the cultural independence of America in addition to providing for the development of the area through the tourist dollar.

Monumentalism was characterised by the belief that natural sites, such as Niagara Falls or the Rockies, were grand, noble and elevated in idea and had something of the enduring, stable and timeless nature of the great architecture of Europe, and proved a significant theme in the establishment of American parks.

Although the national parks in Australia, Canada and New Zealand did not assume the same importance as national monuments, their development nevertheless parallels that of the American park system. The themes of aesthetic romanticism, recreation and the development of 'worthless' or 'waste' lands through tourism characterised the creation of the first national parks in Australia, Canada and New Zealand. Banff National Park in Canada was developed by the Canadian Pacific Railroad as a tourist spa. New Zealand's first parks had lodges and hostels established within them that matched the tourist developments in the North American parks. Australia's first parks, particularly those of Queensland and Tasmania, were also marked by the influence of the desire of government to boost tourism. However, the Australian parks were also noted for their establishment, in unison with railway development, as areas where city-dwellers could find mental restoration in recreation and communion with nature.

With the closing of the American frontier at the end of the nineteenth century the preservation of America's remaining wilderness received new impetus. A massive but unsuccessful public campaign by wilderness preservationists led by John Muir to protect Hetch Hetchy Valley in Yosemite National Park from a dam scheme, a conservation-minded President (Theodore Roosevelt) in the White House, and the emergence of economically oriented 'progressive conservation' under the leadership of Gifford Pinchot all led to wilderness preservation becoming a matter of public importance in the United States.

The United States Forest Service and National Park Service responded to pressures from recreationalists for the creation of designated wilderness areas. Contemporaneously, the development of the science of ecology led to a recognition of the scientific importance of preserving wilderness. The various elements of wilderness preservation blended together in the inter-war years to lay a framework for the establishment of legally protected wilderness areas.

Economic conservation and the development of a scientific perception of wilderness was also influential in Australia, Canada and New Zealand. In Australia, the publication of George Perkins Marsh's (1864 (1965)) book *Man and Nature* stimulated the colonial governments into establishing forest reserves. In addition, significant scientists such as Baron von Mueller, and bodies such as the Australasian Association for the Advancement of Science argued for the preservation of native flora and fauna in both Australia and New Zealand. However, the first national parks in Australia were created for reasons of aesthetics, tourism and recreation with science gaining little recognition. In Canada, progressive conservation proved influential in the creation of forest reserves, and it is significant to note that many of the early Canadian parks were established under forestry legislation. However, the preservation of wilderness lagged behind the efforts of the United States. The declaration of the Wilderness Act in 1964 marked the beginning of the current legislative era of wilderness preservation in the United States. Under the Wilderness Act wilderness is defined as 'an area where the earth and its community of life are untrammelled by man, where man himself is the visitor that does not remain'. The four defining qualities of wilderness areas protected under the Act are that such areas:

- Generally appear to be affected by the forces of nature, with the imprint of man substantially unnoticeable;
- Have outstanding opportunities for solitude or a primitive and unconfined type of recreation;
- Have at least 5,000 acres or be of sufficient size as to make practical its preservation and use in an unimpaired condition;
- May also contain ecological, geological or features of scientific, educational, scenic or historical value.

The protection of wilderness through legal means gave new impetus to the task of improving the process of defining and compiling a wilderness inventory as well as providing for its management, a process that is still continuing today in America as well as in countries such as Australia, which have tended to follow the American model for wilderness and national park protection.

Although wilderness in New Zealand is given administrative protection under a variety of acts, there is no specific legislation for the preservation of wilderness. Similarly, until late 1987 with the passing of the New South Wales Wilderness Act, no wilderness legislation had been enacted in Australia. In Canada, wilderness areas have received a degree of protection under provincial legislation. However, as in Australia and New Zealand, there is no national wilderness act. Yet, in recent years increasing attention has been given to the implications of international heritage agreements, such as the World Heritage Convention, as a mechanism for the preservation of wilderness and other natural areas of international significance.

NATIONAL PARKS AND WILDERNESS AREAS

Environmental history is a field concerned with the role and place of nature in human life. Research and scholarship on the environmental history of national parks and wilderness lies at the intersection of a number of fields of geographic and academic endeavour. Within geography, as with history, the increased awareness of the environment as a social, economic and political issue has led to geographers and historians attempting to chart the history of land use of a given region or site in order to increase understanding of its significance, values and present-day use. Such research is not just an academic exercise. As well as assisting in understanding how current natural resource management problems or user conflicts have developed, such research can also be used to develop interpretive material for visitors as part of a programme of heritage management, an area in which geographers are becoming increasingly involved. Cronan (1990) asserts that good work in environmental history incorporates three levels of analysis.

These are the dynamics of natural ecosystems in time (ecology), the political economies that people erect within these systems (economy), and the cognitive lenses through which people perceive those systems (the history of ideas). Geographers, with their integrative approach to environment, cultural landscapes and land use, would therefore seem to be ideally poised to work in this area. As Mark (1996:153) observed, 'Widening the scope of historical narrative has frequently resulted in more complex interpretation of the past and should point the way toward greater understanding of the past in heritage management.'

National parks are a major focus of heritage management but have been a relatively quiet back-water in traditional historical narrative. Environmental history, however, can place them within the larger context of interaction between nature and culture. For example, a number of extremely valuable park histories which highlight the role of tourism and outdoor recreation in park development have been written on the Yellowstone, Grand Canyon, Rocky Mountain, Olympic, Sequoia and Kings Canyon and Yosemite national parks in the United States; the Albertan and the Ontario national park systems in Canada, and with useful national overviews being provided by Nelson (1970), Hall (1992a) and Dearden and Rollins (1993).

Substantial methodological research is called for when undertaking research on environmental and park histories. In the New Worlds of North America and the Antipodes, travel accounts written during the period of initial European settlement have been utilised by scholars interested in historic environments. They often hope to establish a pre-European settlement landscape as a baseline from which to assess subsequent environmental change. One difficulty with using travel accounts, however, is that they are often written in places where the journalist is not actually travelling; instead the diarist is summarising past events at a convenient place. Another problem is how to tie the usually limited detail (little of which could be utilised quantitatively) to specific localities. The paucity of locality information is often present in even the best accounts, such as those left by collectors of natural history specimens.

The only site-specific records available in many areas about presettlement landscapes are land survey notes. These have been helpful in establishing a historic condition of some forests, riparian habitats and grasslands. Their reliability varies, however, because there can be limitations associated with insufficient description, bias in recording data, contract fraud and land use prior to survey. Another technique which is useful for developing a historical record of land use change or for reconstructing past environments or heritage sites is repeat photography. However, while such techniques may be useful for specific sites or attractions the photographic record of 'ordinary' landscapes, i.e. those which were not subject to the interest of visitors as a view or panorama, is more difficult to construct because of incomplete records.

Cultural landscape documentation is somewhat narrower in scope than environmental history because the question of nature's character is not so central.

Nevertheless, it emphasises change over time and represents a way of integrating nature with culture. In a park setting, its emphasis becomes one of design, material, change, function and use, with one of its main effects on heritage management being the broadening of the focus of historic preservation beyond buildings to the associated landscape and environmental context.

THE VALUES OF WILDERNESS

Decisions affecting environmental policies grow out of a political process, in which 'value choice, implicit and explicit ... orders the priorities of government and determines the commitment of resources within the public jurisdiction'. Therefore, in order to consider the means by which wilderness is utilised, it is essential to understand what the values of wilderness are. As Henning (1987:293) observed: 'In the end, the survival of the wilderness will depend upon values being a respected factor in the political and governmental process.'

The value of wilderness is not static. The value of a resource alters over time in accordance with changes in the needs and attitudes of society. As noted above, ideas of the values of primitive and wild land have shifted in relation to the changing perceptions of western culture. Nevertheless, the dynamic nature of the wilderness resource does not prevent an assessment of its values as they are seen in present-day society. Indeed, such an evaluation is essential to arguments as to why wilderness should be conserved.

Broadly defined, the values of wilderness may be classified as being either anthropocentric or biocentric in nature. The principal emphasis of the anthropocentric approach is that the value of wilderness emerges in its potential for direct human use. In contrast, 'the biocentric perspective places primary emphasis on the preservation of the natural order'. The former approach places societal above ecological values and emphasises recreational and aesthetic rather than environmental qualities. Both perspectives focus on human benefits. However, 'the important distinction between them is the extent to which these benefits are viewed as being independent of the naturalness of wilderness ecosystems'. A more radical, and increasingly popular, interpretation of the notion of the value of wilderness has been provided by what is often termed a deep ecology perspective. Deep ecologists argue that wilderness should be held as valuable not just because it satisfies a human need (instrumental value) but as an end in itself (intrinsically valuable). Instrumental anthropocentric values, derived from a Cartesian conception of nature, are regarded as being opposed to a holistic or systematic view 'in which we come to appreciate the symbiotic interdependencies of the natural world'.

The holistic view broadly corresponds with the ecological conception of wilderness. However, it goes further by arguing that 'the philosophical task is to try and provide adequate justification ... for a scheme of values according to which concern and sympathy for our environment is immediate and natural, and the desirability of protecting and preserving wilderness self-evident', rather than justified purely according to human needs.

We can, however, provide - and it is important that we do so - an answer to the question: 'What is the use of wilderness?' We certainly ought to preserve and protect wilderness areas as gymnasiums, as laboratories, as stockpiles of genetic diversity and as cathedrals. Each of these reasons provides a powerful and sufficient instrumental justification for their preservation. But note how the very posing of this question about the utility of wilderness reflects an anthropocentric system of values. From a genuinely ecocentric point of view the question, 'What is the use of wilderness?' would be as absurd as the question, 'What is the use of happiness?'

Hendee *et al.* (1978) identified three consistent themes in the values associated with wilderness: experiental, mental and moral restorational, and scientific. Experiental values highlight the importance of the 'wilderness experience' for recreationists and tourists. Several themes emerge in an examination of the wilderness experience including the aesthetic, the spiritual and the escapist. Given its essentially personal nature, the wilderness experience is extremely difficult to define.

Associated with the values of the wilderness experience is the idea that wilderness can provide mental and moral restoration for the individual in the face of modern civilisation. This values wilderness as a 'reservoir for renewal of mind and spirit' and in some cases offers 'an important sanctuary into which one can withdraw, either temporarily or permanently, to find respite'. This harks back to the biblical role of wilderness as a place of spiritual renewal and the simple life of Thoreau's Walden Pond. The encounter with wilderness is regarded as forcing the individual to rise to the physical challenge of wilderness with corresponding improvements in feelings of self-reliance and self-worth. As Ovington and Fox (1980:3) wrote: 'In the extreme', wilderness: generates a feeling of absolute aloneness, a feeling of sole dependence on one's own capacities as new sights, smells and tastes are encountered.... The challenge and the refreshing and recreating power of the unknown are provided by unadulterated natural wilderness large enough in space for us to get 'lost' in. Here it is possible once again to depend upon our own personal faculties and to hone our bodies and spirits.

Table. Components of the Wilderness Experience.

Component	Nature of experience	Examples
Aesthetic appreciation	Appreciation of wild nature	Leopold 1921, 1925; Marshall 1930; McKenry 1972a; Smith 1977; Hamilton-Smith 1980; Alexander 1984; Nash 1990.
Religious	The experience of God in the wilderness	McKenry 1972a; Hendee et al. 1978; Wright 1980; Hamilton-Smith 1980; Nash 1990.
Escapist	Finding freedom away from the constraints of city living	McKenry 1972a; Smith 1977; Hendee et al. 1978; Hamilton-Smith 1980; Hawes 1981.
Challenge	The satisfaction that occurs in overcoming dangerous situations and fully utilising physical skills	McKenry 1972a; Smith 1977; Gardner 1978; Hamilton-Smith 1980; Warboys 1980.
Historic/Romantic	The opportunity to re-live or imagine the experiences of pioneers of the 'frontier' that formed national culture	Leopold 1925; Smith 1977; Hamilton-Smith 1980; Ride 1980; Alexander 1984; Johnston 1985
Solitude	The pleasure of being alone in a wild setting	Lee 1977; Smith 1977; Hamilton-Smith 1980; Hawes 1981; Sinclair 1986.
Companionship	Paradoxically, in relation to the previous category, the desire to share the setting with companions	Lee 1977; Smith 1977; Hamilton-Smith 1980.
Discovery/Learning	The thrill of discovering or learning about nature in a natural setting	Smith 1977; Gardner 1978; Hamilton-Smith 1980.
Vicarious appreciation	The pleasure of knowing that wilderness exists without actually ever having seen it	McKenry 1977; Smith 1977; Hawes 1981; Johnston 1985.
Technology	Influence of technological change on outdoor activities	Marsh and Wall 1982.

The third major theme in the values associated with wilderness is that of the scientific values of wilderness. The preservation of wilderness is regarded as an essential component in the scientific study of the environment and man's impact on the environment. Furthermore, wilderness has increasingly come to assume tremendous economic importance because of the value of the genetic material that it contains. However, the multi-dimensional nature of the wilderness resource may lead to value conflicts over the use of wilderness areas.

A fourth theme which is inherent in the values of wilderness is that of economic worth. In addition to the economic significance of genetic resources, wilderness has importance as a tourist and recreation attraction. Indeed, the economic valuation of wilderness and natural areas has now become a critical factor in their designation, although it should be noted that the economic value of tourism has long been used to justify national park creation in areas that would otherwise be deemed worthless. Such a value may also be enhanced through international recognition such as that achieved through listing as a World Heritage site.

Table. The scientific Values of Wilderness.

Value	Description
Genetic resources/ biodiversity	Large natural communities such as those provided for in wilderness areas can serve as sources of genetic materials which are potentially useful to man. As more of the world's natural ecosystems are removed or simplified the remaining natural areas will assume even greater importance as storehouses of genetic material.
Ecological research and biological monitoring	Wilderness areas provide protection for large natural ecosystems. Within these areas a variety of research on ecological processes can occur. Research may consist of ecosystem dynamics, comparative ecology, ethology, surveys of fauna and flora, and the relationship of base ecological data to environmental change.
Environmental baselines	Wilderness areas, representative of particular biomes, can be used as reference areas in the monitoring of environmental change both within the biome and on a global scale.
The evolutionary	Wilderness areas provide the conditions in which the evolutionary continuum of adaptation, continuum extinction and speciation can occur without the direct interference of humans.
Long term	Wilderness areas provide conditions in which flora and fauna conservation can occur, particularly for those species which require large territories to reproduce and be preserved.

McKenry (1977) has provided an analysis of the degree to which the values of wilderness are disrupted by activities such as forestry, mining, grazing and road construction. As soon as the characteristics of the wilderness resource are infringed through the activities of western man then wilderness values are reduced. Emphasis is placed upon the impacts of western society, rather than those of technologically underdeveloped peoples, because as the following discussion will illustrate, the present-day concept of wilderness is a product of western thought. Indeed, geographers such as Nelson (1982, 1986) have argued for the adoption of a human-ecological approach to wilderness and park management which sees the incorporation of the attitudes and practices of indigenous peoples as being an essential part of a contemporary perspective on the notion of wilderness.

IDENTIFYING WILDERNESS

Although the values of wilderness are well recognised, for management and legislative purposes such values need to be turned into a method by which wilderness values can be mapped in space. In addition, such a process can assist in the provision of conservation, scientific and tourism information, technical advice, recognition of management issues and objectives, the integration of conservation and development, and the design of a national conservation system. According to Dasmann's (1973:12) classification of national parks and equivalent reserves, wilderness areas have two principal purposes: 'that of protecting nature (defined as primary) and that of providing recreation for those capable of enduring the vicissitudes of wilderness travel by primitive means.' These purposes reflect the values of wilderness identified in the previous section. 'The area is maintained in a state in which its wilderness or primitive appearance is not impaired by any form of development, and in which the continued existence of indigenous animal and plant species is assured'. However, unlike some of the use limitations of strict natural areas, wilderness is available to recreationists.

Table. Interactions Between Values Associated with Wilderness and Common Disruptive Activities

Common disruptive activities	Water resources	Traditional aboriginal habitat	Wildlife resources and habitat	Plant resources and habitat	Research and education	Wilderness recreation resources	Vicarious appreciation of wilderness	Reserve resource pool
Hydro	1-2	5	3-4	3-4	4-5	4-5	4-5	4-5
Forestry	3-4	5	3-4	3-4	3-4	4-5	4-5	2-3
Mining	3-4	5	3-4	3-4	3-4	4-5	5	4-5
Agriculture	3-4	5	3-4	4-5	3-4	5	5	4-5
Grazing	3-4	4-5	2-3	3-4	2-3	3-4	3-4	2-3
Road	2-3	4-5	2-3	2-3	2-3	4-5	4-5	2-3
Tourism	3-4	5	3-4	2-3	2-3	4-5	4-5	2-3
Off-road	2-3	4-5	2-3	2-3	2-3	4-5	2-3	1-2
Scale of disruption to wilderness values 1 No incompatible interaction (i.e. mutually compatible) 2 Slightly incompatible 3 Substantial incompatibility 4 Slight compatibility only 5 Totally incompatible (i.e. mutually exclusive)								

NATIONAL PARKS AND INDIGENOUS PEOPLES

National parks are a western concept. National parks have their origins in the New World desire to conserve nature and appropriately aesthetic landscapes for economic development through tourism. Until recently, the creation of national parks was marked by the exclusion of aboriginal populations as undesirable elements in the 'natural' landscape. The drawing of boundaries between the natural parks and the rural human landscape available for agriculture, forestry, mining and/or grazing reflecting the Cartesian divide of western society has long sought to separate civilisation and wilderness. However, over the past three decades the separation between natural and cultural heritage has come to be seen as increasingly artificial. In part, this has been due to the renaissance of aboriginal and indigenous cultures in the New Worlds of North America and Australasia as well as greater assertion of native cultural values in post-colonial societies in Africa. Such developments have had enormous influence not only on the ways in which parks are managed but also on how they are established and recreated for tourist consumption.

The influence of the Romantic movement on the establishment of national parks was extremely significant (Hall 1992a). For example, the first call for the establishment of national parks in the US came in 1832 from an artist, George Catlin, who on seeing the slaughter of buffalo on the Great Plains described the waste of animals and humankind to be a 'melancholy contemplation', but he found it 'splendid' when he imagined that there might be in the future '(by some great protecting policy of government) ... a magnificent park', which preserved the Animal and the North American Indian 'in their pristine beauty and wildness'.

'What a beautiful and thrilling specimen for America to preserve and hold up to the view of her refined citizens and the world, in future ages! A nation's Park, containing man and beast, in all the wild and freshness of their nature's beauty!' Catlin's seminal call for 'a nation's park' highlighted the new mood in America towards wilderness. Almost exactly 40 years after Catlin's journal entry, President Ulysses S. Grant signed an Act establishing Yellowstone Park, creating the institution of which Catlin desired 'the reputation of having been the founder' (Catlin 1968:8, 9).

Similarly, John Matson (1892) compared the efforts made in New Zealand to protect wildlife with the absence of such attempts in the Australian colonies and appealed for the creation of 'indigenous parks' in order to preserve the animal and bird life of Australasia. Significantly, Matson quoted a New Zealand 'poet', George Phipps Williams, to conclude his case for the preservation of wildlife and their habitat, in a manner which is reminiscent of Catlin:

- Out in the wilderness is there no desolate space,
- Which you may spare to the brutes of indigenous race?

- Grant us the shelter we need from the pitiless chase.
- Gone are the stateliest forms of the apteryx kind,
- Short is the space that the kiwi is lagging behind;
- Soon you shall painfully seek what you never shall find.
- (George Phipps Williams, *A Plea of Despair*, in Matson 1892:359)

Williams' comments, along with those of Catlin, may seem ill at ease with political and cultural sensibilities at the beginning of the twenty-first century. However, in the late nineteenth century such sentiments were common-place. Maori, along with other aboriginal peoples, were seen as the remnant of a dying race and placing them in parks and reserves, so long as the land was not required for other economic purposes, was often seen as the most appropriate course of action. Despite the initial Romantic sentiments which helped create the momentum for the establishment of parks, humans, including the aboriginal peoples who had often created the park landscapes through their hunting and food-gathering practices, were excluded from the parks through loss of ownership and access rights, management and regulatory actions and policing strategies.

Such measures were the result of ecological and cultural blindness at best, and outright racism and cultural imperialism at worst, with park boundaries serving as the demarcation between the natural and the cultural in European eyes. Although the political status of aboriginal peoples is still a highly contested issue in many societies, substantial shifts have occurred in management practices with respect to aboriginal peoples and their role in national parks over the past 100 years. A number of broad social and political factors in relation to the overall rights of aboriginal peoples have contributed to these changes, including:

- A renaissance of aboriginal culture in a number of western countries which has led to renewed pride in traditional cultural practices;
- The withdrawal of colonial powers in African and Asian states and the development of new modes of administration and management;
- The assertion of ownership of and/or access to natural resources through treaty settlements and other legal channels;
- Changed government policies with respect to native peoples which has led to greater economic and political self-determination;
- Greater political influence of aboriginal peoples.

The management of national parks has been substantially affected and a number of changes have occurred at the micro-level in parallel to the shifts which have occurred at the macro-political level.

Hall (2000c) identified several factors:

- A recognition that many supposedly 'natural' landscapes are the product of a long period of aboriginal occupancy which has created a series of ecological conditions and relationships which are dependent on certain types of human behaviour. This means that the traditional knowledge of native peoples becomes a vital ingredient in effective ecosystem management;

- Growth of the tourist appeal of some indigenous cultural attractions.
- Greater emphasis by park management authorities on the role of various stakeholder groups, including native peoples, in park management and the development of appropriate co-operative management strategies;
- Changed park management practices and strategies which are aimed at specifically satisfying the concerns and needs of native peoples including, in some cases, the management of national park lands owned by native peoples which are then leased to park management agencies.

Dasmann's recognition of wilderness as a discrete land-use category did not appear in the IUCN's (1978) eventual categorisation of conservation areas. However, this does not imply that wilderness has only minimal value as a form of conservation land use. Rather it is a recognition of the difficulties in transferring the notion of wilderness from a North American to a more universal setting (Eidsvik 1985). Nevertheless, increased public awareness of the environment, sustainable development, World Heritage areas, Biosphere Reserves and other sites of international conservation significance highlight the worldwide attention given to the preservation of the earth's remaining wilderness areas. Indeed, the IUCN General Assembly in 1984 recommended 'that all nations identify, designate and protect their wilderness areas on both public and private lands' (Resolution 16/34 in Eidsvik 1987:19). Yet such measures need to have a basis by which wilderness may be identified if it is to succeed. Although a wilderness inventory has been undertaken in the United States, probably the most sustained research programme on wilderness identification occurred in Australia, and it is to this case study that we now turn.

CASE STUDY: WILDERNESS INVENTORY IN AUSTRALIA

One of the key elements in preserving wilderness is the identification of areas of high-quality wilderness that can be incorporated into a national wilderness system. In 1985 the Australian Conservation Foundation and other conservation groups, particularly the Wilderness Society, led the Working Group on Management of National Parks of the Australian Council of Nature and Conservation Ministers (CONCOM) to examine the establishment of a nationwide system of wilderness areas.

CONCOM (1985:7) recommended that 'an inventory of potential wilderness areas should be compiled by all states and Territories, where possible in consultation with user groups.

The inventory would assess areas within existing parks and extend to other land if appropriate. It would be desirable for a consistent approach to be adopted for the surveys.' However, the hopes of CONCOM were not met. Despite both the quality and quantity of research, no consistent approach to evaluating wilderness in Australia has been accepted by all participants in the process of wilderness identification and management, although the Australian Heritage Commission's National Wilderness Inventory Programme came closest. This situation may be due to the academic nature of most wilderness research, the geographic differences between regions, the politics of wilderness preservation, or it may well derive from the intrinsic intangibility of wilderness (Hall 1987, 1992a). Nevertheless, the identification of primitive and remote areas will obviously be critical to the protection and management of wilderness.

WILDERNESS INVENTORIES

Planners and managers now require detailed information to assist in the identification of areas suitable for designation and protection as wilderness, to monitor the status of the resource, and to develop appropriate and effective management prescriptions. There is also a need for the capacity to assess the impact on wilderness of various development proposals so that alternatives may be examined and a suitable response determined.

Definition is the major problem in the inventory of wilderness. The definition, and its accompanying criteria, provide the source from which all else flows. Two different conceptions of wilderness are generally recognised, one anthropocentric, the other biocentric or ecocentric. From the anthropocentric view, wilderness is seen from a perspective in which human needs are considered paramount. Adherents of this approach tend to ascribe a recreational role to wilderness. In contrast, the biocentric approach defines 'wilderness in ecological terms and [equates] wilderness quality with a relative lack of human disturbance'.

The recreational values of wilderness have tended to be dominant in wilderness literature. This is partly the result of the 'Americanisation' of the wilderness concept, where the predominantly recreational perspective of American research has coloured most other studies, but it is also probably related to the way in which the wilderness concept has developed. Nevertheless, over recent years the biocentric concept of wilderness has become increasingly important in research. This increased priority is most likely related to the growth of importance of ecological research relative to recreational research in national park and reserve management and to a recognition that fauna and flora have an intrinsic right to exist.

For each inventory the study area, wilderness definition, dimensional criteria, status of coastal areas, database and status of roadworks is recorded. The status of roadworks criterion is included because it provides a basis of comparison with the 'roadless area' concept which permeates American notions of wilderness and also illustrates one of the major problems in standardising wilderness criteria. As Lesslie and Taylor (1983:23) observed, 'road definition is a major point of contention in the general wilderness literature. Controversy centres on the qualities which make a high grade road an unacceptable intrusion into wilderness and a low grade road a detrimental but nevertheless acceptable intrusion.'

The first Australian study of wilderness of any consequence, the wilderness study of eastern New South Wales and south-east Queensland by Helman *et al.* was designed as a model for future Australian wilderness inventories and it was applied in Victoria and Tasmania. However, the inventory procedures may not be valid for arid and semi-arid environments because they were undertaken in relatively humid, forested and mountainous environments; also, they failed to recognise the remoteness and primitiveness which constitute the key qualities of wilderness. Stanton and Morgan's (1977) study of Queensland identified four key areas as fitting rigid conservation-based criteria. Twenty-four other areas were identified as being 'equivalent to the wilderness areas delineated by Helman *et al.* (1976) in their study of eastern Australia'.

Kirkpatrick's (1980) study of south-west Tasmania identified wilderness as a recreational resource, 'as land remote from access by mechanised vehicles, and from within which there is little or no consciousness of the environmental disturbance of western man'. Kirkpatrick assigned absolute wilderness quality scores, which had not been attempted in Australian wilderness inventories, although it was characteristic of American ones. However, unlike the United States inventories, Kirkpatrick focused on the more readily quantifiable characteristics of wilderness: remoteness and primitiveness.

Remoteness and primitiveness are the two essential attributes of wilderness. Remoteness is measured 'as the walking time from the nearest access point for mechanised vehicles' while primitiveness, which 'has visual, aural and mental components', is 'determined from measures of the arc of visibility of any disturbance ... and the distance to the nearest disturbance'. The identification of remoteness and primitiveness as the essential attributes of a wilderness area helped create the methodological basis for the wilderness inventory of South Australia by Lesslie and Taylor (1983, 1985) and provides the basis for a national survey of wilderness.

Lesslie and Taylor (1983) saw previous wilderness inventory procedures as unsatisfactory because they sought to express a relative concept in absolute terms. They identified four indicators of wilderness quality: remoteness from settlement, remoteness from access, aesthetic primitiveness (or naturalness) and biophysical primitiveness (or naturalness). These indicators were used to provide an inventory of relatively high-quality wilderness areas in South Australia. The attributes of remoteness and primitiveness may be expressed as part of a continuum which indicates the relative wilderness quality of a region. A continuum approach can accommodate the ecological and recreational characteristics of a far wider range of environments than can the inventories formulated for the higher rainfall areas of Australia.

The variation in approaches to wilderness inventory in Australia is 'systematic of confusion concerning the definition of wilderness, since areas which satisfy biocentric considerations need not be consistent with areas which satisfy anthropocentric considerations'.

The area required to satisfy recreational criteria for wilderness may be much smaller than the area required for maintaining the ecological balance of a region. Therefore, the experiental criterion for wilderness remains substantially different to ecological criterion and the concept of 'wilderness experience' must be separated from that of 'wilderness area'. As Lesslie and Taylor (1983:14) observed, there has been an 'almost universal tendency to confuse the *benefits derived from wilderness* with the *nature of wilderness itself*', a point of crucial importance in the delineation, inventory and management of wilderness.

Hence, the two attributes which are definitive of wilderness, *remoteness* from the presence and influences of settled people, and *primitiveness*, the absence of environmental disturbance by settled people, need to be based at the high-quality end of the wilderness continuum in order to accommodate the anthropocentric and biocentric dimensions of wilderness.

In Australia, the methodology of Lesslie and Taylor (1983), and modified in the 1987 Victorian inventory, comes closest to achieving this goal and has served as the model for other studies within the Australian Heritage Commission's National Wilderness Inventory. Furthermore, Lesslie *et al.*'s (1987) methodology is able to indicate low-quality wilderness areas which are not indicated in an inventory along the lines of Helman *et al.* (1976), but which may nevertheless be of significant conservation and recreation value.

In 1987 the Australian government, through the Australian Heritage Commission, initiated a National Wilderness Inventory (NWI) to provide information in order to improve decisions about wilderness conservation. This action was 'a result of its concern over the rapid decline in area and quality of relatively remote and natural lands in Australia and in recognition that an inventory of the remaining resource was the necessary first step in formulating appropriate measures for conservation and management'. The NWI had three main emphases: to compile a national wilderness database; to refine database maintenance procedures and analytical techniques; and to produce information relevant to policy and management issues.

Several inventories were conducted under the auspices of the National Wilderness Inventory, including surveys of Victoria; Tasmania. In 1990 the NWI was accelerated to provide a comprehensive coverage for the whole of Australia.

'The evaluation of wilderness in the National Wilderness Inventory is based upon the notion of wilderness quality as a continuum of remote and natural conditions from pristine to urban'.

A spatial framework utilising the techniques of Geographic Information Systems (GIS) is used to sample variation in values of the four wilderness quality indicators. There are two major advantages in using a GIS to formulate wilderness evaluation databases. First, the approach is open-ended: new data may be added and current data modified.

Indeed, in Australia, 'information about access and landuse is often poorly recorded and lacking in currency. Even the most recently available information may be inaccurate and out of date. This makes the compilation of a reliable database difficult, particularly because of the necessary dependence on published sources for much of the required information' (Lesslie *et al.* 1991b: 13). Second, the process is spatially flexible, enabling scale to be matched to purpose. Furthermore, maps showing the distribution of wilderness identified in the inventory can be generated rapidly and efficiently in order to assist decision-making.

FROM IDENTIFICATION TO PRESERVATION

The purpose of wilderness inventory in Australia has, on the whole, been to identify areas of wilderness quality for the possible enactment of conservation measures by government. Inventories provide a systematic means of ensuring the designation areas of high environmental quality. 'Recognition of wilderness is the necessary first step towards protecting, appreciating and managing wilderness areas'. However, identifying an area as wilderness does not, by itself, ensure that its wilderness qualities can be maintained; this may only be done through the appropriate legislation and management. 'Decisions of this kind are inevitably judgemental, requiring comparative assessments of the social worth of alternative and often conflicting landuse opportunities' (Lesslie *et al.* 1988a: v). Nevertheless, from a management perspective:

The delimitation of wilderness management boundaries for any particular location is a separate question. The major point to be made here is that the commonly accepted practice of placing a wilderness management boundary around a location of high wilderness quality, and ensuring no wilderness degrading activities take place within, will not ensure the retention of high wilderness quality. For instance, a development in lesser quality wilderness on the margin of an area of higher quality wilderness will reduce wilderness quality within the higher quality area.

The lesson to be drawn from this is that areas of lower quality wilderness which fringe areas of high quality are important in maintaining these quality areas. In order to ensure protection of wilderness quality a wilderness management area therefore must include all marginal areas.

Ccncom (1986:8) proposed that the following key criteria be used to identify and evaluate land which has potential as a wilderness area:

- Remoteness and size: a large area, preferably in excess of 25,000 hectares, where visitors may experience remoteness from roads and other facilities.
- Evidence of people: an area with minimal evidence of alteration by modern technology.

However, CONCOM (1985) was not sure that these criteria would reflect differences in landscape and ecological diversity across Australia. The CONCOM criteria may be contrasted with the United States wilderness legislation which suggests as a guideline for minimum wilderness size an area of 5,000 acres (2,023 ha), and where impacted ecosystems may be included if they contribute to the viability and integrity of the wilderness area.

One of the ironies of the criteria for wilderness identification chosen by CONCOM is that they exclude many of the wilderness areas that have already been established under state legislation! According to CONCOM (1986:4), 'Wilderness areas are established to provide opportunities for the visitor to enjoy solitude, inspiration and empathy with his or her natural surroundings'.

The CONCOM position is to preserve the 'wilderness experience', not necessarily the intrinsic qualities of wilderness. However, to preserve wilderness mainly for recreation values is to ignore the significant range of other values of a wilderness area. Unlike the United States government, the Australian government does not have vast areas of federal land upon which wilderness legislation would be readily enforceable. State governments, which under the Australian constitution have primary control over land use, regard the reservation of wilderness areas under appropriate legislation as being a state responsibility.

This situation therefore means that unless the Federal Government exercises its constitutional powers in relation to the environment, any national wilderness system may be achieved only through consensus between the Commonwealth and the various state and Territory governments. Nevertheless, the NWI still serves as a valuable management tool by which to evaluate the potential loss of wilderness quality which new developments might bring and the potential corresponding loss of visitor satisfaction.

- Identification of high value natural resources may not necessarily lead to subsequent action for conservation within the policy and planning process.
- Remoteness and primitiveness are the two essential attributes of wilderness.
- GIS is an extremely valuable tool with which to undertake natural resource inventories.

4

Tectonics

Tectonics is concerned with the processes which control the structure and properties of the Earth's crust, and its evolution through time. In particular, it describes the processes of mountain building, the growth and behavior of the strong, old cores of continents known as cratons, and the ways in which the relatively rigid plates that comprise the Earth's outer shell interact with each other. Tectonics also provides a framework to understand the earthquake and volcanic belts which directly affect much of the global population. Tectonic studies are important for understanding erosion patterns in geomorphology and as guides for the economic geologist searching for petroleum and metallic ores.

EXTENSIONAL TECTONICS

Extensional tectonics is concerned with the structures formed, and the tectonic processes associated with, the stretching of the crust or lithosphere.

DEFORMATION STYLES

The types of structure and the geometries formed depend on the amount of stretching involved. Stretching is generally measured using the parameter β, known as the *beta factor* where $\beta = \frac{t_0}{t_1}$, t_0 is the initial crustal thickness and t_1 is the final crustal thickness. It is also the equivalent of the strain parameter *stretch*.

- *Low beta factor:* In areas of relatively low crustal stretching, the dominant structures are high to moderate angle normal faults, with associated half grabens and tilted fault blocks.
- *High beta factor:* In areas of high crustal stretching, individual extensional faults may become rotated to too low a dip to remain active and a new set of faults may be generated. Large displacements may juxtapose syntectonic sediments against metamorphic rocks of the mid to lower crust and such structures are called detachment faults. In some cases the detachments are folded such that the

metamorphic rocks are exposed within antiformal closures and these are known as metamorphic core complexes.

- *Passive margins:* Passive margins above a weak layer develop a specific set of extensional structures. Large listric regional (i.e. dipping towards the ocean) faults are developed with rollover anticlines and related crestal collapse grabens. On some margins, such as the Niger Delta, large counter-regional faults are observed, dipping back towards the continent, forming large grabenal mini-basins with antithetic regional faults.

GEOLOGICAL ENVIRONMENTS ASSOCIATED WITH EXTENSIONAL TECTONICS

Areas of extensional tectonics are typically associated with:

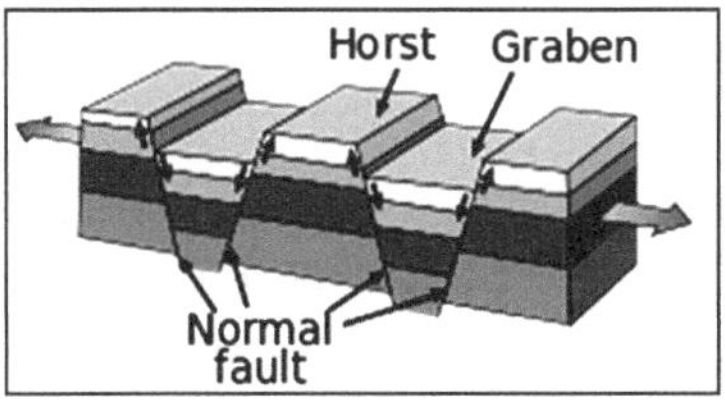

Fig. Horst and graben structure, typical rift related structure (direction of extension shown by red arrows).

Continental rifts

Rifts are linear zones of localized crustal extension. They range in width from somewhat less than 100 km up to several hundred km, consisting of one or more normal faults and related fault blocks. In individual rift segments one polarity (i.e. dip direction) normally dominates giving a half-graben geometry. Other common geometries include metamorphic core complexes and tilted blocks. Examples of active continental rifts are the Baikal Rift Zone and the East African Rift.

Divergent plate boundaries

Divergent plate boundaries are zones of active extension as the crust newly formed at the mid-ocean ridge system becomes involved in the opening process.

Gravitational spreading of zones of thickened crust

Zones of thickened crust, such as those formed during continent-continent collision tend to spread laterally; this spreading occurs even when the collisional event is still in progress. After the collision has finished the zone of thickened crust generally undergoes gravitational collapse, often with the formation of very large extensional faults. Large-scale Devonian extension, for example, followed immediately after the end of the Caledonian orogeny particularly in East Greenland and western Norway.

Releasing bends along strike-slip faults

When a strike-slip fault is offset along strike such as to create a gap i.e. a left-stepping bend on a sinistral fault, a zone of extension or transtension is generated. Such bends are known as *releasing bends* or *extensional stepovers* and often form pull-apart basins or *rhombochasms*. Examples of active pull-apart basins include the Dead Sea, formed at a left-stepping offset of the sinistral sense Dead Sea Transform system, and the Sea of Marmara, formed at a right-stepping offset on the dextral sense North Anatolian Fault system.

Back-arc basins

Back-arc basins form behind many subduction zones due to the effects of oceanic trench roll-back which leads to a zone of extension parallel to the island arc.

Passive margins

A passive margin built out over a weaker layer, such as an overpressured mudstone or salt, tends to spread laterally under its own weight. The inboard part of the sedimentary prism is affected by extensional faulting, balanced by outboard shortening.

THRUST TECTONICS

Thrust tectonics or contractional tectonics is concerned with the structures formed, and the tectonic processes associated with, the shortening and thickening of the crust or lithosphere.

DEFORMATION STYLES

In areas of thrust tectonics two main styles are recognized; thin-skinned deformation and thick-skinned deformation. The distinction is important as attempts to structurally restore the deformation will give very different results depending on the assumed geometry.

- *Thin-skinned deformation:* Thin-skinned deformation refers to shortening that only involves the sedimentary cover. This style is typical of many fold and thrust belts developed in the foreland of a collisional zone. This is particularly the case where a good basal decollement exists such as salt or a zone of high pore fluid pressure.
- *Thick-skinned deformation:* Thick-skinned deformation refers to shortening that involves basement rocks rather than just the overlying cover. This type of geometry is typically found in the hinterland of a collisional zone. This style may also occur in the foreland where no effective decollement surface is present or where pre-existing extensional rift structures may be inverted.

GEOLOGICAL ENVIRONMENTS ASSOCIATED WITH THRUST TECTONICS

- *Collisional zones:* The most significant areas of thrust tectonics are associated with destructive plate boundaries leading to the formation of orogenic belts. The two main types are: the collision of two continental tectonic plates (for example the Arabian and Eurasian plates, which formed the Zagros fold and thrust belt) and collisions between a continent and an island arc such as that which formed Taiwan.
- *Restraining bends on strike-slip faults:* When a strike-slip fault is offset along strike such that the resulting bend in the fault hinders easy movement, e.g. a right stepping bend on a sinistral (left-lateral) fault, this will cause local shortening or transpression. Examples include the 'Big Bend' region of the San Andreas fault, and parts of the Dead Sea Transform.
- *Passive margins:* Passive margins are characterised by large prisms of sedimentary material deposited since the original break-up of a continent associated with formation of a new spreading centre. This wedge of material will tend to spread under gravity and, where an effective detachment layer is present such as salt, the extensional faulting that forms at the landward side will be balanced at the front of the wedge by a series of toe-thrusts. Examples include the outboard part of the Niger delta (with an overpressured mudstone detachment) and the Angola margin (with a salt detachment).

STRIKE-SLIP TECTONICS

Strike-slip tectonics is concerned with the structures formed by, and the tectonic processes associated with, zones of lateral displacement within the crust or lithosphere.

DEFORMATION STYLES

Riedel shear structures

In the early stages of strike-slip fault formation, displacement within basement rocks produces characteristic fault structures within the overlying cover. This will also be the case where an active strike-slip zone lies within an area of continuing sedimentation. At low levels of strain the overall simple shear causes a set of small faults to form. The dominant set, known as R shears, form at about 15° to the underlying fault with the same shear sense. The R shears are then linked by a second set, the R' shear that form at about 75° to the main fault trace. These two fault orientations can be understood as conjugate fault sets at 30° to the short axis of the instantaneous strain ellipse associated with the simple shear strain field caused by the displacements applied at the base of the cover sequence. With further displacement the Riedel fault segments will tend to become fully linked, often with the development of a further set of shears known as 'P shears', which are roughly symmetrical to the R shears with respect to the overall shear direction, until a throughgoing fault is formed. The somewhat oblique segments will link downwards into the fault at the base of the cover sequence with a helicoidal geometry.

Flower structures

In detail many strike-slip faults at surface consist of en echelon and/or braided segments in many cases probably inherited from previously formed Riedel shears. In cross-section the displacements are dominantly reverse or normal in type depending on whether the overall fault geometry is transpressional (i.e. with a small component of shortening) or transtensional (with a small component of extension). As the faults tend to join downwards onto a single strand in basement, the geometry has led to these being termed *flower structure*. Fault zones with dominantly reverse faulting are known as *positive flowers*, those with dominantly normal offsets are known as *negative flowers*. The identification of such structures, particularly where positive and negative flowers are developed on different segments of the same fault, are regarded as reliable indicators of strike-slip.

Strike slip duplexes

Strike slip duplexes occur at the step over regions of faults, forming a lens shaped near parallel arrays of horses. These occur between two or more large bounding faults which usually have large displacement.

An idealized strike-slip fault runs in a straight line with a vertical dip and has only horizontal motion, thus there is no change in topography due to motion of the fault. In reality, as strike slip faults become large and developed, their behavior changes and becomes more complex. A long strike slip fault follows a staircase-like trajectory consisting of interspaced fault planes that follow the main fault direction. These sub parallel stretches are isolated by offsets at first, but over long periods of time they can become connected by step overs in order to accommodate the strike slip displacement. In long stretches of strike-slip the fault plane can start to curve, giving rise to structures similar to step overs.

Right lateral motion of a strike slip fault at a right step over (or overstep) gives rise to extensional bends characterised by zones of subsidence, local normal faults, and pull apart basins. On extensional duplexes, normal faults will accommodate the vertical motion, creating negative relief. Similarly, left stepping at a dextral fault generates contractional bends; shortening the step overs which is displayed by local reverse faults, push-up zones, and folds. On contractional duplex structures, thrust faults will accommodate vertical displacement rather than being folded, as the uplifting process is more energy efficient. Strike slip dulexes are passive structures; they form as a response to displacement of the bounding fault rather than by the stresses from plate motion. Each horse has a length that varies from half to twice the spacing between the bounding fault planes. Depending on the properties of the rocks and the fault, the duplexes will have different length ratios and will develop on either major or subtle offsets, although it is possible to observe duplex structures that develop on nearly straight fault segments. Because the motion of the duplexes may be heterogeneous, the individual horses can experience a rotation with a horizontal axis, which results in the formation of scissor faults. Scissor faults exhibit normal motion at one end of the horse and a thrust motion ant the other end. Because strike slip duplexes structures have more horizontal motion than vertical motion, they are best observed on a map rather than a vertical projection, and are a good indication that the main fault has a strike slip motion.

An example of strike slip duplexes were observed in the Lambertville sill, New Jersey. Flemington and the Hopewell faults, the two main faults in the region, experienced 3km of dip slip and over 20km of strike slip motions to accommodate regional extension. It is possible to trace the lensoidal structures which are interpreted as horses that form duplexes. The lens structures observed in the 3M quarry are 180 meters long and 10 meters wide. The main duplex is 30 m in length and other smaller duplexes are also present.

GEOLOGICAL ENVIRONMENTS ASSOCIATED WITH STRIKE-SLIP TECTONICS

Areas of strike-slip tectonics are associated with:

- *Oceanic transform boundaries:* Mid-ocean ridges are broken into segments offset from each other by transform faults. The active part of the transform links the two ridge segments. Some of these transforms can be very large, such as the Romanche fracture zone, whose active portion extends for about 300 km.
- *Continental transform boundaries:* Transform faults within continental plates include some of the best known examples of strike-slip structures, such as the San Andreas Fault, the Dead Sea Transform, the North Anatolian Fault and the Alpine Fault.
- *Lateral ramps in areas of extensional or contractional tectonics:* Major lateral offsets between large extensional or thrust faults are normally connected by diffuse or discrete zones of strike-slip deformation allowing transfer of the overall displacement between the structures.
- *Zones of oblique collision:* In most zones of continent-continent collision the relative movement of the plates is oblique to the plate boundary itself. The deformation along the boundary is normally partitioned into dip-slip contractional structures in the foreland with a single large

strike-slip structure in the hinterland accommodating all the strike-slip component along the boundary. Examples include the *Main Recent Fault* along the boundary between the Arabian and Eurasian plates behind the Zagros fold and thrust belt, the Liquiñe-Ofqui Fault that runs through Chile and the Great Sumatran fault that runs parallel to the subduction zone along the Sunda Trench.

- *The deforming foreland of a zone of continent-continent collision:* The process sometimes known as indenter tectonics, first elucidated by Paul Tapponnier, occurs during a collisional event where one of the plates deforms internally along a system of strike-slip faults. The best known active example is the system of strike-slip structures observed in the Eurasian plate as it responds to collision with the Indian plate, such as the Kunlun fault and Altyn Tagh fault.

PLATE TECTONICS

Plate tectonics (from the Late Latin *tectonicus*, from the Greek: τεκτονικοζ "pertaining to building") is a scientific theory that describes the large-scale motion of Earth's lithosphere. This theoretical model builds on the concept of continental drift which was developed during the first few decades of the 20th century. The geoscientific community accepted the theory after the concepts of seafloor spreading were later developed in the late 1950s and early 1960s.

The lithosphere, which is the rigid outermost shell of a planet (on Earth, the crust and upper mantle), is broken up into tectonic plates. On Earth, there are seven or eight major plates (depending on how they are defined) and many minor plates. Where plates meet, their relative motion determines the type of boundary; convergent, divergent, or transform. Earthquakes, volcanic activity, mountain-building, and oceanic trench formation occur along these plate boundaries. The lateral relative movement of the plates typically varies from zero to 100 mm annually. Tectonic plates are composed of oceanic lithosphere and thicker continental lithosphere, each topped by its own kind of crust. Along convergent boundaries, subduction carries plates into the mantle; the material lost is roughly balanced by the formation of new (oceanic) crust along divergent margins by seafloor spreading. In this way, the total surface of the globe remains the same. This prediction of plate tectonics is also referred to as the conveyor belt principle. Earlier theories (that still have some supporters) propose gradual shrinking (contraction) or gradual expansion of the globe.

Tectonic plates are able to move because the Earth's lithosphere has greater strength than the underlying asthenosphere. Lateral density variations in the mantle result in convection. Plate movement is thought to be driven by a combination of the motion of the seafloor away from the spreading ridge (due to variations in topography and density of the crust, which result in differences in gravitational forces) and drag, with downward suction, at the subduction zones. Another explanation lies in the different forces generated by the rotation of the globe and the tidal forces of the Sun and Moon. The relative importance of each of these factors and their relationship to each other is unclear, and still the subject of much debate.

KEY PRINCIPLES

The outer layers of the Earth are divided into the lithosphere and asthenosphere. This is based on differences in mechanical properties and in the method for the transfer of heat. Mechanically, the lithosphere is cooler and more rigid, while the asthenosphere is hotter and flows more easily. In terms of heat transfer, the lithosphere loses heat by conduction, whereas the asthenosphere also transfers heat by convection and has a nearly adiabatic temperature gradient. This division should not be confused with the *chemical* subdivision of these same layers into the mantle (comprising both the asthenosphere and the mantle portion of the lithosphere) and the crust: a given piece of mantle may be part of the lithosphere or the asthenosphere at different times depending on its temperature and pressure.

The key principle of plate tectonics is that the lithosphere exists as separate and distinct *tectonic plates*, which ride on the fluid-like (visco-elastic solid) asthenosphere. Plate motions range up to a typical 10–40 mm/year (Mid-Atlantic Ridge; about as fast as fingernails grow), to about 160 mm/year (Nazca Plate; about as fast as hair grows). The driving mechanism behind this movement is described below. Tectonic lithosphere plates consist of lithospheric mantle overlain by either or both of two types of crustal material: oceanic crust (in older texts called *sima* from silicon and magnesium) and continental crust (*sial* from silicon and aluminium). Average oceanic lithosphere is typically 100 km (62 mi) thick; its thickness is a function of its age: as time passes, it conductively cools and subjacent cooling mantle is added to its base. Because it is formed at mid-ocean ridges and spreads outwards, its thickness is therefore a function of its distance from the mid-ocean ridge where it was formed.

For a typical distance that oceanic lithosphere must travel before being subducted, the thickness varies from about 6 km (4 mi) thick at mid-ocean ridges to greater than 100 km (62 mi) at subduction zones; for shorter or longer distances, the subduction zone (and therefore also the mean) thickness becomes smaller or larger, respectively. Continental lithosphere is typically ~200 km thick, though this varies considerably between basins, mountain ranges, and stable cratonic interiors of continents. The two types of crust also differ in thickness, with continental crust being considerably thicker than oceanic (35 km vs. 6 km). The location where two plates meet is called a *plate boundary*. Plate boundaries are commonly associated with geological events such as earthquakes and the creation of topographic features such as mountains, volcanoes, mid-ocean ridges, and oceanic trenches. The majority of the world's active volcanoes occur along plate boundaries, with the Pacific Plate's Ring of Fire being the most active and widely known today. These boundaries are discussed in further detail below. Some volcanoes occur in the interiors of plates, and these have been variously attributed to internal plate deformation and to mantle plumes.

As explained above, tectonic plates may include continental crust or oceanic crust, and most plates contain both. For example, the African Plate includes the continent and parts of the floor of the Atlantic and Indian Oceans. The distinction between oceanic crust and continental crust is based on their modes of formation. Oceanic crust is formed at sea-floor spreading centers, and continental crust is formed through arc volcanism and accretion of terranes through tectonic processes, though some of these terranes may contain ophiolite sequences, which are pieces of oceanic crust considered to be part of the continent when they exit the standard cycle of formation and spreading centers and subduction beneath continents. Oceanic crust is also denser than continental crust owing to their different compositions. Oceanic crust is denser because it has less silicon and more heavier elements ("mafic") than continental crust ("felsic"). As a result of this density stratification, oceanic crust generally lies below sea level (for example most of the Pacific Plate), while continental crust buoyantly projects above sea level.

TYPES OF PLATE BOUNDARIES

Three types of plate boundaries exist, with a fourth, mixed type, characterized by the way the plates move relative to each other. They are associated with different types of surface phenomena. The different types of plate boundaries are:

1. *Transform boundaries (Conservative)* occur where two lithospheric plates slide, or perhaps more accurately, grind past each other along transform faults, where plates are neither created nor destroyed. The relative motion of the two plates is either sinistral (left side toward the observer) or dextral (right side toward the observer). Transform faults occur across a spreading center. Strong earthquakes can occur along a fault. The San Andreas Fault in California is an example of a transform boundary exhibiting dextral motion.
2. *Divergent boundaries (Constructive)* occur where two plates slide apart from each other. At zones of ocean-to-ocean rifting, divergent boundaries form by seafloor spreading, allowing for the formation of new ocean basin. As the continent splits, the ridge forms at the spreading center, the ocean basin expands, and finally, the plate area increases causing many small volcanoes and/or shallow earthquakes. At zones of continent-to-continent rifting, divergent boundaries may cause new ocean basin to form as the continent splits, spreads, the central rift collapses, and ocean fills the basin. Active zones of Mid-

ocean ridges (e.g., Mid-Atlantic Ridge and East Pacific Rise), and continent-to-continent rifting (such as Africa's East African Rift and Valley, Red Sea) are examples of divergent boundaries.

3. *Convergent boundaries (Destructive)* (or *active margins*) occur where two plates slide toward each other to form either a subduction zone (one plate moving underneath the other) or a continental collision. At zones of ocean-to-continent subduction (e.g., Western South America, and Cascade Mountains in Western United States), the dense oceanic lithosphere plunges beneath the less dense continent. Earthquakes then trace the path of the downward-moving plate as it descends into asthenosphere, a trench forms, and as the subducted plate partially melts, magma rises to form continental volcanoes. At zones of ocean-to-ocean subduction (e.g., the Andes mountain range in South America, Aleutian islands, Mariana islands, and the Japanese island arc), older, cooler, denser crust slips beneath less dense crust. This causes earthquakes and a deep trench to form in an arc shape. The upper mantle of the subducted plate then heats and magma rises to form curving chains of volcanic islands. Deep marine trenches are typically associated with subduction zones, and the basins that develop along the active boundary are often called "foreland basins". The subducting slab contains many hydrous minerals which release their water on heating. This water then causes the mantle to melt, producing volcanism. Closure of ocean basins can occur at continent-to-continent boundaries (e.g., Himalayas and Alps): collision between masses of granitic continental lithosphere; neither mass is subducted; plate edges are compressed, folded, uplifted.

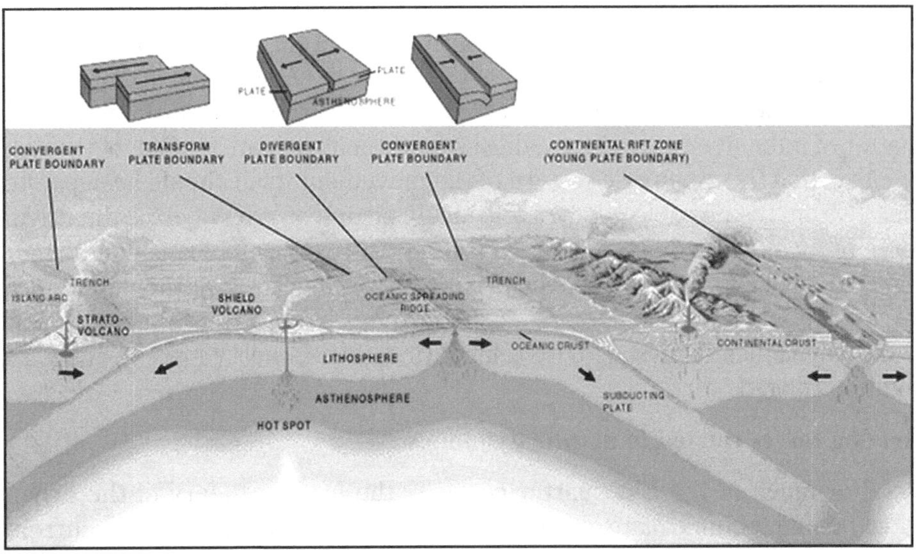

Fig. Three types of plate boundary.

4. *Plate boundary zones* occur where the effects of the interactions are unclear, and the boundaries, usually occurring along a broad belt, are not well defined and may show various types of movements in different episodes.

DRIVING FORCES OF PLATE MOTION

Plate tectonics is basically a kinematic phenomenon. Scientists agree on the observation and deduction that the plates have moved with respect to one another but continue to debate as to how and when. A major question remains as to what geodynamic mechanism motors plate movement. Here, science diverges in different theories.

It is generally accepted that tectonic plates are able to move because of the relative density of oceanic lithosphere and the relative weakness of the asthenosphere. Dissipation of heat from the mantle is acknowledged to be the original source of the energy required to drive plate tectonics through convection or large scale upwelling and doming. The current view, though still a matter of some debate, asserts that as a consequence, a powerful source of plate motion is generated due to the excess density of the oceanic lithosphere sinking in subduction zones. When the new crust forms at mid-ocean ridges, this oceanic lithosphere is initially less dense than the underlying asthenosphere, but it becomes denser with age as it conductively cools and thickens. The greater density of old lithosphere relative to the underlying asthenosphere allows it to sink into the deep mantle at subduction zones, providing most of the driving force for plate movement. The weakness of the asthenosphere allows the tectonic plates to move easily towards a subduction zone. Although subduction is believed to be the strongest force driving plate motions, it cannot be the only force since there are plates such as the North American Plate which are moving, yet are nowhere being subducted. The same is true for the enormous Eurasian Plate. The sources of plate motion are a matter of intensive research and discussion among scientists. One of the main points is that the kinematic pattern of the movement itself should be separated clearly from the possible geodynamic mechanism that is invoked as the driving force of the observed movement, as some patterns may be explained by more than one mechanism. In short, the driving forces advocated at the moment can be divided into three categories based on the relationship to the movement: mantle dynamics related, gravity related (mostly secondary forces), and Earth rotation related.

Driving forces related to mantle dynamics

For much of the last quarter century, the leading theory of the driving force behind tectonic plate motions envisaged large scale convection currents in the upper mantle which are transmitted through the asthenosphere. This theory was launched by Arthur Holmes and some forerunners in the 1930s and was immediately recognized as the solution for the acceptance of the theory as originally discussed in the papers of Alfred Wegener in the early years of the century. However, despite its acceptance, it was long debated in the scientific community because the leading ("fixist") theory still envisaged a static Earth without moving continents up until the major breakthroughs of the early sixties.

Two- and three-dimensional imaging of Earth's interior (seismic tomography) shows a varying lateral density distribution throughout the mantle. Such density variations can be material (from rock chemistry), mineral (from variations in mineral structures), or thermal (through thermal expansion and contraction from heat energy). The manifestation of this varying lateral density is mantle convection from buoyancy forces.

How mantle convection directly and indirectly relates to plate motion is a matter of ongoing study and discussion in geodynamics. Somehow, this energy must be transferred to the lithosphere for tectonic plates to move. There are essentially two types of forces that are thought to influence plate motion: friction and gravity.

- *Basal drag (friction):* Plate motion driven by friction between the convection currents in the asthenosphere and the more rigid overlying lithosphere.
- *Slab suction (gravity):* Plate motion driven by local convection currents that exert a downward pull on plates in subduction zones at ocean trenches. Slab suction may occur in a geodynamic setting where basal tractions continue to act on the plate as it dives into the mantle (although perhaps to a greater extent acting on both the under and upper side of the slab).

Lately, the convection theory has been much debated as modern techniques based on 3D seismic tomography still fail to recognize these predicted large scale convection cells. Therefore, alternative views have been proposed:

In the theory of plume tectonics developed during the 1990s, a modified concept of mantle convection currents is used. It asserts that super plumes rise from the deeper mantle and are the drivers or substitutes of the major convection cells. These ideas, which find their roots in the early 1930s with the so-called "fixistic" ideas of the European and Russian Earth Science Schools, find resonance in the modern theories which envisage hot spots/mantle plumes which remain fixed and are overridden by oceanic and continental lithosphere plates over time and leave their traces in the geological record (though these phenomena are not invoked as real driving mechanisms, but rather as modulators).

Another theory is that the mantle flows neither in cells nor large plumes but rather as a series of channels just below the Earth's crust, which then provide basal friction to the lithosphere. This theory, called "surge tectonics", became quite popular in geophysics and geodynamics during the 1980s and 1990s.

Driving forces related to gravity

Forces related to gravity are usually invoked as secondary phenomena within the framework of a more general driving mechanism such as the various forms of mantle dynamics described above.

Gravitational sliding away from a spreading ridge: According to many authors, plate motion is driven by the higher elevation of plates at ocean ridges. As oceanic lithosphere is formed at spreading ridges from hot mantle material, it gradually cools and thickens with age (and thus adds distance from the ridge). Cool oceanic lithosphere is significantly denser than the hot mantle material from which it is derived and so with increasing thickness it gradually subsides into the mantle to compensate the greater load. The result is a slight lateral incline with increased distance from the ridge axis.

This force is regarded as a secondary force and is often referred to as "ridge push". This is a misnomer as nothing is "pushing" horizontally and tensional features are dominant along ridges. It is more accurate to refer to this mechanism as gravitational sliding as variable topography across the totality of the plate can vary considerably and the topography of spreading ridges is only the most prominent feature. Other mechanisms generating this gravitational secondary force include flexural bulging of the lithosphere before it dives underneath an adjacent plate which produces a clear topographical feature that can offset, or at least affect, the influence of topographical ocean ridges, and mantle plumes and hot spots, which are postulated to impinge on the underside of tectonic plates.

Slab-pull: Current scientific opinion is that the asthenosphere is insufficiently competent or rigid to directly cause motion by friction along the base of the lithosphere. Slab pull is therefore most widely thought to be the greatest force acting on the plates. In this current understanding, plate motion is mostly driven by the weight of cold, dense plates sinking into the mantle at trenches. Recent models indicate that trench suction plays an important role as well. However, as the North American Plate is nowhere being subducted, yet it is in motion presents a problem. The same holds for the African, Eurasian, and Antarctic plates. Gravitational sliding away from mantle doming: According to older theories, one of the driving mechanisms of the plates is the existence of large scale asthenosphere/mantle domes which cause the gravitational sliding of lithosphere plates away from them. This gravitational sliding represents a secondary phenomenon of this basically vertically oriented mechanism. This can act on various scales, from the small scale of one island arc up to the larger scale of an entire ocean basin.

Driving forces related to Earth rotation

Alfred Wegener, being a meteorologist, had proposed tidal forces and pole flight force as the main driving mechanisms behind continental drift; however, these forces were considered far too small to cause continental motion as the concept then was of continents plowing through oceanic crust. Therefore, Wegener later changed his position and asserted that convection currents are the main driving force of plate tectonics in the last edition of his book in 1929.

However, in the plate tectonics context (accepted since the seafloor spreading proposals of Heezen, Hess, Dietz, Morley, Vine, and Matthews during the early 1960s), oceanic crust is suggested to be in motion *with* the continents which caused the proposals related to Earth rotation to be reconsidered. In more recent literature, these driving forces are:

1. Tidal drag due to the gravitational force the Moon (and the Sun) exerts on the crust of the Earth
2. Shear strain of the Earth globe due to N-S compression related to its rotation and modulations;
3. Pole flight force: equatorial drift due to rotation and centrifugal effects: tendency of the plates to move from the poles to the equator ("*Polflucht*");
4. The Coriolis effect acting on plates when they move around the globe;
5. Global deformation of the geoid due to small displacements of rotational pole with respect to the Earth's crust;
6. Other smaller deformation effects of the crust due to wobbles and spin movements of the Earth rotation on a smaller time scale.

For these mechanisms to be overall valid, systematic relationships should exist all over the globe between the orientation and kinematics of deformation and the geographical latitudinal and longitudinal grid of the Earth itself. Ironically, these systematic relations studies in the second half of the nineteenth century and the first half of the twentieth century underline exactly the opposite: that the plates had not moved in time, that the deformation grid was fixed with respect to the Earth equator and axis, and that gravitational driving forces were generally acting vertically and caused only local horizontal movements (the so-called pre-plate tectonic, "fixist theories"). Later studies (discussed below on this page), therefore, invoked many of the relationships recognized during this pre-plate tectonics period to support their theories.

Of the many forces discussed in this paragraph, tidal force is still highly debated and defended as a possible principle driving force of plate tectonics. The other forces are only used in global geodynamic models not using plate tectonics concepts (therefore beyond the discussions treated in this section) or proposed as minor modulations within the overall plate tectonics model.

In 1973, George W. Moore of the USGS and R. C. Bostrom presented evidence for a general westward drift of the Earth's lithosphere with respect to the mantle. He concluded that tidal forces (the tidal lag or "friction") caused by the Earth's rotation and the forces acting upon it by the Moon are a driving force for plate tectonics. As the Earth spins eastward beneath the moon, the moon's gravity ever so slightly pulls the Earth's surface layer back westward, just as proposed by Alfred Wegener. In a more recent 2006 study, scientists reviewed and advocated these earlier proposed ideas. It has also been suggested recently in Lovett (2006) that this observation may also explain why Venus and Mars have no plate tectonics, as Venus has no moon and Mars' moons are too small to have significant tidal effects on the planet. In a recent paper, it was suggested that, on the other hand, it can easily be observed that many plates are moving north and eastward, and that the dominantly westward motion of the Pacific ocean basins derives simply from the eastward bias of the Pacific spreading center (which is not a predicted manifestation of such lunar forces). In the same paper the authors admit, however, that relative to the lower mantle, there is a slight westward component in the motions of all the plates. They demonstrated though that the westward drift, seen only for the past 30 Ma, is attributed to the increased dominance of the steadily growing and accelerating Pacific plate. The debate is still open.

Relative significance of each driving force mechanism

The actual vector of a plate's motion is a function of all the forces acting on the plate; however, therein lies the problem regarding the degree to which each process contributes to the overall motion of each tectonic plate.

The diversity of geodynamic settings and the properties of each plate result from the impact of the various processes actively driving each individual plate. One method of dealing with this problem is to consider the relative rate at which each plate is moving as well as the evidence related to the significance of each process to the overall driving force on the plate. One of the most significant correlations discovered to date is that lithospheric plates attached to downgoing (subducting) plates move much faster than plates not attached to subducting plates. The Pacific plate, for instance, is essentially surrounded by zones of subduction (the so-called Ring of Fire) and moves much faster than the plates of the Atlantic basin, which are attached (perhaps one could say 'welded') to adjacent continents instead of subducting plates. It is thus thought that forces associated with the downgoing plate (slab pull and slab suction) are the driving forces which determine the motion of plates, except for those plates which are not being subducted. The driving forces of plate motion continue to be active subjects of on-going research within geophysics and tectonophysics.

DEVELOPMENT OF THE THEORY

In line with other previous and contemporaneous proposals, in 1912 the meteorologist Alfred Wegener amply described what he called continental drift, expanded in his 1915 book *The Origin of Continents and Oceans* and the scientific debate started that would end up fifty years later in the theory of plate tectonics. Starting from the idea (also expressed by his forerunners) that the present continents once formed a single land mass (which was called Pangea later on) that drifted apart, thus releasing the continents from the Earth's mantle and likening them to "icebergs" of low density granite floating on a sea of denser basalt. Supporting evidence for the idea came from the dove-tailing outlines of South America's east coast and Africa's west coast, and from the matching of the rock formations along these edges. Confirmation of their previous contiguous nature also came from the fossil plants *Glossopteris* and *Gangamopteris*, and the therapsid or mammal-like reptile *Lystrosaurus*, all widely distributed over South America, Africa, Antarctica, India and Australia. The evidence for such an erstwhile joining of these continents was patent to field geologists working in the southern hemisphere. The South African Alex du Toit put together a mass of such information in his 1937 publication *Our Wandering Continents*, and went further than Wegener in recognising the strong links between the Gondwana fragments.

But without detailed evidence and a force sufficient to drive the movement, the theory was not generally accepted: the Earth might have a solid crust and mantle and a liquid core, but there seemed to be no way that portions of the crust could move around. Distinguished scientists, such as Harold Jeffreys and Charles Schuchert, were outspoken critics of continental drift.

Despite much opposition, the view of continental drift gained support and a lively debate started between "drifters" or "mobilists" (proponents of the theory) and "fixists" (opponents). During the 1920s, 1930s and 1940s, the former reached important milestones proposing that convection currents might have driven the plate movements, and that spreading may have occurred below the sea within the oceanic crust. Concepts close to the elements now incorporated in plate tectonics were proposed by geophysicists and geologists (both fixists and mobilists) like Vening-Meinesz, Holmes, and Umbgrove.

One of the first pieces of geophysical evidence that was used to support the movement of lithospheric plates came from paleomagnetism. This is based on the fact that rocks of different ages show a variable magnetic field direction, evidenced by studies since the mid–nineteenth century. The magnetic north and south poles reverse through time, and, especially important in paleotectonic studies, the relative position of the magnetic north pole varies through time. Initially, during the first half of the twentieth century, the latter phenomenon was explained by introducing what was called "polar wander", i.e., it was assumed that the north pole location had been shifting through time. An alternative explanation, though, was that the continents had moved (shifted and rotated) relative to the north pole, and each continent, in fact, shows its own "polar wander path". During the late 1950s it was successfully shown on two occasions that these data could show the validity of continental drift: by Keith Runcorn in a paper in 1956, and by Warren Carey in a symposium held in March 1956.

The second piece of evidence in support of continental drift came during the late 1950s and early 60s from data on the bathymetry of the deep ocean floors and the nature of the oceanic crust such as magnetic properties and, more generally, with the development of marine geology which gave evidence for the association of seafloor spreading along the mid-oceanic ridges and magnetic field reversals, published between 1959 and 1963 by Heezen, Dietz, Hess, Mason, Vine & Matthews, and Morley.

Simultaneous advances in early seismic imaging techniques in and around Wadati-Benioff zones along the trenches bounding many continental margins, together with many other geophysical (e.g. gravimetric) and geological observations, showed how the oceanic crust could disappear into the mantle, providing the mechanism to balance the extension of the ocean basins with shortening along its margins.

All this evidence, both from the ocean floor and from the continental margins, made it clear around 1965 that continental drift was feasible and the theory of plate tectonics, which was defined in a series of papers between 1965 and 1967, was born, with all its extraordinary explanatory and predictive power. The theory revolutionized the Earth sciences, explaining a diverse range of geological phenomena and their implications in other studies such as paleogeography and paleobiology.

Continental drift

In the late 19th and early 20th centuries, geologists assumed that the Earth's major features were fixed, and that most geologic features such as basin development and mountain ranges could be explained by vertical crustal movement, described in what is called the geosynclinal theory. Generally, this was placed in the context of a contracting planet Earth due to heat loss in the course of a relatively short geological time.

It was observed as early as 1596 that the opposite coasts of the Atlantic Ocean—or, more precisely, the edges of the continental shelves—have similar shapes and seem to have once fitted together.

Since that time many theories were proposed to explain this apparent complementarity, but the assumption of a solid Earth made these various proposals difficult to accept.

The discovery of radioactivity and its associated heating properties in 1895 prompted a re-examination of the apparent age of the Earth. This had previously been estimated by its cooling rate and assumption the Earth's surface radiated like a black body. Those calculations had implied that, even if it started at red heat, the Earth would have dropped to its present temperature in a few tens of millions of years. Armed with the knowledge of a new heat source, scientists realized that the Earth would be much older, and that its core was still sufficiently hot to be liquid.

By 1915, after having published a first article in 1912, Alfred Wegener was making serious arguments for the idea of continental drift in the first edition of *The Origin of Continents and Oceans*. In that book (re-issued in four successive editions up to the final one in 1936), he noted how the east coast of South America and the west coast of Africa looked as if they were once attached. Wegener was not the first to note this (Abraham Ortelius, Antonio Snider-Pellegrini, Eduard Suess, Roberto Mantovani and Frank Bursley Taylor preceded him just to mention a few), but he was the first to marshal significant fossil and paleo-topographical and climatological evidence to support this simple observation (and was supported in this by researchers such as Alex du Toit). Furthermore, when the rock strata of the margins of separate continents are very similar it suggests that these rocks were formed in the same way, implying that they were joined initially. For instance, parts of Scotland and Ireland contain rocks very similar to those found in Newfoundland and New Brunswick. Furthermore, the Caledonian Mountains of Europe and parts of the Appalachian Mountains of North America are very similar in structure and lithology.

However, his ideas were not taken seriously by many geologists, who pointed out that there was no apparent mechanism for continental drift. Specifically, they did not see how continental rock could plow through the much denser rock that makes up oceanic crust. Wegener could not explain the force that drove continental drift, and his vindication did not come until after his death in 1930.

Floating continents, paleomagnetism, and seismicity zones

As it was observed early that although granite existed on continents, seafloor seemed to be composed of denser basalt, the prevailing concept during the first half of the twentieth century was that there were two types of crust, named "sial" (continental type crust) and "sima" (oceanic type crust). Furthermore, it was supposed that a static shell of strata was present under the continents. It therefore looked apparent that a layer of basalt (sial) underlies the continental rocks.

However, based on abnormalities in plumb line deflection by the Andes in Peru, Pierre Bouguer had deduced that less-dense mountains must have a downward projection into the denser layer underneath. The concept that mountains had "roots" was confirmed by George B. Airy a hundred years later, during study of Himalayan gravitation, and seismic studies detected corresponding density variations. Therefore, by the mid-1950s, the question remained unresolved as to whether mountain roots were clenched in surrounding basalt or were floating on it like an iceberg.

During the 20th century, improvements in and greater use of seismic instruments such as seismographs enabled scientists to learn that earthquakes tend to be concentrated in specific areas, most notably along the oceanic trenches and spreading ridges. By the late 1920s, seismologists were beginning to identify several prominent earthquake zones parallel to the trenches that typically were inclined 40–60° from the horizontal and extended several hundred kilometers into the Earth. These zones later became known as Wadati-Benioff zones, or simply Benioff zones, in honor of the seismologists who first recognized them, Kiyoo Wadati of Japan and Hugo Benioff of the United States. The study of global seismicity greatly advanced in the 1960s with the establishment of the Worldwide Standardized Seismograph Network (WWSSN) to monitor the compliance of the 1963 treaty banning above-ground testing of nuclear weapons. The much improved data from the WWSSN instruments allowed seismologists to map precisely the zones of earthquake concentration worldwide.

Meanwhile, debates developed around the phenomena of polar wander. Since the early debates of continental drift, scientists had discussed and used evidence that polar drift had occurred because continents seemed to have moved through different climatic zones during the past. Furthermore, paleomagnetic data had shown that the magnetic pole had also shifted during time. Reasoning in an opposite way, the continents might have shifted and rotated, while the pole remained relatively fixed. The first time the evidence of magnetic polar wander was used to support the movements of continents was in a paper by Keith Runcorn in 1956, and successive papers by him and his students Ted Irving (who was actually the first to be convinced of the fact that paleomagnetism supported continental drift) and Ken Creer.

This was immediately followed by a symposium in Tasmania in March 1956. In this symposium, the evidence was used in the theory of an expansion of the global crust. In this hypothesis the shifting of the continents can be simply explained by a large increase in size of the Earth since its formation. However, this was unsatisfactory because its supporters could offer no convincing mechanism to produce a significant expansion of the Earth. Certainly there is no evidence that the moon has expanded in the past 3 billion years; other work would soon show that the evidence was equally in support of continental drift on a globe with a stable radius.

During the thirties up to the late fifties, works by Vening-Meinesz, Holmes, Umbgrove, and numerous others outlined concepts that were close or nearly identical to modern plate tectonics theory. In particular, the English geologist Arthur Holmes proposed in 1920 that plate junctions might lie beneath the sea, and in 1928 that convection currents within the mantle might be the driving force. Often, these contributions are forgotten because:

- At the time, continental drift was not accepted.

- Some of these ideas were discussed in the context of abandoned fixistic ideas of a deforming globe without continental drift or an expanding Earth.
- They were published during an episode of extreme political and economic instability that hampered scientific communication.
- Many were published by European scientists and at first not mentioned or given little credit in the papers on sea floor spreading published by the American researchers in the 1960s.

Mid-oceanic ridge spreading and convection

In 1947, a team of scientists led by Maurice Ewing utilizing the Woods Hole Oceanographic Institution's research vessel *Atlantis* and an array of instruments, confirmed the existence of a rise in the central Atlantic Ocean, and found that the floor of the seabed beneath the layer of sediments consisted of basalt, not the granite which is the main constituent of continents. They also found that the oceanic crust was much thinner than continental crust. All these new findings raised important and intriguing questions.

The new data that had been collected on the ocean basins also showed particular characteristics regarding the bathymetry. One of the major outcomes of these datasets was that all along the globe, a system of mid-oceanic ridges was detected. An important conclusion was that along this system, new ocean floor was being created, which led to the concept of the "Great Global Rift". This was described in the crucial paper of Bruce Heezen (1960), which would trigger a real revolution in thinking. A profound consequence of seafloor spreading is that new crust was, and still is, being continually created along the oceanic ridges. Therefore, Heezen advocated the so-called "expanding Earth" hypothesis of S. Warren Carey. So, still the question remained: how can new crust be continuously added along the oceanic ridges without increasing the size of the Earth? In reality, this question had been solved already by numerous scientists during the forties and the fifties, like Arthur Holmes, Vening-Meinesz, Coates and many others: The crust in excess disappeared along what were called the oceanic trenches, where so-called "subduction" occurred. Therefore, when various scientists during the early sixties started to reason on the data at their disposal regarding the ocean floor, the pieces of the theory quickly fell into place.

The question particularly intrigued Harry Hammond Hess, a Princeton University geologist and a Naval Reserve Rear Admiral, and Robert S. Dietz, a scientist with the U.S. Coast and Geodetic Survey who first coined the term *seafloor spreading*. Dietz and Hess (the former published the same idea one year earlier in *Nature*, but priority belongs to Hess who had already distributed an unpublished manuscript of his 1962 article by 1960) were among the small handful who really understood the broad implications of sea floor spreading and how it would eventually agree with the, at that time, unconventional and unaccepted ideas of continental drift and the elegant and mobilistic models proposed by previous workers like Holmes.

In the same year, Robert R. Coats of the U.S. Geological Survey described the main features of island arc subduction in the Aleutian Islands. His paper, though little noted (and even ridiculed) at the time, has since been called "seminal" and "prescient". In reality, it actually shows that the work by the European scientists on island arcs and mountain belts performed and published during the 1930s up until the 1950s was applied and appreciated also in the United States.

If the Earth's crust was expanding along the oceanic ridges, Hess and Dietz reasoned like Holmes and others before them, it must be shrinking elsewhere. Hess followed Heezen, suggesting that new oceanic crust continuously spreads away from the ridges in a conveyor belt–like motion. And, using the mobilistic concepts developed before, he correctly concluded that many millions of years later, the oceanic crust eventually descends along the continental margins where oceanic trenches – very deep, narrow canyons – are formed, e.g. along the rim of the Pacific Ocean basin. The important step Hess made was that convection currents would be the driving force in this process, arriving at the same conclusions as Holmes had decades before with the only difference that the thinning of the ocean crust was performed using Heezen's mechanism of spreading along the ridges. Hess therefore concluded that the Atlantic Ocean was expanding while the Pacific Ocean was shrinking. As old oceanic crust is "consumed" in the trenches (like Holmes and others, he thought this was done by thickening of the continental lithosphere, not, as now understood, by underthrusting at a larger scale of the oceanic crust itself into the mantle), new magma rises and erupts along the spreading ridges to form new crust. In effect, the ocean basins are perpetually being "recycled," with the creation of new crust and the destruction of old oceanic lithosphere occurring simultaneously. Thus, the new mobilistic concepts neatly explained why the Earth does not get bigger with sea floor spreading, why there is so little sediment accumulation on the ocean floor, and why oceanic rocks are much younger than continental rocks.

Magnetic striping

Beginning in the 1950s, scientists like Victor Vacquier, using magnetic instruments (magnetometers) adapted from airborne devices developed during World War II to detect submarines, began recognizing odd magnetic variations across the ocean floor. This finding, though unexpected, was not entirely surprising because it was known that basalt—the iron-rich, volcanic rock making up the ocean floor—contains a strongly magnetic mineral (magnetite) and can locally distort compass readings. This distortion was recognized by Icelandic mariners as early as the late 18th century. More important, because the presence of magnetite gives the basalt measurable magnetic properties, these newly discovered magnetic variations provided another means to study the deep ocean floor. When newly formed rock cools, such magnetic materials recorded the Earth's magnetic field at the time.

As more and more of the seafloor was mapped during the 1950s, the magnetic variations turned out not to be random or isolated occurrences, but instead revealed recognizable patterns. When these magnetic patterns were mapped over a wide region, the ocean floor showed a zebra-like pattern: one stripe with normal polarity and the adjoining stripe with reversed polarity. The overall pattern, defined by these alternating bands of normally and reversely polarized rock, became known as magnetic striping, and was published by Ron G. Mason and co-workers in 1961, who did not find, though, an explanation for these data in terms of sea floor spreading, like Vine, Matthews and Morley a few years later.

The discovery of magnetic striping called for an explanation. In the early 1960s scientists such as Heezen, Hess and Dietz had begun to theorise that mid-ocean ridges mark structurally weak zones where the ocean floor was being ripped in two lengthwise along the ridge crest. New magma from deep within the Earth rises easily through these weak zones and eventually erupts along the crest of the ridges to create new oceanic crust. This process, at first denominated the "conveyer belt hypothesis" and later called seafloor spreading, operating over many millions of years continues to form new ocean floor all across the 50,000 km-long system of mid-ocean ridges.

Only four years after the maps with the "zebra pattern" of magnetic stripes were published, the link between sea floor spreading and these patterns was correctly placed, independently by Lawrence Morley, and by Fred Vine and Drummond Matthews, in 1963, now called the Vine-Matthews-Morley hypothesis. This hypothesis linked these patterns to geomagnetic reversals and was supported by several lines of evidence:

1. The stripes are symmetrical around the crests of the mid-ocean ridges; at or near the crest of the ridge, the rocks are very young, and they become progressively older away from the ridge crest;
2. The youngest rocks at the ridge crest always have present-day (normal) polarity;
3. Stripes of rock parallel to the ridge crest alternate in magnetic polarity (normal-reversed-normal, etc.), suggesting that they were formed during different epochs documenting the (already known from independent studies) normal and reversal episodes of the Earth's magnetic field.

By explaining both the zebra-like magnetic striping and the construction of the mid-ocean ridge system, the seafloor spreading hypothesis (SFS) quickly gained converts and represented another major advance in the development of the plate-tectonics theory. Furthermore, the oceanic crust now came to be appreciated as a natural "tape recording" of the history of the geomagnetic field reversals (GMFR) of the Earth's magnetic field. Today, extensive studies are dedicated to the calibration of the normal-reversal patterns in the oceanic crust on one hand and known timescales derived from the dating of basalt layers in sedimentary sequences (magnetostratigraphy) on the other, to arrive at estimates of past spreading rates and plate reconstructions.

Definition and refining of the theory

Concepts:

- In 1965, Tuzo Wilson who had been a promotor of the sea floor spreading hypothesis and continental drift from the very beginning added the concept of transform faults to the model, completing the classes of fault types necessary to make the mobility of the plates on the globe work out.
- A symposium on continental drift was held at the Royal Society of London in 1965 which must be regarded as the official start of the acceptance of plate tectonics by the scientific community, and which abstracts are issued as Blacket, Bullard & Runcorn (1965). In this symposium, Edward Bullard and co-workers showed with a computer calculation how the continents along both sides of the Atlantic would best fit to close the ocean, which became known as the famous "Bullard's Fit".
- In 1966 Wilson published the paper that referred to previous plate tectonic reconstructions, introducing the concept of what is now known as the "Wilson Cycle".
- In 1967, at the American Geophysical Union's meeting, W. Jason Morgan proposed that the Earth's surface consists of 12 rigid plates that move relative to each other.
- Two months later, Xavier Le Pichon published a complete model based on 6 major plates with their relative motions, which marked the final acceptance by the scientific community of plate tectonics.
- In the same year, McKenzie and Parker independently presented a model similar to Morgan's using translations and rotations on a sphere to define the plate motions.

IMPLICATIONS FOR BIOGEOGRAPHY

Continental drift theory helps biogeographers to explain the disjunct biogeographic distribution of present-day life found on different continents but having similar ancestors. In particular, it explains the Gondwanan distribution of ratites and the Antarctic flora.

PLATE RECONSTRUCTION

Reconstruction is used to establish past (and future) plate configurations, helping determine the shape and make-up of ancient supercontinents and providing a basis for paleogeography.

Defining plate boundaries

Current plate boundaries are defined by their seismicity. Past plate boundaries within existing plates are identified from a variety of evidence, such as the presence of ophiolites that are indicative of vanished oceans.

Past plate motions

Tectonic motion first began around three billion years ago.Various types of quantitative and semi-quantitative information are available to constrain past plate motions. The geometric fit between continents, such as between west Africa and South America is still an important part of plate reconstruction. Magnetic stripe patterns provide a reliable guide to relative plate motions going back into the Jurassic period. The tracks of hotspots give absolute reconstructions, but these are only available back to the Cretaceous. Older reconstructions rely mainly on paleomagnetic pole data, although these only constrain the latitude and rotation, but not the longitude. Combining poles of different ages in a particular plate to produce apparent polar wander paths provides a method for comparing the motions of different plates through time. Additional evidence comes from the distribution of certain sedimentary rock types, faunal provinces shown by particular fossil groups, and the position of orogenic belts.

Formation and break-up of continents

The movement of plates has caused the formation and break-up of continents over time, including occasional formation of a supercontinent that contains most or all of the continents. The supercontinent Columbia or Nuna formed during a period of 2,000 to 1,800 million years ago and broke up about 1,500 to 1,300 million years ago. The supercontinent Rodinia is thought to have formed about 1 billion years ago and to have embodied most or all of Earth's continents, and broken up into eight continents around 600 million years ago. The eight continents later re-assembled into another supercontinent called Pangaea; Pangaea broke up into Laurasia (which became North America and Eurasia) and Gondwana (which became the remaining continents). The Himalayas, the world's tallest mountain range, are assumed to have been formed by the collision of two major plates. Before uplift, they were covered by the Tethys Ocean.

Gallery of past configurations

Interpretive simulation of past continental movement and shorelines, with time given in millions of years ago (Ma). For more complete timeline of images.

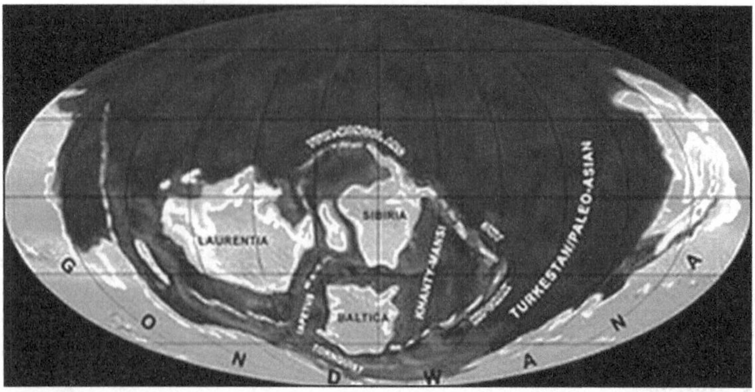

500 Ma

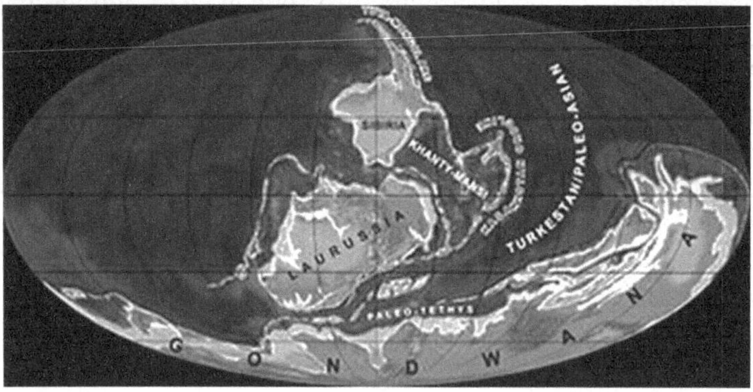

400 Ma

CURRENT PLATES

Depending on how they are defined, there are usually seven or eight "major" plates: African, Antarctic, Eurasian, North American, South American, Pacific, and Indo-Australian. The latter is sometimes subdivided into the Indian and Australian plates.

There are dozens of smaller plates, the seven largest of which are the Arabian, Caribbean, Juan de Fuca, Cocos, Nazca, Philippine Sea and Scotia.

The current motion of the tectonic plates is today determined by remote sensing satellite data sets, calibrated with ground station measurements.

OTHER CELESTIAL BODIES (PLANETS, MOONS)

The appearance of plate tectonics on terrestrial planets is related to planetary mass, with more massive planets than Earth expected to exhibit plate tectonics. Earth may be a borderline case, owing its tectonic activity to abundant water (silica and water form a deep eutectic.)

- *Venus:* Venus shows no evidence of active plate tectonics. There is debatable evidence of active tectonics in the planet's distant past;

however, events taking place since then (such as the plausible and generally accepted hypothesis that the Venusian lithosphere has thickened greatly over the course of several hundred million years) has made constraining the course of its geologic record difficult. However, the numerous well-preserved impact craters have been utilized as a dating method to approximately date the Venusian surface (since there are thus far no known samples of Venusian rock to be dated by more reliable methods). Dates derived are dominantly in the range 500 to 750 million years ago, although ages of up to 1,200 million years ago have been calculated. This research has led to the fairly well accepted hypothesis that Venus has undergone an essentially complete volcanic resurfacing at least once in its distant past, with the last event taking place approximately within the range of estimated surface ages. While the mechanism of such an impressive thermal event remains a debated issue in Venusian geosciences, some scientists are advocates of processes involving plate motion to some extent. One explanation for Venus' lack of plate tectonics is that on Venus temperatures are too high for significant water to be present. The Earth's crust is soaked with water, and water plays an important role in the development of shear zones. Plate tectonics requires weak surfaces in the crust along which crustal slices can move, and it may well be that such weakening never took place on Venus because of the absence of water. However, some researchers remain convinced that plate tectonics is or was once active on this planet.

- *Mars:* Mars is considerably smaller than Earth and Venus, and there is evidence for ice on its surface and in its crust. In the 1990s, it was proposed that Martian Crustal Dichotomy was created by plate tectonic processes. Scientists today disagree, and believe that it was created either by upwelling within the Martian mantle that thickened the crust of the Southern Highlands and formed Tharsis or by a giant impact that excavated the Northern Lowlands. Valles Marineris may be a tectonic boundary. Observations made of the magnetic field of Mars by the *Mars Global Surveyor* spacecraft in 1999 showed patterns of magnetic striping discovered on this planet. Some scientists interpreted these as requiring plate tectonic processes, such as seafloor spreading. However, their data fail a "magnetic reversal test", which is used to see if they were formed by flipping polarities of a global magnetic field.
- *Galilean satellites of Jupiter:* Some of the satellites of Jupiter have features that may be related to plate-tectonic style deformation, although the materials and specific mechanisms may be different from plate-tectonic activity on Earth. On 8 September 2014, NASA reported

finding evidence of plate tectonics on Europa, a satellite of Jupiter—the first sign of such geological activity on another world other than Earth.

- *Titan, moon of Saturn:* Titan, the largest moon of Saturn, was reported to show tectonic activity in images taken by the Huygens Probe, which landed on Titan on January 14, 2005.
- *Exoplanets:* On Earth-sized planets, plate tectonics is more likely if there are oceans of water; however, in 2007, two independent teams of researchers came to opposing conclusions about the likelihood of plate tectonics on larger super-earths with one team saying that plate tectonics would be episodic or stagnant and the other team saying that plate tectonics is very likely on super-earths even if the planet is dry.

SALT TECTONICS

Salt tectonics is concerned with the geometries and processes associated with the presence of significant thicknesses of evaporites containing rock salt within a stratigraphic sequence of rocks. This is due both to the low density of salt, which does not increase with burial, and its low strength.

PASSIVE SALT STRUCTURES

Structures may form during continued sedimentary loading, without any external tectonic influence, due to gravitational instability. Pure halite has a density of 2160 kg/m. When initially deposited, sediments generally have a lower density of 2000 kg/m^3, but with loading and compaction their density increases to 2500 kg/m^3, which is greater than that of salt. Once the overlying layers have become denser, the weak salt layer will tend to deform into a characteristic series of ridges and depressions, due to a form of Rayleigh–Taylor instability. Further sedimentation will be concentrated in the depressions and the salt will continue to move away from them into the ridges. At a late stage, diapirs tend to initiate at the junctions between ridges, their growth fed by movement of salt along the ridge system, continuing until the salt supply is exhausted. During the later stages of this process the top of the diapir remains at or near the surface, with further burial being matched by diapir rise, and is sometimes referred to as *downbuilding*. The Schacht Asse II and Gorleben salt domes in Germany are an example of a purely passive salt structure. Such structures do not always form when a salt layer is buried beneath a sedimentary overburden. This can be due to a relatively high strength overburden or to the presence of sedimentary layers interbedded within the salt unit that increase both its density and strength.

ACTIVE SALT STRUCTURES

Active tectonics will increase the likelihood of salt structures developing. In the case of extensional tectonics, faulting will both reduce the strength of the overburden and thin it. In an area affected by thrust tectonics, buckling of the overburden layer will allow the salt to rise into the cores of anticlines.

If the pressure within the salt body becomes sufficiently high it may be able to push through its overburden, this is known as *forceful* diapirism. Many salt diapirs may contain elements of both active and passive salt movement. An active salt structure may pierce its overburden and from then on continue to develop as a purely passive salt diapir.

REACTIVE SALT STRUCTURES

In those cases where salt layers do not have the conditions necessary to develop passive salt structures, the salt may still move into relatively low pressure areas around developing folds and faults. Such structures are described as *reactive*.

SALT DETACHED FAULT SYSTEMS

When one or more salt layers are present during extensional tectonics, a characteristic set of structures are formed. Extensional faults propagate up from the middle part of the crust until they encounter the salt layer. The weakness of the salt prevents the fault from propagating through. However, continuing displacement on the fault offsets the base of the salt and causes bending of the overburden layer.

Eventually the stresses caused by this bending will be sufficient to fault the overburden. The types of structures developed depend on the initial salt thickness. In the case of a very thick salt layer there is no direct spatial relationship between the faulting beneath the salt and that in the overburden, such a system is said to be *unlinked*.

For intermediate salt thicknesses, the overburden faults are spatially related to the deeper faults, but offset from them, normally into the footwall; these are known as *soft-linked* systems. When the salt layer becomes thin enough, the fault that develops in the overburden is closely aligned with that beneath the salt, and forms a continuous fault surface after only a relatively small displacement, forming a *hard-linked* fault.

In areas of thrust tectonics salt layers act as preferred detachment planes. In the Zagros fold and thrust belt, variations in the thickness and therefore effectiveness of the late Proterozoic Hormuz salt are thought to have had a fundamental control on the overall topography.

SALT WELD

When a salt layer becomes too thin to be an effective detachment layer, due to salt movement, dissolution or removal by faulting, the overburden and the underlying sub-salt basement become effectively *welded* together. This may cause the development of new faults in the cover sequence and is an important consideration when modeling the migration of hydrocarbons. Salt welds may also develop in the vertical direction by putting the sides of a former diapir in contact.

ECONOMIC IMPORTANCE

A significant proportion of the world's hydrocarbon reserves are found in structures related to salt tectonics, including many in the Middle East, the South Atlantic passive margins (Brazil, Gabon and Angola) and the Gulf of Mexico.

5

Geographical Settlement

SEDENTISM

REQUIREMENTS FOR PERMANENT SETTLEMENTS

It is difficult to settle down permanently—to become sedentary—in a landscape without on-site agricultural or cattle-breeding resources, since sedentism requires:

- Sufficient year-round local natural resources;
- Sufficient easily-accessible local natural resources.

Both situations require good preservation and storage technologies. For example cooking, smoking, drying and fermenting of foods, as well as good containers such as pottery, baskets or special pits in which to securely store food whilst making it available. It was only at locations where the resources of several major ecosystems overlapped that enabled the earliest sedentism to occur. For example where a river met the sea, at lagoon environments along the coast, at river confluences, or where flat savanna met hills and mountains with rivers.

BEFORE AGRICULTURE

During the last 30 years archaeological research has shown the earliest sedentism started before one began with on-site agriculture and cattle breeding, and most researchers now believe that sedentism was a prerequisite for the first agriculture to occur. Sedentism, both without agriculture and with this economy, usually meant more people, sturdier houses, new stone tools, more jewelry, burials or cemeteries, more long-distance goods and also clear signs of stratification.

At sedentary sites usually more people lived together for a longer time compared to earlier base camp sites or annual gathering sites. This created deeper cultural layers and thus generally richer archaeological materials. There are also indications that the use of rock art is connected to sedentism, both pre-agricultural and agricultural forms.

REGIONS

A year-round sedentary site, with its usually larger population, generates a substantial demand on local resources, a demand that, for example in the Middle East, could have triggered the first attempts to cultivate plants on-site. In the Middle East the Natufian culture was the first to become sedentary at around 12000 BC.

The Natufians were sedentary during a period of more than 2000 years before they at some sites started to cultivate plants around 10000 BC. However, the first sedentary sites consisted of pre-agricultural ones, and they appeared during the Upper Paleolithic in Moravia in Europe and on the Russian Plain already during the interval of c. 25000-17000 BC.

The Jomon culture in Japan, which was primarily a coastal culture, was sedentary from c. 12000 to 10000 BC until the cultivation of rice at some sites in northern Kyushu. In northernmost Scandinavia, there are several early sedentary sites without evidence of agriculture or cattle breeding. They appear from c. 5300-4500 BC and are all located optimally in the landscape for extraction of major ecosystem resources. In northern Sweden the earliest indication of agriculture occurs at previously sedentary sites, and one example is the Bjurselet site used during the period c. 2700-1700 BC, famous for its large caches of long distance traded flint axes from Denmark and southernmost Sweden. The evidence of small scale agriculture at that site can be seen from c. 2300 BC.

EFFECTS OF SEDENTISM

Sedentism increased contacts and trade, and the first Middle East cereals and cattle in Europe, could have spread through a stepping stone process, where the productive gift was exchanged through a network of large pre-agricultural sedentary sites, rather than a wave of advance spread of people with agricultural economy, and where the smaller sites found in between the bigger sedentary ones, did not get any of the new products. Not all contemporary sites during a certain period were sedentary. Evaluation of habitational sites in northern Sweden indicates that less than 10 percent of all the sites around 4000 BC, were sedentary. At the same time, only 0.5-1 percent of these represented villages with more than 3-4 houses. This means that the old nomadic or migratory life style continued in a parallel fashion for several thousand years, until somewhat more sites turned to sedentism, and gradually switched over to agricultural sedentism.

The shift to sedentism is coupled with the adoption of new subsistence strategies, specifically from foraging to agricultural and animal domestication. The development of sedentism led to the rise of population aggregation and formation of villages, cities, and other community types. In North America, evidence for sedentism emerges around 4500 BC.

FORCED SEDENTISM

Forced sedentism or sedentarization occurs when a dominant group restricts the movements of a nomadic group. Nomadic populations have undergone such a process since the first cultivation of land; the organization of the modern society have imposed demands that have pushed aboriginal populations to adopt a fixed habitat.

There are many examples of forced sedentarization with detrimental effects on minority groups in developed countries. This is mainly caused by lack of sufficient integration into the greater society, old traditions and identity withering and the broken travel cycle of the year, meaning that there may be lack of jobs and activity through significant parts of the year leaving the population reliant on government funded programs.

This can cause great social decline, and also weaken the ethnic identity of the population affected, as examples show of North American indigenous peoples such as the Inuit in the mid-20th century.

THE PROCESS OF URBANIZATION

URBANISM AND URBAN PLANNING

Urbanisation or the process of intense city growth due to prolific economic activities around the city core, often at the expense of the rural or agricultural hinterlands, is largely a product of the 20th Century particularly in the wake of the Industrial Revolution and the advent of the Automobile Industry.

The word urban or urban living can be traced to the original latin word - urbs: meaning a city. The township or city as we know it today represents a place for human activities of a fairly sophisticated nature and not merely a cumulation of numbers. Cities had been established for more than 5,000 years ago mainly in the river valleys of Mesopotamia, the Nile in Egypt, ancient Greece and Crete, the Yang Tse Kiang valley in China and Mohenjo Daro in the Indus Valley. All these places revealed a remarkably advanced state of civilisation and town building achievements. In order to qualify for township or city status the denizens need to break away from its traditional agrigarian and servitudal heritage and claim forth the rights of citizenship to live a civil life. To fully justify the word 'city' man has to attain the most advanced state of social organisation.

Urbanisation means the radical transformation of society and a deep-seated change in human psychology where the environment has made him more aware of the isolation of the individuals and his growing mobility through the modern transportation system and choice of employments. The undisciplined growth of the city has resulted in the uprooting of traditional homes where the individual is swallowed up by the immence scale of thing, exposing him to all kinds destructive influences. At the lowest level is the whole lot of unhappy homes, broken marriages and other ills resulting in the spate of vandalism, graffity and expression of rage such as found in the act of mugging, road-bullying and gangsterism. At the next level is the growing number of society especially the younger generation becoming dependent on drugs and its cancerous nature. At the highest level, in my opinion, is the growing number of H.I.V. Positives found in society due to the supposedly affluence lifestyle we live in today which promote sexual aggravation and unhealthy social practice. Evidently all these three main categories have now become a scurge in our own towns and cities and need very urgent reparations. Although a lot of organisations have been set up to attend to the immediate problems it is felt that a lot can be done through careful planning of the urban dwelling and its physical organisation.

The urban revolution has given rise to new cultural, economic and political trends where the individual is lost in the conglomeration of lonely people working in large concerns, rubbing elbows with strangers in complete anonymity and where relationships are just casual and fleeting. In such a situation the importance of community building is obvious. There is a need for the home to retain its intimate character and neighbourliness as a source of warmth and friendship. There must be room to allow for the town dwellers to make for themselves a circle of friends, creating solid community ties within the framework of the town. Although it is difficult to influence the trends of development with its wide divergent need but useful experience of the past should serve as a guide to the future.

TOWN DESIGN

The design of the town and city involves the meticulous hand of the Masterplanner who must be both an artist and a technician. A qualified town planner does not necessarily make a good town designer. He may have a lot of ideas and sound theories to put into practice but he will need the sensitivity of the the artist to make his planning concept emerge as a praiseworthy physical entity. The beautiful city is a visual experience which requires concerted efforts to reconcile the intrinsic quality of the terrain onto the two-dimensional plan that take into considerations breathtaking vistas. Exquisite natural vegetations and other element of surprises that can put the beholder into a state of awe. It is also widely believed that Mother Earth has an inborn spirituality that guides its future destiny governed by her relationship with the Cosmos. The 'genii loci' which means the spirit of the place in Latin will inevitably determine the future success or otherwise of the city based on its original siting.

The juxtaposition of the early cities that stood the test of time, required painstaking effort in the proper siting by the planner to ensure a healthy and vantage position and to avoid soggy ground, prone to fogs and other ills. The lay of the land or topography should not encourage draughts and strong winds through the artificially formed spaces and lend towards pollution. Hence the important of Fung Shui and geomancy in the laying of the chinese cities and prominent buildings which remain a landmark to this day and the believe that such practice could avoid the depressive attributes of the locality and enhance all the positive ambience. Oftentime the early city builders were architects and military strategist whose contributions to the future growth of the city as a centre of commerce and military fort could not be questioned. Sir Christopher Wren for London, General La Fayette for New York and Captain Sir Francis Light for both Adelaide in Australia and George Town in Penang are some of the famous names that were responsible for city designs across the continents whose handiworks are still appreciated today.

PRESENT APPROACH TO PLANNING

The present day approach to town building where sporadic housing estates are allowed to come together as adjoining growth centers to form larger township is disasterous not only to the future traffic circulation but also to the social units and community well-being. The rows and rows of barrack like terrace blocks built in a rigid pattern to maximise the number of units will no doubt satisfy the developer but will do nothing towards the preservation of the family unit and the quality of life within the built neighbourhoods. With the current system of planning approval the planners are more concerned with satisfying standards from within each housing estate rather than meeting the need of the whole conglomeration of housing estates whose threshold requirements in term of basic facilities and social amenities may differ quite drastically.

Planners fail to grasp the global implications of the fusion that takes place between the independently planned housing estates especially in relation to the disruptive nature of the resultant circulation pattern or road networks. Let us look at a real situation today namely the much talked about traffic crawl in Subang Jaya. When it was first built the overall planning was commendable with its wide dual carriageway roads, up to date town centre design and spacious well equipped playgrounds; the whole set up was a breeze. Subsequently more housing estates by other developers were approved either directly adjoining it or within close proximity to it. Such was the case when Wangsa Baiduri, Subang Perdana, Sunway project and the spate of housing developments that took place at the nearby Puchong area following in their wakes.

Of course the planner has no inkling of the volume of cross towns traffic that are going to be generated by the phenomenal increase in the number of work places, places of entertainment, commercial attractions and other Nodes that sprung up in the locality causing havoc to the crucial origin and destination factors in the traffic pattern. The four lane dual carriageway, the round abouts and even the traffic lights are no longer adequate to meet the cross-town flow let alone cater for the doubling in the number of houses in Subang Jaya itself through its USJ expansion that is still going on and contributing to the growing nightmare. Yet all these could have been avoided if proper scrutiny of the regional growth pattern is made and a forcast attempted on the direction and size of all future developments at the outset. Once the upper limit of all future housing density for the whole region is evolved then it is possible to calculate the ultimate traffic volume and flow in order to design the requisite arterial roads and superhighways to effeciently accomodate the anticipated growth in vehicular traffic.

Unfortunately the government and taxpayers will have to fork out the vast amount of money needed to correct the problem which has become compounded with continuing growth.

MEGACITY

A megacity is usually defined as a metropolitan area with a total population in excess of 10 million people. Some definitions also set a minimum level for population density. A megacity can be a single metropolitan area or two or more metropolitan areas that converge. The terms conurbation, metropolis and metroplex are also applied to the latter. The terms megapolis and megalopolis are sometimes used synonymously with megacity]

In 2011, 21 megacities were in existence – with conurbations such as Mumbai, Tokyo, New York City, and Mexico City having populations in excess of 10 million inhabitants. Greater Tokyo already has 35 million, which is greater than the entire population of Australia and New Zealand combined.

HISTORY

In 1800, only 3% of the world's population lived in cities, a figure that has risen to 47% by the end of the twentieth century. In 1950, there were 83 cities with populations exceeding one million; by 2007, this number had risen to 468. If the trend continues, the world's urban population will double every 38 years. The UN forecasts that today's urban population of 3.2 billion will rise to nearly 5 billion by 2030, when three out of five people will live in cities.

This increase will be most dramatic on the least-urbanized continents, Asia and Africa. Surveys and projections indicate that all urban growth over the next 25 years will be in developing countries. One billion people, one-sixth of the world's population, now live in shanty towns. In many poor countries overpopulated slums exhibit high rates of disease due to unsanitary conditions, malnutrition, and lack of basic health care. By 2030, over 2 billion people in the world will be living in slums. Over 90% of the urban population of Ethiopia, Malawi and Uganda, three of the world's most rural countries, already live in slums.

By 2025, according to the Far Eastern Economic Review, Asia alone will have at least 10 megacities, including Mumbai (33 million), Shanghai (27 million),

Karachi, Pakistan (26.5 million), Dhaka, Bangladesh (26 million) and Jakarta, Indonesia (24.9 million people). Lagos, Nigeria has grown from 300,000 in 1950 to an estimated 12.5 million today, and the Nigerian government estimates that the city will have expanded to 25 million residents by 2015.

LARGEST CITIES

Growth

For almost a thousand years, Rome was the largest, wealthiest, and most politically important city in Europe. Rome's population passed a million by the end of the 1st century BC. Its population declined to a mere 20,000 during the Early Middle Ages, reducing the sprawling city to groups of inhabited buildings interspersed among large areas of ruins and vegetation.

Baghdad was likely the largest city in the world from shortly after its foundation in 762 AD until the 930s, with some estimates putting its population at over one million.

Chinese capital cities Chang'an, Kaifeng also experienced huge population booms during prosperous empires. According to the census in the year 742 recorded in the New Book of Tang, 362,921 families with 1,960,188 persons were counted in Jingzhao, the metropolitan area including small cities in the vicinity.

The medieval settlement surrounding Angkor, the one-time capital of the Khmer Empire which flourished between the 9th and 15th centuries, could have supported a population of up to one million people.

In 1950, New York City was the only urban area with a population of over 10 million. Geographers had identified 25 such areas as of October 2005, as compared with 19 megacities in 2004 and only nine in 1985. This increase has happened as the world's population moves towards the high (75–85%) urbanization levels of North America and Western Europe. The 1990 census marked the first time the majority of US citizens lived in cities with over 1 million inhabitants.

In the 2000s, the largest megacity is the Greater Tokyo Area. The population of this urban agglomeration includes areas such as Yokohama and Kawasaki, and is estimated to be between 35 and 36 million. This variation in estimates can be accounted for by different definitions of what the area encompasses.

While the prefectures of Tokyo, Chiba, Kanagawa, and Saitama are commonly included in statistical information, the Japan Statistics Bureau only includes the area within 50 kilometers of the Tokyo Metropolitan Government Offices in Shinjuku, thus arriving at a smaller population estimate. A characteristic issue of megacities is the difficulty in defining their outer limits and accurately estimating the populations.

The twenty-five largest mega cities, according to these criteria are:

Rank	Megacity	Country	Continent	Population	Annual Growth
1	Tokyo	Japan	Asia	34,200,000	0.60%
2	Guangzhou	China	Asia	24,900,000	4.00%
3	Seoul	South Korea	Asia	24,500,000	1.40%
4	Delhi	India	Asia	23,900,000	4.60%
5	Mumbai	India	Asia	23,300,000	2.90%
6	Mexico City	Mexico	North America	22,800,000	2.00%
7	New York City	USA	North America	22,200,000	0.30%
8	São Paulo	Brazil	South America	20,800,000	1.40%
9	Manila	Philippines	Asia	20,100,000	2.50%
10	Shanghai	China	Asia	18,800,000	2.20%
11	Jakarta	Indonesia	Asia	18,700,000	2.00%
12	Los Angeles	USA	North America	17,900,000	1.10%
13	Osaka	Japan	Asia	16,800,000	0.15%
14	Karachi	Pakistan	Asia	16,700,000	4.90%
15	Kolkata	India	Asia	16,600,000	2.00%
16	Cairo	Egypt	Africa	15,300,000	2.60%
17=	Buenos Aires	Argentina	South America	14,800,000	1.00%
17=	Moscow	Russia	Europe	14,800,000	0.20%
19	Dhaka	Bangladesh	Asia	14,000,000	4.10%
20	Beijing	China	Asia	13,900,000	2.70%
21	Tehran	Iran	Asia	13,100,000	2.60%
22	Istanbul	Turkey	Europe & Asia	13,000,000	2.80%
23=	London	United Kingdom	Europe	12,500,000	0.70%
23=	Rio de Janeiro	Brazil	South America	12,500,000	1.00%
25	Lagos	Nigeria	Africa	12,100,000	3.20%

Another list defines megacities as urban agglomerations instead of metropolitan areas. As of 2010, there are 25 megacities by this definition.

CHALLENGES

Slums

According to the United Nations, the proportion of urban dwellers living in slums decreased from 47 percent to 37 percent in the developing world between 1990 and 2005. However, due to rising population, the absolute number of slum dwellers is rising.

The majority of these come from the fringes of urban margins, located in legal and illegal settlements with insufficient housing and sanitation. This has been caused by massive migration, both internal and transnational, into cities, which has caused growth rates of urban populations and spatial concentrations not seen before in history. These issues raise problems in the political, social, and economic arenas. Slum dwellers often have minimal or no access to education, healthcare, or the urban economy.

Homelessness

Megacities often have significant numbers of homeless people. The actual legal definition of homelessness varies from country to country, or among different entities or institutions in the same country or region.

Traffic congestion

Traffic congestion is a condition on road networks that occurs as use increases, and is characterized by slower speeds, longer trip times, and increased vehicular queueing.

Urban sprawl

A flat land area in the greater Los Angeles area almost completely filled with houses, buildings, roads, and freeways. Areas constructed to capacity contribute to urban expansion. Urban sprawl, also known as suburban sprawl, is a multifaceted concept, which includes the spreading outwards of a city and its suburbs to its outskirts to low-density, auto-dependent development on rural land, with associated design features that encourage car dependency. As a result, some critics argue that sprawl has certain disadvantages, including, longer transport distances to work, high car dependence, and inadequate facilities e.g.: health, cultural. etc. and higher per-person infrastructure costs. Discussions and debates about sprawl are often obfuscated by the ambiguity associated with the phrase. For example, some commentators measure sprawl only with the average number of residential units per acre in a given area. But others associate it with decentralization (spread of population without a well-defined center), discontinuity (leapfrog development), segregation of uses, etc.

Gentrification

Gentrification and urban gentrification denote the socio-cultural changes in an area resulting from wealthier people buying housing property in a less prosperous community. Consequent to gentrification, the average income increases and average family size decreases in the community, which may result in the informal economic eviction of the lower-income residents, because of increased rents, house prices, and property taxes. This type of population change reduces industrial land use when it is redeveloped for commerce and housing. In addition, new businesses, catering to a more affluent base of consumers, tend to move into formerly blighted areas, further increasing the appeal to more affluent migrants and decreasing the accessibility to less wealthy natives.

Environmental problems

Air pollution

Air pollution is the introduction of chemicals, particulate matter, or biological materials that cause harm or discomfort to humans or other living organisms, or damages the natural environment into the atmosphere. Many urban areas have significant problems with smog, a type of air pollution derived from vehicular emission from internal combustion engines and industrial fumes that react in the atmosphere with sunlight to form secondary pollutants that also combine with the primary emissions to form photochemical smog.

Smog is also caused by large amounts of coal burning, which creates a mixture of smoke and sulfur dioxide. World coal consumption was about 6,743,786,000 short tons in 2006 and is expected to increase 48% to 9.98 billion short tons by 2030. China produced 2.38 billion tons in 2006. India produced about 447.3 million tons in 2006. 68.7% of China's electricity comes from coal. The USA consumes about 14% of the world total, using 90% of it for generation of electricity.

IN FICTION

- Many of the following fictional cities were inspired by Fritz Lang's 1927 film, Metropolis and the influential depiction of Los Angeles in Ridley Scott's 1982 film, Blade Runner.
- Megacities are a common backdrop in dystopian science fiction, with examples such as the Sprawl in William Gibson's Neuromancer, and Mega-City One, a megalopolis of over 400 million people across the east coast of the United States, in the Judge Dredd comic. In Demolition Man a megacity called "San Angeles" was formed from the joining of Los Angeles, Santa Barbara, San Diego and the surrounding metropolitan regions following a massive earthquake in 2010.
- Fictional planet-wide megacities (ecumenopoleis) include Trantor in Isaac Asimov's Foundation series of books and Coruscant in the Star Wars universe. Other examples are 'City Europe' in David Wingrove's Chung Kuo series of books, Holy Terra and the hive cities of Necromunda in Warhammer 40,000 and Ravnica in the eponymous Magic: The Gathering expansion.
- The Fifth Element features a parody of New York City set in 2263. Buildings are so high that people use flying cars to get around and the ground level of the Earth is obscured by pollution.
- The 1973 film Soylent Green, based on Harry Harrison's novel Make Room, Make Room, depicted New York City in 2022 with a population of 40 million. It is not said how large the city is, but the main character does make the comment that a wanted criminal is "over the city line in Philadelphia" implying that it has sprawled that far.
- The MMORPG game "Guild Wars" has a massive, fictional megacity on its southern continent, Cantha, called Kaineng City which is very run down, corrupted, and in colossal slums and poverty. The city is a

daily struggle for survival infested with crime, plagues, starvation, and a massive sewer system called the "undercity". Another MMORPG game City of Heroes is set in the fictional megacity known as Paragon City, which contains two other cities: Galaxy City and Skyway City. In the two novels based on the game as well as the official timeline for the game, Paragon City has existed at least as far back as the early to mid-19th century.

- The sprawling metropolis featured in The Matrix series of films can be considered a megacity. It is based on Sydney, Chicago and Oakland, California. While the city is never referenced by name in the films, in the MMORPG The Matrix Online, the city itself is called the Mega City.

6

Weather and Climate

BASICS DEFINITIONS

WEATHER

Weather is the state of the atmosphere, to the degree that it is hot or cold, wet or dry, calm or stormy, clear or cloudy. Most weather phenomena occur in the troposphere, just below the stratosphere. Weather refers, generally, to day-to-day temperature and precipitation activity, whereas climate is the term for the average atmospheric conditions over longer periods of time. When used without qualification, "weather" is understood to be the weather of Earth. Weather is driven by density (temperature and moisture) differences between one place and another. These differences can occur due to the sun angle at any particular spot, which varies by latitude from the tropics.The strong temperature contrast between polar and tropical air gives rise to the jet stream.

Weather systems in the mid-latitudes, such as extratropical cyclones, are caused by instabilities of the jet stream flow. Because the Earth's axis is tilted relative to its orbital plane, sunlight is incident at different angles at different times of the year. On Earth's surface, temperatures usually range ±40 °C (100 °F to "40 °F) annually. Over thousands of years, changes in Earth's orbit affect the amount and distribution of solar energy received by the Earth and influence long-term climate and global climate change. Surface temperature differences in turn cause pressure differences. Higher altitudes are cooler than lower altitudes due to differences in compressional heating.

Weather forecasting is the application of science and technology to predict the state of the atmosphere for a future time and a given location. The atmosphere is a chaotic system,so small changes to one part of the system can grow to have large effects on the system as a whole. Human attempts to control the weather have occurred throughout human history, and there is evidence that human activity such as agriculture and industry has inadvertently modified weather patterns. Studying how the weather works on other planets has been helpful in understanding how weather works on Earth. A famous landmark in the Solar System, Jupiter's Great Red Spot, is an anticyclonic storm known to have existed for at least 300 years. However, weather is not limited to planetary bodies. A star's corona is constantly being lost to space, creating what is essentially a very thin atmosphere throughout the Solar System. The movement of mass ejected from the Sun is known as the solar wind.

CLIMATE

Climate encompasses the statistics of temperature, humidity, atmospheric pressure, wind, rainfall, atmospheric particle count and other meteorological elements in a given region over a long period of time. Climate can be contrasted to weather, which is the present condition of these same elements and their variations over shorter time periods. The climate of a location is affected by its latitude, terrain, and altitude, as well as nearby water bodies and their currents. Climates can be classified according to the average and the typical ranges of different variables, most commonly temperature and precipitation.

The most commonly used classification scheme was originally developed by Wladimir Köppen. The Thornthwaite system, in use since 1948, incorporates evapotranspiration in addition to temperature and precipitation information and is used in studying animal species diversity and potential impacts of climate changes. The Bergeron and Spatial Synoptic Classification systems focus on the origin of air masses that define the climate of a region. Paleoclimatology is the study of ancient climates.

Since direct observations of climate are not available before the 19th century, paleoclimates are inferred from proxy variables that include non-biotic evidence such as sediments found in lake beds and ice cores, and biotic evidence such as tree rings and coral. Climate models are mathematical models of past, present and future climates. Climate change may occur over long and short timescales from a variety of factors; recent warming is discussed in global warming. Climate is commonly defined as the weather averaged over a long period of time. The standard averaging period is 30 years, but other periods may be used depending on the purpose. Climate also includes statistics other than the average, such as the magnitudes of day-to-day or year-to-year variations. The Intergovernmental Panel on Climate Change (IPCC) glossary definition is:

- Climate in a narrow sense is usually defined as the "average weather," or more rigorously, as the statistical description in terms of the mean and variability of relevant quantities over a period of time ranging from months to thousands or millions of years. The classical period is 30 years, as defined by the World Meteorological Organization (WMO). These quantities are most often surface variables such as temperature, precipitation, and wind. Climate in a wider sense is the state, including a statistical description, of the climate system.

The difference between climate and weather is usefully summarized by the popular phrase "Climate is what you expect, weather is what you get." Over historical time spans there are a number of nearly constant variables that determine climate, including latitude, altitude, proportion of land to water, and proximity to oceans and mountains.

These change only over periods of millions of years due to processes such as plate tectonics. Other climate determinants are more dynamic: for example, the thermohaline circulation of the ocean leads to a 5 °C (9 °F) warming of the northern Atlantic ocean compared to other ocean basins. Other ocean currents redistribute heat between land and water on a more regional scale. The density and type of vegetation coverage affects solar heat absorption, water retention, and rainfall on a regional level.

Alterations in the quantity of atmospheric greenhouse gases determines the amount of solar energy retained by the planet, leading to global warming or global cooling. The variables which determine climate are numerous and the interactions complex, but there is general agreement that the broad outlines are understood, at least insofar as the determinants of historical climate change are concerned.

AIR TEMPERATURE

- Temperature is a measure of the level of sensible heat (temperature measured by a thermometer) of matter, whether it is gaseous (air), liquid (water), or solid (rock or dry soil).
- Air temperature is the intensity aspect of sun's energy that strikes the earth's surface.
- Because the amount of energy from the sun reaching the earth varies from day to day, from season to season, and from latitude to latitude, temperatures also vary.
- The earth as a whole receives a constant flow of radiant short-wave energy from the sun. The earth also radiates long-wave energy to space.
- During the day, the flow of short-wave radiation absorbed exceeds long -wave energy emitted, and the surface temperature increases.
- At no short-wave radiation strikes the darkened side of the earth. But, long-wave energy is still emitted from the surface. Therefore, surface temperatures decrease.

AIR PRESSURE AND WIND

The wind blows because of differences in air pressure from one location to another. Wind blows from areas of high pressure toward areas of low pressure. If the high pressure area is very close to the low pressure area, or if the pressure difference is very great, the wind can blow very fast.

WHAT IS AIR PRESSURE

Imagine a group of acrobats at the circus. One climbs up and stands on another's shoulders. The weight of the acrobat on top puts more pressure on the one below. Then another acrobat climbs up and stands on the second acrobat's shoulders. Now there's even more pressure on the acrobat on the bottom because he is under the weight of the two acrobats above him. It's the same with air. Yes, air has weight, and probably more than you think. In fact, the weight of the air on your desk at school weighs about 11,000 pounds. That's about the same weight as a school bus! Since air pressure pushes in all directions, the air pressure pushing up from under your desk balances out the air pushing down on it, so the desk doesn't collapse under the weight. Just like an acrobat with two people stacked on his shoulders would want to move to where there wasn't so much pressure on him, air moves from areas where the pressure is higher to where it is lower.

CAUSES OF AIR PRESSURE

Air pressure depends on the density of the air, or how close together its molecules are. You know that a hard rubber ball is more dense than a Styrofoam ball and that ice cream is more dense than whipped cream. Air lower in the atmosphere is more dense than air above, so air pressure down low is greater than air pressure higher up. Temperature also makes changes in air pressure. In cold air, the molecules are more closely packed together than in warm air, so cold air is more dense than warm air.

RISING AND SINKING AIR

Since warm air is less dense and creates less air pressure, it will rise; cold air is denser and creates greater air pressure, and so it will sink. When warm air rises, cooler air will often move in to replace it, so wind often moves from areas where it's colder to areas where it's warmer. The greater the difference between the high and low pressure or the shorter the distance between the high and low pressure areas, the faster the wind will blow. Wind also blows faster if there's nothing in its way, so winds are usually stronger over oceans or flat ground. Meteorologists can forecast the speed and direction of wind by measuring air pressure with a barometer.

WIND DIRECTION

Although wind blows from areas of high pressure to areas of low pressure, it doesn't blow in a straight line. That's because the earth is rotating. In the northern hemisphere, the spin of the earth causes winds to curve to the right (to the left in the southern hemisphere). This is called the coriolis effect. So in the northern hemisphere, winds blow clockwise around an area of high pressure and counter-clockwise around low pressure.

OCEAN CURRENTS

DEFINITIONS

The movement of ocean water is one of the two principal sources of discrepancy between dead reckoned and actual positions of vessels. Water in motion is called a current; the direction toward which it moves is called set, and its speed is called drift. Modern shipping speeds have lessened the impact of currents on a typical voyage, and since electronic navigation allows continuous adjustment of course, there is less need to estimate current set and drift before setting the course to be steered. Nevertheless, a knowledge of ocean currents can be used in cruise planning to reduce transit times.

Ocean current models are an integral part of ship routing systems. Oceanographers have developed a number of methods of classifying currents in order to facilitate descriptions of their physics and geography. Currents may be referred to according to their forcing mechanism as either wind driven or thermohaline. Alternatively, they may be classified according to their depth (surface, intermediate, deep or bottom). The surface circulation of the world ocean is mostly wind driven. Thermohaline currents are driven by differences in heat and salt and are associated with the sinking of dense water at high latitudes; the currents driven by thermohaline forcing are typically subsurface. Note that this classification scheme is not unambiguous; the circumpolar current, which is wind driven, extends from the surface to the bottom. A periodic current is one for which the speed or direction changes cyclically at somewhat regular intervals, such as a tidal current. A seasonal current is one which changes in speed or direction due to seasonal winds. The mean circulation of the ocean consists of semi-permanent currents which experience relatively little periodic or seasonal change. A coastal current flows roughly parallel to a coast, outside the surf zone, while a longshore current is one parallel to a shore, inside the surf zone, generated by waves striking the beach at an angle. Any current some distance from the shore may be called an offshore current, and one close to the shore an inshore current.

CAUSES OF OCEAN CURRENTS

The primary generating forces are wind and differences in density of the water caused by variations in heat and salt. Currents generated by these forces are modified by such factors as depth of water, underwater topography including shape of the basin in which the current is running, extent and location of land, and deflection by the rotation of the earth.

WIND DRIVEN CURRENTS

The stress of wind blowing across the sea causes a surface layer of water to move. Due to the low viscosity of water, this stress is not directly communicated to the ocean interior, but is balanced by the Coriolis force within a relatively thin surface layer, 10-200m thick. This layer is called the Ekman layer and the motion of this layer is called the Ekman transport. Because of the deflection by the Coriolis force, the Ekman transport is not in the direction of the wind, but is 90° to the right in the Northern Hemisphere and 90° toward the left in the Southern Hemisphere. The amount of water flowing in this layer depends only upon the wind and the Coriolis force and is independent of the depth of the Ekman layer and the viscosity of the water.

The large scale convergence or divergence of Ekman transport serves to drive the general ocean circulation. Consider the case of the Northern Hemisphere subtropics. To the south lie easterly winds with associated northward Ekman transport. To the north lie westerly winds with southward Ekman transport. The convergence of these Ekman transports is called Ekman pumping and results in a thickening of the upper ocean and a increase in the depth of the thermocline. The resulting subsurface pressure gradients, balanced by the Coriolis force, give rise to the anticyclonic subtropical gyres found at mid latitudes in each ocean basin. In subpolar regions, Ekman suction produces cyclonic gyres. These wind driven gyres are not symmetrical.

Along the western boundary of the oceans, currents are narrower, stronger, and deeper, often following a meandering course. These currents are sometimes called a stream. In contrast, currents in mid-ocean and at the eastern boundary, are often broad, shallow and slow-moving. Sometimes these are called drift currents. Within the Ekman layer, the currents actually form a spiral.

At the surface, the difference between wind direction and surface wind-current direction varies from about 15° along shallow coastal areas to a maximum of 45° in the deep oceans. As the motion is transmitted to successively deep layers, the Coriolis force continues to deflect the current. At the bottom of the Ekman layer, the current flows in the opposite direction to the surface current. This shift of current directions with depth, combined with the decrease in velocity with depth, is called the Ekman spiral. The velocity of the surface current is the sum of the velocities of the Ekman, geostrophic, tidal, and other currents. The Ekman surface current or wind drift current depends upon the speed of the wind, its constancy, the length of time it has blown, and other factors. In general, however, wind drift current is about 2 percent of the wind speed, or a little less, in deep water where the wind has been blowing steadily for at least 12 hours.

CURRENTS RELATED TO DENSITY DIFFERENCES

The density of water varies with salinity, temperature, and pressure. At any given depth, the differences in density are due only to differences in temperature and salinity. With sufficient data, maps showing geographical density distribution at a certain depth can be drawn, with lines connecting points of equal density. These lines would be similar to isobars on a weather map and serve an analogous purpose, showing areas of high density and those of low density. In an area of high density, the water surface is lower than in an area of low density, the maximum difference in height being about 1 meter in 100 km. Because of this difference, water tends to flow from an area of higher water (low density) to one of lower water (high density). But due to rotation of the earth, it is deflected by the Coriolis force or toward the right in the Northern Hemisphere, and toward the left in the Southern Hemisphere. This balance, between subsurface pressure fields and the Coriolis force, is called geostrophic equilibrium. At a given latitude, the greater the density gradient (rate of change with distance), the faster the geostrophic current.

OCEANIC CIRCULATION

A number of ocean currents flow with great persistence, setting up a circulation that continues with relatively little change throughout the year. Because of the influence of wind in creating current, there is a relationship between this oceanic circulation and the general circulation of the atmosphere. The oceanic circulation is shown on the chart following this page with the names of the major ocean currents. Some differences in opinion exist regarding the names and limits of some of the currents, but those shown are representative. Speed may vary somewhat with the season. This is particularly noticeable in the Indian Ocean and along the South China coast, where currents are influenced to a marked degree by the monsoons.

Southern Ocean Currents

The Southern Ocean has no meridional boundaries and its waters are free to circulate around the world. It serves as a conveyor belt for the other oceans, exchanging waters between them. The northern boundary of the Southern Ocean is marked by the Subtropical Convergence zone. This zone marks the transition from the temperate region of the ocean to the polar region and is associated with the surfacing of the main thermocline. This zone is typically found at 40°S but varies with longitude and season. In the Antarctic, the circulation is generally from west to east in a broad, slow-moving current extending completely around Antarctica.

This is called the Antarctic Circumpolar Current or the West Wind Drift, and it is formed partly by the strong westerly wind in this area, and partly by density differences. This current is augmented by the Brazil and Falkland Currents in the Atlantic, the East Australia Current in the Pacific, and the Agulhas Current in the Indian Ocean. In return, part of it curves northward to form the Cape Horn, Falkland, and most of the Benguela Currents in the Atlantic, and the Peru Current in the Pacific. In a narrow zone next to the Antarctic continent, a westward flowing coastal current is usually found. This current is called the East Wind Drift because it is attributed to the prevailing easterly winds which occur there.

Atlantic Ocean Currents

The trade winds set up a system of equatorial currents which at times extends over as much as 50° of latitude or more. There are two westerly flowing currents conforming generally with the areas of trade winds, separated by a weaker, easterly flowing countercurrent. The North Equatorial Current originates to the northward of the Cape Verde Islands and flows almost due west at an average speed of about 0.7 knot. The South Equatorial Current is more extensive. It starts off the west coast of Africa, south of the Gulf of Guinea, and flows in a generally westerly direction at an average speed of about 0.6 knot.

However, the speed gradually increases until it may reach a value of 2.5 knots, or more, off the east coast of South America. As the current approaches Cabo de Sao Roque, the eastern extremity of South America, it divides, the southern part curving toward the south along the coast of Brazil, and the northern part being deflected northward by the continent of South America. Between the North and South Equatorial Currents, the weaker North Equatorial Countercurrent sets toward the east in the general vicinity of the doldrums. This is fed by water from the two westerly flowing equatorial currents, particularly the South Equatorial Current. The extent and strength of the Equatorial Countercurrent changes with the seasonal variations of the wind.

It reaches a maximum during July and August, when it extends from about 50° west longitude to the Gulf of Guinea. During its minimum, in December and January, it is of very limited extent, the western portion disappearing altogether. That part of the South Equatorial Current flowing along the northern coast of South America which does not feed the Equatorial Countercurrent unites with the North Equatorial Current at a point west of the Equatorial Countercurrent. A large part of the combined current flows through various passages between the Windward Islands and into the Caribbean Sea. It sets toward the west, and then somewhat north of west, finally arriving off the Yucatan peninsula.

From there, the water enters the Gulf of Mexico and forms the Loop Current; the path of the Loop Current is variable with a 13-month period. It begins by flowing directly from Yucatan to the Florida Straits, but gradually grows to flow anticyclonically around the entire Eastern Gulf; it then collapses, again following the direct path from Yucatan to the Florida Straits, with the loop in the Eastern Gulf becoming a separate eddy which slowly flows into the Western Gulf. Within the Straits of Florida, the Loop Current feeds the beginnings of the most remarkable of American ocean currents, the Gulf Stream. Off the southeast coast of Florida this current is augmented by the Antilles

Current which flows along the northern coasts of Puerto Rico, Hispaniola, and Cuba. Another current flowing eastward of the Bahamas joins the stream north of these islands. The Gulf Stream follows generally along the east coast of North America, flowing around Florida, northward and then northeastward toward Cape Hatteras, and then curving toward the east and becoming broader and slower. After passing the Grand Banks, it turns more toward the north and becomes a broad drift current flowing across the North Atlantic. The part in the Straits of Florida is sometimes called the Florida Current. A tremendous volume of water flows northward in the Gulf Stream. It can be distinguished by its deep indigo-blue color, which contrasts sharply with the dull green of the surrounding water.

It is accompanied by frequent squalls. When the Gulf Stream encounters the cold water of the Labrador Current, principally in the vicinity of the Grand Banks, there is little mixing of the waters. Instead, the junction is marked by a sharp change in temperature. The line or surface along which this occurs is called the cold wall. When the warm Gulf Stream water encounters cold air, evaporation is so rapid that the rising vapor may be visible as frost smoke. Investigations have shown that the current itself is much narrower and faster than previously supposed, and considerably more variable in its position and speed. The maximum current off Florida ranges from about 2 to 4 knots.

Northward, the speed is generally less, and it decreases further after the current passes Cape Hatteras. As the stream meanders and shifts position, eddies sometimes break off and continue as separate, circular flows until they dissipate. Boats in the Newport-Bermuda sailing yacht race have been known to be within sight of each other and be carried in opposite directions by different parts of the same current. This race is generally won by the boat which catches an eddy just right. As the current shifts position, its extent does not always coincide with the area of warm, blue water. When the sea is relatively smooth, the edges of the current are marked by ripples. A recirculation region exists adjacent to and southwest of the Gulf Stream. The flow of water in the recirculation region is opposite to that in the Gulf Stream and surface currents are much weaker, generally less than half a knot. As the Gulf Stream continues eastward and northeastward beyond the Grand Banks, it gradually widens and decreases speed until it becomes a vast, slow-moving current known as the North Atlantic Current, in the general vicinity of the prevailing westerlies. In the eastern part of the Atlantic it divides into the Northeast Drift Current and the Southeast Drift Current.

The Northeast Drift Current continues in a generally northeasterly direction toward the Norwegian Sea. As it does so, it continues to widen and decrease speed. South of Iceland it branches to form the Irminger Current and the Norway Current. The Irminger Current curves toward the north and northwest to join the East Greenland Current southwest of Iceland. The Norway

Current continues in a northeasterly direction along the coast of Norway. Part of it, the North Cape Current, rounds North Cape into the Barents Sea. The other part curves toward the north and becomes known as the Spitsbergen Current. Before reaching Svalbard (Spitsbergen), it curves toward the west and joins the cold East Greenland Current flowing southward in the Greenland Sea.

As this current flows past Iceland, it is further augmented by the Irminger Current. Off Kap Farvel, at the southern tip of Greenland, the East Greenland Current curves sharply to the northwest following the coastline. As it does so, it becomes known as the West Greenland Current, and its character changes from that of an intense western boundary current to a weaker eastern boundary current. This current continues along the west coast of Greenland, through Davis Strait, and into Baffin Bay. In Baffin Bay the West Greenland Current generally follows the coast, curving westward off Kap York to form the southerly flowing Labrador Current. This cold current flows southward off the coast of Baffin Island, through Davis Strait, along the coast of Labrador and Newfoundland, to the Grand Banks, carrying with it large quantities of ice.

Here it encounters the warm water of the Gulf Stream, creating the cold wall. Some of the cold water flows southward along the east coast of North America, inshore of the Gulf Stream, as far as Cape Hatteras. The remainder curves toward the east and flows along the northern edge of the North Atlantic and Northeast Drift Currents, gradually merging with them. The Southeast Drift Current curves toward the east, southeast, and then south as it is deflected by the coast of Europe. It flows past the Bay of Biscay, toward southeastern Europe and the Canary Islands, where it continues as the Canary Current. In the vicinity of the Cape Verde Islands, this current divides, part of it curving toward the west to help form the North Equatorial Current, and part of it curving toward the east to follow the coast of Africa into the Gulf of Guinea, where it is known as the Guinea Current. This current is augmented by the North Equatorial Countercurrent and, in summer, it is strengthened by monsoon winds. It flows in close proximity to the South Equatorial Current, but in the opposite direction. As it curves toward the south, still following the African coast, it merges with the South Equatorial Current.

The clockwise circulation of the North Atlantic leaves a large central area between the recirculation region and the Canary Current which has no well-defined currents. This area is known as the Sargasso Sea, from the large quantities of sargasso or gulfweed encountered there. That branch of the South Equatorial Current which curves toward the south off the east coast of South America, follows the coast as the warm, highly-saline Brazil Current, which in some respects resembles a weak Gulf Stream. Off Uruguay it encounters the colder, less-salty Falkland or Malvinas Current forming a sharp meandering front in which eddies may form. The two currents curve toward the east to form the broad, slow-moving, South Atlantic Current in the general vicinity of the prevailing westerlies and the front dissipates somewhat.

This current flows eastward to a point west of the Cape of Good Hope, where it curves northward to follow the west coast of Africa as the strong Benguela Current, augmented somewhat by part of the Agulhas Current flowing around the southern part of Africa from the Indian Ocean. As it continues northward, the current gradually widens and slows. At a point east of St. Helena Island it curves westward to continue as part of the South Equatorial Current, thus completing the counterclockwise circulation of the South Atlantic. The Benguela Current is also augmented somewhat by the West Wind Drift, a current which flows easterly around Antarctica. As the West Wind Drift flows past Cape Horn, that part in the immediate vicinity of the cape is called the Cape Horn Current. This current rounds the cape and flows in a northerly and northeasterly direction along the coast of South America as the Falkland or Malvinas Current.

Pacific Ocean Currents

Pacific Ocean currents follow the general pattern of those in the Atlantic. The North Equatorial Current flows westward in the general area of the northeast trades, and the South Equatorial Current follows a similar path in the region of the southeast trades. Between these two, the weaker North Equatorial Countercurrent sets toward the east, just north of the equator. After passing the Mariana Islands, the major part of the North Equatorial Current curves somewhat toward the northwest, past the Philippines and Taiwan. Here it is deflected further toward the north, where it becomes known as the Kuroshio, and then toward the northeast past the Nansei Shoto and Japan, and on in a more easterly direction.

Part of the Kuroshio, called the Tsushima Current, flows through Tsushima Strait, between Japan and Korea, and the Sea of Japan, following generally the northwest coast of Japan. North of Japan it curves eastward and then southeastward to rejoin the main part of the Kuroshio. The limits and volume of the Kuroshio are influenced by the monsoons, being augmented during the season of southwesterly winds, and diminished when the northeasterly winds are prevalent.

The Kuroshio (Japanese for "Black Stream") is so named because of the dark color of its water. It is sometimes called the Japan Current. In many respects it is similar to the Gulf Stream of the Atlantic. Like that current, it carries large quantities of warm tropical water to higher latitudes, and then curves toward the east as a major part of the general clockwise circulation in the Northern Hemisphere. As it does so, it widens and slows, continuing on between the Aleutians and the Hawaiian Islands, where it becomes known as the North Pacific Current.

As this current approaches the North American continent, most of it is deflected toward the right to form a clockwise circulation between the west coast of North America and the Hawaiian Islands called the California Current. This part of the current has become so broad that the circulation is generally weak. Near the coast, the southeastward flow intensifies and average speeds are about 0.8 knot. But the flow pattern is complex, with offshore directed jets often found near more prominent capes, and poleward flow often found over the upper slope and outer continental shelf. It is strongest near land. Near the southern end of Baja California, this current curves sharply to the west and broadens to form the major portion of the North Equatorial Current. During the winter, a weak countercurrent flows northwestward, inshore of the southeastward flowing California Current, along the west coast of North America from Baja California to Vancouver Island.

This is called the Davidson Current. Off the west coast of Mexico, south of Baja California the current flows southeastward during the winter as a continuation of part of the California Current. During the summer, the current in this area is northwestward as a continuation of the North Equatorial Countercurrent. As in the Atlantic, there is in the Pacific a counterclockwise circulation to the north of the clockwise circulation. Cold water flowing southward through the western part of Bering Strait between Alaska and Siberia, is joined by water circulating counterclockwise in the Bering Sea to form the Oyashio. As the current leaves the strait, it curves toward the right and flows southwesterly along the coast of Siberia and the Kuril Islands. This current brings quantities of sea ice, but no icebergs. When it encounters the Kuroshio, the Oyashio curves southward and then eastward, the greater portion joining the Kuroshio and North Pacific Current. The northern branch of the North Pacific Current curves in a counterclockwise direction to form the Alaska Current, which generally follows the coast of Canada and Alaska. When the Alaska Current turns to the southwest and flows along the Kodiak Island and the Alaska Peninsula, its character changes to that of a western boundary current and it is called the Alaska Stream.

When this westward flow arrives off the Aleutian Islands, it is less intense and becomes known as the Aleutian Current. Part of it flows along the southern side of these islands to about the 180th meridian, where it curves in a counterclockwise direction and becomes an easterly flowing current, being augmented by the northern part of the Oyashio. The other part of the Aleutian Current flows through various openings between the Aleutian Islands, into the Bering Sea. Here it flows in a general counterclockwise direction. The southward flow along the Kamchatka peninsula is called the Kamchatka Current which feeds the southerly flowing Oyashio. Some water flows northward from the Bering Sea through the eastern side of the Bering Strait, into the Arctic Ocean.

The South Equatorial Current, extending in width between about 4°N latitude and 10°S, flows westward from South America to the western Pacific. After this current crosses the 180th meridian, the major part curves in a counterclockwise direction, entering the Coral Sea, and then curving more sharply toward the south along the east coast of Australia, where it is known as the East Australian Current. The East Australian Current is the weakest of the subtropical western boundary currents and separates from the Australian coast near 34°S. The path of the current from Australia to New Zealand is known as the Tasman Front, which marks the boundary between the warm water of the Coral Sea and the colder water of the Tasman Sea. The continuation of the East Australian Current east of New Zealand is the East Auckland Current.

The East Auckland Current varies seasonally: in winter, it separates from the shelf and flows eastward, merging with the West Wind Drift, while in winter it follows the New Zealand shelf southward as the East Cape Current until it reaches Chatham Rise where it turns eastward, thence merging with the West Wind Drift. Near the southern extremity of South America, most of this current flows eastward into the Atlantic, but part of it curves toward the left and flows generally northward along the west coast of South America as the Peru Current or Humboldt Current. Occasionally a set directly toward land is encountered. At about Cabo Blanco, where the coast falls away to the right, the current curves toward the left, past the Galapagos Islands, where it takes a westerly set and constitutes the major portion of the South Equatorial Current, thus completing the counterclockwise circulation of the South Pacific. During the northern hemisphere summer, a weak northern branch of the South Equatorial Current, known as the New Guinea Coastal Current, continues on toward the west and northwest along both the southern and northeastern coasts of New Guinea. The southern part flows through Torres Strait, between New Guinea and Australia, into the Arafura Sea. Here, it gradually loses its identity, part of it flowing on toward the west as part of the South Equatorial Current of the Indian Ocean, and part of it following the coast of Australia and finally joining the easterly flowing West Wind Drift. The northern part of New Guinea Coastal Current both curves in a clockwise direction to help form the Pacific Equatorial Countercurrent and off Mindanao turns southward to form a southward flowing boundary current called the Mindanao Current. During the northern hemisphere winter, the New Guinea Coastal Current may reverse direction for a few months.

Indian Ocean Currents

Indian Ocean currents follow generally the pattern of the Atlantic and Pacific but with differences caused principally by the monsoons, the more limited extent of water in the Northern Hemisphere, and by limited communication with the Pacific Ocean along the eastern boundary. During the northern hemisphere winter, the North Equatorial Current and South Equatorial Current flow toward the west, with the weaker, eastward Equatorial Countercurrent flowing between them, as in the Atlantic and Pacific (but somewhat south of the equator). But during the northern hemisphere summer, both the North Equatorial Current and the Equatorial Countercurrent are replaced by the Southwest Monsoon Current, which flows eastward and southeastward across the Arabian Sea and the Bay of Bengal. Near Sumatra, this current curves in a clockwise direction and flows westward, augmenting the South Equatorial Current, and setting up a clockwise circulation in the northern part of the Indian Ocean. Off the coast of Somalia, the Somali Current reverses direction during the northern hemisphere summer with northward currents reaching speeds of 5 knots or more.

Twice a year, around May and November, westerly winds along the equator result in an eastward Equatorial Jet which feeds warm water towards Sumatra. As the South Equatorial Current approaches the coast of Africa, it curves toward the southwest, part of it flowing through the Mozambique Channel between Madagascar and the mainland, and part flowing along the east coast of Madagascar. At the southern end of this island the two join to form the strong Agulhas Current, which is analogous to the Gulf Stream. This current, when opposed by strong winds from Southern Ocean storms, creates dangerously large seas. South of South Africa, the Agulhas Current retroflects, and most of the flow curves sharply southward and then eastward to join the West Wind Drift; this junction is often marked by a broken and confused sea, made much worse by westerly storms. A small part of the Agulhas Current rounds the southern end of Africa and helps form the Benguela Current; occasionally, strong eddies are formed in the retroflection region and these too move into the Southeastern Atlantic. The eastern boundary currents in the Indian Ocean are quite different from those found in the Atlantic and Pacific. The seasonally reversing South Java Current has strongest westward flow during August when monsoon winds are easterly and the Equatorial jet is inactive. Along the coast of Australia, a vigorous poleward flow, the Leeuwin Current, runs against the prevailing winds.

Arctic Currents

The waters of the North Atlantic enter the Arctic Ocean between Norway and Svalbard. The currents flow easterly, north of Siberia, to the region of the Novosibirskiye Ostrova, where they turn northerly across the North Pole, and continue down the Greenland coast to form the East Greenland Current. On the American side of the Arctic basin, there is a weak, continuous clockwise flow centered in the vicinity of 80°N, 150°W. A current north through Bering Strait along the American coast is balanced by an outward southerly flow along the Siberian coast, which eventually becomes part of the Kamchatka Current. Each of the main islands or island groups in the Arctic, as far as is known, seems to have a clockwise nearshore circulation around it. The Barents Sea, Kara Sea, and Laptev Sea each have a weak counterclockwise circulation. A similar but weaker counterclockwise current system appears to exist in the East Siberian Sea.

OCEANIC CURRENT PHENOMENA

Ocean Eddies And Rings

Eddies with horizontal diameters varying from 50-150 km have their own pattern of surface currents. These features may have either a warm or a cold core and currents flow around this core, either cyclonically for cold cores or anticyclonically for warm cores. The most intense of these features are called rings and are formed by the pinching off of meanders of western boundary currents such as the Gulf Stream. Maximum speed associated with these features is about 2 knots. Rings have also been observed to pinch off from the Agulhas retroflexion and to then drift to the northwest into the South Atlantic. Similarly, strong anticyclonic eddies are occasionally spawned by the loop current into the Western Gulf Mexico. In general, mesoscale variability is strongest in the region of western boundary currents and in the Circumpolar Current. The strength of mesoscale eddies is greatly reduced at distances of 200-400 km from these strong boundary currents, because mean currents are generally weaker in these regions. The eddies may be sufficiently strong to reverse the direction of the surface currents.

Undercurrents

At the equator and along some ocean boundaries, shallow undercurrents exist, flowing in a direction counter to that at the surface. These currents may affect the operation of submarines or trawlers. The most intense of these flows, called the Pacific Equatorial Undercurrent, is found at the equator in the Pacific. It is centered at a depth of 150m to the west of the Galapagos, is about 4 km wide, and eastward speeds of up to 1.5 m/s have been observed. Equatorial Undercurrents are also observed in the Atlantic and Indian Ocean, but they are somewhat weaker. In the Atlantic, the Equatorial Undercurrent is found to the east of 24°W and in the Indian Ocean, it appears to be seasonal. Undercurrents also exist along ocean boundaries. They seem to be most ubiquitous at the eastern boundary of oceans. Here they are found at depths of 100-200m, may be 100 km wide, and have maximum speeds of 0.5 m/s.

Ocean Currents And Climate

Many of the ocean currents exert a marked influence upon the climate of the coastal regions along which they flow. Thus, warm water from the Gulf Stream, continuing as the North Atlantic, Northeast Drift, and Irminger

Currents, arrives off the southwest coast of Iceland, warming it to the extent that Reykjavik has a higher average winter temperature than New York City, far to the south. Great Britain and Labrador are about the same latitude, but the climate of Great Britain is much milder because of the relatively warm currents. The west coast of the United States is cooled in the summer by the California Current, and warmed in the winter by the Davidson Current. Partly as a result of this circulation, the range of monthly average temperature is comparatively small. Currents exercise other influences besides those on temperature. The pressure pattern is affected materially, as air over a cold current contracts as it is cooled, and that over a warm current expands. As air cools above a cold ocean current, fog is likely to form. Frost smoke occurs over a warm current which flows into a colder region. Evaporation is greater from warm water than from cold water, adding to atmospheric moisture.

Ocean Current Observations

Historically, our views of the surface circulation of the ocean have been shaped by reports of ocean currents provided by mariners. As mentioned at the start of this chapter, these observations consist of reports of the difference between the dead reckoning and the observed position of the vessel. These observations were routinely collected until the start of World War II. Two observation systems are generally used for surface current studies. The first utilizes autonomous free-drifting buoys which are tracked by satellite or relay their position via satellite. These buoys consist of either a spherical or cylindrical surface float which is about 0.5m in diameter with a drogue at a depth of about 35m. The second system utilizes acoustic Doppler current profilers. These profilers utilize hull mounted transducers, operate at a frequency of 150 kHz, and have pulse repetition rates of about 1 second. They can penetrate to about 300m, and, where water is shallower than this depth, track the bottom. Merchant and naval vessels are increasingly being outfitted with acoustic Doppler current profilers which, when operated with the Global Positioning System, provide accurate observations of currents.

MOISTURE IN THE ATMOSPHERE

The troposphere is also known as the weather sphere. This is due to the water vapor in the air. After the tropopause, water vapor doesn't exist in the atmosphere.

MEASUREMENT OF WATER IN THE AIR

The amount of water in the air can be measured in different ways. The specific humidity of air is a measure of how much water is in the air. Warmer air can hold more water than colder air. When the air reaches its capacity, it is saturated. This capacity doubles for about every 11°C rise in temperature. The term more often used is relative humidity. This is the measure of how much water is in the air divided by how much it can hold. The relative humidity reading is given as a percent. The relative humidity for saturated air is 100 percent.

FINDING RELATIVE HUMIDITY

The relative humidity can be found by two different methods. One involves the use of a hygrometer. This is a pointer attached to a piece of hair. As the humidity increases, the hair stretches out. This is your typical "bad-hair day." When the humidity drops, the hair shrinks, causing the needle to point in a different direction. The other method requires the use of two thermometers and a chart.

The thermometers and chart all use the Celsius scale. If you are getting the readings from a station model and need to find the relative humidity, you need to convert the temperature readings from Fahrenheit to Celsius. Station models show the surface observations and weather data for a specific city. One of the thermometers measures the air temperature. This is the dry-bulb reading. The other thermometer has a wet wick on the bottom of the bulb. Water evaporating from the wick into the air takes energy with it, cooling off the thermometer. As the relative humidity increases, less water can evaporate into the air. This makes the temperature readings between the two thermometers closer. If the air is much drier, the thermometers have readings that are much farther apart. The difference between the wet and dry-bulb temperatures is called the wet-bulb depression. The wet-bulb temperature is always lower or the same as the dry-bulb temperature. If the temperatures are the same, the relative humidity is 100 percent. The wet-bulb depression is used with the dry-bulb temperature and a chart to determine the relative humidity. The instrument with the wet and dry-bulb thermometers is called a psychrometer. A sling psychrometer is a handheld device with the two thermometers that spins around.

DEW POINT

The temperature at which water vapor condenses into liquid water is called the dew point. If the dew point is below 0°C, it is called the frost point. These are important numbers in helping to determine where to post frost and freeze warnings. The dew-point temperature is found in a similar manner to that of relative humidity. The dry-bulb and wet-bulb temperatures are determined. If the water vapor comes in direct contact with the cooler surface, it can condense onto it. Fog can occur when warm air moves into an area that has a cold surface temperature. An advected fog forms in this situation. This also can be a reverse situation, where cooler air moves over a warmer surface. Ground fog forms by radiational cooling at night. These are common in humid valleys and near rivers and lakes.

CLOUDS

A cloud is formed when air is cooled to its dew-point temperature. The air cools as it rises away from the Earth's surface. If that temperature is above 0°C, the cloud is made of water droplets. If the cloud forms below 0°C, the cloud is made from ice and snow crystals and supercooled water. Cloud formations fall into three categories. Cirrus clouds are very high clouds that are made from ice crystals. They are the thin, feathery clouds you see on a nice day. Stratus clouds are the layered, sheet-like clouds. They are found at lower altitudes. Cumulus clouds are the puffy, cottonlike clouds formed by vertical rising of air. Other clouds are made from combinations and variations of these clouds. The name of a cloud may also contain a prefix or suffix that tells you more about the cloud. Alto (high) and nimbus (rain) are some examples of these.

CLOUD DEVELOPMENT

As a parcel of air rises upward, it cools. The air expands and cools because of the decreasing pressure. The rate at which it cools depends on the amount of moisture in the air. If dry air rises, it cools at a rate of 1°C/100 m. This is the dry adiabatic lapse rate. By adding moisture, this rate changes to 0.6°C/100 m. This is the moist adiabatic lapse rate. The high specific heat of the water is the reason for the difference in the rates. When air at the surface is heated, it rises upward. The air is warmer than the air surrounding it and is less dense, which makes it buoyant.

This is why clouds appear to "float" in the sky. The clouds can continue to develop vertically. Eventually, a cumulonimbus cloud may form. These are thunderstorm clouds that can be associated with heavy rain, hail, strong winds, and tornadoes. These clouds form in an unstable air mass that has air that is moving due to density differences. A cloud can form in a stable air mass, but it rises for other reasons. These are layered clouds that form from air that is forced upward by the land (mountains) or by radiational cooling as the air mixes with a cooler layer of air. Some clouds that form have a flat base and billow out on top.

The bottom of the cloud is the place where the air temperature is the same as the dew-point temperature. This is the point known as the condensation level. The height of the cloud base can be found with a simple formula or a chart. To use the formula, take the difference between the temperature and dew point at the surface and divide it by 0.8°C (the amount that the dew-point temperature gets closer to the air temperature in 100 m). The result is multiplied by 100, which gives you the lifting condensation level or the height that a cloud can form at. Cloud base altitude can also be found by using the air temperature and the dew point temperature. When the lines meet, read along the side that is labeled "Altitude." This is the height of the cloud base in kilometers. Eventually the cloud and air temperatures become equal. The cloud isn't buoyant at this point and begins to spread out. This creates the classic anvil-shaped tops that are seen at cloud tops.

PRECIPITATION

In order for water vapor to condense, certain conditions are needed. The air must cool down. This can occur in several different ways. It can come in contact with a colder surface; it can radiate heat; it can mix with colder air; or it can expand as it rises upward. The other ingredient that is needed is condensation nuclei.

This provides a surface for condensation to occur. These particles can be dust, salt, sulfate, or nitrate particles (these form acid rain) in the air. Scientists have seeded clouds to enhance nucleation and produce needed rain. Silver iodide crystals are put into clouds to provide a surface for condensation to occur. In some instances, water vapor can condense and form water droplets (homogenous nucleation), but this is rare. The type of precipitation that forms depends on the air temperature.

If this is above the freezing point, rain forms. If the air temperature is below 0°C, snow forms. Updrafts in a cloud move rain droplets around. As they collide, they collect and get larger. When the drop gets too heavy to stay in up the cloud, it falls to the Earth. Small droplets of rain (less than.02 cm in diameter) are called drizzle. Drops larger than these are called rain. When much larger drops of rain fall, they fall apart into smaller drops by vibrations caused by friction with the air. Hail forms in a tall cloud with strong updrafts. An ice crystal or frozen raindrop moves though the cloud collecting water droplets. As the hailstone rises up in the cloud, the outer layer freezes. When it falls downward, it gathers more water droplets. This circulation process continues until the hailstone falls to the ground. When you cut a hailstone in half, you can see rings. Like rings in a tree, they can tell the hailstone's history of formation. Some hailstones can reach the size of a softball. These can be very damaging to crops, animals, cars, and other property.

7

Understanding Demand and the Financial Ecosystem

THE EVOLVING FINANCIAL LANDSCAPE

Historically, the promise of poverty alleviation through micro-credit was tied primarily to one product—the productive loan invested in a micro-enterprise— delivered primarily by one type of provider—a micro-finance institution (MFI). Yet reality belies the premise of this model: clients do not always use loans for productive purposes; they have either limited capacity to use investment credit or more pressing needs for products that support consumption or income smoothing. Today, there is broad recognition that access to capital is only one of the inputs required for economic development and poverty alleviation.

Furthermore, there is wide acknowledgment that the poor, like anyone, require and use a variety of financial services for a variety of purposes. And some of these services work better than others, for reasons we are just beginning to understand. Since the original *Micro-finance Handbook* was written, the field of micro-finance has changed substantially, particularly in the last few years. Many events have influenced the landscape for financial services for the poor, but three significant "big picture" influences warrant discussion and are the subject of this opening chapter.

The first has been a shift from a narrow focus on the institution and its performance to a much broader focus on clients—understanding their behavior, financial service needs, and how various providers can better meet these needs. This shift has been brought on by the recognition—supported by significantly better data and more robust research—that outreach and, perhaps more important, impact have not been as expected. This is also the result of a widening view of micro-finance. No longer limited to investing in micro-enterprises, micro-finance now encompasses all financial services and how to provide them in a way that improves the quality of life of poor women and men. The second important shift, which greatly influences this book, has been from a narrow supply- led view to a broader focus on the financial ecosystem. In addition to a renewed focus on consumers (demand), proponents of the " systems" approach acknowledge the variety of providers and services, including the substantial role of the informal sector. They also acknowledge the need for effective rules that govern the system and supporting functions such as credit bureaus or payment systems. The result has been a much more holistic view of the sector and a more coordinated effort by government and industry to focus on increasing financial inclusion and, ultimately, making markets work better for the poor.

The third shift has been the massive opportunity to expand outreach through new business models based on branchless banking using technology and agent networks. However, while the opportunity seems vast, to date only a few branchless banking applications have reached significant scale. At the time of writing, this area of tremendous promise requires a lot more work and testing to understand and determine ways to take advantage of the opportunities that technology presents.

This chapter considers each of these influences and places the new landscape in context. It will be of interest to readers seeking to understand some of the major influences in micro-finance today. Each of the topics is introduced here and elaborated in more detail in various chapters that follow.

FOCUS ON CLIENTS

Almost everywhere, people involved in micro-finance are talking about clients. As a result, the language of micro-finance is changing. Initially *micro-credit* became *micro-finance* with the recognition of the need for savings services; today policy makers and industry players use terms like *inclusive finance, access to finance, financial ecosystems*, and *financial inclusion*. Focusing on clients is a welcome and necessary shift. However, the end game cannot simply be to develop new products or make adjustments within institutions; an institutional response alone is not enough. We need to understand consumer behavior and how it influences financial service needs and use.

While the ultimate solution may be a better product or service, an easier way to access an account, or a lower-cost delivery option, to get there we need to appreciate the nuances and contextual factors that affect how poor women and men behave and which financial services are of most benefit to them, for what purpose, and why. For example, market research conducted with MFI clients in Bolivia indicates that clients identify respect as their greatest priority; product attributes are important, but they are not the most important consideration. Clients want to preserve their dignity when interacting with a financial institution, and they want to borrow without fear or humiliation. To accomplish these goals, they need to understand the services they use and the contracts they sign, and providers need to value and invest in customer service. The solution is unlikely to be simply new or more products.

Understanding how consumer behavior translates into financial service needs requires understanding the uniqueness and heterogeneity of clients and how life-cycle events, livelihoods, geography, income levels, and gender influence their behavior. The following section discusses the characteristics that define and influence client behavior and financial service needs, while chapter 2 provides an overview of how clients use financial services based on findings from *Portfolios of the Poor*.

Age, Life-Cycle, and Family Structure

Financial needs and vulnerabilities change as people move through the life-cycle—from dependence on family to independence and from school to work, marriage, family responsibilities, and retirement. Sons migrate in search of more income; young mothers manage childbirth expenses, health care, and nutrition; parents struggle to educate their children. Widows are threatened with loss of land and other assets to their husbands' relatives. Elderly clients face acute vulnerabilities, including loss of productivity due to deteriorating health, physical immobility, and the loss of family support as children become independent and develop their own financial commitments. These changes result in the need for different financial services at different life-cycle stages.

Other life-cycle events, such as celebrations, religious ceremonies, or building a home, require lump sums that are often hard to accumulate without adequate financial services. Financial exclusion is strongly influenced by age, with youth facing significant hurdles. To be relevant, financial service providers must modify products, services, and delivery channels to accommodate differences in life-cycle and age. Providers can respond to differing needs by developing age-specific products, such as youth savings accounts or pension funds. Family structure can also affect how financial services are used. In many communities, the concept of family extends well beyond spouses, siblings, children, and grandparents. Cousins, distant relatives, and even neighbors are an integral part of a family. Polygamy further increases the size and complexity of the family structure. A large family may live together in one compound, often combining financial resources in order to meet daily needs or respond to emergencies. Similarly, income is often shared among the larger family. While saving may be difficult for an individual, sharing income facilitates risk management in the absence of formal services. In many contexts, community elders control assets and decide how they will be distributed throughout a given community. Thus an individual's ability to access services may depend on his or her social position relative to that of more senior members in the community.

Livelihoods, Geography, and Income Levels

The financial pressures of managing inconsistent income to cover daily expenses, unexpected emergencies, and life-cycle events weigh heavily on the poor. Although millions of people—from the poorest of the poor to the economically active poor to small business operators to salaried workers—face similar pressures, their responses and need for financial services vary depending on their livelihoods and where they live, which, in turn, affect their income level.

Historically, micro-finance has focused on micro-entrepreneurs, with loan products designed primarily for traders with daily or weekly cash flow and in need of short-term working capital. However, by focusing on productive credit, micro-finance providers may have missed serving the majority of the potential market. As demonstrated in figure, of the 1.6 billion working poor, less than 500 million are micro-entrepreneurs or salaried wage workers; the rest earn their income, likely low and irregular, from farming, casual labor, fishing, and pastoral activities. They, like anyone, need access to financial services to manage their daily lives, and they need a variety of products to address a multitude of financial service needs.

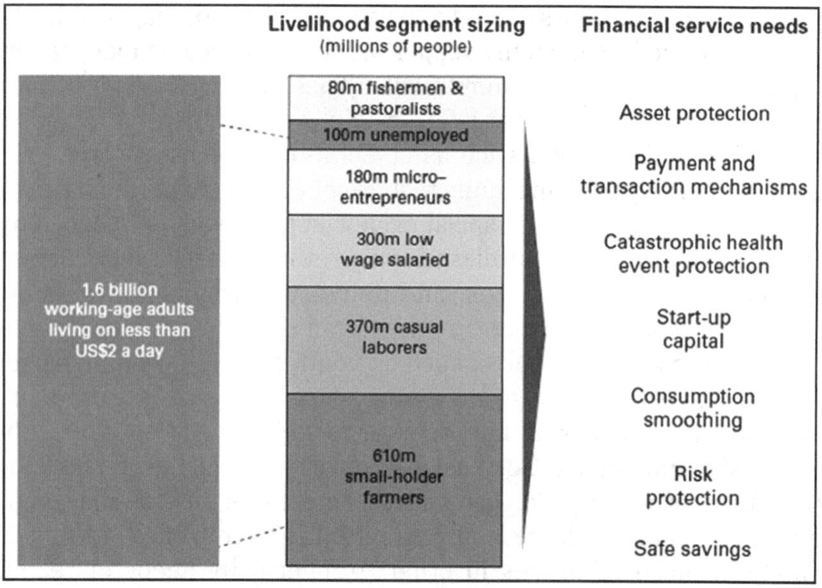

Fig. Financial Service Needs for Different Livelihood Segments

Geography matters as well. For example, people living in rural areas likely earn income from agricultural activities that generate very different cash flows than traditional "micro-enterprises." Financial services for smallholder farmers need to suit their cash flows and consider the production and marketing risks specific to a given crop. However, in general, it is more expensive for providers to operate in rural areas, limiting clients' choices and challenging providers to reach scale, particularly where population density is low, access to markets or supplies is limited, and infrastructure is undeveloped. Rural areas often have higher covariance risk due to the lack of a diversified economic base and the risk of crop failure or drought; in some rural areas, a history of poorly designed rural credit programs (subsidized and/or directed credit, no savings mobilization) can affect people's perceptions of financial services.

And while having a bank account may seem more useful for an employee who receives regular wages than for, say, a laborer who is paid in cash, farmers, wage earners, and laborers would all benefit from having access to a safe place to save for lump-sum expenditures or respond to an emergency or new opportunity. In addition to *how* consumers generate income, the *amount* of income affects their access to and need for financial services. To meet varying income levels, products and services need to have characteristics—minimum balances, eligibility criteria, fees, and benefits—appropriate to each level.

Over the years, we have learned that the economically active poor rather than the poorest of the poor stand to benefit the most from access to financial services (without other interventions). "The majority of the world's estimated 150 million micro-credit clients are thought to live just below and, more often, just above the poverty line". From the perspective of both the client and the provider, it is generally more expensive to transact in smaller amounts with greater frequency. For providers, smaller transaction amounts also result in a smaller revenue base— for example, people with lower incomes generally have lower savings balances, less capacity to take on debt, and fewer opportunities to generate income. Together, this makes it very difficult to provide financial services to the extremely poor.

For the extremely poor, cash or asset transfers, rather than micro-credit, are often a better solution, at least initially. If possible, placing cash transfers into a bank account appropriate for the poor can also support financial inclusion. While the majority of providers serve the economically active poor, an innovative model for providing financial services to the poorest in Bangladesh, developed by BRAC, is being replicated in countries around the world.

Ethnicity, Caste, and Religion

Building and maintaining a level of trust in all circumstances can improve financial inclusion, and it is particularly important when different ethnic or religious groups are involved. Caste, while not solely an ethnic factor, can pose cultural barriers similar to ethnic differences. In countries where caste systems or religion are central to a community's social organization, individuals may be systematically denied access because they are from a lower caste or a different religion.

Islamic finance is possibly the best-known example of religion influencing financial transactions. Islamic finance is based on Islamic or sharia law, but despite the term "law," Islamic finance is based largely on cultural norms. According to Karim, Tarazi, and Reille, "Indeed, sharia compliance in some societies may be less a religious principle than a cultural one—and even the less religiously observant may prefer sharia-compliant products." A key overriding principle of Islamic finance is the need to provide for the welfare of the community by prohibiting practices considered unfair or exploitative. Fundamental to the provision of Islamic financial services is the inability to give or receive a fixed, predetermined rate of return. This principle is banned based on two sharia precepts: money has no intrinsic worth, and providers of funding must share the business risk. While these principles reflect widely held beliefs, sharia-compliant regulatory frameworks are just beginning to be developed.

Religion and ethnicity can also affect the ability of women to access services. For example, in some cultures women are home-bound for religious reasons and unable to meet with providers outside the home or to form groups with other women. Similarly, some cultures prohibit male staff from visiting female clients. Gender-based rules and norms can have a significant impact on both the financial service needs of women and their ability to access and use services.

Gender

Recognizing gender issues in micro-finance, as in any project intervention, means more than targeting a programme towards women. It means recognising the position of women in relation to men as actors in society: in the context of husbands and families; local community and authority; and more broadly their position in society at the national level as governed by laws and custom. Then it is necessary to act to support women to overcome the obstacles they face in these relationships which prevent them from using financial services to achieve what they wish for themselves. Women often lack control over cash management within their household and may be dependent on their husband to access financial services.

Moreover, rules often prevent women from owning assets or participating in wage-earning activities outside the household. For example, in Morocco, women's mobility outside the home is restricted, and women's work is often associated with shame, as it reflects a man's inability to be the sole financial provider.

Altogether, the need for and ability to use and benefit from financial services depend to a great extent on age and life-cycle income levels, cultural context, and gender. The more we understand client characteristics and influences on their behavior, the better equipped we will be to increase financial inclusion in a meaningful way.

THE FINANCIAL ECOSYSTEM

While understanding the behavior and needs of clients is paramount, many stakeholders are also concerned with the wider financial ecosystem and how it affects financial inclusion (or exclusion). Financial inclusion efforts focus on how the supply of financial services (products and services provided by sustainable institutions) can better meet demand; they also acknowledge the functions within the wider market system that support financial transactions.

The contents of this book are shaped by the market system approach. This approach provides a practical means of assessing consumer behavior, the demand for and supply of financial services, and the rules and functions that support transactions. Whether financial service needs translate into demand that is met by a financial service provider depends on many factors, including the degree to which providers are sufficiently informed to identify client *needs*, potential clients have *information* about providers, and *trust* exists between the two.

Beyond this, a provider's ability to develop and offer an appropriate product is shaped by its capacity in relation to *product development* and *delivery channels* and by its incentives to improve them. For example, do *regulations* encourage the development and expansion of services? Do the *laws* on collateral requirements promote overall financial inclusion? Can providers access *funding* to support growth?

Do they have the right *legal form* and networks to do so? Do *credit bureaus* exist, and are they effective? Does the accessible *infrastructure* promote overall financial inclusion? Equally important, how do the *attitudes* and *norms* among both consumers (for example, to loan repayment) and providers (for example, to risk and reward) influence financial inclusion? This section describes the financial market system, specifically the functions within it and the roles played by various market actors. A market system necessarily includes both private and public sector actors as well as civil society and, indeed, consumers themselves. Because the term *market* is often equated only with the private sector, the term *ecosystem* is used interchangeably with market system in this book.

FUNCTIONS OF THE MARKET SYSTEM

There are three main sets of functions in a market system, each carried out by various market players, including the private sector, government, NGOs, community groups, representative associations, and consumers.

- *Core*. Transactions between providers and clients (supply and demand)
- *Rules*. Informal and formal rules that shape the behavior of market players, including consumers
- *Supporting functions*. The collection of functions that provide information and services supporting the development and expansion of the core

Understanding financial market systems involves breaking down each of these functions into more detail to identify specific elements within them and the main players who are likely to be directly engaged.

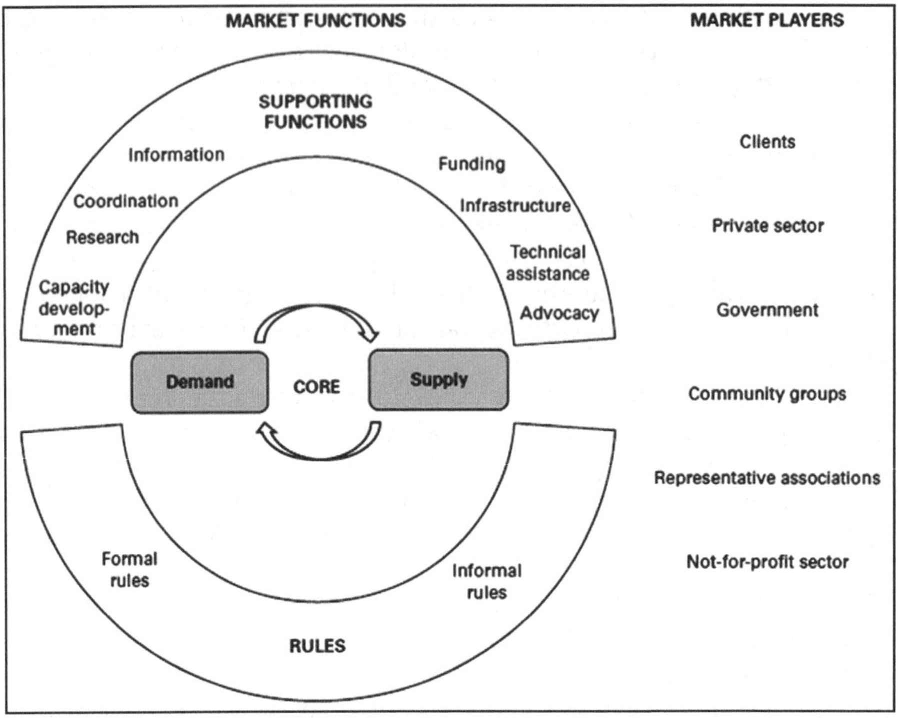

Fig. Sylized View of the Finanical Ecosystem

Each set of functions can be viewed in isolation, yet in practice functions only have value when seen as integral parts of a wider ecosystem. By incorporating the interests and incentives of clients and other key market players and the influence of rules and supporting functions with regard to financial service provision, the market system framework acknowledges that only by understanding the entire system can we address the constraints to and take advantage of the opportunities for increasing financial inclusion.

The Core

Offering a combination of the appropriate instruments and an understanding of how these can be used practically within the context of current livelihoods and existing social and cultural norms will enable and encourage people to shift towards improved management of their finances. The heart of the market systems approach is to understand the demand side and support customer-focused development and innovation driving the supply side.

For financial market systems to work more inclusively and successfully, two characteristics must be present. First, the number of transactions must increase; expanding the access frontier to include previously excluded people is a key indicator of financial system development and an official goal of many financial authorities. Second, products must accurately address the needs of clients, improving their lives or businesses. A better-functioning core is therefore manifested in more and better-quality transactions. The key players in the core of the market are clients (demand) and financial service providers (supply), connected to each other by products (supply). The following discussion provides a brief overview of demand and supply. More detailed discussions are provided in the chapters that follow.

Demand: Clients

As discussed in the previous section on clients, poor households are in continual need of financial tools to improve their productivity and secure the best possible consumption and investment choices, all the while managing potential or existing risks. Understanding demand requires both an understanding of the financial service needs of clients and, as well, their behavior with regard to existing financial services. Analyzing data from financial diaries collected across Bangladesh, India, and South Africa, Collins et al. suggests a much more complex picture of demand than previously assumed: "The authors of the book, *Portfolios of the Poor*, found that households used between eight and 10 different types of mostly informal financial instruments with very high turnovers—often 10 times the asset values through the year and more than 100 percent of their income. This reveals a remarkable resourcefulness, but when transaction costs don't scale with transaction size, fragmenting transactions over many informal instruments can be very costly. Therefore, they not only need financial tools, they need *well-performing* and *cost-effective* financial tools". The poor often prefer the informal sector on most dimensions important to consumers (access, flexibility, product features, and service quality). However, informal financial mechanisms may entail cost, inconvenience, embarrassment, and sometimes depletion of the very social capital on which they are built. More needs to be understood about how the informal sector expands outreach, if and how those relying on the informal sector are underserved, and how the quality of consumers' lives could be improved as a result of access to formal financial services. Chapter 2 provides a more detailed discussion of demand and how we can learn from the informal sector and the behavior of clients.

Supply: Providers

While most of the first micro-finance institutions were established as NGOs, the sector has evolved to include many types of providers. Specialized commercial banks providing a range of financial services have proven that the poor are "bankable," while member-based community groups have shown that financial services can be provided directly by the community on a sustainable basis. Providers are discussed in detail in part II of this book; an overview of the types of providers is included here and illustrated in figure.

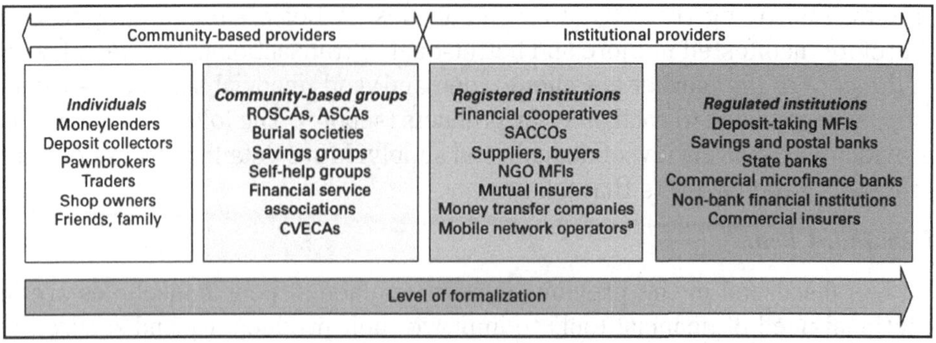

Fig. The Range of Finanical Service Providers

While financial service providers are often characterized as formal, semiformal, or informal, traditionally referring to their regulatory status, we classify them as either community-based (generally informal with no legal status) or institutional (generally more formal and in some cases regulated). Community-based providers include both individuals (such as friends and family, moneylenders, shop owners, traders, and deposit collectors) and groups, including indigenous groups, such as ROSCAs and accumulating savings and credit associations (ASCAs), and facilitated groups trained by external agencies, such as Savings Groups (SGs) and Self-Help Groups (SHGs). While more formal than ROSCAs, these facilitated groups are not considered to be "institutions," as they, for the most part, are not legally licensed as financial service providers, have few expenses, and provide services primarily within the group itself. Institutional providers include member-owned financial cooperatives and NGOs, which are normally registered and possibly supervised, as well as banks (private and public), deposit-taking MFIs, and non-bank financial institutions (NBFIs) such as insurance companies and leasing companies, which are normally regulated in some fashion.

No single type of organization presents an optimal solution to reaching all market segments with all types of financial services. In remote rural areas, the low cost structure and proximity of user-owned and managed providers constitute significant advantages over more structured MFIs or commercial banks. However, credit unions and banks have the advantage of being able to offer a wider variety of products or a broader spectrum of terms and conditions and may be more reliable than community-based providers.

New entrants such as mobile network operators (MNOs) can offer services conveniently in rural areas, although relatively few have achieved scale. While recent years have witnessed a considerable increase in the commercial provision of micro-finance and the emergence of publicly listed micro-finance companies, informal providers remain the main source of financial services for the vast majority of the poor. For example, FinAccess data provide strong evidence that Kenyan consumers use a portfolio of financial services. Of those using regulated formal services, only 11 percent rely solely on a formal service, 31 percent use a semiformal service, 13 percent use an informal service, and the remaining 45 percent use all three categories of services. Similarly, more than half of those who have a semiformal provider as their most formal source of finance also use an informal source. Furthermore, this pattern of multiple service use has increased from 2006 to 2009. In 2009, a mere 2.5 percent of Kenyans relied *solely* on the regulated formal sector.

Supply: Products

Clients benefit from having access to products that match the way they live and conduct business and support them in addressing challenges. The irregularity and limited size of cash flows mean that products that permit frequent, small, incremental transactions are more useful and convenient than, for example, services that require a minimum transaction amount or take significant time to access. Products provided directly in the community are generally used frequently because they are accessible, convenient, and in close proximity to where poor people live. The main financial services include savings, credit, payments, and insurance and are described in part III of this book. While financial products and services are generally defined by standard characteristics such as term, size, price, returns, and eligibility, their appeal to consumers often depends on their reliability, accessibility, flexibility, safety, and affordability.

For example, products are accessible when providers explain product features so that clients understand the commitment they are making. Products are safe if they are well-structured and meet client needs in a transparent way without doing harm.

Increasingly, more flexible terms and conditions are being offered, including the ability to repay loans early, receive increases in existing loans, and open savings accounts with no minimum balance. Payment services, loans for housing and education, or savings accounts specifically for youth, as well as more complex products such as leasing and insurance are beginning to reach low-income populations. As services become more client-centered, product delivery is also developing through innovative channels.

Rules and Supporting Functions

Rules and supporting functions influence the effectiveness of transactions (the core of the market) and provide an enabling environment to allow markets to grow, adapt, and succeed in changing circumstances. Ensuring that they improve and increase transactions supports financial inclusion. Who establishes and enforces rules and who provides supporting functions differs by function. Some functions, such as regulations, are appropriately considered a "public good"; the key players are the government and policy makers and, on occasion, business associations. Others, such as credit bureaus or rating agencies, are more appropriately provided by private sector firms.

Rules

A broad term used to define the *rules of the game*, rules include formal rules (regulations and standards) and informal rules (social conventions and cultural norms). Formal or informal rules—the rules themselves and their enforcement—govern participation and behavior in financial market systems and strongly influence financial market outcomes. Formal rules have a defined, written set of responsibilities that are allocated to specific parties, which together create the de jure parameters that shape behavior (of clients and providers). Informal rules are usually unwritten and are invariably more nebulous and ill-defined than formal rules; they manifest themselves in attitudes, behavioral norms, social organizations, and common practices. These informal rules often drive incentives and behavior and determine the extent to which formal rules are adhered to.

The key players in relation to formal rules are government organizations and industry associations. The increasing complexity of financial systems and new innovations within them—such as the emergence of mobile banking—pose new challenges for rule makers in terms of not only what rules should be, but who should make and implement them. Formal rules play a public or collective role in market systems, leveling the playing field for providers and consumers.

Formal rules affect clients by setting legal frameworks and industry standards that influence market access, the range of products, and the competitive landscape, which, in turn, affect providers and their ability to serve their markets appropriately. For example, the legal ability to enforce contracts and register assets, the existence of a national identification system, or the protection of public deposits are all critical parts of the "formal rule" system. Formal rules are discussed in more detail in chapters 3, 17, and 19. Informal rules are an integral part of local culture, value systems, and practices. By definition, they are not the responsibility of one player. Although particular individuals or organizations may exert considerable influence, informal rules emerge organically and are the result of traditions and habits influenced by social institutions, such as gender, religion, caste, tradition, inheritance rights, and landownership. For example, according to micro-LINKS wiki, "Typically these gender norms are expressed through informal (and formal) rules that lead to discriminatory property and inheritance laws, for example, different access to resources, and to restrictions on the tasks or places of work that women may occupy." Norms suggest a standard of conduct that people believe they ought to follow to avoid sanctioning.

Social and cultural norms surrounding attitudes toward money, sharing, and authority can greatly influence the type of financial services that are most useful in a given community. Trust, for example, plays an integral role in the decision to use a particular financial service or adopt a set of financial behaviors. In societies with high social capital, where systems and structures have been developed to build trust and foster social and economic transactions beyond the family and kin group, it will be easier and less costly to build sustainable systems for financial intermediation. Informal rules can contribute to the effectiveness of formal rules when the norm is compliance or when formal rules codify informal norms already widely accepted, such as Islamic finance principles now being incorporated into regulatory frameworks. Informal rules may also emerge in response to formal rules that do not work well for a particular group or do not exist.

For example, a village leader can "vouch" for borrowers in the absence of a credit bureau or can verify property ownership in the absence of a housing registry. Given that informal rules reflect long-held beliefs and social structures, they typically are difficult to change (although some can be addressed by corrective regulation or judicial decision). Informal rules also influence the supply side of the market. They may be manifested in, for example, industry norms in relation to innovation and risk, which, in turn, drive attitudes and practices to develop new products. And for providers of all sizes, the level of trust clients have, as well as the norms regarding repayment of loans, is critical in determining the incentives for increased financial inclusion.

For example, historical experience such as conflict or disaster can create social dynamics that persist for generations, such as a lingering lack of trust, a lack of available resources, infrastructure, and opportunities, and overall difficulty in establishing relationships and creating solidarity in the community. Communities marked by significant ethnic conflict may be less receptive initially to peer-based group lending models that have historically worked very well in micro-finance. Alternatively, a community where cash is less prevalent than in-kind assets potentially requires unique financial services outside traditional credit and savings products. While some informal rules may appear unproductive, they serve an important purpose, such as providing a social safety net. These rules might include shared access to income, common understanding of property, and rigid social structures, as discussed earlier. However, social institutions do change and evolve in response to new technologies or interaction with new cultures. For example, mobile money may make it easier to transfer money from urban to rural areas, thus resulting in less reliance on community solidarity to manage risks and deal with emergencies. Understanding informal rules provides insight into what will work within a particular community.

Supporting Functions

Supporting functions provide the resources, information, and services that shape financial market behavior and enable markets to grow, adapt, and succeed in changing circumstances. Weak supporting functions (and inappropriate rules) leave markets vulnerable, lacking the necessary depth to be sustainable and fit into a changing world. The composition and nature of supporting functions, and who provides them, vary from one context to another but are concerned generally with information and communication, capacity building, coordination, resource development, and innovation. All of these support the core function—the exchange between clients (demand) and service providers (supply). Because they differ from one context to another, there is no comprehensive list of supporting functions. However, the following are some of the main functional areas:

- *Capacity development.* Concerned with developing capacity of various players including policy makers and providers. It therefore may involve training services or other means by which employees learn new skills. In more established markets, capacity development for the industry as a whole may involve coordination among private and public players. *Coordination.* The capacity (within a market system) to go beyond the limitations of individual perspectives, understand the system as a whole, and support its development. This is a noncommercial, collective, public role and therefore is likely to be the domain of government or representative industry (and perhaps consumer) associations.
- *Advocacy.* Efforts to provide an appropriate voice in the financial market system, especially for providers and consumers, and to ensure that their views contribute to public functions such as regulations and standards.
- *Information.* Refers loosely to the "information environment," for example, in relation to emerging trends and products (aimed at both providers and consumers) and to more specific information-based products and services. The key players include specialized service companies and government or associations in relation to public information on, for example, standards and legal rights.
- *Research.* The provision of knowledge-based products or services related to, for example, the demand and supply sides of the core, impact assessment and the implications of wider trends.
- *Funding.* Can take various forms, such as equity or debt. The key players here are private investors, but in practice, especially for micro-finance, a range of social investors are active, often supported by donor funds, not usually seeking a commercial (or indeed any financial) return.
- *Infrastructure.* The range of technical and other support services required to enhance the efficiency of the overall system. This could include credit bureaus, deposit insurance, and accounting services.

The key players are likely to be private sector companies and public regulatory authorities.

Implications of the Market System Framework: Providers and Facilitators

While all organizations engaged in financial inclusion may agree that development of the system as a whole represents a worthy aim, they do not all have the same role or perspective. Organizations differ with respect to several factors, for example, their legal status (for-profit business, NGO, association, government), funding sources (grants, debt, equity, client-generated revenues), scale, and motivations. However, perhaps the most basic but useful distinction is between organizations that see themselves as *market players* with a continuing direct role within the market system and *facilitators* that see themselves as external actors with a mandate to act as temporary catalysts in stimulating others in the market.

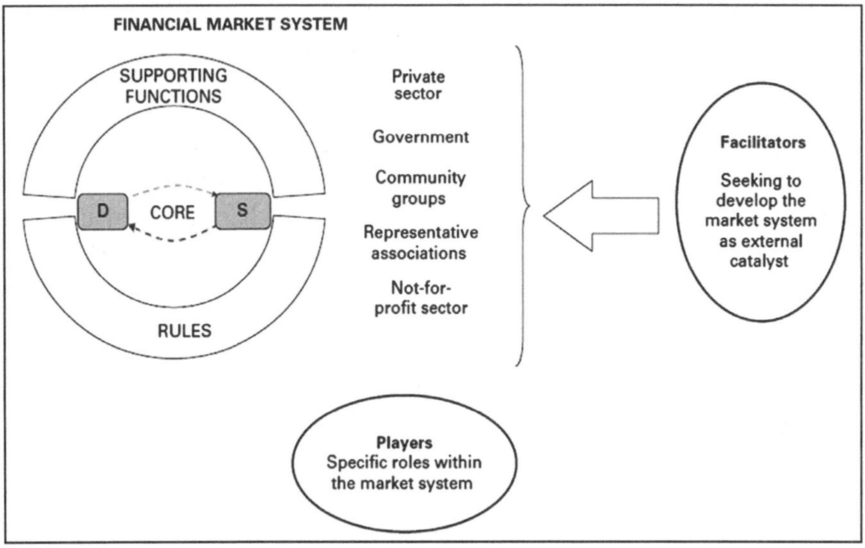

Fig. Market system players and Facilitators

Knowing your place in the financial services landscape is an important step in determining what you should do and how you should do it.

- *Market system players*. Organizations or individuals with an active and continuing role delivering functions in the financial ecosystem. This includes providers of financial services, regulators, and other developers and enforcers of formal rules and providers of supporting functions. These entities are part of the system and envisage remaining part of it in the future.
- *Facilitators*. External players, standing outside the system, whose role is to facilitate positive changes in the market system. Facilitators are most often donors and development agencies that are funded by

donors. (Investors who provide debt or equity to providers are considered to be market players, as they provide funding, an important supporting function.) Grant funding is used (or should be) to facilitate the market and to develop the capacity of market players in the system. While facilitators work in a variety of ways, their role is to use resources to address constraints, allowing the system to function more effectively and inclusively. Facilitation is therefore a public role (not commercial); it is temporary (not permanent) and requires understanding and capacity to intervene with appropriate and timely resources (financial, human, and political). And while in the short to medium term, the role of the facilitator may involve multiple activities—including direct roles in the market if required—in the longer term, the strategic purpose of facilitation is, by definition, *not* to have any continuing role in the market system.

In the long term, who should be a market player (that is, provide a product or service, public or private) and who should pay for those products or services? There is relatively little disagreement about who should fulfill some functions in the financial system. Financial service delivery is generally accepted as appropriately provided by the private sector, while the development of regulatory frameworks, for example, merits public subsidy. Historically however, ambiguity over the nature of some functions has provided justification for extensive donor subsidy in micro-finance. Donors that fund market players directly or themselves play market roles only have a valid rationale for participating in the short term. If the financial market system is to be truly facilitated and a position reached where long-term financial inclusion has been achieved and facilitation is no longer required, facilitators must figure out how to play a role without becoming a market player and how to implement their vision of how the market system should function without them in the future.

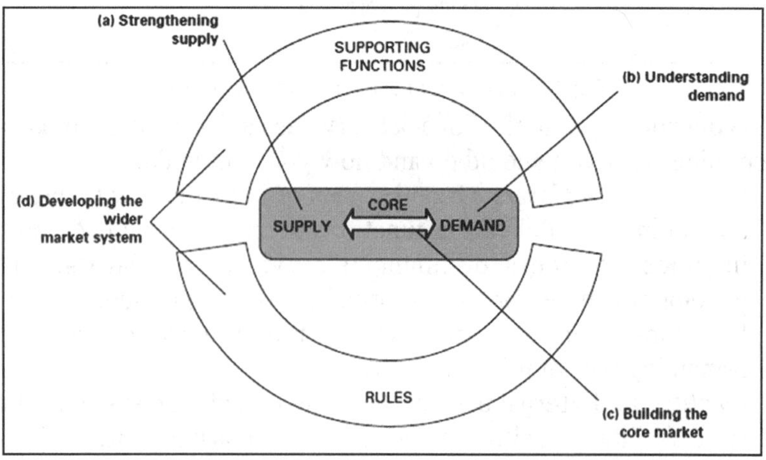

Fig. Evolution of intervention foucs from financial institutions to Financial systems

Figure illustrates the evolution of taking a financial system approach rather than an institutional approach— from:

- Strengthening supply to
- Understanding demand and from
- Building the core market to
- Developing the wider market system.

BANKING WITHOUT BRANCHES

The third significant influence on financial services for the poor is the opportunity presented by technology to increase financial inclusion. Building on the previous discussion of the financial ecosystem, this introduction to branchless banking focuses on the new market players— MNOs and agent networks—within the system and the emerging new business models that result. Chapter 12 provides a more technical discussion of each of the various transaction or access points—for example, mobile phones, Internet, automated teller machines (ATMs)— and the development and management of an agent network; it also includes a glossary of branchless banking terms. Cost and proximity drive the delivery of financial services. Historically, providing services in close proximity to clients entailed high costs for both the provider and the client. However, financial service providers are increasingly finding innovative ways to integrate the delivery of financial services into the everyday lives of clients.

While community-based providers are already largely "branchless," for institutional providers, branchless banking is changing the way clients and providers interact and is poised to lower the costs of delivery significantly and to reach financially excluded households that cannot be served profitably using conventional branch-based approaches—especially in remote, sparsely populated areas and urban slums. Banking without branches requires alternative access points for client transactions. These include self-serve solutions such as mobile phones or ATMs, staff-based transaction points such as mobile branches that visit underserved areas on specific days, and third-party agents including retailers (or in some cases, MFIs) using card-reading point-of-sale (POS) devices, mobile phones, or Internet-connected computing devices. Branchless product offerings range from individual money transfers and government cash transfers to full-service banking, allowing deposits, withdrawals, and, if relevant, loan disbursement and payments or even insurance premium payments or payouts.

In providing an overview of branchless banking and the associated new business models, it is helpful to define a few terms. *Mobile money* refers to a type of electronic money that can be transferred over a mobile phone. The issuer of mobile money may (depending on the local law and the business model) be an MNO or a third party, including a bank. *Mobile banking* is the use of a mobile phone to access financial services and execute financial transactions connected to a bank account. This covers both transactional and nontransactional services, such as viewing financial information on a mobile phone. An *agent* is any third party acting on behalf of a bank or other financial service provider (including an electronic money issuer or distributor) in its dealings with customers. Agents perform "cash-in" (the exchange of cash for electronic value) and "cash-out" (the exchange of electronic value for cash) services.

New Market Actors: A Wider Ecosystem

Branchless banking is primarily about the emergence of different kinds of businesses, often with new kinds of players, to deliver multiple financial services to a mass market through technologyenabled business models that operate very differently from more traditional financial service delivery models. Branchless banking services require an ecosystem of players. For example, mobile banking, a subset of branchless banking, requires partnerships between MNOs and banks or other financial service providers and agents. Mobile banking solutions "are hard to build because they require strong multiparty orchestration, in principle spanning several regulatory domains, and the proposition is severely weakened if any one element of the solution is not properly primed. Indeed, the commercial arrangements between the parties are what holds the system together". This discussion focuses on agent networks and MNOs as the two main new entrants to financial service provision.

Agent Networks

While branchless banking channels offer clients more convenience and access points, POS devices on their own cannot accept deposits; Internet and mobile channels by themselves have no cash transaction capability; and mobile branches may not visit often enough to meet all the needs of clients. Thus these channels individually cannot replace traditional channels altogether. This is where agents enter the picture. An agent network is a group of retailers with existing businesses or retail locations who (primarily) provide cash-in, cash-out services.

An agent may be any retailer conveniently located with reliable cash flow who can service clients seeking to deposit, withdraw, or send funds to a third party. Providers such as banks or MNOs often establish agent networks through a range of distribution networks, including airtime sellers, shopkeepers, retailers, traders, petrol stations, post offices, or kiosks in markets. Agents charge transaction fees, but because they serve areas where most institutional providers are unable to reach, these fees are often lower than the cost of traveling to a bank branch or using a traditional money transfer company. Agents can facilitate transactions via several access devices, including a POS device, a mobile phone handset, a tablet, or a personal computer.

A client can deposit cash with an agent in one location, and those same funds can be withdrawn immediately by another client at a different location. Agents must have an account at a bank that has a secure, real-time transaction-processing capability, either online using wireless or Internet connectivity or offline using smartcards capable of updating balances and recording transactions. A payments system or network is needed that allows the agent's bank to account for and settle transactions with all participating client banks. Consumer protection safeguards are also required to minimize exposure of bank clients to agent risk. Some providers use agents for more than simple transactions, such as providing account balances or notifying clients of payments coming due, delivering credit products, and, if properly licensed, delivering insurance products. Based on a representative case in the Mexican market, as much as 20 percent of the transactions coming into branches could be handled by agents. Depending on the regulatory environment, sometimes MFIs can act as agents for larger commercial banks or for MNOs. This strategy allows micro-finance customers to gain exposure to mobile banking and can also help MFIs to differentiate themselves from the competition and bring enhanced liquidity to their branches. Agents provide the customer interface. Therefore, when developing a network of agents, providers must address the operational challenges in a way that fosters a positive and consistent customer experience that will create and maintain trust in the system. Strategies for enrolling, training, incentivizing, managing, and retaining agents are critical considerations for all providers that use agents to deliver financial services. Providers can hire and manage their own agents, or they can outsource this function.

Mobile Network Operators

Mobile network operators provide the ability to use mobile phones for financial services—either directly to consumers or on behalf of other financial service providers, usually through an agent network. MNOs can provide money transfer and payment services directly without being linked to another financial service provider (mobile money), or they can partner with a bank or other provider to increase outreach both in terms of numbers as well as available products (mobile banking). The role of MNOs in mobile banking can vary from simply selling text-messaging services to providing a full-fledged parallel banking infrastructure (although it is still early in the process to fully understand what this involves). Which role(s) a bank or other financial service provider wants the MNO to play depends on how much it wants to integrate mobile banking services into its core business and its ability to implement technology-based deployments. Customer experience is determined directly by the technology platform used and the ability to access cash-in, cash-out services. These and other issues are still being worked out, and expectations for the future are uncertain.

New Business Models: Partnerships for Branchless Banking

Developing partnerships between financial service providers and MNOs is not easy. A key consideration when developing partnerships is how flexible the service will be in terms of transmitting and receiving funds from clients with other financial service providers or MNOs. MNOs may partner with multiple financial institutions, increasing the ability of clients to transact across financial institutions (interoperability), but diminishing the unique added value for the financial partners. At the same time, banks and other providers that partner with only one MNO restrict the use of the service to clients of that MNO. Financial service providers must balance the need for universal, multi-MNO solutions with the practicality of outsourcing more functions to a single MNO.

At the outset, it can be expensive to engage in mobile banking; partners may be scarce and the incentives to reach a broad mass of people may not be aligned between the necessary actors. Some providers, including MNOs, do not have the high market share that might translate into the volume of transactions needed for mobile services to break even. Furthermore, adequate back-office and transaction-switching capability as well as sufficient internal controls are required, which smaller providers may not have or not have access to. To increase adoption rates, banks and others need to drive awareness of the service and ensure strong branding.

While mobile banking reduces the cost of service delivery and increases convenience for both providers and clients, significant efforts are required to allay security fears and natural resistance to new technologies. In addition, negotiations between the MNO and the financial service provider need to consider the customer service interface (for example, the MNO's customer call center) and the marketing and cross-selling of bank services to telephone customers. MNOs can use their extensive agent networks and retailers to provide cash-in, cash- out services and to sign up customers for banking services.

The MNO's brand can be leveraged to appeal more directly to clients with stronger affiliations to mobile phones and mobile brands than to banking. This may be particularly appealing for efforts to increase financial inclusion among youth. However, using the MNOs' distribution and marketing channels also has revenue implications: fees are split among the MNO as a brand, the MNO as a transaction channel provider, and the bank as financial intermediary. And lastly, in many countries, regulation of MNOs by the banking authorities is not yet clear, although this is beginning to change as new models emerge and the various stakeholders better understand the systemic risks inherent in mobile banking.

Ultimately, significant regulatory factors define the options for mobile banking, including regulatory restrictions on outsourcing cash-in, cash-out functions, know-your-customer (KYC) obligations, and limits on mobile money transactions. In fact, the maximum amount allowed for transfers is generally relatively low, which may limit the use of this service. Other issues include data security and customer privacy regarding e-banking, account issuance of non-banks, and taxation. At the time of writing, various new technology- enabled business models are emerging: those that provide money transfer services (mobile money), those that link MNOs with bank services (mobile banking), and agent banking being established by large retailers.

Branchless Banking and MFIs

MFIs, both regulated and NGOs, have generally not played a critical role in branchless banking; rather they have used the new technology to enhance customer service and reduce costs. For example, as MFIs become licensed, they can join the national payments system, gaining the use of ATMs and cards or POS devices to provide services through new channels. While some MFIs are able to take advantage of opportunities made available through technology, many struggle, and the expectations and hopes for what might have been have not materialized at any scale. MFIs require superior customer service skills, sophisticated back-office systems, and strong leadership and technical skills to achieve the organizational changes required, and many are simply not there yet. However, MFIs and other smaller providers can engage in branchless banking in several ways:

- Use mobile phones (or personal digital assistants, notebooks, or any other technology) to collect data in the field
- Use mobile financial services to update or replace practices related to the core business, for example, use mobile payments for loans and insurance premiums
- Act as an agent on behalf of a bank or an MNO.

Together, these three drivers—a focus on understanding clients better; acknowledgment of the multiplayer, multifunction nature of the financial ecosystem; and the opportunities technology presents—can support increased financial inclusion. The following chapters provide much more detail on each of these areas, describing the functions and roles within the financial market system and how they can work better for the poor.

CLIENTS

No matter how it is measured, the number of people without access to financial services is very large indeed. In 1976, when Muhammad Yunus in Bangladesh started the experiment that led to the Grameen Bank, he focused on the very poor. As micro-finance grew, it attracted the "economically active poor," people who might be expected to take loans to run a small business, for example. More recently with the drive for "financial inclusion," attention has turned to the "unbanked" poor—poor people not using formal financial services of any sort (including micro-finance, sometimes referred to as "semiformal" services). Just over half of the world's adult population is unbanked, most of them poor: In Africa, four out of five adults are unbanked, and in South Asia, three out of five. In rich countries, by contrast, fewer than one in ten adults lacks a formal means to save or to borrow. All these numbers—of the extremely poor, the moderately poor, and the unbanked poor—dwarf the number of clients already served by micro-finance, estimated at 190 million at the end of 2009. "The Evolving Financial Landscape," we discussed who the poor are, how they differ, and how various influences such as life-cycle stages, geography, livelihoods, and informal rules and norms, such as gender, affect their access to financial services. This chapter examines financial services from the point of view of poor people. It looks at the kinds of tools that the poor need to manage their money, shows why they need them, and assesses the extent to which they already have access to them. It describes the key characteristics of good quality pro-poor formal financial tools and shows how and why the poor, the extremely poor, and the unbanked poor might use and benefit from such services if they were more widely available.

THE POOR AND FINANCIAL SERVICES: DIVERSE NEEDS AND COMMON PROBLEMS

The poor, as broadly defined in the opening paragraph, make up half or more of the world's population, and although they are somewhat clustered regionally, above all in Africa and Asia, in all other respects they are diverse. It follows that their financial behavior is similarly diverse. The borrowing and saving patterns of an agricultural day-laboring household are not the same as those of a farmer, let alone those of a household that depends on a small shop or workshop in an urban slum, or on low-paid wage jobs in a factory, or on domestic service.

Even where livelihoods are similar, innate differences between households will generate different financial patterns, according to the age, the gender, and the health of the household members. Research shows that women and men tend to have different attitudes toward household resources and their allocation, including financial resources. At an individual level, personality counts: Some people are more cautious than others and may therefore be more averse to loans and more ready to save. Conversely, there are overarching cultural traditions—for example, the preference for certain types of savings- and-loan clubs among the ethnic Chinese or among the slum dwellers of Nairobi—that give a distinctive shape to the financial behavior of whole groups of people. The degree of monetization of a country's or of a district's economy will affect the scope for financial intermediation. And, last, a household's financial service needs change over time with life-cycle events: for example, as the children are educated and leave home and productive activities in the household decline. Nevertheless, poverty presents poor people with a number of financial management problems that cut across differences in traditions, livelihoods, and household composition. These commonalities are the subject of this chapter. Here general observations about poor people and their money management needs are presented, beginning with the most basic question of all: Why do poor people need financial tools in the first place? To answer that question, we need to move into the villages and slums and find out more about how poor people manage their money.

THE "FINANCIAL PORTFOLIOS" OF THE POOR

Finance is the intersection of money and time. Looking at one element in the absence of the other tells less than half the story. One-off surveys that focus on the finances of poor households may identify which savings institutions are used or what types of loans are outstanding, but say little or nothing about how the timing of cash flows is managed to accumulate savings or repay loans. To see how poor households try to reconcile constrained incomes with expenditure needs, and how financial tools, no matter how crude, are employed to achieve that end, we need to look at their household finances as a totality, as a *portfolio* of tools, each with its particular cash flow. To understand how and why poor households choose and use their financial tools, we need to observe how these portfolios change over time: "What has been missing is a close look at how portfolios function: not just how well the pieces work, but how well they work together.

Focusing on *how* gives new insight into the day-to-day nature of poverty and yields concrete ideas for creating better solutions for it". For the book *Portfolios of the Poor,* the authors conducted year-long "financial diaries" in urban and rural sites in Bangladesh, India, and South Africa, to better understand this threedimensional view of household finances. These were not "diaries" that the households themselves kept, but reports from interviews carried out by trained investigators, speaking the local language, on a frequent and regular basis throughout a full year. The investigators recorded as full an account as possible of income and expenditure, and focused especially closely on financial flows—flows in and out of savings and loan tools. At the same time, they probed for an understanding of how circumstances, preferences, and aspirations shaped the financial decisions the households made. From these "diaries" it was often possible to construct not just the balance sheets of the household accounts but also—and much more revealing—cash flow statements showing the activity that lay behind the balance sheets, all set in the context of the particular household's circumstances. Altogether, data for about 250 households were gathered, supplemented by a further 50 households from Bangladesh collected in a subsequent and slightly modified "diary" exercise.

Active Money Managers

The "diary" research revealed that poor people use financial tools intensely. At first this finding seems counterintuitive. It is easy to suppose that very small incomes lead to a "hand-to-mouth" existence in which income is consumed as soon as it arrives and there is no need and no scope for intermediation and thus no need for the financial tools that make it possible. This turns out not to be the case.

The poor, rather, tend to be intensive money managers, constantly seeking ways to set a bit of money aside or to borrow. This is not *in spite* of incomes being small, but precisely *because* they are small. Small incomes are often unreliable and irregular, so there is an ever-present need to make sure there is enough money to put food on the table every day and not just on those days when money comes in. Small incomes, even if they arrive regularly, also mean that large-scale but unavoidable expenditures—for marriage, education, homemaking, and festivals, for bicycles, fridges, fans, televisions, and mobile phones, and for business and bribes and so on—can almost never be found from current income, and so must be saved or borrowed, or both.

The same applies to emergencies, which, no matter what form they take, almost always require large sums of money if they are to be coped with successfully. The poor's need for ways to save and to borrow—their need for financial services—is greater than the needs of the nonpoor: not in monetary value, of course, but in intensity. Being able to take a dollar from a bank, or borrow it from a helpful neighbor, may allow a mother to take her child to the clinic and have her conjunctivitis cleared up; not being able to do so may lead to her daughter going blind in later life. Managing money well is an essential life skill that most poor people take very seriously.

To manage their money, the households that took part in the "diaries" research pushed and pulled more money through *informal* tools than through formal savings, loan, or insurance accounts at banks, insurance companies, or micro-finance institutions (MFIs). This was true even where banks were near at hand (as in South Africa) or where MFIs had already reached the slum or the village (as in the Bangladesh case). This can be partly understood from the "supply side." Banks are mostly set up to serve corporate clients and wealthier individuals and were never designed to cater to the needs of the poor.

MFIs *are* built to serve the poor, but so far at least, they have focused most sharply on one particular financial service they believe will help poor people to climb out of poverty—the short-term loan for small-business investment. Investing in a business may indeed provide the potential to increase incomes, but it is rarely the financial service in greatest demand. Many MFIs and other service providers now recognize this and are beginning to offer a broader range of products tailored to the poor, but most of these services are relatively new and have yet to reach large numbers of clients. If we look at the "demand side" and see things from the point of view of poor households it is easier to understand why they rely most often on informal devices and services. They need ways to build sums of money: small sums to keep the household fed and clothed, and bigger amounts for life-cycle expenses of all kinds and for emergencies. Because such sums can be built only by capturing money squeezed from already very small cash flows, they need tools that help them do exactly that—set aside a little money each day or each week or month that can be used to build savings or to repay loans. Such tools need to be close at hand, and flexible enough to catch as many deposits and repayments as possible. The financial diaries revealed that saving at home, often in very small values, is the most common and frequent kind of transaction carried out by poor householders as they seek to protect money from many competing demands. Then comes borrowing and lending small sums in the village or slum, among family and friends, and often interest free. To build larger sums, poor people typically save through savings groups of various sorts (some of them very sophisticated) or use larger-scale informal borrowing, often from moneylenders and usually with interest.

UNDERSTANDING THE POOR'S FINANCIAL SERVICE NEEDS

Research exercises such as the financial diaries reveal the complexity of money management among the poor and the intimate way in which it shapes and is shaped by the circumstances of individuals and their households. Nevertheless, the research also provides an opportunity to look at the financial lives of poor people in aggregate, and when that is done, dominant themes emerge that respond to the set of most pressing financial needs faced by all poor people. One of these is short-term cash flow management to deal with day-to-day life—what economists might call "consumption smoothing." Another is the problem of how to deal with emergencies when they arise, or "risk management." A third is how poor households struggle to assemble the large sums of money they need to take care of major life-cycle events and to build up household assets. For some households, an important part of this last category includes the financing of productive activities, such as setting up and stocking small businesses, or buying assets for self-employment, such as rickshaws.

Cash Flow Management and Income Smoothing

When the World Bank says that a percentage of the world's population lives on US$2 a day, it means that the *average* monthly income, multiplied by 12 and divided by 365, comes to US$2. But most people who live on low incomes do not actually receive US$2 each and every day. Many poor people derive their income from one or several informal activities that produce income sporadically. An Indian slum dweller may pull a rickshaw most days, but not on days when he cannot find one to hire, or it is raining heavily, or he is too ill, or the streets are blocked by a demonstration. Meanwhile his wife has a low-grade job in a garments factory where, in theory, she gets paid monthly, but in practice she can never be sure when her floor supervisor is going to get around to paying her, or how much he is going to hold back for how long. Income irregularity and unreliability make up one leg of a "triple whammy" of financial handicaps faced by the poor.

The other legs are low incomes and the lack of adequate financial tools. The effect of all three working together and reinforcing each other is reflected most sharply in the poor's struggle to manage life on a day-to-day basis. If income really did come in at a reliable US$2 a day, not only would planning expenditures be much easier, but the poor might also be offered better financial services by lenders or deposit collectors who would know their clients could save or repay at least a small amount every day. But with US$8 coming in one day and then nothing for a week, just putting food on the table each day becomes a logistical problem that needs help from financial tools if it is to be solved.

Widening the timescale reveals an extra layer of *seasonal* problems. Farmers or traders whose income is "lumpy," arriving with the harvest or with the good trading months when festivals occur, can face two intertwined cash flow management problems. First, they have to find a way to retain liquidity throughout the year, perhaps by keeping back most of the harvest and then selling it in smaller amounts from time to time. Second, they have to make sure the money raised by such sales is stored somewhere where it can be called on for daily expenditure without being eroded by the many other demands they face.

It is not surprising, then, that the financial diaries showed that day-to-day money management, both in towns and in villages, is the most intensive part of the poor's money management efforts. Almost everywhere housewives keep a little money back each time they shop, but they also put a handful of grain into a "reserve" bag each time they cook a meal. They borrow and lend, close by in their slum or village, both small sums of money and small amounts of rice, kerosene, salt, and soap. The disadvantages of one financial tool lead to the use of another, sometimes in a chain.

For example, because saving money in the home is so hard when there are so many requests for help or for loans from family and neighbors, demands for candies or a drink by children and husbands, or the temptations offered by peddlers, people often use "moneyguards"—other trusted people in their extended family or neighborhood with whom they can keep a little money out of harm's way. Because moneyguards are not always reliable— they may not have the money on hand the day it is needed—the poor end up borrowing from other neighbors (often interest free if the sum is small), or buying goods on credit at the local shop, or going into rent arrears. Then, when the rent arrears have built to the point where the landlord begins to threaten eviction, they borrow larger sums, with interest, from a moneylender. To repay the moneylender, saving efforts have to be redoubled, or assets have to be sold off. But selling off assets—for example, selling roof sheets to repay a creditor—simply creates another essential item that requires the poor to save. No wonder households in the financial diaries told the researchers that "All this keeps us awake at night," or confided that "I hate having to borrow money from other people—but there is no life without money, so we just have to do it."

But although day-to-day money management is where the majority of financial services are used, this does not show up much in the balance sheets of the poor. Year-end balances of most "diary" households revealed rather low levels of household savings and of local borrowing and lending. It is only when cash flows are examined that this intensity of use can be seen. Typically a household's annual financial cash flow was many times the value of their financial assets and liabilities.

The ratio of cash pushed and pulled through financial tools to average annual income varied between about 75 percent and 175 percent in India, a similar amount in Bangladesh, and a figure somewhat higher in South Africa. This is because much day-to-day management involves short-term, rapidly revolving exchanges of cash. Many of the smallest loans from neighbors were repaid in a matter of days. "Big flows and small balances" is a good general description of poor-owned portfolios, and they are matched in the experiences of MFIs that have a track record of offering unusually convenient passbook savings to poor communities. When examining the accounts at BURO, an MFI in Bangladesh, researchers found that the annual flow through the passbook savings product was four and a half times the value of the year-end savings balance. Poor people need to save short term to form small sums that can be withdrawn to cope with everyday life. Saving, for the poor, is a *verb* before it is a *noun*: something you do rather than something you possess. More often than not, saving is a way of coping with small and unreliable incomes rather than a way of building capital.

Dealing with Emergencies and Anticipating Risk

When emergencies strike, poor people, like everyone else, need large amounts of capital if they are to have a chance of fending off the worst effects of the event. In wealthy countries, and among the better-off in poorer ones, insurance is available to provide that capital, in the right amount at the right time. Insurance is a fast-growing and exciting part of micro-finance, but it has reached few poor households so far (though many micro-lenders do provide insurance against debt if a borrower dies holding a loan, either as an option for the borrower or built into the price of the loan). Lacking formal insurance, most poor people must look for other ways to anticipate risk and to deal with emergencies when they occur. Poor households are peculiarly vulnerable to emergencies. Many live in fragile ecosystems: Pushed to the margins by poverty, they are closer than others to seas that breed cyclones or rivers that flood, or farmland prone to drought.

Close to one-fifth of the burden of disease in developing countries can be attributed to environmental risk—with unsafe water, poor sanitation, and poor hygiene as leading risk factors causing premature deaths. The poor may live in provisional slums with uncertain legal status where they can be pushed out by landlords or governments at short notice, or suffer from fires ignored by the municipality. Unable to buy suitable drugs or quality feed, their animals die younger and produce less than those of wealthier farmers. Cooking over an open flame near homes built of bamboo walling or straw roofs, they experience a higher risk of destructive fires. That same wood smoke damages lungs and eyes, an example of how health problems start more often and are cured less easily among the poor than among the population in general.

In Bangladesh, half of the households studied in the diaries project suffered serious financial disruption from ill health during the study year, and in India the figure was two in five. One in five of the Bangladesh households lost a home during the year, and four out of five of the South African households had to contribute to expensive funeral ceremonies, many of them related to the HIV/AIDS pandemic. How did they cope when these crises struck?

Often they did not: The illness was never properly cured, the home or the job was lost for good, and the cousin was given only the most basic of burials. The question then becomes, How did they *try* to cope? When disaster strikes, people pull in whatever resources they can reach. Assets may be sold or, in the case of precious metals, pawned.

If there is time for the deal, any land in the household's ownership may be mortgaged out. Savings may be exhausted. Social networks are called on for gifts in kind or in money, and for interest-free or low-cost loans. Nonessential spending is foregone. Without access to insurance services poor people use whatever financial tools they have available to them to manage risk. Nevertheless, when a particular risk is especially expensive, or has an unusually high likelihood of happening, poor households may try to buy protection from it, using formal insurance or informal substitutes. Such is the case in South Africa of funeral insurance, where many poor households anticipate having to pay out for funerals and invest in devices specifically designed to deal with this event.

Many of the "diary" households belonged to an informal *burial society* into which they pay monthly premiums and in return receive financial benefits to help cover the high costs of burials. Some of the same households also paid into formal *funeral insurance policies*. Many households used both the informal and the formal schemes, so the financial diaries authors were able to compare how well they worked. Within an overall financial portfolio of 8 to 12 financial instruments, South African diaries households usually had at least one burial society and one formal funeral insurance policy. These households spent, on average, 3 percent of gross monthly income in total on all of their funeral cover instruments.

On pure economic terms, formal funeral insurance has about the same value as informal burial insurance: Formal funeral insurance tends to cost more on average per month than informal burial insurance, but it also pays out more. Looking beyond economics, burial societies have the advantage of providing a great deal of physical assistance and moral support around the time of the funeral. Fellow members take on a significant role in preparing and serving the feast during the burial, often providing the cookware and eating utensils. However, burial societies can be quite unreliable. Evidence suggests that close to 10 percent of them run out of money. Therefore, although many poor households may continue to belong to burial societies for the social benefits they provide, formal insurance providers have a clear contribution to make in this market by continuing to offer good value products with reliable service.

Building Bigger Sums for Life-Cycle Events, Assets, and Businesses

The constant threat of emergencies requires households to find large sums of money *quickly*. But they are by no means the only reason why poor households need to build large sums. All of us, including the poor, need to be frequent big spenders, to deal with life's big events—annual festivals, ceremonies to celebrate birth, marriage and death, costs for education and home building, and assets to make life better, such as fans and televisions. Some will also want to build large sums to establish a new business or expand an existing one, or to invest in a large asset for self-employment, such as owning one's own rickshaw rather than hiring one on a daily basis, or buying or leasing-in more land to farm. Others will migrate to find work, in the big city or overseas, and will need to finance these often costly journeys.

How do they go about building these bigger sums? We have seen that most of the financial tools used by poor people are informal. But informal sector finance is not geared to handling large sums of money over protracted periods of time. It is not safe to hold large amounts of savings at home, or in a savings club, because the longer these savings have to be kept, and the greater their value, the greater the risk of loss or theft or misuse. Similarly, even the greediest moneylender is not willing to lend large sums to the poor because large loans need lengthy repayment periods, and the longer the loan is held the greater grows the risk of default. So, even though these kinds of large expenditure can usually be anticipated, rather than being needed suddenly, poor people nevertheless find themselves building up sums piecemeal, just as they do when faced with an emergency. It is not unusual for a big asset to be bought with a mix of savings, loans, gifts from family, and the proceeds from the sale or mortgaging of other assets. The piecemeal approach also characterizes the way that savings for large-scale expenditures are assembled.

Certain items, notably gold jewelry, roof sheets (and bricks and cement blocks and lengths of timber), and, in many households, livestock, are used as long-term stores of value, and although the terms of most informal financial tools are short, they can be used to finance these savings-in-kind. ROSCAs are particularly good at this. ROSCAs, short for rotating savings and credit associations, are savings clubs in which members pay regularly into a pot that is taken in its entirety by one of their number in rotation and are common around the world. Pumza was in a four-member daily ROSCA, and Enayet's sister belonged to a much bigger monthly ROSCA run by fellow workers at her garments factory.

ROSCAs are often deliberately designed to make it easier to obtain expensive items. In the Philippines, for example, rural school teachers use ROSCAs to help furnish their homes after marriage: They persuade their colleagues to join a ROSCA and use the proceeds to buy sofas and chairs. Where MFIs have become common, as in much of South Asia, the short terms that characterize their lending (mostly about one year) lead to similar uses of the sums loaned. To the consternation (and sometimes disapproval) of MFI field officers, MFI clients may take a loan ostensibly for business investment and use it to buy gold jewelry.

From the clients' point of view, buying such a store of savings is as legitimate a use for a loan as any other, especially when other opportunities to save (or invest) are so scarce. The piece of jewelry may serve as decoration until called on to help finance something on a much larger scale, such as the wedding of the young woman whose neck it adorns. In all three countries in the financial diaries studies, most of the rural sample owned their home and the parcel of land on which it stood, often through inheritance. The better-off also had land to farm (in the case of India and Bangladesh) or a large compound (in the case of South Africa).

In the urban areas renting a home was more common. In some cases, such as in some slums in Dhaka, Bangladesh, families owed the physical structure of a simple timber-and tin-sheet oneroom home and perched it rent free on land owned officially by the government or some other institutional landlord. In South Africa some of the diaries households owned a permanent brick home, although others with shaky tenure in the urban areas could simultaneously be building a home in the rural areas. Financing the ownership of a home, then, was a challenge being faced by only a minority of the diary households—but where that was the case, the challenge was considerable, and the solution to it required huge self-discipline, as the case of Jonas and Mimimi, from South Africa, shows. Although many MFIs and other providers are beginning to offer housing loans or contractual savings products to invest in a home, these tools were not available to this couple. Therefore, like many others around the world, they did their home building in a piecemeal fashion.

Much of what is observed about the financing of domestic assets is also true of productive assets. They too are often acquired through a range of sources including gifts, asset sales, remittances from family members working in the big city or overseas, and savings and loans. The savings may have been held until needed in lower-value items acquired through saving or borrowing short term in the informal sector. Once again, community-based devices such as the ROSCA, with its simple and flexible formula, can be a powerful way of assembling cash for working assets.

In Vietnam fishing communities have used "auction ROSCAs" (ROSCAs in which the order in which the lump sum is taken is determined not by lottery but by bidding for it at each draw) to raise money for boats and equipment. So high is the demand for capital that club members sometimes forego as much as 50 percent of the sum in bidding for it. In Bangladesh rickshaw drivers run "rickshaw ROSCAs" to build a big enough sum to buy their own rickshaws. At some gathering place, often the garage where their hired rickshaws are parked overnight, each rickshaw driver in the club sets aside a fixed contribution from his daily earnings, and when there is enough in the kitty to buy a rickshaw it is decided by lottery which member of the club is to receive it. By a clever twist, which illustrates well the sophistication that often characterizes ROSCAs, after a club member has received his rickshaw he puts in double the usual amount each day: He can afford it because now he does not have to pay rent for a rickshaw.

This has the effect of accelerating the ROSCA so that the next rickshaw purchase comes along sooner, reducing the length of time that members' investments are at risk. A few men have used these clubs so successfully that they have acquired fleets of rickshaws, and then graduated to motorized rickshaws. Note, however, that not every Dhaka rickshaw driver wants to own his own rickshaw. Costs and risks are associated with owning such assets. A rickshaw needs maintenance. It needs to be stored somewhere safely at night. It has to be protected from confiscation by police officers running extortion rackets.

Not every poor rickshaw driver can manage these tasks, so many prefer not to try. It is not only because they cannot afford them—or do not have access to the right financial products at the opportune time—that poor people own few productive assets or invest in few productive activities: Other aspects of their poverty may make it unprofitably hard to benefit from investment. Nor does every self-employed person want to join a dedicated ROSCA of this sort, again for reasons to do with the financial facts of his or her life. The pressure to keep up with the payment schedule is severe, and if one cannot be sure that one's cash flow will allow one to pay on time every time, it may be better to avoid the commitment. This is not just because of the immediate consequences of default—the shame and maybe a bit of rough treatment at the hands of other members—but, more importantly, because the inability to keep up the repayment schedule is a very good indicator that one's financial position is not strong enough to maintain the asset once it is acquired.

Many rickshaw drivers who struggle to meet ROSCA dues or repay MFI loans used to buy a rickshaw end up having to sell their machine, almost always at a big discount, because they lack the means to bring financial stability to other aspects of their life. That leads to an important observation: All poor households need financial tools to handle their basic needs—day-to-day consumption smoothing, dealing with emergencies, and building sums to pay for life's big occasions. If those basic needs are not being at least partially met, lending to poor people *exclusively* for productive investment may not be wise. At best, the loans meant for business will be diverted to the more basic needs.

At worst the loan will go into a business that will prove short lived or loss making in the face of other financial demands made on the borrower. In the case of Bangladesh, one of the world's most mature micro-finance markets, MFI lenders have by and large learned to turn a blind eye to the fact that many poor clients use their MFI loans primarily or even exclusively for nonproductive purposes—even though some of these MFIs continue to insist in public that loans are given only for micro-enterprise investment. A set of financial diaries carried out to examine how informal devices and MFI services fit into the financial lives of the rural poor in Bangladesh sheds light on this: Productive investment is only one of a range of uses that people borrow from MFIs. Other evidence suggests that business owners can benefit from small, flexible cash infusions in a cash flow crunch, but that they may not lead to business growth.

Financial diaries done with a modest sample of small business owners in South Africa showed that business owners were able to start operating with fairly small sums of upfront capital. However, to keep their business in operation, they need frequent fresh infusions of capital. Rarely did these business owners dream of expanding their business, or imagine that they would make more money if they did. They were rather more concerned about just keeping it going, to provide a stable, if small, source of income. Enterprise borrowing, then, is not for everyone. Nevertheless, a good proportion of MFI borrowers respond well to the micro-credit dream of enabling poor people to borrow to establish and expand businesses. Most MFIs began with the primary purpose of providing loans to the poor to start or expand a small business, but the early hope that every poor person can become a successful entrepreneur is now giving way to an understanding that enterprise lending is best when targeted at clients selected for their aptitude for business and their stable domestic finances.

As a result, the enterprise- investment side of micro-finance is gradually moving away from loans with weekly repayment schedules that may not match the cash flow patterns of small business, and toward loans given to and tailored for individuals rather than group-based borrowers. This should leave room for group-based saving and borrowing for the nonentrepreneurial poor to adapt better to their wide range of nonbusiness money-management needs.

HOW GOOD ARE THE FINANCIAL TOOLS USED BY THE POOR?

So far this chapter has provided numerous examples of how poor people choose and use their financial tools. In this section we step back to review the overall quality of these services and devices. Understanding better the strengths and weaknesses of the present set of tools should help to structure thinking about how micro-finance might, in the future, add more value to the financial lives of the poor.

Convenient, Frequent, and Flexible—But Not Always Reliable

The most convenient tools of money management are ones that can be organized by the users themselves, without the need to interact with others, without the need to travel, available at any time of the day or night, and at little or no cost. It is not surprising then that the financial diary research found almost every poor household held—or tried to hold—savings at home. But this level of convenience and flexibility comes with obvious drawbacks: It is just too easy to take back these savings, so only those with exceptionally strong willpower (and there are such people) are able to build or keep large sums at home. Security is another obvious weakness of home savings: They are vulnerable to theft or misuse, or to being lost in floods or storms, and at the very least they will lose value to inflation.

Self-help home saving, then, illustrates the trade-off very commonly found in informal finance—between convenience on the one hand, and low reliability, short-termism, and insecurity on the other. One way to mitigate these drawbacks is to form a financial relationship with somebody else. "Moneyguards"—people trusted to hold money safely on one's behalf—are common. They may be neighbors, relatives, or employers. Often the transactions take place in both directions: The diary research found several households that both take in and put out money in this way, at the same time. Moneyguarding is closely related to casual interest-free borrowing and lending among kin or neighbors. Sometimes it is hard to tell them apart: In Bangladesh diary households might say they had "put" some money that week with a neighbor, and they would give vague answers when asked to specify whether this was a loan or a savings deposit or a repayment on a loan. Nothing better illustrates the complex ways in which a community's aggregate cash savings flow back and forth between its members.

This ambiguity is, like much in the informal sector, a strength and a weakness: It enables a good deal of interaction to take place, but at low levels of reliability that in turn place limits on the values and durations of this kind of intermediation. Where greater certainty or larger sums are needed, a price is usually demanded. Village or slum moneylenders who lend as a business ask for interest, and many who lend merely to fulfill family or social obligations do likewise. The interest is often at a high rate, either to compensate for the evident risk of lending to very poor people (in the case of professional lenders) or, in the case of those lending as an obligation, to help limit the amount of money being lent. There is more on the social aspects of this kind of lending below. One way to borrow free of social entanglements is to use a pawnbroker.

The limitation here is that poor people rarely hold much in the way of pawnable goods, so very large sums cannot usually be obtained by this route. The mortgaging of land has other disadvantages: The land mortgaged may have been the household's main income source, and the larger sums that can be had from mortgaging land often prove very difficult, if not impossible, to repay, so the land is in effect lost for good. MFIs have been much better able than banks to approximate the convenience of informal finance. They have done this in various ways. First, they got physically close to their clients, by holding meetings right in the village or slum. Soon, they settled on a form of lending in which repayments were made easy by being small and frequent—often weekly, at the meeting, sometimes even daily, through itinerant collectors.

It was this level of convenience and frequency— rather than anything to do with micro-enterprise development, or "group solidarity"—that led to micro-credit's extreme popularity in its early days. Provided that their household cash flows were strong enough to come up with a small weekly toll, people could borrow for whatever purpose was most pressing at the time. Later, when some of the disadvantages of a credit-only regime became apparent (such as the risk of overindebtedness), MFIs, where regulators allowed them to, introduced passbook savings that could be deposited into or withdrawn from at will, at the village or slum meeting.

Nevertheless, most general lending to the poor by MFIs (as opposed to their lending to micro-enterprises) is short term and therefore of low value relative to incomes: A typical loan may have a term of 11 months and be worth the equivalent of two or three months' household income. This is very useful for consumption smoothing but not for the bigger sums that all households need from time to time.

To accumulate big sums, with most MFIs, borrowers still need to build a series of modest sums through successive rounds of borrowing, and find their own ways of storing their value— most commonly by holding them in nonfinancial assets such as jewelry or livestock.

Disciplined—But Only in the Short Term

Saving on your own is hard. Saving with a moneyguard helps impose some distance but not enough discipline. Saving within a bigger group, as in a ROSCA or an ASCA (accumulating savings and credit association, described in chapter 6, "Community-Based Providers"), offers much more discipline, relying on the power of group pressure and sanctions to keep the transactions flowing regularly. Many poor people are well aware of the flip side of informal finance's flexibility and convenience—its lack of discipline—and this helps to explain the popularity of devices like the ROSCA. Researchers have also suggested that when people are distracted by the problems of poverty, and have to juggle several income flows from different sources and deal with the individual cash flows of numerous financial tools, they can lose sight of their longer-term financial position.

By joining a group such as a ROSCA poor people may inject enough regularity into their financial lives to help them plan for and meet longer- term goals. In earlier sections we have seen how ROSCAs help their members build sums that can be used to meet emergencies or acquire assets. ROSCAs can fail, but as well as offering a disciplined environment that encourages regular saving, they have other advantages. One is that because they never require cash to be stored (at each meeting the money goes straight to that meeting's taker) there is no risk of the treasurer dipping into the fund. Another is that the combined eyes of all the members ensure that transactions will be more than usually transparent and verifiable.

These virtues offset the moderate risk of the ROSCA going wrong because a member simply fails to pay in after he or she has taken his or her turn at the lump sum. Other features of ROSCAs make them suitable for poor people: They require no bookkeeping, so the illiterate are rarely confused by more literate members of the group. They are without cost: Money goes straight from the depositors to the taker in what must be the world's swiftest and cheapest form of financial intermediation. And they are close at hand and convenient: People set up ROSCAs right where they live or work and hold meetings at times that suit them. Poor people find it easier to form larger sums through ROSCAs than they do through saving at home or saving with partners such as moneyguards. Nevertheless, really big sums—enough to buy a home or business outright or fund a pension annuity—cannot usually be formed through ROSCAs because, like all informal schemes, ROSCAs become riskier the longer they run, the more members they have, and the bigger the amounts transacted. ROSCAs are time bound: As soon as every member has received the "prize" once, it comes automatically to an end, although the members are, of course, free to start another cycle and accumulate another modest sum.

ROSCAs illustrate another typical informalfinance trade-off—security versus longevity and volume. The group-based approach to financial services to the poor has been taken up by outsiders in various ways. The oldest and most impressive is the credit union movement, now found throughout the world. Credit unions take the basic idea behind all ROSCAs and ASCAs—the idea of a group of people coming together voluntarily to pool their savings—and submit it to enough formalization to allow the credit union to become a permanent formal institution, providing the members with ongoing services and, crucially, enough security to allow members to build up large deposits over the long term, or pay steadily into insurance or pension policies. What has stopped this admirable system from becoming the obvious first choice for poor people around the world is that the degree of formal organization needed to keep a credit union stable requires levels of education and financial sophistication that are simply not available in most of the world's poorer village and slums.

Credit unions are inventions of the nineteenth century. More recently, nongovernmental organizations (NGOs) have taken up the basic idea of the savings club and used it to work with poor people on a range of development issues, not just finance. The largest endeavor of this kind is India's Self-Help Group (SHG) movement, which counts its members in millions. SHGs are basic savings clubs linked to formal banks, which recognize them as legal entities and lend to them at favorable rates. More recent still is the Savings Groups movement, which has been building steadily over the last 20 years and follows a rather different course.

The NGOs that promote savings groups prefer to tackle the weaknesses of savings clubs, especially problems of poor governance, by training members in the use of improved practices. Because these savings groups are standalone entities not linked to banks or other institutions, they are seen as particularly suitable to remote and sparsely populated areas. Micro-credit MFIs, as is well known, of course, lend through groups. But MFI groups in the fastest- growing micro-credit traditions, such as that based on the work of Grameen Bank, are not mutual entities that own or share their own group funds, but simply groups of retail customers brought together by the MFI to reduce service delivery costs.

Social Embeddedness—A Strength and a Weakness

The discipline that ROSCAs offer is in part a result of the social relationships they embody: Being a member of the group creates an obligation to contribute or to be shamed in front of the group. However, this discipline is often tempered by flexibility in the way in which the ROSCA responds to clients' needs. The essential feature of the group is that it represents a source of liquidity that members can access *one way or other*. This can involve direct negotiation at a group meeting to obtain the payout because of a pressing need, shock, or emergency, or members can negotiate directly with each other to change the order in which the payout is received or borrow the payout from the member who did receive it. Groups organize themselves in many ways, and they vary in how flexible they are prepared to be, but the key feature is that by jointly creating a source of liquidity, members have a right to make claims on that resource and to be listened to by other members, either formally at the club meeting or at its margins.

This feature can be referred to as "negotiability." Although the mechanism differs, this negotiability is also a feature of moneylending. Moneylending is often seen as exploitative, but the social relationships in which people are engaged may be complex, involving labor exchange and land rental as well as money. In such contexts "moneylenders" may act as patrons who assist their "clients," and this remains true even when such help could result in cycles of debt that are ultimately damaging to the long-term welfare of the borrower.

In these cases, with few competing options, poor people often prefer to retain such avenues of access to resources than to avoid them. Another way in which the informal sector operates through social relationships is in the ways people assist each other, especially family and friends. Poor people may help their friends and relatives in ways that are quite open-ended. If a child needs school fees and parents cannot provide, another relative—or even a friend—may help.

Such assistance creates a debt that takes the form of a future obligation to reciprocate. It may not be reciprocated in cash, or in school fees, but in a completely different form such as labor, lending animals, or taking care of a child. It is a form of saving with others that is not directly financial and in which the return is unknown at the time, but is indeed an obligation. In this way debts are not to be avoided: They create relationships of reciprocity that can be drawn on in the future. In the case of Enayet the loans his parents took were never repaid in full and were on the way to being "forgiven"—but public disapproval and comment ensures that the borrowers cannot forget that the obligation represented by the unpaid debt continues.

The social relationships in which informal financial services are embedded are both one of their greatest strengths as well as their greatest weakness. For those who are able to manage "negotiability" successfully they offer flexibility and responsiveness for risk management in particular, but also for productive investment and asset building. However, such relationships are not open to all, and the poorest people are less able to engage with them because they are less able to reciprocate, although they may also be the recipients of assistance from time to time.

CREATING BETTER FINANCIAL SERVICES FOR THE POOR

The picture this chapter has painted of the current state of financial services for poor people has numerous implications for micro-finance. They are overwhelmingly positive.

Taken together, they suggest that micro-finance enjoys big opportunities to grow in both quality and quantity:

- First, the picture implies a very high demand from poor people for financial services. This is seen in the intensity with which poor households use whatever financial tools they have at hand.
- Second, it implies that this high level of demand is by no means fully met, neither in volume nor in quality. This is seen in the failure of the existing, largely informal, tools to satisfy in full the financial needs of the poor, in the low levels of reliability that characterize much informal intermediation, and in the still very modest numbers of poor people reached by MFIs and other formal providers.
- Third, it implies that a great deal of the demand from poor people is *not* for the products and services that the micro-finance industry has emphasized during its first three decades. In particular, the demand for savings (including insurance) may outstrip the demand for loans; the demand for general-purpose loans may outstrip the demand for loans for micro-business investment; and the demand for longterm saving, borrowing, and insurance instruments is at least a strong as the demand for short-term savings and loans.
- Fourth, it implies that much of the methodology that micro-finance has already developed will be relevant to meeting this demand. Techniques for getting close to clients and enabling them to transact frequently, through out-of-branch banking of the sort seen in weekly village or slum meetings or in mobilephone banking, will remain vital. Breaking the formation of sums down into small bitesize pieces, as in Grameen- or village bank– style weekly savings and repayments or via daily collection agents, will still be essential. Above all, the MFI's superior level of reliability and transparency, relative to much informal finance, needs to be retained and strengthened.
- Fifth, it shows where micro-finance will have to improve and extend its products and delivery systems. Two very important goals are finding ways to introduce greater flexibility into loan terms and repayment schedules (while still offering discipline) and finding ways of enabling the poor to engage in much longer-term intermediation, through longterm commitment savings plans (including insurance and pension plans) and loan terms longer than the six months to one year common to much micro-lending at present.
- Sixth, it suggests that the demand by poor people for financial services may be quite similar across regions and districts, which implies that although micro-finance practitioners will need to modify their work to suit each location, a core set of needs is present that can be met by broadly similar products. This is seen in the remarkable

congruence of behaviors observed in the two South Asian nations and in South Africa—countries that have very different histories, cultures, and levels of economic and financial development.

A key challenge for formal service providers has been the struggle to get close enough to the poor to compete with the proximity and frequency of informal tools. Informal tools are certain to keep their advantage in this respect, and it would be foolish to think that formal services will entirely replace them. But by finding ways to contact their clients where they are, in the village or slum, and doing so as often as they can, through regular weekly or daily routines, or via cell phones and bank agents, formal services should be able to gain a much bigger share of the everyday financial intermediation of the poor than they have at present. Recent innovations that will help them do this include mobile-phone banking and legislation to allow banks to operate through agents—either peripatetic as in India's recent "banking correspondent" provisions or as a supplemental business for local shops, as in Brazil. Another challenge for formal providers is to make products more flexible, to respond better to the irregular cash flows of poor clients.

Here again there is cause for optimism: Worries about internal control, and a sensible concern to keep things simple, caused early micro-credit pioneers to begin with rigid payment schedules, such as the strict weekly repayments of Grameen-style micro-lending. But with experience and the astute use of technology they are now able to offer "passbook" savings—savings accounts where the client can deposit or withdraw as much as he or she likes at any time—and flexible loan repayments, at least for modest value loans. Because they are permanent institutions, it is much easier for MFIs and other formal providers to offer long-term intermediation. Formal commitment savings plans for the poor (which include endowment and other forms of insurance, and pension plans) will be a huge growth area for micro-finance.

They offer the discipline that poor people so often seek when they use group-based devices such as ROSCAs but add value by having much longer terms, allowing much larger sums to be formed. They can also offer a "one-stop shop" for such services. In East Africa it is common for people to take membership in several ROSCAs at once, each with its own term, frequency, and value, so that the user can ensure that different spending needs— weekly consumption, quarterly rents, or annual school fees, for example—can be met. This range of plans can be offered, more reliably, by a formal provider that is in regular frequent contact with its clients. These challenges are well worth formal providers tackling. Informal finance, where poor people conduct most of their financial lives, can suffer from low reliability and an inability to offer long terms to create large-value sums. These are major deficiencies, and formal services can and should offer something better. Reliability, in the sense of ensuring that agreed contracts are honored, is fundamental.

The poor live in environments that are continuously changing; most have neither cash flows, nor living arrangements, nor environmental and social conditions that are static or *reliable*. Bringing more reliability into financial tools will provide a significant boost to the ability of the poor to plan and envision a future beyond the short term. This requires services that are offered in a timely manner and under clear conditions, with terms that are upheld and with opportunities to easily ask questions and seek redress. A minimum "menu" of financial services for *all* poor clients in the second decade of the twentyfirst century would ideally include passbook savings and flexible small-scale loans (for shortto- medium- term money management), medium-term loans (such as up to three years) with structured repayments suited to whatever is known about the client's household cash flow, and medium-to-long-term commitment savings. As techniques for doing so evolve, providers should aim to add pensions, and insurance cover, starting with the risks that are easiest to calculate, such as life insurance, but aiming eventually at the more difficult ones, above all health and agriculture.

To carefully selected segments of clients, providers should also learn how to offer longerterm loans for productive investments tailored to business cash flow, and for big life-enhancing investments (in homes, household goods, and education) tailored to repayment capacity shown to exist by the transaction records of successive loans. There is nothing in the history of micro-finance to suggest that offering these services to a majority of the world's poorest households cannot be achieved in this decade.

THE ROLE OF GOVERNMENT AND INDUSTRY IN FINANCIAL INCLUSION

Tailoring a country's financial system to enable financial markets to work better for the poor involves the combined efforts of public and private players. It is relatively recent, and commendable, that both government and the financial services industry acknowledge the importance of increasing financial inclusion. But financial inclusion is not simply about numbers or attracting more clients to the range of providers. "Responsible" financial inclusion increases access to financial services in ways that are safe for consumers, enabling their participation informed by knowledge and choice. Increasingly shared by public and private actors, this vision requires coordinated efforts from both. Governments are investing authority in policies and rules that shape behavior in market systems; their imprint is wide-ranging, from infrastructure to legally mandated outreach targets. Industry players are rallying around codes of conduct intended to increase transparency and fair treatment of consumers and are defining performance in financial, social, and environmental terms. Both spheres share the responsibility for "responsible" finance, building financial inclusion on a foundation of consumer protection. This chapter outlines the role of government (through its policies, regulation, and other support for a stable financial sector) and industry (through standards and guidelines) in promoting financial inclusion, as both separate and sometimes overlapping arenas of activity. In addition, it recognizes coordination and advocacy as important functions within the market system. This chapter provides a high-level perspective on the roles of government and industry, largely related to formal rules that help to shape the financial market system; more detailed information on the specifics of regulation is provided in chapter 17. It will be of interest to policy makers, industry associations, financial service providers, and other stakeholders seeking to understand the enabling environment for financial services.

THE ROLE OF GOVERNMENT IN FINANCIAL INCLUSION

Micro-finance is now seen as an integral part of an inclusive financial system. As a result, financial inclusion has become an important policy goal that complements the traditional pillars of monetary and financial stability, as well as other regulatory objectives such as consumer protection.

Government as Rule Maker

Governments have increasingly embraced financial inclusion as one of their policy objectives. Data from the Financial Access 2010 Survey show that in 90 percent of economies, at least some aspect of the financial inclusion agenda is under the purview of the main financial regulator. Furthermore, "As rule makers, governments determine not only what efforts may be undertaken to promote financial inclusion, but also by whom, how, and when. In addition to prudential and consumer protection rule making, governments can enable innovative financial inclusion business models, including permitting the entry of new actors into the financial service sector". Rather than provide financial services directly, the government's role is to maintain macroeconomic stability and provide appropriate regulatory and supervisory frameworks.

And while the assumption still holds that the private sector plays the central role in providing financial services, there is much more awareness of the reasons why market forces will not—without an appropriate enabling environment, infrastructure support, and adequate consumer protection and financial capability— achieve the goal of improving financial inclusion. Policy making is a complex process bringing together various actors who use a multitude of tools and strategies to promote financial inclusion. Policy decisions influence where resources are allocated and how priorities are established within political, economic, and social institutions. Policies are designed to guide decision makers and to achieve an intended purpose. They typically outline general principles, but they do not carry the force of law. Policy makers recognize the potential for economic growth and poverty alleviation through the development of a more inclusive financial services sector. In doing so, they also acknowledge three primary barriers to financial inclusion:

- Supply-side barriers such as transaction costs, the inability to track an individual's financial history, and lack of knowledge about how to serve poorer customers
- Demand-side barriers that restrict the capacity of individuals to access available services and products, including socioeconomic and cultural factors, lack of formal identification systems, and low levels of financial literacy
- Poor regulatory frameworks, including consumer protection mechanisms that hinder the quantity and quality of financial products and services.

The main participants in developing formal rules include the legislature (typically the parliament), the government unit (the relevant ministry and government bureaucracy), and the regulator (the central bank or regulatory authority). A legislative process in micro-finance normally starts with a mostly technical discussion among the experts and the regulator, but eventually depends on the support of the legislature to implement legal changes. Educating lawmakers about the rationale and objectives of proposed rules early on can help to overcome any potential resistance and create a joint understanding of what is needed to achieve an enabling environment for financial services for the poor.

Infrastructure Support

The government has traditionally played a strong role in ensuring that infrastructure is in place and providing oversight. The front-end infrastructure includes client access points, such as post offices, automated teller machines, point-of-sale devices, and retail agents, all of which are subject to specific rules and regulations. The back-end infrastructure includes automated clearinghouses, real-time gross settlement systems, retail payment switches, and cash distribution networks. Not least because of the growing importance of branchless banking models, the payment system infrastructure has received a lot of attention, as it constitutes the rails for the cost-effective provision of financial services.

If the government (for example, the central bank) does not run these systems, at least it nurtures them and sets the general rules of operations. In addition to service delivery infrastructure, several other supporting functions should be considered in the government's domain for financial inclusion. For example, credit bureaus allow clients to build a credit history and help providers to reduce the risk of serving them, a deposit insurance system protects clients against loss of savings, and a land registry system facilitates access to loans using land as collateral. Nonfinancial infrastructure also has a bearing on financial inclusion. For example, roads for traveling to the nearest service point, electricity for recharging mobile phones or running real-time communication systems between remote areas, agents, and head offices, and national identification systems all promote access to financial markets. In all these areas, the government plays a crucial role, either as provider or as regulator and promoter.

Promoting Savings through Government Payments

The government can potentially play an important role in promoting savings and catalyzing volumes by moving its social transfers, wages, and pension payments onto electronic channels and ensuring that these channels are linked to easily accessible, basic transaction accounts. Its policy with regard to social safety nets and government- to-person (G2P) payments can thus have an important impact on the viability of innovative delivery channels and draw more clients into the formal financial sector. Both the government and the poor benefit as G2P payments can often be delivered at substantially lower cost and with less "leakage" if they are delivered electronically.

Consumer Protection

In an environment of increasingly complex financial products and services, effective consumer protection is important for the overall sustainability of the financial market system. Participation in the formal financial sector must pose fewer risks for vulnerable, low-income people who have little experience with formal finance and low levels of financial literacy and capability. Governments have an important role in providing the legal and enforcement muscle to ensure that financial institutions do not undermine consumer protection by intentionally capitalizing on their advantages in information, knowledge, and power. Effective consumer protection legislation, applied equitably across providers, can facilitate comparison shopping and healthy competition, leading to improved products and practices. Despite limited regulatory and supervisory capacity and challenges in enforcing legal contracts in the countries where micro-finance is needed most, governments can ensure that providers disclose prices and other characteristics of credit products in a consistent manner using agreed terminology and definitions; and they can set rules for client privacy, out-of-court redress mechanisms, or rigorous safety of data storage and transmission to protect customer funds and information. Some examples of consumer protection regulations include the following:

- The National Bank of Cambodia requires that micro-finance institutions (MFIs) state their interest on a declining balance rather than a flat-rate basis.
- South Africa's sweeping National Credit Act addresses over-indebtedness and reckless lending by defining these terms under the

law. It sets clear rules governing disclosures, credit reporting, and advertising, among other practices.

- Indonesian regulators require regulated providers to have written procedures and a formal complaints unit.

For countries characterized as "low-access environments" (where levels of financial access and financial literacy are low and regulators face significant capacity constraints), the Consultative Group to Assist the Poor (CGAP) recommends that the government agenda for consumer protection pursue three basic goals: transparency, fair treatment, and effective recourse. *Transparency* covers broad disclosure of relevant product terms and conditions, including pricing, fees, and default provisions. When such disclosure rules require all providers of the same type of product to use standardized formulas as well as plain language to communicate relevant charges, consumers are better able to compare products. Disclosure requirements are considered more market friendly and effective at reducing costs to the borrower than mandated interest rate ceilings.

Transparency targets two interrelated objectives— increased *consumer comprehension*, allowing consumers to understand and choose appropriate products, and increased *market competition*, stimulated as consumers engage in comparison shopping. Disclosure regulations should govern both content provided to the consumer and how it is communicated for effective comprehension. Disclosure of the various cost components and other product terms can be overwhelming to consumers and counterproductive to the objective of enhancing their comprehension. For example, creditors in Armenia are required to advise customers orally regarding terms, costs, risks, and obligations associated with a service. A standardized summary sheet of product costs and terms used by all providers is one of the most useful tools for ensuring that consumers have information they can understand and compare. Standardized forms are also easier for providers, particularly smaller and less sophisticated ones, as they save time and resources by not having to develop their own disclosure forms to meet regulatory requirements. The perspective of the individual consumer is critical to tailoring disclosure regulations. Loan pricing provides a good example. Because nominal interest rates do not reflect the total cost of a loan, regulations should mandate that pricing be expressed using one or more of the following methods:

- Total financial cost of credit,
- Repayment schedules, and
- Annual percentage rate (APR) or effective interest rate.

While the use of APRs and EIRs allows for greater comparability, total loan cost and the amount and frequency of repayment may be easier for low-income consumers to comprehend. Limited data suggest that borrowers tend to focus on the amount of the installment payment rather than the interest rate, because their main concern is whether their cash flow will cover loan payments. For example, policy makers in Peru and Ghana standardize the calculation of APR or EIR with regulators specifically to address the capacity constraints of smaller, less formal institutions. Allowing for the monthly presentation of APRs or EIRs is another practical option introduced in the Philippines. Monthly APRs or EIRs may be more appropriate for loans of less than a year and more comprehensible to consumers.

Fair treatment covers ethical staff behavior, the sale of appropriate products, and acceptable marketing and reasonable collections practices. Rules governing truth in advertising support transparency through disclosure. Codes of ethics guard against overly aggressive responses to delinquency. Zero tolerance of delinquency, a cornerstone of institutional performance, can result in abusive collections with adverse effects on poor households. In India, Ghana, and elsewhere, regulators have established rules governing fair debt collection and prohibiting intimidation and coercion. *Effective recourse* is necessary for consumer trust in the formal financial system; when things go wrong, consumers need to know they have a way to communicate their complaints and resolve their issues.

Consumer recourse mechanisms such as specialized help desks within financial institutions not only handle complaints, but also often handle questions and can play a role in facilitating consumer comprehension of disclosed information. Sometimes the regulatory agency takes responsibility for this function, and sometimes it assigns the role to an industry association, ombudsman, or other entity. Rules governing these processes should specify all aspects of customer complaints, including the method of submission, location, and time frame for resolution. Providers need to display such information clearly and communicate it directly to clients. While these three goals—transparency, fair treatment, and recourse—are basic to protecting consumers, it may not be feasible or practical to address all of them at once. An incremental approach to developing a set of disclosure policies and regulations may be necessary, taking into consideration compliance costs for industry and supervisory capacity of government.

A starting point might be to tackle the most critical yet discrete transparency issues in a given context. At an intermediary level, governments can target broader consumer comprehension. Finally, regulators can reinforce market competition by requiring broad dissemination of comparable metrics for total costs (such as APRs and EIRs) and other key terms through advertising and media channels, allowing market forces to apply pressure on providers. Extensive dissemination of new disclosure requirements, coupled with sufficient time for implementation, can help to reduce the industry's costs of compliance. Consumer testing can be used to refine disclosure rules at each stage and build a stronger disclosure regime over time. However, even where provided for by law, broad application and enforcement of consumer protection regulations can be difficult to achieve in practice. Challenges include consistent application of rules and coordination among multiple regulators where supervisory authority is divided. Micro-insurance provides a good example of this.

Building Financial Capability

Although historically governments may have focused on limiting harmful credit products through interest rate caps and debt forgiveness, the focus has shifted toward the need to empower financial service users, to inform them, and to give them tools to protect their rights. CGAP identifies consumer financial capability, government regulation, and industry codes of conduct as the three principal consumer protection strategies. Consumers need to know their rights in order to exercise them.

These include the right to understand product choices, often offered by competing providers, and the right to choose the services that are best for them. Consumers need to develop relationships with financial service providers on the basis of knowledge and choice as opposed to fear. Ill-informed consumers and unsupervised providers can undermine the impact of financial inclusion efforts; this risk is especially high in a context of rapid, often technology-driven, change in the financial service marketplace. Given the asymmetries in knowledge, as well as access to information and skills between providers and consumers, governments can help to meet the challenges— educational, regulatory, and financial—of empowering consumers to use financial services effectively and participate in their own protection. However, with limited experience in addressing this need, government strategies to support responsible finance are key to learning what works. Three overlapping terms are used in relation to the concept of consumer financial capability: financial literacy, capability, and education.

Financial literacy is the ability to understand basic information about financial products and services. *Financial capability* is the ability to apply that knowledge, to make informed decisions, and to take effective actions regarding the current and future management of money. It includes the ability to save, borrow, and spend wisely, to generate more stable cash flows, and to manage the challenges associated with costly life-cycle events. Challenges of money management are never static, and neither are the solutions, especially given the unpredictable and seasonal incomes that are common among the poor. Financial capability is an evolving state of competency subject to ever-changing personal and economic circumstances.

Financial education is a key tool, coupled with experience using financial services, to build financial literacy and capability. It introduces people to good money management practices with respect to earning, spending, saving, borrowing, and investing. Its power lies in its potential to be relevant to anyone and everyone, from the person who contemplates moving savings from under the mattress to a Savings Group to the saver who tries to compare account features between competing banks. Serving multiple, interrelated purposes, financial education promotes personal financial management, product uptake and use, and consumer awareness and protection.

Matching the content of financial education to the target group is essential to making it relevant. Target groups for financial education can be defined by age, gender, employment status, or relationship to a specific financial product. For example, financial education targeted to youth is likely to focus on negotiating with parents about spending money, the value of saving, and planning for the future. Finally, to ensure financially capable consumers, financial education must be integrated with hands-on experience; consumers need to choose and use financial products and services if they are to understand their full benefits.

Financial Inclusion Strategies

A financial inclusion strategy clearly defines and aligns a shared vision among policy makers and other stakeholders for achieving an inclusive financial sector. It also raises awareness of and secures commitment to sound practices and establishes the means for communication and coordination around implementation to avoid gaps or duplication of efforts. In 2010, 45 percent of the countries participating in the Financial Access 2010 Survey had a dedicated strategy document for promoting financial inclusion. Regulators in countries with a financial inclusion strategy also have, on average, more financial inclusion topics under their purview and more resources and staff working on these matters.

Financial inclusion strategies are developed through a consultative process among the key stakeholders in financial inclusion (government, regulators, the industry, and consumer associations) and approved by a government body. They typically include a diagnostic of the current state of the sector to ensure "evidence-based policy making," policy objectives, strategies, and an action plan for implementation. Financial inclusion strategies need to consider existing capacity as well as the need for reform and capacity building. An important element is the process itself: bringing a diverse range of actors to the same table whose only common denominator may be their potential to affect the financial ecosystem and getting them to agree on a shared vision for the sector.

The action plan for implementation needs to consider all elements of the financial market system: the core (clients and providers and the products they exchange) and the rules (formal and informal) and supporting functions (infrastructure, funding, and information). Only a combined effort of all stakeholders is likely to have a significant impact on the overall goal of making markets work for the poor. While financial inclusion strategies have the potential to lead to better structured and more evidence-based policy-making processes, they have suffered from several shortcomings:

- *Many strategies are driven by donors.* Government must have strong interest in and ownership of the process and the outcome.
- *The outcome can only be as good as the analysis.* At times, the diagnostic does not include all relevant actors and institutions; the analysis should be conducted by a team of experts with a diverse set of skills and be updated regularly.
- *The common vision does not sufficiently consider the local context.* This is particularly the case if the document is drafted by an international consultant without much involvement of local actors.
- *The strategy is not disseminated widely or updated regularly.* The success of implementation depends on broad dissemination, a clear allocation of rules, sufficient funding, and the setting of realistic targets; the strategy should be a "living document."

The extent to which financial inclusion strategies have improved access to finance is difficult to know, as we do not know how the sector would have developed without a strategy.

What we do know is that financial inclusion strategies, if taken seriously, are a powerful instrument for convening stakeholders who have a potential impact on financial inclusion and helping them to come to a common understanding on how to reach this goal. National strategies that focus on *responsible* financial inclusion, as opposed to simply *access* to finance, might lead to significantly greater benefits for households and service providers alike. While many financial inclusion strategies may not focus on consumer protection and financial capability, they should.

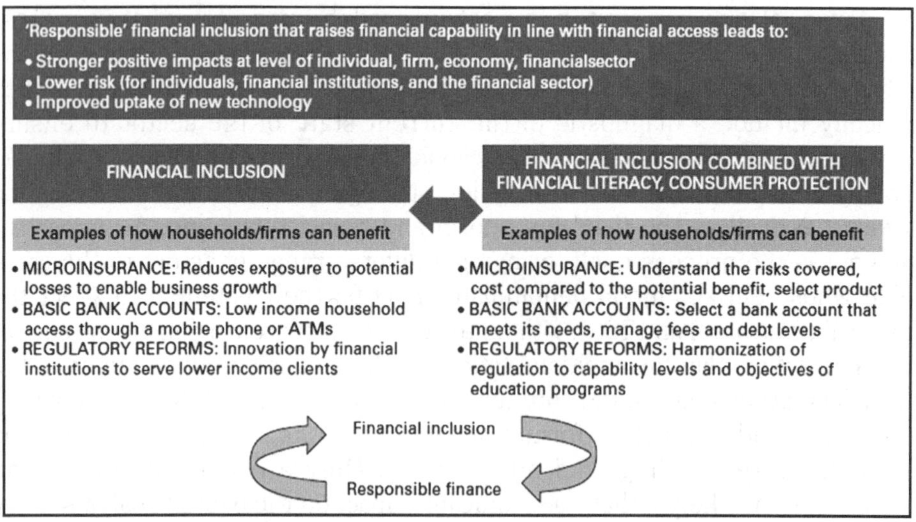

Fig. Financial inclusion strategies and responsible finance

Legal Mandates

Some countries use quantitative financial inclusion targets or specific product offerings mandated by law as tools to promote the provision of financial services to underserved populations or geographic areas. These *financial inclusion mandates* can be seen as a complement to other financial regulations and incentives (for example, tax advantages for providers to reach poorer segments of the population). Mandates appear to be a simple and effective tool for achieving financial inclusion targets; assuming that enforcing compliance is possible, predefined targets can be reached (for example, everybody has access to certain products or all districts are served by at least one branch). However, in practice this might not always be the case. Priority sector lending targets are the bestknown example of financial inclusion targets. Priority sector lending usually requires a certain percentage of a provider's loan portfolio to be dedicated to sectors such as agriculture, micro- and small businesses, housing, or micro-finance.

Basic or "no frills" bank accounts, designed for low-income clients with low or no fees, are another example of financial inclusion mandates; in some countries (including Belgium and France in the European Union, Indonesia, and Mexico) banks are required by law to offer basic accounts. Expert opinions about the usefulness of legal mandates are divided. Opponents give the following reasons:

- In a market economy, it is assumed that providers know best how to serve the market. It is also assumed that a decision *not* to offer a certain product is informed by economic factors. If mandated to do so, providers will incur losses that have to be recovered elsewhere.
- Targets can be achieved at lowest cost if they focus on those providers that are best positioned to contribute to their achievement. On a more practical level, it is difficult to set up rules in a way that does not encourage regulatory avoidance (for example, providers choosing a different legal form, moving to another jurisdiction, or bending the rules).
- The achievement of targets has to be monitored, and an effective enforcement mechanism, including penalties for nonachievement, has to be established, which requires additional resources.

Proponents, however, argue that mandates to explore new markets are needed to counter the complacency of financial institutions. When mandates are imposed (if applied to all so that no individual provider's competitive position is compromised), financial institutions will do their best to comply with the targets at the lowest cost and eventually may even be able to cover their costs. In some cases (South Africa and Germany), the mere threat of a legal mandate prohibiting commercial banks from refusing any customer the opportunity to open a bank account was sufficient to lead the banking industry, of its own accord, to offer basic accounts to everybody. The ultimate decision whether to mandate financial inclusion in law depends on the specific context of a country.

Global Standards and Standard-Setting Bodies

The term "standards" encompasses many things in the financial sector. Standards may be general or specific, and they may be national or international. Standards for supervision are largely set by international financial standard-setting bodies; they reflect national and global experience with different types of institutions and the risks and benefits of different activities. While standards represent formal rules, they are typically "soft law"; there is no technical means of enforcing them, although there may be consequences (in terms of reputation and pricing) for failure to comply with them.

In some cases, the threat of these consequences can have significant impact on the actions of a government or its regulator. Global standard-setting bodies set standards and provide guidance for the regulators of financial institutions. Due to the historical emphasis on setting standards for existing institutions and their clients and the supervision of such institutions, many standards have not yet considered the issues of particular relevance to providing the poor with financial services. Moreover, these standards may inhibit new approaches, including technical and nontechnical innovations, and new products and services that the poor need. However, the global standard setters have begun to consider how existing standards might need to be revised in order to facilitate financial inclusion. This effort requires understanding the risks of financial exclusion as well as the changing risks and benefits of increased financial inclusion. In addition, attention is required to understand the situation of poor countries with high levels of financial exclusion and weak supervisory capacity (both staffing and experience) and to adjust standards accordingly.

Of the various standard-setting bodies, the three most relevant to financial services for the poor are the Basel Committee on Banking Supervision (BCBS), the Financial Action Task Force (FATF), and the International Association of Insurance Supervisors (IAIS). The BCBS formulates standards and guidelines for the supervision of banks and other deposit-taking institutions and is best known for its international standards on capital adequacy and its Core Principles for Effective Banking Supervision (known as the Basel Core Principles). In December 2011, the BCBS proposed revised principles intended to address the postcrisis lessons for promoting sound supervisory systems.

These proposed principles are significant for the prominence given to the principle of proportionality. In 2010 the BCBS issued guidelines on applying the Basel Core Principles to micro-finance activities of depository institutions. The guidelines highlight the importance of a proportionate (risk-based) approach as well as the key differences between a micro-loan portfolio and a commercial loan portfolio.

The key differences include:

- The particularities of the labor-intensive micro-lending methodology,
- The licensing requirements, which should reflect different risks than those of commercial banks,
- The particular provisioning and reserve requirements that should be applied to micro-loans, and
- The need for different liquidity requirements.

The FATF is the global standard-setting body for anti-money-laundering and combating the financing of terrorism (AML/CFT) rules. It is organized as a task force–style body with 34 member countries and two regional organizations (the European Commission and the Gulf Cooperation Council). The FATF recommendations articulating standards for national regimes on AML/CFT have recently been revised to incorporate a risk-based approach that is critical to financial inclusion efforts. For example, under the revised recommendations, a mobile money account with strict transaction limits does not require the same customer due diligence rules as a current account with no limits.

Specifically, FATF recommendations outline the measures that countries, financial institutions, and related businesses should institute. While the recommendations are not legally binding, countries that do not adhere to them run the risk of being considered a haven for illicit transactions or criminal activity. This can result in international sanctions and higher borrowing costs, among other consequences. The IAIS is a broad-based forum composed of insurance regulators and supervisors from some 190 jurisdictions in almost 140 countries. Its stated mission is to promote effective and globally consistent regulation and supervision of the insurance industry in order to develop and maintain fair, safe, and stable insurance markets for the benefit and protection of policyholders. The IAIS issues standards and guidance material and has recently revised its Insurance Core Principles to incorporate the principle of proportionality. Specifically, the Insurance Core Principles state, "Supervisors need to tailor certain supervisory requirements and actions in accordance with the nature, scale, and complexity of individual insurers. In this regard, supervisors should have the flexibility to tailor supervisory requirements and actions so that they are commensurate with the risks posed by individual insurers as well as the potential risks posed by insurers to the insurance section or the financial system as a whole".

COORDINATION AND ADVOCACY

An important element of policy and rule making for financial inclusion is the interaction of various stakeholders and how those interactions shape policy outcomes. The development and implementation of formal rules are not a one-off event; rules need to be revised regularly in light of experience and learning. As with every other part of the financial market system, the process of how rules are developed and who is involved needs to be understood and supported in a way that encourages pro-poor regulation. How rules develop depends on the level of accountability and responsiveness among rule makers to the advocacy "voice" of different interest groups and the wider political economy around financial regulation. This means that coordinating bodies, such as the G-20 Global Partnership for Financial Inclusion, and advocacy groups, such as associations of providers or consumer groups, are important players in relation to the rules regarding financial services. Each group has its own motivation and objectives, which may or may not always result in what is best for the ultimate beneficiary of policies, the wider public.

Coordination

Coordination of policy makers and various stakeholders interested in financial services for the poor is a key element in designing and implementing effective financial inclusion reforms and policies. This is particularly important as new partnerships develop between providers, including banks and mobile network operators, or as retailers and agents become involved in the delivery of financial services. A lack of coordination can increase risks such as improper sequencing of regulatory changes or regulatory changes in one sector that undermine efforts in other areas.

Alliance for Financial Inclusion

More and more policy makers and representative bodies are beginning to coordinate formally with one another to influence financial inclusion. For example, as of 2012, government institutions from 78 countries had joined the global Alliance for Financial Inclusion (AFI), a network of financial policy makers that promotes peer learning and the implementation of effective policies that advance the goal of financial inclusion: A global policy response based on leadership from developing countries, closer international cooperation, and strong and coordinated partnerships between relevant public and private sector stakeholders at national and international levels could be the most effective way to support countries at all levels of policy development ... Dialogue between policy makers and the industry is also a powerful tool for deciphering and mitigating risks that help to create regulation and foster innovations in access. A good example of coordination efforts is the Maya Declaration initiated by AFI to commit policy makers to prioritize financial inclusion. Other coordination and advocacy efforts include the G-20 Global Partnership for Financial Inclusion and the Responsible Finance Forum.

Global Partnership for Financial Inclusion

In 2010 the G-20 recognized financial inclusion as a key pillar of the global development agenda and created the Global Partnership for Financial Inclusion as an implementing body open to G-20 countries, non-G-20 countries, and other relevant stakeholders. The G-20 principles for innovative financial inclusion play an increasing role as a point of reference for policy makers and other stakeholders seeking to promote increased financial inclusion.

Responsible Finance Forum

The Responsible Finance Forum is an interinstitutional community of practice for exchanging knowledge and building consensus on responsible finance. It was created to support participating institutions, including development agencies and development finance institutions, in sharing knowledge and information on development efforts and potential collaborations, to build on responsible finance frameworks and foster broadbased dialogue and facilitate convergence of views, and to support coordinated action. The Responsible Finance Forum considers issues related to consumer protection regulation, industry action, and financial capability, with an emphasis on more transparent, inclusive, and equitable financial sectors.

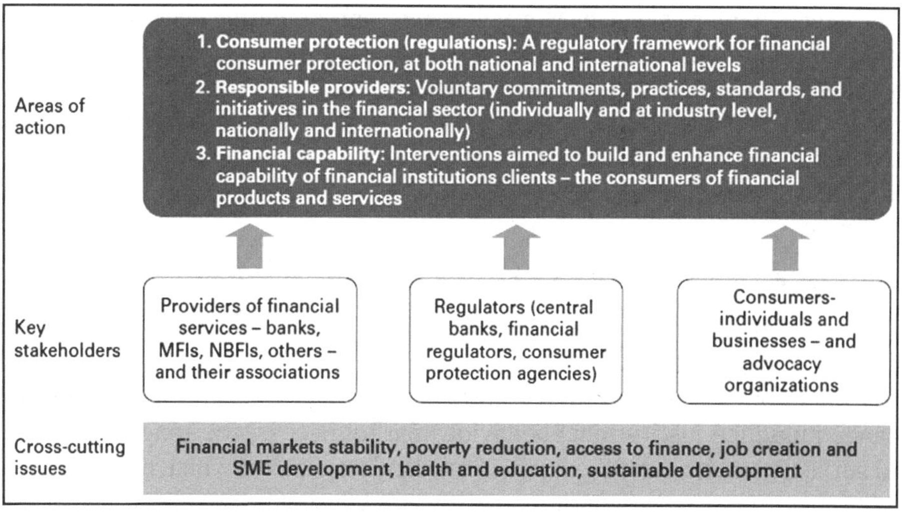

Fig. Responsible Finance: A multiple-stakeholder Approach

Advocacy

Industry networks or associations often take a central role in advocating the interests of providers. As associations are formed on the premise of common interests, they can effectively communicate members' shared concerns about a particular issue. The activities that constitute advocacy are generally developed on the basis of member needs, internal capacities, and the external political environment. For example, regional or international associations, whose membership typically comprises national-level networks and providers from multiple countries, engage in policy in a more indirect manner. Regional associations often publish information on industry practices or lobby market players on issues affecting their members across countries and markets. By doing so, they facilitate the work of local association representatives. National associations can influence policy more directly by engaging with local authorities who can pursue direct changes to various laws or secondary legislation (for example, regulations and guidelines). They can pursue specific actions that advance an advocacy strategy—letter writing, publicity campaigns, or direct lobbying with policy makers—to communicate or publicize their support for change on a particular issue. Industry associations often provide policy advocacy as a service to members. If implemented effectively, advocacy can strengthen the voice of providers and their associations and thus help to design rules that are tailored to their specific needs. While clients should be the main beneficiaries of financial inclusion efforts, their voice is rarely heard; often, they lack the technical expertise to lobby effectively for their interests. In addition, their divergent interests pose a challenge to collective action. Although consumer associations try to overcome both of these challenges, they are not yet widespread in micro-finance. More effective representation occurs through the intersection of client and provider interests. While the interests of providers and clients are not identical (for example, they differ with regard to product pricing), the fact that providers depend on the satisfaction of their clients creates substantial overlap. Furthermore, because clients constitute an important voting bloc, policy makers should be motivated to consider their current and potential interests.

THE ROLE OF INDUSTRY IN FINANCIAL INCLUSION

Financial inclusion calls for better outreach, appropriate products and services, and consumer trust. Responsible finance emphasizes value, respect, and protection of the consumer. Efforts by providers to encourage responsible finance influence institutional behavior, market access, the range of products and services on offer, and the competitive landscape, all of which have an impact on the functioning of the market and the suitability of financial services. Given that financial services for the poor are most prevalent in countries with limited supervisory capacity, often providers may need to take the lead in promoting responsible finance.

Industry Standards and Guidelines

Standards of practice and codes of conduct that financial service providers and other market actors abide by can contribute to financial inclusion and help to build the industry's commitment to consumer protection. In recent years, multilateral agencies have promulgated many initiatives to provide guidelines and principles, and the titles of their documents define the targeted areas: the "United Nations Principles for Investors in Inclusive Finance," the "World Bank

Draft Guidelines for Consumer Financial Protection," and the "Organisation for Economic Co-operation and Development (OECD) Principles and Good Practices for Financial Awareness and Education." Often these are living documents, open to review and revision as members respond to issues raised by stakeholders and better understand what is missing or inadequate in the standards or codes.

However, enforcement can be challenging: There is typically no legal consequence for failure to comply, and influential financial institutions may use their power to discourage the self-regulatory body (for example, a micro-finance association) from taking action. Without enforcement, such standards can only exert a weak influence. CGAP has developed numerous guidelines for the industry based on consensus from various stakeholders, including, for example, "Micro-finance Investment Vehicle Disclosure Guidelines"; "Good Practice Guidelines for Funders of Micro-finance"; "Regulation and Supervision Consensus Guidelines"; "Information Systems Implementation Guidelines"; "Disclosure Guidelines for Financial Reporting by Micro-finance Insitutions"; "The Role of Funders in Responsible Finance"; "Due Diligence Guidelines for the Review of Micro-credit Loan Portfolios"; "Developing Deposit Services for the Poor"; and "Definitions of Selected Financial Terms, Ratios, and Adjustments for Micro-finance." Other industry representative bodies such as the Social Performance Task Force, the Smart Campaign on Client Protection Principles, and Micro-finance Transparency have all launched initiatives and advocacy campaigns.

The Social Performance Task Force

The Social Performance Task Force, with more than 1,000 members in 2011, represents the primary stakeholders in financial services for the poor: practitioners, donors and investors, industry associations, technical assistance providers, rating agencies, and academics. It defines social performance as the "effective translation of a micro-finance organization's mission into practice in line with commonly accepted social values." Its mission is to promote standards by which providers can manage the double (and, for some, triple) bottom line that is at the core of providing financial services to the poor. Seeking to ensure that services focus on clients, the Social Performance Task Force promotes the following:

- Efforts to serve increasing numbers of poorer and more excluded people sustainably
- Systematic assessment of the target population's specific needs to improve the relevance and quality of services
- Benefits for micro-finance clients, their families, and communities, including increased social capital, assets, income, and access to services; reduced vulnerability; and fulfillment of basic needs

- Social responsibility of the provider toward its clients, employees, and the community it serves.

Tools covering a wide range of purposes support the measurement and achievement of strong social performance.

The Smart Campaign

- Under the broader umbrella of social performance management, the Smart Campaign, initiated in 2009 by the Center for Financial Inclusion at ACCION International, advocates consumer protection principles and has recruited hundreds of organizations and individuals to endorse them. The shift from assumed to explicit articulation of consumer protection measures followed debates about pricing and profits in micro-finance, as well as the emerging crises related to over-indebtedness and abusive practices. The Smart Campaign has advanced seven consumer protection principles: *Appropriate product design and delivery.* Providers will take adequate care to design products and delivery channels in such a way that they do not cause clients harm. Products and delivery channels will be designed taking client characteristics into account.
- *Prevention of over-indebtedness.* Providers will take adequate care in all phases of their credit process to determine that clients have the capacity to repay without becoming overindebted. In addition, providers will implement and monitor internal systems that support the prevention of over-indebtedness and will foster efforts to improve market-level credit risk management (such as sharing credit information).
- *Transparency.* Providers will communicate clear, sufficient, and timely information in a manner and language that clients can understand so that they can make informed decisions. The need for transparent information on pricing, terms, and conditions of products is highlighted.
- *Responsible pricing.* Pricing, terms, and conditions will be set in a way that is affordable to clients, while allowing financial institutions to be sustainable. Providers will strive to provide positive real returns on deposits.
- *Fair and respectful treatment of clients.* Financial service providers and their agents will treat their clients fairly and respectfully. They will not discriminate. Providers will ensure adequate safeguards to detect and correct corruption as well as aggressive or abusive treatment by their staff and agents, particularly during the loan sales and debt collection processes.
- *Privacy of client data.* The privacy of individual client data will be

respected in accordance with the laws and regulations of individual jurisdictions. Such data will only be used for the purposes specified at the time the information is collected or as permitted by law, unless otherwise agreed with the client.

- *Mechanisms for complaint resolution.* Providers will have in place timely and responsive mechanisms for handling complaints and resolving problems for their clients and will use these mechanisms both to resolve individual problems and to improve their products and services.

Of the seven principles, over-indebtedness and transparency receive the most attention. Efforts to prevent over-indebtedness have included more careful assessments of client debt capacity, staff incentive schemes focused on portfolio quality, and attempts to identify or limit the number of loans a client carries from multiple lenders. In addition, lenders have found that the policies developed for markets with minimal competition need to be adjusted for more mature markets with multiple providers. The Smart Campaign conducts a global campaign to garner support for these principles. It also promotes activities that help providers to move from endorsement to implementation, including developing numerous tools for assessment, training, and client protection and education. Both the Social Performance Task Force and the Smart Campaign also work with micro-finance rating agencies and investors to achieve alignment between their rating frameworks or due diligence processes and consumer protection principles.

Micro-Finance Transparency

Pricing is central to the debates regarding profits and the broader social responsibility of financial service providers. The true prices of micro-loans are not always measured accurately or reported and remain widely misunderstood. Consequently, the need for the industry to improve the disclosure of interest rates and the standardization and communication of costs is a priority. Micro-Finance Transparency (MFTransparency) is a global initiative committed to promoting pricing transparency in the micro-finance sector. The organization aims to achieve its mission in the following ways: data collection, standardization, and dissemination; training and capacity building for financial institutions; development of educational materials; and consulting with regulators and policy makers on price disclosure legislation. Micro-loans often have higher interest rates than mainstream commercial loans because they are more expensive to make and manage. This challenge has driven many providers to quote prices that are significantly lower than the effective prices. Once providers in a specific market begin to employ confusing product pricing, it becomes very difficult for any single provider to maintain transparent pricing. Standardized forms of disclosure can help to address this problem.

Compliance

Industry associations and individual financial providers have an important role to play in promoting responsible finance through standards. However, industry standards rely on compliance with self-imposed codes of conduct and explicit rejection of strong incentives for deceptive behavior. Furthermore, membership of industry associations rarely comprises all relevant providers, which limits the scope of protection and may place compliant providers at a competitive disadvantage. For example, although the consumer protection principles advanced by the Smart Campaign are intended to benefit both financial service providers and their clients and pricing transparency initiatives are intended to benefit clients, the asymmetries between what providers endorse and what clients understand have the potential to undermine those efforts. Identifying the priorities of consumers and providers highlights potential barriers to translating principles of responsible finance into effective practice, as significant distance separates clients from financial institutions.

Bibliography

A. Ahmad: *Economic Geography*, Omega Publication, Delhi, 2010.

A.M. Bagulia: *Encyclopaedia of Economic Geography (3 Vols-Set)*, Anmol Publication, Delhi, 2005.

Abha Lakshmi Singh: *Economics and Geography of Agricultural Land Reclamation*, B.R. Publication, Delhi, 1997.

Ahmad Husain: *Economic Geography*, Vishvabharti Publication, Delhi, 2006.

Anil Kumar Thakur and Deepa Rawat: *Economic Geography and Development*, Deep and Deep Publication, Delhi, 2011.

Bahura Ekka: *Economic Geography*, Shree Publication, Delhi, 2005.

Frank Van Den Bossche: *Elements of Jaina Geography : The Jambudvipasamgrahani of Haribhadra Suri*, Motilal Banarsidass, Delhi, 2007.

G. Remcay: *Encyclopaedia of Geography (2 Vols-Set)*, Sarup Publication, Delhi, 2004.

G.E. Marindin: *Encyclopaedia of Classical Mythology and Culture (Including Art, Biography and Ancient Geography)*, Aryan Publication, Delhi, 1996.

H.M. Saxena: *Economic Geography*, Rawat Publications, Delhi, 2013.

I Singh: *Encyclopaedia of Geography (5 Vols-Set)*, Alfa Publication, Delhi, 2007.

I. Singh: *Economic Geography*, Alfa Publication, Delhi, 2006.

Indira Singh and Satnam Singh: *Encyclopaedia of Indian Geography (3 Vols-Set)*, Reprint Publication, Delhi, 2006.

K.R. Singh: *Econogeography*, Arise Publication, Delhi, 2012.

M A Bangash: *Economic Geography*, Anmol Publication, Delhi, 2006.

M. Abbas Khan: *Encyclopaedia of Indian Geography (3 Vols-Set)*, Anmol Publication, Delhi, 2005.

Manorama Sinha: *Electoral Geography of India*, Adhyayan Publication, Delhi, 2007.

Pradeep Sharma: *Economic Political Geography*, Discovery Publication, Delhi, 2007.

R. Jagannathan: *Economic Geography*, Dominant Publication, Delhi, 2012.

R. Jagannathan: *Elements of Geography*, Anmol Publication, Delhi, 2011.

Rajendra Yadav: *Economic Geography*, Ritu Publications, Delhi, 2015.

Raninder Kaur: *Economic Geography*, Sublime Publication, Delhi, 2006.

S. Evelyn Thomas: *Economic and Regional Geography (2 Vols-Set)*, Sumit Enterprises, Delhi, 2003.

Seema Jalan: *Electoral Geography*, Rawat Publication, Delhi, 2015.

Siya Ram Sharma: *Economic Geography*, Murari Lal Publication, Delhi, 2008.

Subodh Kapoor: *Encyclopaedia of Ancient Indian Geography (2 Vols-Set)*, Cosmo Publication, Delhi, 2002.

T.C. Sharma: *Economic Geography of India*, Rawat Publication, Delhi, 2013.

Vivek Sharma: *Encyclopaedia of Geography*, Anmol Publication, Delhi, 2006.

Index

N

P

R

S

T

U

W